MW01092189

Cognitive Search

Evolution, Algorithms, and the Brain

Strüngmann Forum Reports

Julia Lupp, series editor

The Ernst Strüngmann Forum is made possible through the generous support of the Ernst Strüngmann Foundation, inaugurated by Dr. Andreas and Dr. Thomas Strüngmann.

This Forum was supported by funds from the Deutsche Forschungsgemeinschaft (German Science Foundation) and the Stiftung Polytechnische Gesellschaft

Cognitive Search

Evolution, Algorithms, and the Brain

Edited by

Peter M. Todd, Thomas T. Hills, and Trevor W. Robbins

Program Advisory Committee:
Thomas T. Hills, John M. McNamara,
Jeroen G. W. Raaijmakers, Trevor W. Robbins,
and Peter M. Todd

The MIT Press

Cambridge, Massachusetts
London, England

Series Editor: J. Lupp
Assistant Editor: M. Turner
Photographs: U. Dettmar
Lektorat: BerlinScienceWorks

MIT Press books may be purchased at special quantity discounts
for business or sales promotional use. For information, please email
special_sales@mitpress.mit.edu or write to Special Sales Department,
The MIT Press, 55 Hayward Street, Cambridge, MA 02142.

The book was set in TimesNewRoman and Arial.
Printed and bound in the United States of America.

Library of Congress Cataloging-in-Publication Data

Cognitive search : evolution, algorithms, and the brain / edited by Peter M.
Todd, Thomas T. Hills, and Trevor W. Robbins.
      p.   cm. — (Strüngmann Forum reports)
Includes bibliographical references and index.
ISBN 978-0-262-01809-8 (hardcover : alk. paper)
1. Cognition. 2. Searching behavior. 3. Memory. 4. Brain. 5. Information
retrieval. I. Todd, Peter M. II. Hills, Thomas Trenholm. III. Robbins,
Trevor W.
BF311.C5527   2012
153—dc23
                                                         2012003903

10 9 8 7 6 5 4 3 2 1

Contents

The Ernst Strüngmann Forum

Founded on the tenets of scientific independence and the inquisitive nature of the human mind, the Ernst Strüngmann Forum is dedicated to the continual expansion of knowledge. Through its innovative communication process, the Ernst Strüngmann Forum provides a creative environment within which experts scrutinize high-priority issues from multiple vantage points.

This process begins with the identification of themes. By nature, a theme constitutes a problem area that transcends classic disciplinary boundaries. It is of high-priority interest, requiring concentrated, multidisciplinary input to address the issues involved. Proposals are received from leading scientists active in their field and are selected by an independent Scientific Advisory Board. Once approved, a steering committee is convened to refine the scientific parameters of the proposal and select the participants. Approximately one year later, the central meeting, or Forum, is held to which circa forty experts are invited.

Preliminary discussion for this theme began in 2008, and on February 5–7, 2010, the steering committee was convened. Working together, the committee (Thomas T. Hills, John M. McNamara, Jeroen G. W. Raaijmakers, Trevor W. Robbins, and Peter M. Todd) identified key issues for debate and selected the participants for the Forum. Chaired by Peter M. Todd and Trevor W. Robbins, the Forum was held in Frankfurt am Main from February 20–25, 2011.

The activities and discourse surrounding a Forum begin well before participants arrive in Frankfurt and conclude with the publication of this volume. Throughout each stage, focused dialog is the means by which participants examine the issues anew. Often, this requires relinquishing long-established ideas and overcoming disciplinary idiosyncrasies which otherwise might inhibit joint examination. When this is accomplished, new insights emerge.

This volume attempts to convey the synergy that arose from a group of diverse experts, each of whom assumed an active role, and is comprised of two types of contributions. The first provides background information on key aspects of the overall theme. Originally written before the Forum, these chapters have been extensively reviewed and revised to provide current understanding on these key topics. The second (Chapters 4, 9, 15, and 20) summarizes the extensive group discussions. These chapters should not be viewed as consensus documents nor are they proceedings; they are intended to transfer the essence of the discussions, expose the open questions that still remain, and highlight areas in need of future enquiry.

An endeavor of this kind creates its own unique group dynamics and puts demands on everyone who participates. Each invitee contributed not only their time and congenial personality, but a willingness to probe beyond that which is evident, and I extend my gratitude to all. A special word of thanks goes to the steering committee, the authors of the background papers, the reviewers of the papers, and the moderators of the individual working groups: David W. Stephens, Trevor W. Robbins, Jeroen G. W. Raaijmakers, and Robert L. Goldstone. To draft a report during the Forum and bring it to its final form in the months thereafter is no simple matter, and for their efforts, I am especially grateful to the rapporteurs: John M. C. Hutchinson, Catharine A. Winstanley, Thorsten Pachur, Curt Burgess, and Lael J. Schooler. Most importantly, I wish to extend my sincere appreciation to Peter M. Todd, Thomas T. Hills, and Trevor W. Robbins for their commitment to this project.

A communication process of this nature relies on institutional stability and an environment that encourages free thought. The generous support of the Ernst Strüngmann Foundation, established by Dr. Andreas and Dr. Thomas Strüngmann in honor of their father, enables the Ernst Strüngmann Forum to conduct its work in the service of science. In addition, the following valuable partnerships are gratefully acknowledged: the Scientific Advisory Board, which ensures the scientific independence of the Forum; the German Science Foundation and the Stiftung Polytechnische Gesellschaft, for their financial support of this theme; and the Frankfurt Institute for Advanced Studies, which shares its vibrant intellectual setting with the Forum.

Long-held views are never easy to put aside. Yet when this is achieved, when the edges of the unknown begin to appear and gaps in knowledge are able to be defined, the act of formulating strategies to fill these gaps becomes a most invigorating exercise. It is our hope that this volume will convey a sense of this lively exercise and play its part in furthering understanding of the evolution, function, and mechanisms of search for resources in the mind as well as in the world.

Julia Lupp, Program Director
Ernst Strüngmann Forum
http://www.esforum.de

List of Contributors

Bernard W. Balleine   Brain and Mind Research Institute, School of Medical Sciences, University of Sydney, Camperdown, NSW 2050, Australia

Melissa Bateson   Institute of Neuroscience, Newcastle University, Newcastle upon Tyne, NE2 4HH, U.K.

Ethan S. Bernstein   Harvard Business School, Boston, MA, U.S.A.

Joshua W. Brown   Department of Psychological and Brain Sciences, Indiana University, Bloomington, IN 47405, U.S.A.

Christian Büchel   Institut für Systemische Neurowissenschaften, Universitätsklinikum Hamburg-Eppendorf, 20246 Hamburg, Germany

Curt Burgess   Department of Psychology, University of California, Riverside, CA 92521, U.S.A.

Roshan Cools   Radboud University Nijmegen Medical Centre, Donders Institute for Brain, Cognition and Behaviour, Centre for Cognitive Neuroimaging and Department of Psychiatry, 6500 HB Nijmegen, The Netherlands

Iain Couzin   Department of Ecology and Evolutionary Biology, Princeton University, NJ 08544, U.S.A.

Eddy J. Davelaar   Department of Psychological Sciences, Birkbeck College, University of London, London WC1E 7HX, U.K.

Nathaniel D. Daw   Center for Neural Science and Department of Psychology, New York University, New York, NY 10003, U.S.A.

Michael R. Dougherty   Department of Psychology, University of Maryland, MD 20742, U.S.A.

Reuven Dukas   Department of Psychology, Neuroscience and Behavior, McMaster University, Ontario L8S 4K1, Canada

Daniel Durstewitz   Central Institute for Mental Health, Research Group Computational Neuroscience, 68159 Mannheim, Germany

Tim W. Fawcett   School of Biological Sciences, University of Bristol, Bristol BS8 1UG, U.K.

Wai-Tat Fu   Department of Computer Science, University of Illinois at Urbana-Champaign, IL 61801, U.S.A.

Sergey Gavrilets   Department of Ecology and Evolutionary Biology, Department of Mathematics, National Institute for Mathematical, and Biological Sciences, University of Tennessee, TN 37996, U.S.A.

Luc-Alain Giraldeau   Faculté de Sciences, Université du Québec à Montréal, Québec H3C 3P8, Canada

Robert L. Goldstone   Department of Psychological and Brain Sciences, Indiana University, Bloomington, IN 47405, U.S.A.

Helga A. Harsay Amsterdam Center for the Study of Adaptive Control in Brain and Behavior (Acacia), Department of Psychology, University of Amsterdam, 1018 WB Amsterdam, The Netherlands

Thomas T. Hills Department of Psychology, University of Warwick, Coventry CV4 7AL, U.K.

Bernhard Hommel Leiden University, Cognitive Psychology Unit and Leiden Institute for Brain and Cognition, 2333 AK Leiden, The Netherlands

John M. C. Hutchinson Senckenberg Museum für Naturkunde, 02806 Görlitz, Germany

David Lazer Department of Political Science, Northeastern University, Boston, MA 02115, U.S.A.

Michael D. Lee Department of Cognitive Sciences, University of California at Irvine, CA 92697-5100, U.S.A.

James A. R. Marshall Department of Computer Science/ Kroto Research Institute, University of Sheffield, Sheffield S3 7HQ, U.K.

John M. McNamara School of Mathematics, University of Bristol, Bristol BS8 1TW, U.K.

Frederic Méry Laboratoire Evolution, Génomes et Spéciation, CNRS, 91198 Gif sur Yvette, France

Derek E. Nee Department of Psychological and Brain Sciences, Indiana University, Bloomington, IN 47405, U.S.A.

Frank Neumann School of Computer Science, The University of Adelaide, Adelaide SA 5005, Australia

John P. O'Doherty HSS and Computation and Neural Systems, California Institute of Technology, Pasadena, CA 91125, U.S.A.

Thorsten Pachur Faculty of Psychology, University of Basel, 4055 Basel, Switzerland

Cyriel M. A. Pennartz Swammerdam Institute for Life Sciences, University of Amsterdam, 1090XH Amsterdam, The Netherlands

Sean M. Polyn Department of Psychology, Vanderbilt University, Nashville, TN 37240, U.S.A.

Jeroen G. W. Raaijmakers Department of Psychology, University of Amsterdam, 1018 WB Amsterdam, The Netherlands

A. David Redish Department of Neuroscience, University of Minnesota, Minneapolis, MN 55455, U.S.A.

K. Richard Ridderinkhof Amsterdam Center for the Study of Adaptive Control in Brain and Behavior (Acacia), Department of Psychology, and Cognitive Science Center Amsterdam (CSCA), University of Amsterdam, 1018 WB Amsterdam, The Netherlands

Trevor W. Robbins Behavioural and Clinical Neurosciences Institute, University of Cambridge, Cambridge CB2 3EB, U.K.

Lael J. Schooler Max Planck Institute for Human Development, 14195 Berlin, Germany

Jeremy K. Seamans Department of Psychiatry and Brain Research Centre, University of British Columbia, Vancouver, BC V6T 2B5, Canada

David W. Stephens Ecology, Evolution, and Behavior, University of Minnesota, MN 55108, U.S.A.

Peter M. Todd Cognitive Science Program, Indiana University, Bloomington, IN 47405, U.S.A.

Jan M. Wiener The School of Design, Engineering and Computing, Bournemouth University, Dorset BH12 5BB, U.K.

Catharine A. Winstanley Department of Psychology, University of British Columbia, Vancouver, BC V6T 1Z4, Canada

Bruce Winterhalder Department of Anthropology, University of California, Davis, CA 95616-8522, U.S.A.

Jeremy M. Wolfe Harvard Medical School, Cambridge, MA 02139, U.S.A.

1

Building a Foundation
for Cognitive Search

Peter M. Todd, Thomas T. Hills, and Trevor W. Robbins

Over a century ago, William James, the father of modern psychology, proposed that humans search through memory much the same way as they rummage through a house looking for a lost set of keys (James 1890). This recognition of commonalities between search in physical and information domains—including space, memory, and the Internet—has become increasingly salient as information resources expand and our capacity to search successfully for such information gains greater economic and personal importance.

Just as animals spend much of their time searching for resources, including territory, food, and mates, so too do humans—albeit our search is often conducted in different kinds of spaces. We search for items in visual scenes (e.g., a favorite brand on a crowded supermarket shelf or a weapon in a luggage X-ray image), for historical facts or shopping deals on Internet sites, for new friends or opportunities in a social network. We search our memories for past experiences and solutions to novel problems. In all these cases, just as in James's search for lost keys, the structures of resources and information in the world govern how we search and what we will find.

Search—the behavior of seeking resources or goals under conditions of uncertainty—is a common and crucial behavior for most organisms. It requires individuals to achieve an adaptive trade-off between exploration for new resources distributed in space or time and exploitation of those resources once they are found. Because this search problem is common to so many aspects of our lives, search behavior has been studied in a diverse range of scientific disciplines and paradigms: theoretical biologists study the characteristics of evolutionary search in high-dimensional spaces; behavioral ecologists analyze animals foraging for food; experimental psychologists investigate search in vision, memory, decision making, and problem solving; neuroscientists study the neural mechanisms of goal-directed behavior in humans and other animals; psychiatrists and clinical neuroscientists analyze aberrant volition such as drug-seeking behavior in addiction and attentional control in attention deficit hyperactivity disorder (ADHD); computer scientists develop information-search algorithms for mining large-scale databases and for individual navigation of the World Wide Web; social psychologists investigate how people seek and choose mates and friends; and political scientists study how groups look for solutions to problems.

Search behavior is so ubiquitous that it is constantly being examined, reexamined, and redefined by many disciplines. At the same time, these disciplines often proceed in their investigations independently of one another and even without awareness of the parallels with research going on in other fields. This has put search at an interdisciplinary "blind spot" in the study of human and animal cognition. Furthermore, although the various fields that compose cognitive science have each furthered our understanding of cognition at various levels of analysis, the success of these endeavors has contributed to a modular view of the mind, comprising separate processes independently evolved to solve specific problems. Little attention has been paid to how the processes may share similar algorithms, neurocognitive control systems, or common ancestry.

Individual fields have, however, started to uncover a number of such commonalities among search processes. Recent molecular and comparative biological findings of neural mechanisms in multiple species that control the search for and evaluation of resources support a putative common ancestral precursor for many of the search behaviors in animal foraging. Computer scientists have extended the principles of foraging for food to the study of human "information foraging" in knowledge environments such as the World Wide Web. Characterizations from network science of large-scale mental spaces (such as lexicons) and social spaces (such as friendship networks) have provided structurally similar terrains for modeling search behavior in those domains. Cognitive neuroscience has explored how interactions between the prefrontal cortex and basal ganglia mediate response selection among a variety of goal-directed behaviors, including trade-offs between exploration and exploitation. Similar neuronal and molecular machinery may handle problems as diverse as spatial target search (involving the parietal cortex), retrieval from memory (hippocampus and prefrontal cortex), and abstract decision making (anterior cingulate, prefrontal cortex, and dopamine-dependent functions of the striatum). These diverse goal-directed processes are central to cognition and rely on the integration of search-related architectures. Findings such as these lead to the surprising conclusion that the same cognitive and neural processes may underlie much of human behavior comprising cognitive search—both in the external world and in internal memory (reviewed in Hills 2006).

The pressing need to integrate these insights further has led to the current book, which provides a cross-cutting perspective on the underlying commonalities of cognitive search in different search domains, as studied through different disciplinary lenses. This perspective was developed at the Ernst Strüngmann Forum on Cognitive Search: Evolution, Algorithms, and the Brain. This Forum convened 44 scientists to discuss what can be learned about cognitive search from the study of animal behavior, psychology, neurobiology, and computer science, who sought to identify the commonalities and distinctions among the findings on search in these fields. The chapters in this book capture the beginnings of the foundation that was constructed for a common intellectual ground between the varied disciplines studying search behavior and cognition. This new conceptual base also highlights important directions for future research, including investigations on the underlying neuromolecular and evolutionary origins of human goal-directed cognition and the applications that follow from seeing human behavior as grounded in different types of search.

Central Themes in Cognitive Search

This book is organized around four main themes central to search behavior:

1. its evolutionary origins, adaptive functions, and main characteristics as described from an ecological perspective;
2. its neural and neurochemical underpinnings in the brain;
3. its cognitive manifestations and mechanisms in domains commonly studied by psychologists;
4. its algorithmic application to high-dimensional spaces including evolutionary search over genotypes, social search in social networks, and information search on the World Wide Web.

These themes framed the discussion of the four corresponding working groups at the Forum, and are similarly reflected in the four sections of this volume. Each section comprises background chapters followed by a group-authored chapter that summarizes the discussions and debates that arose. Here we give an overview of the questions that drove each group's discussions.

Group 1: Evolution of Search, Adaptation, and Ecology

This working group focused on the biological origins of search and the ultimate adaptive functions it plays for different species, and was guided by the following questions:

*   What adaptive problems has search evolved to solve (e.g., food, habitat, mates, social partners, information, specific memories)?
*   What are the common features of those problems (e.g., patchy vs. uniform distribution, competition, degree of uncertainty)?
*   What are the common features of the solutions (e.g., individual vs. group foraging, exploration vs. exploitation, local vs. global, parallel vs. serial)?
*   What is the evolutionary history and fate of strategies (e.g., phylogeny, homology, exaptation)?

Much of this group's discussion (see Hutchinson et al., this volume) centered around defining search behavior (and what is not search), and on creating typologies of different kinds of search defined by features such as the distribution of resources in space and time and whether or not the resources are ephemeral. The intent was to provide a wide range of examples of different kinds of search and where they occur, and to build an ecological basis for thinking about search in other domains. Social search, including the dual roles that individuals may have in terms of finding resources versus scrounging them from others, was another central topic.

Group 2: Search, Goals, and the Brain

Focusing on the conserved proximate mechanisms—brain structures, neural circuits, and neurochemical modulations—that underlie search behavior across multiple domains, this group was guided by the following questions:

- What are the shared molecular and neural processes that control spatial and nonspatial attention and search?
- How does the brain implement goal maintenance and switching, and exploration versus exploitation trade-offs?
- How is the neuromodulation of search processes (e.g., via the molecular signaling functionality of dopamine) controlled and conserved across species and behaviors?
- What can be learned from pathologies of goal-directed search such as obsessive-compulsive disorder, ADHD, and Parkinson's disease?

After discussing definitions of search and its connection to goal seeking, Winstanley et al. (this volume) worked to come up with a model of the neural mechanisms underlying goal-directed behavior that brings together much of what is currently known in the literature. This provided a useful jumping-off point for discussions with the other groups, particularly the psychologists in Group 3. Relatively less progress was made on the questions related to pathologies, which remains an important direction for further research.

Group 3: Mechanisms and Processes of Cognitive Search

This working group focused on the cognitive and memory mechanisms involved in search, as studied by psychology and cognitive science, and the possibility of a general cognitive search process. Discussions were guided by the following questions:

- What are the psychological components (e.g., exploration, sampling, evaluation, stopping rules) in common to various types of cognitive search (e.g., visual, memory, spatial), and how do these compare to the components of search in external environments?

- Do the shared aspects of cognitive models of memory recall and recognition, visual search, and lexical retrieval point to a common underlying mental search process, and what methods (e.g., priming between search tasks) could be used to study this?
- What are appropriate ways to represent mental search spaces, and what do these representations presume about the underlying search processes?
- How is cognitive search directed and controlled (e.g., focus of attention, cue selection, feeling of knowing, inhibition of return)?

Pachur et al. (this volume) centered on search tasks that have been traditionally studied in laboratory experiments, including search through memory of paired-associate lists, visual search in simple two-dimensional arrays of images, and the search for information or cues to be used in making decisions. Group members agreed that more emphasis needs to be put on real-world tasks, such as searching for memories of routes to known locations in one's environment or for objects in a natural visual scene.

Group 4: Search Environments, Representation, and Encoding

This working group focused on how people search through high-dimensional environments (beyond two or three dimensions), such as social networks or collections of information, and on comparisons with search processes in evolution and computer science. Organizing questions included:

- How are different search domains structured and represented to searchers (e.g., patches of resources, topological distributions in physical, mental, and social environments)?
- Where do these search space structures come from, and how are they formed (e.g., evolution, ontogeny, network growth)?
- What are the similarities and differences between mechanisms and behaviors for search in high-dimensional (e.g., information) versus low-dimensional (e.g., physical) spaces?
- How does the structure and dimensionality of the environment impact the search process? Are different strategies appropriate in predictable ways across memory search, World Wide Web search, and social network search?
- How can we facilitate individual and group search in different environments (e.g., in the semantic web or social networks)?

Schooler et al. (this volume) considered ways that search has been implemented in computer science, where search is a central concept for developing algorithms that find solutions to problems or information sought by users. Social scientists reported related studies in which people search their social networks for others who may have parts of solutions that they need to solve problems cooperatively. The theory of neutral networks from genetics was discussed as a way for agents to search along "ridges" in a high-dimensional space so that they can avoid getting stuck in local maxima. Semantic space models relating concepts in memory or on the World Wide Web were also considered as prime targets for developing better methods for search.

Synergy and Future Directions

Throughout the Forum, issues arose that cut across the different groups, leading to even wider interdisciplinary conversations. For example, biologists and psychologists in Groups 1 and 3 explored the many commonalities between the basic principles underlying animal search for resources and those governing human cognition. Just as animals often search spatial patches, like berries on separate bushes, so humans also search patchy memory representations, hunting for useful clusters of information in their own minds and then exploiting what they find. To sustain their intake rate, foraging animals have evolved rules that guide them to leave a patch when their rate of finding things falls below that which they could achieve if they look elsewhere; the psychologists in Group 3 debated evidence that people behave similarly when searching in memory or a visual scene. Computer scientists in Group 4 argued that information search on the World Wide Web follows similar principles: users give up on websites when their "information scent" falls below the level indicating further profitable exploration in that direction. The brain architecture underlying such goal-directed searching behavior and the seeking of memories to guide voluntary action toward those goals was also the main focus of neuroscientists in Group 2.

Open questions raised at the Forum demonstrate that we are just at the beginning of understanding the intertwined evolutionary, psychological, and neurological bases of the great range of search behaviors of humans and other animals. The most pressing and promising avenues for research include:

- further elucidating the underlying similarities and differences of search in different domains (e.g., Web search, memory search, visual search, mate search, search for food);
- specifying the neural and cognitive mechanisms governing search across different domains;
- exploring the phylogeny of search and how one type of search could evolve into another;
- studying individual differences in search behavior, their genetic bases, and the possible adaptive nature of mixed strategies;
- determining the usefulness of considering some clinical conditions as aberrations of search, leading to too much exploration (e.g., ADHD) or too much focus (e.g., obsessive-compulsive disorder), and possibly

sharing neuromodulatory mechanisms similar to those that control search in other species (e.g., dopamine);

- seeking new treatments for goal-directed pathologies (e.g., drug addiction, Parkinson's disease, ADHD) based on knowledge of the brain mechanisms of search;

- building tools that structure the increasingly overwhelming information environment to work with people's search mechanisms and help them successfully find satisfactory results.

Further interdisciplinary cross-fertilization and scientific inquiry will increase our knowledge of the foundations of cognitive search, which will in turn find use in a variety of new applications. These include clinical treatments and "brain training" to improve strategic search and focus; greater vigilance and control of attention in airport baggage checking, medical image screening and diagnosis, and intelligence analysis; enhanced use of the wisdom of crowds in social problem solving; and better decision making through insights into the evolutionary origins of our abilities to think rationally about finding and using resources. With a greater understanding of how various forms of search are related to each other, we will enhance our search for all that we seek.

Evolution of Search, Adaptation, and Ecology

2

The Evolution of Cognitive Search

Thomas T. Hills and Reuven Dukas

Abstract

Search can be defined as an attempt to arrive at a goal at an unknown location in the physical environment, as well as in time, memory, or any other space. Search is necessary because the quantity and quality of resources essential to survival and reproduction vary in space and time. In addition to exploration through actual body movement in their environment, animals search their external information space through selective allocation of attention and their internal information space to retrieve relevant items from memory. This chapter integrates data on search in three distinct domains—physical movement, attention to external information, and locating items in memory—to highlight the remarkable similarities between these three domains. First, resources in all three domains are typically distributed in patches. Second, in each of the three domains, animals typically keep searching in patches where they have recently found resources and leave areas when none are found or where they have already depleted the resources. Third, the neurobiological mechanisms modulating the exploration for and exploitation of resources in all three domains involve dopamine as well as, in many vertebrates, regions of the prefrontal cortex and striatum. It is suggested that, throughout evolution, animals co-opted existing strategies and mechanisms used to search their physical space for exploring and exploiting internal and external information spaces. The cross-disciplinary integration of theory and data about search can be used to guide future research on the mechanisms underlying cognitive search.

Introduction

Search is one of the most fundamental of all organismal behaviors. Bacteria seek out essential nutrients and steer clear of noxious compounds (Koshland 1980; Eisenbach and Lengeler 2004), plant roots search for water and nutrients (Hutchings and de Kroon 1994; McNickle et al. 2009), and the protozoan *Paramecium* exhibits chemotaxis as well as thermotaxis, geotaxis, and thigmotaxis (movement in response to touch) (Jennings 1906; Saimi and Kung 1987). In general, organisms that move are capable of searching for optimal abiotic settings, such as temperature, humidity, and sunlight, as well as the best places for finding nutrients, avoiding danger, and securing sexual partners.

In addition to physically moving through the environment, animals may search within the information space for cues indicating relevant resources. The information space may be external (e.g., requiring the direction of attention in pursuit of cues that signal prey) or internal (e.g., requiring the directed activation of memory). Regardless of whether physical movement is involved, search entails navigating some space in pursuit of resources; that is, an individual has to decide whether to move (its body or its attention) or stay where it is, and, if it moves, where it should move to. In the domain of physical space, such search problems have been studied extensively in behavioral ecology (Stephens et al. 2007). Research on information search, in both external and internal environments, is developing rapidly (e.g., Fu and Gray 2006; Stephens and Krebs 1986; Hills and Hertwig 2010; Pirolli 2007; Wilke et al. 2009).

In this chapter, we are interested in drawing attention to the potential evolutionary parallels between search across external and internal domains. How might search in external and internal domains be related in an evolutionary sense? Three potential types of evidence can be used to address this question:

1. The neurobiological mechanisms that guide search in different animals may be functionally homologous, deriving from a common ancestral function that was also used to solve search-related problems.
2. Different environments may pose similar kinds of problems for search, generally involving navigating heterogeneous resource distributions to find locations containing resources that maximize fitness.
3. The underlying search strategies may share similar characteristics across different environments and domains.

We begin by providing a definition of search and then briefly review the three characteristics of environmental structure, search strategies, and neural mechanisms involved in search tasks in external and internal domains. The domain of physical movement of individuals in space is taken as a starting point, followed by allocation of attention to external cues and a closing discussion on search in memory.

What Do We Mean by Search?

Search can be defined as an attempt to arrive at a goal at an unknown location in the physical environment, time, memory, or any other space. Finding a resource typically involves at least two components: an *exploration phase* that investigates possible locations as to where the resource might be located and an *exploitation phase* that involves resource acquisition. Often, the exploration and exploitation phases are not mutually exclusive, as animals may sample and exploit during exploration and continue exploring while exploiting.

Because exploration typically takes time away from exploitation, modulation between the two can be represented as an optimal control problem in which organisms attempt to minimize the time spent exploring for resources but still acquire sufficient information to maximize resource exploitation. When the search task involves a distinct individual target, the optimization problem is to choose the movement strategy that would minimize the time needed to find that target. Typically, however, biologically important resources show large variation in quality, and they vary over time and space. Thus an adaptive search usually involves a fitness-maximizing decision about the optimal balance between exploration and exploitation. More exploration can lead to finding better resources but to less time available for exploiting those resources. This trade-off between exploration and exploitation is common to both external and internal search problems.

External Search: Movement

The Structure of the External Resource Environment

All organisms encounter variation in the quantity and quality of resources. In terrestrial systems, physical factors (including the topography, soil types, winds, solar radiation, and precipitation) shape the spatial structure of temperature and availability of minerals and water. These, in turn, generate a variable spatial distribution of plant species and of the organisms associated with them. Such distribution may be either continuous or broken; the latter implies that distinct patches vary in the quality and quantity of a given resource, each surrounded by regions lacking that resource. Further diurnal and seasonal variation in abiotic factors adds temporal variation in organismal activity and productivity. This combination of spatial and temporal variation in essential abiotic and biotic resources means that an individual's exact location in time and space can dramatically affect its fitness. Hence individuals can be modeled as attempting to optimize their spatial position over time.

Search Strategies in External Space

Confined to the question of physical movement, the central issue concerning search in space is whether or not an organism should stay where it is or move elsewhere. Organisms should make this decision in response to heterogeneity in the density of resources in the surrounding environment—an area of study that has been extensively examined (Stephens et al. 2007; Stephens and Krebs 1986). One approach for examining adaptive "nonrandom" foraging behavior involves testing for area-restricted search, which refers to an individual's ability to restrict search to the local area where it has recently found resources before transitioning to more wide-ranging, global exploration (Kareiva and Odell 1987). Area-restricted search is related to patch-based models of foraging, like

14   *T. T. Hills and R. Dukas*

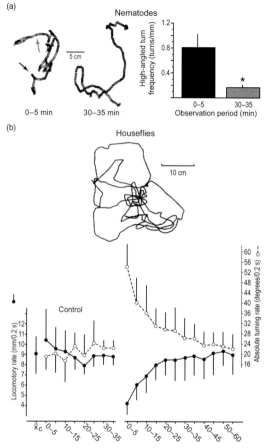

Figure 2.1   Evidence of resource-contingent foraging in (a) nematodes (*Caenorhab-ditis elegans*), (b) houseflies (*Musca domestica*), (c) bumblebees (*Bombus bimacula-tus*), and (d) humans (*Homo sapiens*). (a) The left panel shows the foraging paths for *C. elegans* 0–5 min after encountering food and 30–35 min later. The black arrow indicates a high-angled turn; the gray arrow denotes a region of the path with no turning. The right panel shows that high-angled turns are significantly more likely to occur for the interval more recently associated with food (Hills et al. 2004). (b) The top panel shows a 69 s path for *M. domestica* immediately after it encounters food (at the central dot). The lower panel shows the quantitative comparison of turning angle (open circles) and locomotory rate (closed circles) for control flies (on the left) and flies immediately after encountering food (on right) (redrawn from White et al. 1984). (c) The top panel shows a significantly decreasing flight distance to the next flower following sequences of one, two, or three rewarding flowers for *B. bimaculatus*. The lower panel shows a significantly increasing flight distance after a series of one, two, or three nonrewarding flowers (data from Dukas and Real 1993). (d) The top panel shows typical paths for humans foraging in a three-dimensional environment with invisible resources arrayed in distributed or clustered arrangements. The lower panel illustrates that humans show significantly increased turning after encounters with resources in clustered environments than in distributed environments (Kalff et al. 2010).

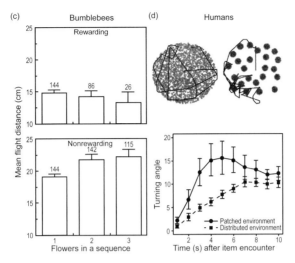

Figure 2.1 (cont'd)

the marginal value theorem (Charnov 1976), but is often employed when patch boundaries are difficult to detect or are otherwise "fuzzy" (Benhamou 1992; Adler and Kotar 1999).

One of the most primitive forms of search transitions between local and global foraging is the run-and-tumble behavior of bacteria such as *Escheria coli*. *E. coli* exhibit a change in behavior upon detecting increasing or decreasing food concentration gradients (Eisenbach and Lengeler 2004; Koshland 1980). When *E. coli* encounter increasing resources as they move, they engage in directed "runs" of swimming behavior using their flaggelar motor. When they experience decreasing resources, the direction of the flaggelar motor changes and this causes the bacteria to tumble randomly before engaging in another directed swim. This behavior appears to serve as a method for moving toward high concentration gradients and away from low concentration gradients. Thus, bacteria show evidence of area-restricted search by attempting to stay in areas with higher resource density, but move away from areas with lower resource density.

Figure 2.1 illustrates patterns of area-restricted search observed for several classes of animal species: nematodes (*Caenorhabditis elegans*), houseflies (*Musca domestica*), bumblebees (*Bombus bimaculatus*), and humans (*Homo sapiens*). In each case, the central result is that the animal responds to low resource densities by traveling away from them and to high resource densities by staying near them. In nematodes (*C. elegans*), individuals engage in high-angled turns (or pirouettes) following recent encounters with resources, but reduce their number of pirouettes as the time since the last encounter increases (Hills et al. 2004). Similar patterns of increased turning in response to resource encounters have been observed in flies (White et al. 1984), bumblebees (Dukas and Real 1993), and humans (Kalff et al. 2010). This pattern of density-contingent foraging in space is ubiquitous across metazoans (Bell 1990; Hills 2006).

Neural Mechanisms of Search in External Space

What are the neural modulators of spatial search? Despite the abundance of evidence that animals can respond to changing resource densities in space, the neural mechanisms that control this ability are not well understood. Here we focus primarily on dopamine, because other neuromodulators (e.g., norepinephrine and serotonin) are less well understood from a comparative perspective, though they are potentially critical to search and other reward-seeking behaviors (Barron et al. 2010; Cools, this volume).

In nematodes (*C. elegans*), the modulation between local area-restricted perseveration and wider-ranging exploration is governed, at least in part, by a relationship between presynaptic dopaminergic neurons modulating downstream glutamatergic locomotory interneurons. Higher levels of dopamine increase turning angles, whereas lower levels reduce turning angles. Selectively killing dopaminergic neurons or applying a dopaminergic antagonist (raclopride) removes the capacity for area-restricted search (Hills et al. 2004). Dopaminergic mechanisms also facilitate the increased turning that fruit flies (*Drosophila melanogaster*) show under the influence of cocaine (Bainton et al. 2000), and this has even been found to extend to associative learning for places in the flatworm, *Dugesia japonica* (Kusayama and Watanabe 2000). In rats (*Rattus norvegicus*), turning increases in response to agonists for dopaminergic receptors (Robertson and Robertson 1986), and modulation between explorative and exploitative behaviors is mediated by midbrain dopaminergic neurons (Fink and Smith 1980). In random foraging experiments, injection of a specific antagonist for the dopaminergic receptor subtype D1 into the nucleus accumbens of rats significantly impaired performance, measured by an increase in wrong entries into maze arms (Floresco and Phillips 1999).

Perseveration in response to resources is known to involve a significant dopaminergic component across animal phyla (for a recent review, see Barron et al. 2010). In part, this may be due to the relationship between dopaminergic processing and reward sensitivity. Numerous observations of dopaminergic activity in response to rewards as well as novel and aversive stimuli have been made and given rise to terms like "reward detector" and "novelty detector" (Salamone et al. 1997). Critically, dopaminergic neurons adjust their firing rates in response to unpredicted stimuli that are associated with fitness, such as appetitive and aversive stimuli (Salamone et al. 1997). Dopaminergic neurons are also involved in learning to predict outcomes associated with conditioned stimuli (Ljungberg et al. 1992; Kusayama and Watanabe 2000). In vertebrates, the dopaminergic neurons most often associated with goal-directed behaviors are located in the thalamus, striatum, and frontal cortex. These appear to work together to control goal-directed movement in physical space and the focus of attention.

Attentional Search for External Information

The Structure of the External Information Space

As noted above, animals encounter nonrandom distributions of abiotic and biotic resources as they move through their physical environment. This means that the cues indicating the availability and quality of relevant resources (including food, predation, potential mates, and competitors) also show nonrandom distribution in time and space. Hence individuals can rely on the spatial and temporal structure of certain information for locating resources.

It is obvious that, in many species, search involves movement in physical space but the issue of search within the external information space is less apparent. Intuitively, one might argue that individuals should just process all incoming relevant information. It is indeed possible for some organisms with very limited perceptual ability to adopt such an inclusive strategy. In animals with extensive perceptual ability, it is clearly optimal to tune out all irrelevant information. Often, however, even the flow of relevant information exceeds the information processing rate of both the sensory organs and the brain (Dukas 2002, 2009). In humans, for example, only the fovea, which occupies about 0.01% of the retina and $1.7°$ of the visual field, transmits high-quality visual information. In primates, in general, the optic nerve transmits only approximately 2% of the information captured by the retina, and only about 1% of that information is processed by the visual cortex (Van Essen and Anderson 1995). In short, an individual's sensory organs can capture only a small proportion of the incoming information flow, and the rate of information capture by the sensory organs far exceeds the brain's rate of information processing. This necessitates a strategy for allocating attention to the most relevant cues in the information space at any given time.

Search Strategies for External Information

External information can be envisioned as a multidimensional space generated by the information flow from all sense organs. At any given time, animals must choose what information to attend to. This is analogous to the location choices that animals make in their physical space (discussed above). In the information space, animals should attend to the portion of information flow that would have the greatest effect on fitness (Dukas and Ellner 1993). For example, when human subjects were more likely to find targets at certain angles of the visual field, they devoted more attention to and had higher detection rates at these angles than subjects searching for randomly distributed targets (Shaw and Shaw

1977). Similarly, human subjects tend to focus their visual attention in the vicinity of a recently detected target but switch their attention to other spatial locations if no target is found at this area within a short giving-up time. This behavior, which is reminiscent of area-restricted search, is called *inhibition of return* (Klein 2000; Posner and Cohen 1984). In general, animals foraging in natural settings should focus their attention on the sensory cues associated with the most profitable food and most likely danger (Dukas 2002). Whereas much of the research on attention has been done in the visual domain, auditory and olfactory studies have revealed similar patterns of animals focusing on the most relevant cues at any given time (Skals et al. 2005; Fritz et al. 2007; Cross and Jackson 2010).

Animals searching for resources in the physical environment must often choose the search rate (distance moved per unit time) that would maximize their rate of finding resources (Dukas 2002; Gendron and Staddon 1983). Similarly, animals have to choose their range of information processing, which should be negatively related to the difficulty of processing certain information (Dukas and Ellner 1993). That is, animals can distribute attention broadly (e.g., devote little attention per unit area) when handling easy information but must adopt a narrow focus of attention when handling difficult information. Consider, for example, blue jays (*Cyanocitta cristata*) that were trained to search for two prey types: a caterpillar, which could appear in the center of the visual field at a probability of 0.5, and a moth, which could appear in either right or left peripheries of the visual field at a probability of 0.25 per side. Jays were three times more likely to detect the peripheral moth targets when the central caterpillar was conspicuous (i.e., easy to detect) than when it was cryptic and hence difficult to detect. This result is consistent with the prediction that the jays would process information from the whole visual field when the primary task is easy, but would narrow down their focus of attention to the center field when the primary task is difficult (Dukas and Kamil 2000). Jays modulated their focus of attention, reducing the area from which they processed information when the task became more difficult (see also Wolfe, this volume).

Neural Mechanisms Controlling Attention to External Information

Exactly as dopamine is a key neuromodulator of search in physical space, it plays an important role in search within the external information space. In general, dopamine is involved in subjects' ability to focus and sustain attention on relevant cues. For example, mice (*Mus musculus*) that were genetically manipulated to eliminate selectively phasic firing of dopaminergic neurons showed selective impairment in using relevant cues for learning. This suggests that the phasic firing of dopaminergic neurons modulates selective attention to relevant information (Caron and Wightman 2009; Zweifel et al. 2009). In humans, subjects with a subtype of the dopamine transporter gene associated with higher dopamine levels in the striatum (a region of the brain associated with attention) show a different pattern of inhibition of return than control subjects (Colzato et al. 2010a). This suggests involvement of dopamine in the spatial allocation of attention over time.

Dopamine deficit is currently the leading theory for explaining attention deficit hyperactivity disorder (ADHD), a mental disorder characterized by a reduced ability to focus and sustain attention and by an excessive level of activity. Brain imaging studies indicate smaller sizes and lesser activation of brain regions related to dopamine in individuals with ADHD. Allelic variation in two genes, the dopamine receptor D4 and the dopamine transporter, has been linked to ADHD, and the principal drug for treating ADHD, methylpheni-date (Ritalin®), increases synaptically released dopamine (Iversen and Iversen 2007; Swanson et al. 2007). Together, these examples provide strong evidence that dopamine modulates the focus of attention to external information simi-larly to the way it modulates perseverative local foraging in external space.

Internal Information Search

Having focused on search via physical movement in the environment as well as through selective tuning to external information, we now explore search for information in memory or for solutions to problems that require internal manipulation of information.

The Structure of Internal Information

As demonstrated above, external stimuli often present themselves in a nonran-dom, spatially autocorrelated fashion—with rewards associated with a specific location likely to signal rewards close to that location in the near future. Does the structure of relationships between items in memory also implicate an au-tocorrelated structure, and do we see evidence of this structure in recall from memory?

Studies of written language—presumably reflecting the internal structure of cognitive information—find evidence for a strongly clustered environment. With nodes representing words and links representing relations between words, these language networks often reveal a small-world structure, indicating that words are much more likely to appear together in small clusters of related items than one would expect by chance (Cancho and Solé 2001). A similar small-world structure has also been identified in internal search when people are asked to say the first word that comes to mind after hearing another word (i.e., free association) (Steyvers and Tenenbaum 2005). Moreover, this struc-ture of language and free association networks is well correlated with the order in which children learn about language (Hills et al. 2010a). This indicates that the patchy internal structure of memory may be tightly linked with the patchy external structure of information.

Search Strategies for Internal Information

Research on free recall from natural categories and list learning consistently finds that groups of semantically similar words are produced together (Bousfield 1953; Romney et al. 1993). This clustering in output is often considered to be the result of a dynamic search process that modulates between local and global search policies. One of the most prominent and successful memory search models, the search of associative memory model, employs this dynamic local-to-global search policy (Raaijmakers and Shiffrin 1981). Local search is assumed to occur via item level similarity, with recently recalled items in memory activating other related items in memory. Global search activates items in relation to the overarching category and context such as according to their typicality or frequency of occurrence in that category. For example, in the animal fluency task—"say all the animals you can think of"—a person might search globally and produce "dog" and then search locally for similar items, like "wolf" and "fox," before transitioning to a global search and producing "cow." In the model, transitions from local to global search occur when local resources become depleted, such as when there is nothing similar to "fox" that has not already been produced. Interestingly, this model of memory search was developed in cognitive psychology independent of models in behavioral ecology, but it shares the signature behavioral pattern associated with area-restricted search in physical space: modulating between exploration and exploitation in response to recent experience with the resource environment.

Similar evidence for local perseveration due to memory activation has been found in experiments based on word priming. In these experiments, a person is first shown a word prime (e.g., BIRD) and then asked to determine whether a second shown word target is a true word or a nonword (e.g., ROBIN or ROLIN, respectively). Relative to an uninformative word prime, Neely (1977) demonstrated both facilitation (faster response times) and inhibition (slower response times) in people's ability to determine the identity of the word target by manipulating whether the word target was expected or unexpected following the word prime. This elegantly demonstrates that expectations create local activation in memory following the presentation of a prime, and that this can both reduce the time it takes to recognize objects associated with those memories and also increase the time it takes to recognize objects that are not associated with those memories.

Research on sequential solutions in problem-solving tasks also demonstrates that people show local perseveration in internal search environments. For example, people tend to produce solutions that are more clustered together (i.e., similar) than one would expect by random generation; for example, in math search tasks (Hills 2010) and anagram search tasks (Hills et al. 2010b). In one case, Hills et al. (2010b) had participants search within scrambled sets of letters for multiple words. Participants would see a letter set, like BLNTAO, and they could find "BOAT," "BOLT," etc. An analysis of the string similarity

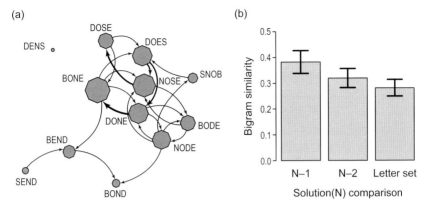

Figure 2.2 Behavior in an anagram search task. (a) Visual depiction of the between-word transitions produced by all participants in the letter set NSBDOE. Participants looked for words they could make from letters in the letter set (using four or more letters). Nodes represent solutions and links between nodes represent transitions between words, with the arrow showing which word came second. Node size is proportional to the number of participants who provided that solution for this letter set. Link thickness is proportional to the number of participants who made that transition. For visual clarity, only transitions that took place more than twice are represented with a link. (b) The bigram similarity of the present word solution to previous ($N-1$) and two-back ($N-2$) solutions and to the original letter set, showing that solutions tended to have the highest string similarity to solutions produced nearby. Error bars are standard error of the mean. Reprinted with permission from Hills et al. (2010b).

(e.g., bigram similarity comparing the number of shared letter pairs: "BO," "OA," etc.) between subsequent solutions determined that participants tended to produce solutions that were most similar to their last solution. This was true even though previous solutions were not visible. Results indicate that participants were searching locally around previous solutions, before transitioning to a global search strategy (Figure 2.2).

Neural Mechanisms in Internal Information Search

Several studies have found that the trajectories taken through long-term memory are related to working memory span (Rosen and Engle 1997), which is well known to be tightly connected with dopaminergic processing (Cools and D'Esposito 2009). Rosen and Engle (1997) found that participants with higher working memory spans tend to produce longer sequences of clustered items in a category fluency task than individuals with lower working memory spans. Hills and Pachur (2012) used a social fluency task ("say all the people that you know") and had participants reconstruct the social network over which they were searching. Using semantic memory models, they found that participants with lower working memory spans transitioned more frequently between global and local cues in memory than individuals with higher working memory spans. This passage is similar to the transition between exploratory and exploitative behavior described above for spatial and attentional foraging.

Cools and D'Esposito (2009) suggest that a proper balance between prefrontal and striatal dopamine levels is the key modulator of cognitive stability and cognitive flexibility and that this proper balance is also related to working memory. This is similar to Kane and Engle's (2002) interpretation that the cognitive control of attention (i.e., the ability to focus on one subgoal to the exclusion of other, distracting stimuli) is the underlying factor that determines working memory span. Furthermore, they suggest that this ability is mediated by prefrontal cortex modulation of activity in other areas of the brain. In other words, individuals with higher working memory spans are better at exploiting local information in internal search, whereas individuals with lower working memory spans tend to leave patches of local information more readily.

Prospects

The data we have presented above indicate three central points about external and internal search:

1. The environments in which organisms search both externally and internally share similar structural properties, and resources tend to be patchily distributed.
2. Various search strategies often rely on this patchiness to focus search around areas where resources have been recently found, and thus to facilitate resource acquisition based on their nonrandom distribution.
3. The neural mechanisms that control search—especially those involving dopamine, the prefrontal cortex, and the striatum—are often shared across species and search environments.

Although the data help us integrate information about the structure, strategies, and mechanisms of search in external and internal environments, we still lack substantial knowledge about the cognitive ecology of search. Below we highlight key issues that require further research.

Physical Search as an Evolutionary Precursor of Cognitive Search

Might the similarity between external physical search and internal information search indicate an origin for goal-directed cognition (i.e., cognitive control) from an evolutionary precursor devoted to spatial foraging and feeding related behaviors? Across metazoans (i.e., vertebrates and invertebrates), we find similar mechanisms modulating physical search for resources (Barron et al. 2010). As outlined above, in vertebrates (especially mammals) we find roughly the same mechanisms modulating search for information. This suggests a potential evolutionary homology between search in physical space and cognitive search, with the derived form broadening the domains of search to information (Hills 2006). What other evidence would provide support for or against this hypothesis?

The comparative evolutionary approach to search raises several other questions. Are different forms of cognitive search domain-specific or domain-general? Recent research demonstrated priming in humans from external to internal search (Hills et al. 2008), based on empirical data indicating that prior experience in spatial foraging influenced a subsequent search in an "internal" problem-solving task. In this experiment, participants who first searched in a visuospatial task for clustered or diffuse resources subsequently searched for word solutions in anagrams as if those solutions were also more or less clustered, respectively. This may indicate a domain-general search process, consistent with our understanding of executive processing in cognition as a method for navigating hierarchical subgoals (Hills et al. 2010b). Which other forms of search are guided by such a domain-general process, or by different domain-specific processes (e.g., mate search)?

Do flexible cognitive capacities rely on balancing neuromodulation, similar to the cognitive search trade-off between exploration and exploitation outlined above? Many pathologies of goal-directed behavior (e.g., ADHD, Parkinson's, stereotypies in autism, drug addiction) involve dopamine in a way that would be predicted from the neural control of animal foraging behavior, with more (or less) synaptic dopamine leading to higher (or lower) levels of perseveration and attentional focus (Hills 2006). Cools and Robbins (2004) argue that there is a balance between too-high and too-low dopamine levels and that this generates the "optimal state of mind"; patterns of behavior associated with too much or too little dopamine are consistently inflexible, often being too compulsive or impulsive for the demands of the environment. Flexibility is potentially one of the guiding selective forces in the evolution of the brain, as relatively larger brains appear to confer greater flexibility—an observation called the *cognitive buffer hypothesis* (Sol 2009). Can we better operationalize what flexibility means, in terms of searching for information? What might be the various evolutionary origins of this flexibility?

What Are the Biological Mechanisms of Cognitive Search?

In our analysis of the neural mechanisms underlying search, we focused on the common denominator of neuromodulation by dopamine, which, in vertebrates, is localized principally in the prefrontal cortex and striatum. Whereas this shared characteristic of neuromodulation by dopamine is intriguing and deserves further exploration, a fuller examination must also include more specific details about other brain regions, neuromodulators, and patterns of neuronal firings involved in search within each of the distinct spaces discussed here. Are there additional common mechanisms at this deeper level of analysis? Can existing knowledge about biological mechanisms of search within one domain, such as selective attention in external space (Knudsen 2007; Salamone et al. 1997), help us understand mechanisms of search in another area (e.g., retrieval from an internal information space) (see also Winstanley et al., this volume)?

The Organization of Internal Information

Thus far we have focused on similarities across search environments and search mechanisms; however, important differences do exist. Perhaps the most significant distinction between external and internal search environments is that searchers typically cannot control the distribution of targets in the external environment but may affect the way they store their own information. That is, natural selection may have shaped the architecture of internally stored information to maximize some utility, such as the speed of recall or the numbers of items recalled. Existing models and data on search in external space may be able to help us understand the selective pressures and constraints operating on the structure of internal search environments.

How Are Algorithms for Search Shared across Domains?

What other dimensions can be used to characterize search? Part of the power of search as a paradigm is our ability to use search algorithms in one domain to inform research in other domains. In this discussion we highlighted the trade-off between exploitation and exploration, which is closely aligned with models of patch foraging. Similar search strategies borrowed from behavioral ecology have recently been applied to human information processing, for example, in terms of giving-up rules in problem solving (Wilke et al. 2009) and information-foraging strategies that capitalize on the structure of linked pages in the World Wide Web (Fu and Pirolli 2007). There are, however, other ways to implement search policies and many dimensions along which they may be defined. Given that some characterizations of search (e.g., exploitation versus exploration) lend themselves better to comparative analysis—both across organisms and algorithms—understanding how we define the dimensions of search and characterize different search policies may help us integrate our understanding of search and cognitive abilities more effectively.

Acknowledgments

We thank Lauren Dukas, Luc-Alain Giraldeau, David Redish, Peter Todd, and an anonymous referee for comments on the manuscript, and participants of the Ernst Strüngmann Forum for helpful suggestions. Our work has been supported by a grant from the Swiss National Research Foundation (100014 130397/1) (TH) and by the Natural Sciences and Engineering Research Council of Canada, Canada Foundation for Innovation and Ontario Innovation Trust (RD).

3

Ecological and Behavioral Approaches to Search Behavior

David W. Stephens, Iain Couzin, and Luc-Alain Giraldeau

Abstract

This chapter offers a selective review of behavioral and ecological perspectives on search behavior. Basic results from foraging theory are presented and their relationship to search is discussed. Techniques for the statistical description of searching motion are outlined, with a focus on the correlated random walk and the so-called Lévy flights—a technique that holds considerable promise. The problems of search in groups are reviewed at several levels. Both cooperative search (as conducted, e.g., by members of a social insect colony) and group movements of extremely selfish animals are considered. Finally, a review is provided of the producer-scrounger game, which considers the interactions within groups when some individuals parasitize the search behavior of others. The implications of these ideas are discussed and potential future directions for future enquiry are highlighted.

Introduction

Movement is basic to an animal's way of life. Indeed, many readers will realize that the word "animal" refers to movement. Animals move to obtain their food, whereas plants do not. It follows that search is a primitive and fundamental aspect of the animal way of life. By search we typically mean the behavior associated with finding and identifying resources (Bell 1991). Any study of the diversity of ways in which animals find and identify resources will be connected to nearly every level of biological organization: from sensation to motor control, from cell biology to evolution.

Two Basic Observations about Animal Search

When we search for a set of lost keys, the activity we undertake to find them has a definite end. Once we find the keys, we are done and the "search" is over. In contrast, many important types of animal search are repeated. An animal searching for food is not, typically, searching for a single food item but rather for food in general; an animal may encounter and consume many separate items before a given bout of "search" ends. This is an important distinction because single-shot and iterated search are quite different economically. In an iterated search process, the way an animal treats items discovered early in the sequence can affect what happens later. Specifically, actions taken early in the sequence can have opportunity costs that do not arise in single-shot search processes. This is not to say that animals never engage in single-shot searches; they may search for a single nest site, or possibly a single mate. However, iterated search is probably the norm, even though we tend to think of search as a single-shot process.

Search can be conceptualized in two distinct ways. A literal modeling of search considers the patterns of movement required to find resources in the environment, and the statistical characterizations of search that we outline below take this approach. However, some models of search focus instead on the problem of identifying suitable resources. In models of this type, the animal "examines" potential resources and sequentially accepts or rejects them. Models of processes like this often ignore movement completely and, instead, characterize the properties of "acceptable" and "unacceptable" items. For example, some models of "mate search" consider a situation where a female examines prospective mates in sequence. These models consider "search" in the sense that they specify the properties of acceptable and unacceptable males. Notice that in this conceptualization of search, movement is not strictly required; the targets that are examined by the searcher could pass by a stationary searcher, or the searcher could actively move from one to the other. Although these two aspects of search are often considered separately, a complete analysis of search must consider them together (indeed it is possible imagine a single mechanism that combines these functions).

Search and Foraging Theory

Although search occurs in many biological contexts, search for food holds a central position in biological ideas about feeding, and a well-articulated body of theory exists about some of the basic food acquisition decisions animals make. Two are relevant here, because they have direct implications for search behavior, diet choice, and patch exploitation. Diet choice models consider an animal moving through its habitat encountering foods items in sequence; as it encounters items, it must decide whether to accept or reject them. If the forager accepts an item, it gains some amount of food, e (often measured in calories), and spends a fixed time (h) handling and consuming this item. Foods vary in their qualities (e values) and handling times (h values). If the forager rejects the item, it continues searching until it discovers another item. When it discovers another item, it again makes an accept-reject decision.

While the details of the diet choice model, and many other foraging models, are fully described elsewhere (Stephens and Krebs 1986), we make two points about this "diet selection" process. First, it envisions an iterated rather than single-shot search, and this makes the handling time variable important. A long handling time increases the opportunity cost of accepting an item, because the time a forager spends handling is time it cannot spend searching for new items. Second, crudely speaking, the model predicts that environmental richness should determine a forager's selectivity; this follows from the idea of iterated search and the opportunity costs of accepting an item with a long handling time. In a rich habitat (where the forager can obtain high-quality items quickly), it can be costly to accept an item because searching further is likely to yield a better item, so we predict that animals should be specialists; that is, they should only accept a narrow range of good prey types in rich environments. In contrast, when the environment is poor (low-quality items that are difficult or time consuming to find), accepting an item carries a smaller opportunity cost, and we predict that animals should be generalists, consuming a relatively wide range of food types.

In patch exploitation problems (for the original development, see Charnov 1976; for a comprehensive treatment, see Stephens and Krebs 1986), we imagine that foragers encounter clumps of food. The interesting thing about food clumps or patches is that they tend to get worse as the forager exploits them. When a forager first enters a patch, it acquires food quickly because the patch is "fresh" and unexploited, but as it continues to hunt there, it becomes more difficult to extract the next unit of food value. Patches typically decline in marginal intake rate. Because of this, the forager faces a dilemma: searching for another fresh patch is costly and time consuming, but the value of the current patch is inevitably declining. Using rationale that closely resembles our discussion of diet selection, patch exploitation theory predicts that animals should stay longer and extract more from patches when the environment is poor. While this is an intuitively reasonable (and empirically well-supported) result, it is clearly relevant to our thinking about the biology of search. It focuses our attention on the balance between "searching" and "exploiting" and suggests that habitat richness influences how this balance is struck.

Moreover, patch exploitation theory gives us insight into the ecological rationale of foraging movement; that is, for the existence of searching movements. Consider animals that live in the rocky intertidal zone around the world. Between the tides, we find incredibly exotic invertebrates—from colorful sea slugs to sedentary barnacles. Some of these animals, like sea slugs, move about while searching for food, and we say that they are "widely foraging" animals. Others, like the barnacle and the many filter-feeding organisms, are "sit-and-wait" foragers. The difference is striking in the intertidal zone because there are many sedentary foragers, but both strategies are common and taxonomically widespread. For example, web-building spiders, ant-lions, and flycatchers can all be characterized as sit-and-wait foragers.

Why do some animals sit and wait? In patch exploitation models, animals leave patches (to search for new resources) because exploiting reduces patch quality. There are, however, situations where patch quality does not decline. The flux of photons impinging on a leaf does not change when the leaf absorbs some of the photons; similarly, the concentration of plankton that washes over a barnacle in the intertidal zone is virtually unchanged by the barnacle's filtering. In both cases, of course, the organism in question does not move. Sit-and-wait foragers, therefore, represent an end point of the patch exploitation spectrum. This application of patch exploitation theory illustrates the basic rationale of animal search. To be specific, we see sit-and-wait foraging as an extreme case of the marginal value theorem; for these animals, the patch does not deplete, and thus there is no reason to move to another patch.

Some Types of Search

Although animal biologists recognize the central role of search in behavior, it has seldom been the subject of a unified and coherent treatment. Instead, it tends to come up as a component of other topics, such as "searching for mates," or "spatial cognition." Here, we briefly review several of these topics and point out recurrent themes in the study of search.

Gradient Climbing

Animals may follow concentration gradients to reach goals. The concentration and concentration differences involved in these gradients can be stunningly small. For example, anadromous fish (fish that live in the ocean as adults but breed in freshwater streams, such as salmon or sea lampreys) find appropriate streams using olfaction. As you can imagine, the olfactory signature of a stream many kilometers out to sea must be incredibly faint. Sea lampreys follow a gradient of bile acids released by lamprey larvae (intriguingly lamprey larvae are sit-and-wait foragers that live in the substrate of freshwater streams, whereas adults widely forage for free-living fish that they parasitize). Animals that follow olfactory "plumes" (e.g., spawning lamprey) commonly initiate this search with wide zig-zagging movements, which helps them to detect small differences in concentration.

Saltatory Search

A surprising number of animals search in a jerky way. While searching, these animals show a repeating pattern of moving and pausing. A robin foraging on a lawn will typically show this behavior, as will many planktivorous fish. This distinctive behavior has attracted the attention of behavioral biologists starting with Andersson (1981). Although there are several possible explanations, the simplest is that movement degrades the forager's ability to detect prey (or possibly predators). This degradation would, we assume, be similar to the difficulties in focusing a moving camera. Under this hypothesis, we view the pauses in "pause-travel" search as opportunities to scan new territory accurately for prey. Interestingly, pigeons can famously stabilize their visual apparatus while walking steadily: although a walking pigeon typically does not exhibit the pause-travel pattern of a foraging robin, its head bobs in a manner that holds the position of the eyes steady while the body literally moves underneath them.

Area-Restricted Search

Many animals change their patterns of movement in response to foraging success. The effect of these behavioral changes is to keep the predator in the region of its foraging success. For example, a predacious coccinelid beetle larva will increase its rate of turning and decrease its movement speed after it captures an aphid. Investigators assume that this behavior functions to keep the predator in the neighborhood of a clump of prey, and it follows that we would not expect area-restricted search in predators that exploit uniformly distributed (i.e., nonpatchy) resources; acknowledging, of course, that patchiness is a nearly ubiquitous feature of feeding environments. Although these links have not been fully developed, area-restricted search is connected to two aspects of search already discussed. Obviously, it is strikingly connected to the zig-zagging movements we see in animals detecting olfactory plumes. It is also clearly related to the very general and well-studied problem of patch exploitation, yet we know of little work that establishes or develops the connection between these ideas (for a possible counter example, see Waage 1979). There seem to be two barriers to developing this connection. First, the two approaches focus on different aspects of the clump exploitation problem. Studies of area-restricted search seem to focus on recognizing a clump of food, whereas patch exploitation studies focus on leaving a clump. Second, the theory of patch exploitation assumes that animals can easily recognize well-defined patches; in these models, patches have well-defined and recognizable boundaries. In contrast, the clumps in area-restricted search are loosely defined and may be difficult to recognize.

The Phylogeny of Search

In this review, we aim to give the reader a glimpse of the diversity of search behavior by using examples from a wide range of taxa and ecological situations. We do not feel, however, that we can offer an authoritative statement about "the phylogeny of search." Constructing "a phylogeny of search" is a daunting undertaking. As this review will show, search is a behavior with many dimensions, and it is not clear which attribute of search one would study phylogenetically. Put another way, biologists categorize search in many ways: generalist versus specialist, saltatory versus continuous, area-restricted search versus not. Which of these "characters" should one choose to represent "search" in a phylogenetic analysis? It may make perfect sense to analyze separate attributes of search phylogenetically, but a phylogeny of search generally is likely to be too vague to be satisfying.

A similar question is whether one can construct a coherent taxonomy of search that not only recognizes different types of search (as we have done above), but recognizes the connections between them. We recommend the paper by Mueller and Fagen (2008), which attempts to do this. Mueller and Fagen's approach is ambitious in that it both recognizes different categories of search (e.g., nonoriented vs. oriented) and attempts to synthesis explanatory and descriptive approaches to search. While Mueller and Fagan's approach will probably not satisfy all investigators, it does seem to be a very useful step in the right direction.

Development and Search

As discussed, search can be characterized in many ways. An obvious question that arises is whether the attributes of search vary as an animal grows and develops. Clearly, this is true for specific types of animals. For example, for insects with a complete "egg-larva-pupa-adult" life cycle, differences between the two active stages, larva and adult, are the rule. Butterfly larvae (caterpillars) are usually foliovores, and their search is typically restricted to finding the most palatable leaves on a plant, whereas adults typically feed on nectar and hence they actively search for flowers. One could surely find thousands of similar examples, where juveniles and adults eat different things, and so search differently. Because growth occurs in juveniles and reproduction takes place in adults, it is reasonable to expect that the "goals" of search behavior will differ accordingly. Beyond this rather crude and biologically obvious observation, we know of no formal generalizations about this phenomenon.

In the remainder of our discussion, we develop two themes in the biological study of search. First, we briefly review the surprisingly subtle problem of describing animal movement mathematically. In doing so, we show that the simplest model, the random walk, falls short. In addition, we consider the statistical properties of movement and how these properties may (or may not) be influenced by scales of measurement. Second, we take up the problem of search in and by groups of animals. We consider this problem at two levels: by extending our ideas about the statistical description of movement to groups and by considering group search at a more strategic level. Within groups, individuals can "parasitize" the successes of their group mates, and this leads to a fascinating and dynamic game in which some individuals "produce" and others "scrounge" (the so-called producer-scounger game), which has been a key success story of experimental behavioral ecology.

Describing Search

In this section, we conceptualize search as a probabilistic process. In this view, search influences the probability that animals will find food or mates, evade predators, encounter appropriate habitat, or experience physiological stress (Turchin 1991; Adler and Gordon 1992; Fourcassie and Traniello 1995). Since search movements are typically probabilistic (Bovet and Benhamou 1988; Alt and Hoffmann 1990; Tourtellot et al. 1990), this makes it difficult to describe search via deterministic kinematic equations of classical physics.

Discretizing Search Paths

A typical approach used when analyzing the spatial aspects of search is to segment trajectories into successive linear "moves." In some cases, researchers use natural end points to create these segments (see, e.g., Kareiva and Shigesada 1983), but one can partition continuous paths into units of equal distance or time (a move being the displacement observed at the end of a predetermined constant time interval). In some cases, the data may not contain a time base (i.e., the path of an animal may be estimated from tracks, e.g., the slime trail of a snail or footprints of a mammal) without necessitating direct observation of movement. The type of discretization depends not only on the type of data, but also on the biological questions that are being asked.

Regardless of how one chooses path segments, all discretizing techniques face some common problems. Figure 3.1 shows the discretization of an ant search trajectory, recorded using digital tracking software, which demonstrates discretization based on different move-lengths. Figure 3.2 shows histograms of the estimated turning angles made by the ant for each of our four example trajectories. The turning angles can also be used to calculate statistical measures of movement. Useful measures include the mean and standard deviation of the distribution of turning angles, as well as skew and kurtosis. Skew indicates the degree of asymmetry of the distribution around the mean. (A positive skew value implies an asymmetric tail extending toward the positive values, and negative skew implies an asymmetric tail extending toward negative values.) Kurtosis describes the peakedness of a distribution, relative to the normal distribution. Positive kurtosis indicates a relatively peaked (leptokurtic) distribution and negative kurtosis indicates a flatter (platykurtic) distribution than the normal distribution. Table 3.1 shows these statistics calculated for the trajectories a–d shown in Figure 3.1 and 3.2. From the histograms in Figure 3.2 and corresponding data in Table 3.1, it is clear that analyses based on different move-lengths have a large influence on the measured statistical properties.

In general, short move-lengths generate a leptokurtic distribution of turning angles with little skew (Figure 3.2a), whereas larger move-lengths generate platykurtic distributions (Figure 3.2d). Different move-lengths can, therefore, emphasize different aspects of the trajectory. Even a path with an obvious bias

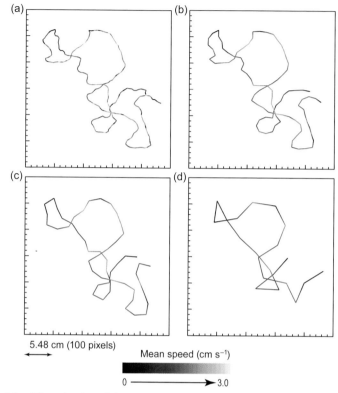

5.48 cm (100 pixels)

Mean speed (cm s⁻¹)

0 ————————➤ 3.0

Figure 3.1 Discretization of the same trajectory of an ant (*Myrmica ruginodis*) using different move-lengths: (a) 8 pixels (0.44 cm), (b) 24 pixels (1.32 cm), (c) 40 pixels (2.19 cm), and (d) 80 pixels (4.38 cm). Distance was measured as the Euclidean distance between end points. The color at the mid-point of each path segment represents the mean speed of the ant recorded between the previous and next vertex. As move-length increases, the velocity information becomes increasingly "smoothed." Redrawn after Couzin (1999).

in turning may appear to have little or no skew if the move-length is short. In segmenting the trajectory to such a degree, the variance of turning is low, and the animal's path appears relatively linear. If move-length is increased, the variance in turning angle increases, and the distribution of turns becomes

Table 3.1 Statistics of trajectories shown in Figure 3.2.

Trajectory	Mean angle	Standard deviation degrees (radians)	Kurtosis	Skew
(a)	−2.08	26.30 (0.46)	3.19	−0.21
(b)	−6.35	40.35 (0.70)	0.45	−0.04
(c)	−11.13	46.87 (0.82)	−0.61	0.05
(d)	−27.52	72.12 (1.26)	−1.29	−0.47

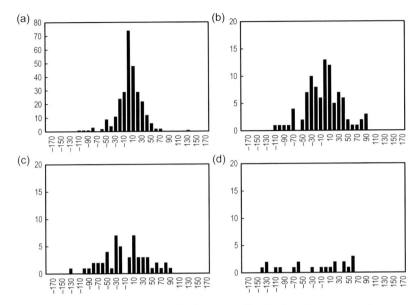

Figure 3.2 Histograms showing the frequency distribution of turning angles corresponding to the trajectories in Figure 3.1. X-axis values represent turning angles (negative = counterclockwise; positive = clockwise). Redrawn after Couzin (1999).

increasingly platykurtic, tending toward a uniform distribution. Thus, there is typically some intermediate move-length that produces the most informative characterization of movement.

Correlated Random Walk Models of Animal Search

The pure random walk model, analogous to Brownian motion, is typically too simple to represent animal movement because it does not account for the correlation of an organism's current direction with that of its previous direction (resulting from head-to-tail polarization). Correlated random walks introduce a first-order correlation between the steps of a path by allowing a nonuniform distribution of changes in direction to be incorporated. The change of direction between one step and the next is taken from a circular distribution. In most cases the distribution is taken to be symmetrical around the current orientation. Suitable circular distributions include the von Mises distribution and the more commonly used normal (Gaussian) distribution wrapped around a trigonometrical circle (for the disadvantages of the von Mises distribution, see Bovet and Benhamou 1988). Once this distribution is specified, we can simulate the trajectory numerically (see Figure 3.3).

The correlated random walk is useful because we can readily compare it to data, and it shares statistical properties with discretized natural animal trails.

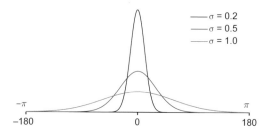

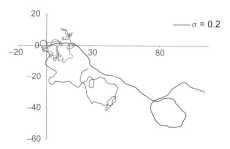

Figure 3.3   Correlated random walk simulation models of animal search trajectories with various values of the standard deviation σ (in radians) of the distribution of changes of direction of successive steps. $V_i = 1$. Trajectories start at the origin with the simulated organisms' initial orientation along the positive X-axis. The parent distributions are shown in the upper plot. Redrawn after Couzin (1999).

Specifically it tends toward linearity at very small spatial scales and behaves like Brownian motion (random walk) at large scales (this is analogous to the transition from a leptokurtotic to an increasingly uniform distribution of turning angles as move-length increases in Figure 3.2). The correlated random walk model can easily be modified to represent more accurately the motion of particular organisms, because it can describe the biases in direction and turning that might be caused by biological processes such as gravitaxis, phototaxis, or memory of previous positions or movements.

Scale-Free Models of Animal Search

Our development above suggests that the scale at which we consider a search path (i.e., how we divide it into segments) can affect our measurements of the path's statistical properties. The reader may reasonably wonder whether one could construct a scale-free description of search trajectories. Fractal analyses (Mandelbrot 1977; Sugihara and May 1990) offer one possibility, but current thinking favors another approach. Scale invariance arises naturally in a class of stochastic processes, known as Lévy processes. Lévy flights are a type of random walk (Bartumeus 2005; Viswanathan et al. 1996), and they have been shown to facilitate optimal search under a set of constraint conditions. In a pattern reminiscent of area-restricted search or patch exploitation, Lévy flights consist of "walk clusters": within-cluster movements consist of relatively short step-lengths, but longer displacements characterize between-cluster movements. This pattern, however, repeats at all spatial and temporal scales, and this repetition generates fractal or scale-invariant patterns (Bartumeus 2005; note that Lévy flights represent a specific stochastic mechanism that can generate scale invariance, whereas fractal measures provide a tool to characterize all forms of scale invariance).

In Lévy flights, the frequency of step-lengths are not described by the normal distribution with a finite variance, as is the case for simple Brownian motion. Instead the step-lengths have a probability distribution with longer power-law tails (see Benhamou 2007; Plank and James 2008; Reynolds and Rhodes 2009; Reynolds and Bartumeus 2009). Lévy behavior has also been found in a wide range of biological systems, from unicellular organisms to humans (Schuster and Levandowsky 1996; Brockmann et al. 2006).

A forager performing longer step-lengths (longer power-law tails) can increase its probability of encountering new patches and can efficiently visit nearby sites, when compared to Brownian motion. Lévy processes also lead to superdiffusion, a diffusion process that increases faster than linearly with time, thereby resulting in more spreading (Bartumeus 2007), allowing a forager to reach more distant sites. Lévy-type statistics have been found in intermittent movement patterns, for example, in the time between reorientations (Bartumeus 2007), and theoretical models have shown that these reorientations can change the statistical patterns of the animal's movement at large scales, particularly with regard to the diffusive properties of movement or spatial trajectory (Bartumeus 2007).

Some empirical evidence shows that there is a change in the distribution of flight times from an exponential to an inverse square power-law distribution when resource abundance or predictability decreases, for example, in the heterotrophic dinoflagellate *Oxyrrhis marina* as preferred prey *Rhodomonas sp.* become scarce (Bartumeus et al. 2002). Similar results have also been found in marine predators and seabirds (Bartumeus et al. 2010). However, in the field of animal movement, the presence of power-law distributions in empirical data has been a controversial issue that has generated much debate (Bartumeus 2007, 2009; Sims et al. 2008). For example, complex patterns of motion can result from individuals interacting with their environment. Prey distributions can display Lévy-like fractal patterns (Sims et al. 2008). Consequently, when organisms employ mechanisms to detect resources, through sampling prey directly or responding to cues such as odor, it may be difficult to determine what components of search result from true stochastic processes.

As the discussion above shows, we can describe searching movements in various ways, from Lévy flights to correlated random walks. If we accept for the moment that we have an agreed set of statistics to describe search, then one might ask how these descriptions of search could be correctly applied: Are they properties of species, of individuals, or of environments? As yet, there is no simple answer. Obviously the locomotor apparatus of the species matters, so that species is one dimension we would consider, but clearly the nature of the resources being searched for (widely distributed individual items of food, food clumps, or mates) could have a profound effect on statistical properties of search.

Collective Search

Cooperative Search

Colonial animals like social insects may search cooperatively in the sense that the benefits of discovered food items accrue to the colony or group. Ants, for example, search collectively, generating what has been described as a diffuse search network (Detrain et al. 1991; Gordon 1995; Adler and Gordon 1992); see Figure 3.4. Adler and Gordon (1992) developed a simple correlated random walk model to investigate how the movement patterns of individuals within a group affect the success of group search. They found that high turning rates lowered food discovery rates, because excessive turning leads individuals to search the same space repeatedly. For all group sizes, more linear paths led to higher discovery rates, but excessive turning hurt smaller groups more. In a crowded area, however, the entire surface is likely to be searched by some

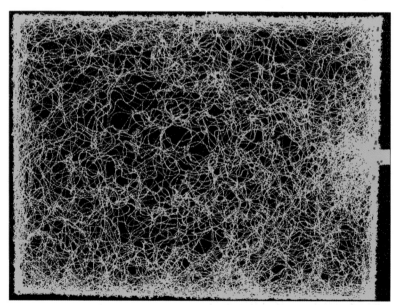

Figure 3.4   Ants (*Myrmica ruginodis*) creating a network of search paths in an empty experimental arena (40 cm × 30 cm). Ten minutes of search are shown. Data from Couzin (1999).

individual, even if individual movement is sub-optimal. Adler and Gordon predicted, on the basis of this idea, that at higher densities, linear paths are less important to food discovery and consequently turning rates may increase as ant density increases.

Gordon (1995) tested the predictions of this model with the Argentine ant, *Linepithema humile*, and reported that as the density of ants in the experimental arena increased, there was an increase in the tortuosity of ant paths. Although several problems exist with Gordon's analysis, another study revealed that although tortuosity of collective search in *Myrmica ruginodis* ants does increase as a function of density, the ants themselves do not regulate their behavior (Couzin 1999); when calculating statistical properties of searching ants, no behavioral modulation is observed, except when two ants collide (Figure 3.5). Individual ants did, however, regulate search as a function of the amount of time spent in the arena (Figure 3.6).

Some investigators have suggested that grouping can improve the efficiency of search in a gradient. This phenomenon has been termed the "many wrongs"

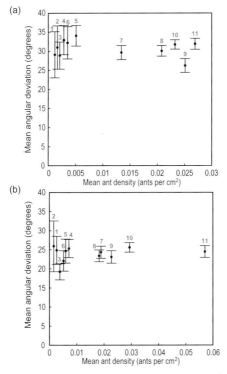

Figure 3.5 Mean angular deviation (indicative of path tortuosity or sinuosity) as a function of density (a) 0–10 minutes and (b) 50–60 minutes. Error bars show the 95% confidence interval for each value. Gray numbers associate values with colony identity. Redrawn after Couzin (1999).

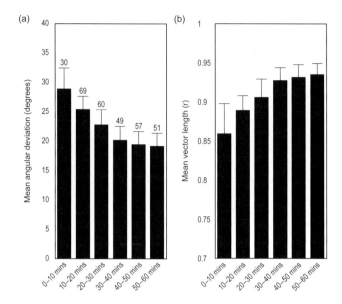

Figure 3.6   Temporal change in search pattern over time for a *Myrmica ruginodis* colony. The decrease in angular deviation is shown in (a); the increase in mean vector length is depicted in (b). Error bars indicate the 95% confidence interval; figures above the bars give the respective number of ants tracked. Redrawn after Couzin (1999).

principle and can be thought of as follows: given inherent error in sensing local gradients (through sensory and/or environmental noise), individuals can benefit by interacting (specifically aligning direction of travel with others) since this means they can act as a distributed "array" of sensors, noise being attenuated by individuals taking into account not only their own samples but the directions chosen by others. Individuals can thus balance their own assessment with the perceived assessment of others.

A numerical study of this phenomenon by Grünbaum (1997) supports this idea. Moreover data from schooling fish reveal how animals might adjust their sensitivity to the behavior of others. Studies show that schooling killifish (Hoare et al. 2004) and stickleback fish exhibit a reduced schooling tendency when they can gather reliable information directly from the environment, but their tendency to group with others increases when this information is perceived to be unreliable or scarce.

Collective Search by Extremely Selfish Organisms

While cooperative search among social insects represents one end of the spectrum of collective search, apparently coordinated group movements can arise from spectacularly selfish motives. In two species of swarming insects— the desert locust (*Schistocerca gregaria*) and the Mormon cricket (*Anabrus simplex*)—an interaction between nutritional state and aggregation influences patterns of movement (Bazazi et al. 2011). When placed in groups, protein-deprived insects readily swarm, whereas those replete with protein march slowly, if at all. It may surprise some readers to know that locusts and crickets can be aggressively cannibalistic; indeed in their depauperate habitats, other crickets and locusts can be a critical source of protein and salt (Simpson et al. 2006; Bazazi et al. 2008). Protein deprivation promotes cannibalism (Bazazi et al. 2008, 2010, 2011), which can, in turn, generate an autocatalytic movement process. Hungry individuals tend to approach those moving away from them, in an attempt to cannibalize them, and avoid those moving toward them, to avoid being cannibalized—the outcome being that protein-deprived insects readily form directional mobile swarms (Romanczuk et al. 2009; Bazazi et al. 2011). The insects appear to be forming a cooperative search for new resources, but in fact they are on a forced march. If an insect stops, it risks being eaten. The directed motion of the group may itself confer an advantage in allowing individuals to better find distributed sources of food in the environment.

Exploiting the Search of Others: The Producer-Scrounger Game

As the stunning example of group movement mediated by attempts to commit and avoid cannibalism shows, the interactions between individuals can dramatically change the character of animal groups. Other group-level characteristics can emerge from the individual search decisions of group members. While locusts may move to avoid cannibalism, in other settings movement patterns may be created by the possibility of stealing or otherwise usurping resources discovered by others. Group-living animals commonly exploit resources that others have uncovered, captured, or otherwise made available. Behavioral ecologists call this scrounging (Barnard 1984), and the dynamic between animals that "produce" and those that "scrounge" has become a central topic in social foraging theory. In the simplest analysis, one can think of this dynamic as an information-sharing process. Information sharing assumes that all animals engage in a single search process, much like the searching activity of solitary animals, and that this single process can lead to either finding food or detecting someone that has already found food, whichever comes first.

This view of group resource exploitation pervaded until Barnard and Sibly (1981) used evolutionary game theory to analyze group foraging. The game they proposed pits a "producer" strategy that only searches for its food, against a "scrounger" strategy that only detects and feeds from discoveries of producers. This producer-scrounger game implicitly assumes that feeding from the discovery of a partner and feeding from one's own discovery are end products of two distinct and mutually exclusive search strategies: producer, the usual form of searching for resources that leads to food discovery, and scrounger, which consists in looking for eating individuals. This producer-scrounger game is characterized by strong frequency-dependence of payoffs to scroungers and,

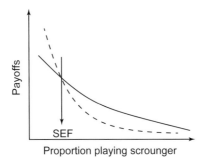

Figure 3.7 Payoffs to producer (solid line) and scrounger (dashed line) strategies as a function of the frequency of individuals playing the role of scrounger. The lines cross at the stable equilibrium frequency (SEF), at which point payoffs are equal for each alternative.

under most conditions, we can expect to observe a stable mixture of the two search strategies within a population (Giraldeau and Caraco 2000; Figure 3.7).

A considerable amount of experimental evidence has accumulated that is consistent, at least qualitatively, with predictions of the producer-scrounger game (for a review, see Giraldeau and Dubois 2008). For example, a version of the producer-scrounger game designed to measure the maximization of food intake predicts that the stable equilibrium frequency of the scrounger strategy depends directly on the fraction of each resource clump that goes to the exclusive use of its discoverer: the finder's share (Vickery et al. 1991). It also predicts that the larger the finder's share, for whatever reason, the fewer scroungers are expected to be part of the stable mixture (Giraldeau and Livoreil 1998; Coolen et al. 2001; Morand-Ferron and Giraldeau 2010).

Are Producer and Scrounger Mutually Exclusive Search Modes?

Although it has garnered qualitative experimental support over the years, the most intriguing aspect of the producer-scrounger game remains its assumption of mutually exclusive producer and scrounger search strategies (originally made to simplify the analysis of the game). If the game is to apply to a group of foraging animals, it has to be that when individuals search as a producer they cannot detect scrounging opportunities—or in any event fail to act upon those detected—and vice versa. To many it seems utterly unrealistic to assume that a bird looking for food on the ground, for example, remains unable to detect a companion that has discovered food some short distance away. The incompatibility assumption seems especially difficult to accept in light of evidence that birds feeding from food on the ground can still detect approaching predators.

To test this assumption, behavior patterns that correspond to producer and scrounger must be identified. Coolen, Giraldeau, and Lavoie (2001) set out to accomplish this task, using flocks of nutmeg mannikins (*Lonchura punctulata*), small granivorous estrildid finches, as they foraged for seeds hidden in wells spread over a foraging grid. They observed that the orientation of the head while hopping predicted whether a bird would produce or scrounge food (Figure 3.8). Specifically, birds that hop with their beaks pointed down tend to be producers, while those that hop with their beaks parallel to the substrate tend to scrounge (Figure 3.8a). Evidence of incompatibility comes from the observation that hopping with the head pointing up leads to scrounging (Figure 3.8); the more hopping with the head pointed down an individual engages in, the less likely it is to feed as a result of scrounging (Figure 3.8c). Remarkably, hopping with the head pointed down was never observed to immediately precede a scrounging event.

Spatial Consequences of Producer-Scrounger Search Modes

Searching for food as a producer or scrounger is expected to have an effect on the spatial position that foragers prefer. Using a genetic algorithm, Barta et al. (1997) found that a group of birds which engaged in "producer only" behavior should evolve search movements that maintain a greater average distance between each group member. When scroungers predominate, however, we expect that individuals will stay closer to one another (Figure 3.9a). One of the main reasons for this is that producers benefit from steering clear of their group mates, because this reduces competition, whereas scroungers need to stay close to group mates so that they can scrounge effectively (Figure 3.9a). As a result, the predicted movement rules for scroungers shift them into central positions where scrounging is most efficient.

Empirical support consistent with such movement rules has been provided by Flynn and Giraldeau (2001). In their experiment, they used flocks of six nutmeg mannikins that had to find food by flipping lids that covered wells filled with sand. Some wells contained seeds, and only birds that had been pretrained to flip lids could act as producers. Flynn and Giraldeau manipulated the number of producers in a flock, thus creating a high- and a low-scrounging flock. In addition, they videotaped trials from above and scored the flock geometry from 2149 frames of the video records. Results show that high-scrounging flocks were more compact than low-scrounging flocks. Groups with fewer scroungers and hence more producers spread out more, so that they occupied significantly larger areas than the more densely packed flocks in which scroungers predominated. Accordingly, the mean interindividual distances in the high-scrounging flocks were significantly greater than in the low-scrounging flocks. Individuals that were not trained to find food, and thus were forced to search as scroungers, were found on average closer to the geometric center of the flock than the birds that played producer. These experimental results are entirely consistent with the predictions described above. Clearly, therefore, an individual's foraging strategy affects its preferred location within a group, which in turn affects the flock's geometry.

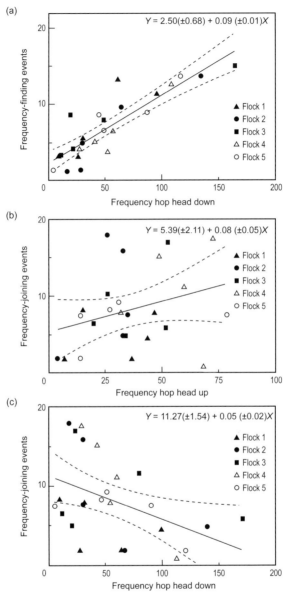

Figure 3.8   The relationship between hopping in one head position and finding events for 25 individuals tested in flocks of five. (a) The mean frequency of finding events increased as a function of the frequency with which subjects hopped with the head down. (b) The mean frequency of joining events increased as a function of the frequency with which the subject hopped with the head upright. (c) The mean frequency of joining decreased with an increased frequency of hopping with the head down. The equations give the linear regression models and the coefficients' standard errors. Reprinted with permission from Coolen et al (2001).

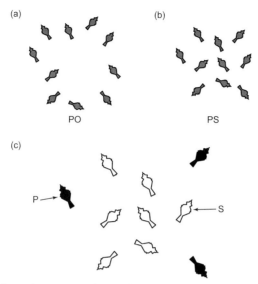

Figure 3.9 Schematic representation of the consequences of movement rules for individuals within a flock that contains (a) only producers (PO) or (b) both producers and scroungers (PS). PS flocks are denser (c) because scroungers (S) evolve movement rules that tend to bring them to the center of the flock, thus minimizing their distance to producers (P). After Barta et al. (1997).

Discussion

Search is a fundamental problem in animal biology, and we presented several perspectives on the analysis and description of search behavior. We considered the terminology and classification of search behavior (e.g., widely foraging vs. sit-and-wait, area-restricted search, saltatory search), and discussed connections between search behavior and the fundamental foraging problem of patch exploitation, which predicts when foraging animals should leave a food patch to search for another. As the theory suggests, animals are clearly sensitive to the richness of their habitats when they make these decisions.

We considered the statistical description of movement patterns. The simple idea of a correlated random walk fits many data, but the resulting statistics of the movement depend critically on the scale at which the investigator segments the path. This led us to ask whether one can find scale-independent descriptions of search paths, which in turn led us to Lévy flights. Lévy flights capture the idea that movement consists of many small steps, with a few relatively large steps, and it does this in a scale-independent way.

Many animals search in groups, and we considered three aspects of this important phenomenon. In cooperative group search, social foragers share a common interest in maximizing returns to the colony, and we asked what parameters of search (e.g., turning rate) maximize the collection of food from a given area. Broadly, these models suggest that straight line search will maximize food recovery, yet foraging ants turn quite frequently, and they turn more in larger groups, which suggests an interesting paradox for further analysis. Swarming desert orthorpterans (crickets and locusts) are the stunning antithesis to cooperative search. These animals live in harsh "low protein" environments and are aggressive cannibals. It seems that their swarm patterns of movement are generated by efforts to attack those in front and escape those behind.

At a different level of analysis, we discussed the producer-scrounger game, which considers how some individuals in a group (the scroungers) parasitize the food discoveries of others (the producers). This situation has been well-studied experimentally, and results suggest an impressive flexibility in the extent to which individuals depend on their own search behavior. We find more "producers" in groups when the producer can keep a larger portion of the food it discovers.

Although we have focused on specific aspects of search in this chapter, we recognize that search is a rich phenomenon with many dimensions. The classic dichotomy of sit-and-wait versus widely foraging searchers is far from a hard-and-fast categorization. Some sit-and-wait foragers, like barnacles, are literally glued to the substrate; others, like web-building spiders, create food-trapping mechanisms that may persist for days or weeks; still others, like fly-catching birds, may occupy a given waiting station for less than an hour. Thus, classical categories are, at best, end points of a continuum. Moreover, the sit-and-wait versus active distinction is only one way of categorizing search. Consider the properties of targets: In the searches of our daily lives (e.g., searching for our keys), we naturally think of passive targets, but many biological targets move. So we might categorize search in terms of whether the targets move or not. However, if targets move, this opens another set of possibilities. Targets could actively evade the searching animal, as many prey animals surely must; or targets could actively advertise their presence, as when males advertise to searching females; of course, even a target movement that is random with respect to search could shape the behavior of the searcher.

We appreciate that our reluctance to offer a phylogeny of search may frustrate readers, even though we have offered many ways to categorize and measure search. As we see it, creating a phylogeny of search faces three serious problems. First one must choose an appropriate "search character" to study phylogenetically: Should we choose some variable that expresses a position on the continuum between widely foraging animals and sit-and-wait foragers? Should we use the measured properties of the distribution of "move distances"? Or should we use the frequency of scrounging in a group? Second, each of these "characters" depends on the animal's environment, so one must somehow specify a set of test environments that fairly represents each species' abilities and predispositions. Third, one must specify the taxa and taxonomic level to study phylogenetically. For examples, "all animals" is both overbroad and impractical. Even if we settle on a given group, say birds, we must still decide whether to consider species or genera or orders. Clearly there is a phylogenetic "signal" in search. Yet, it does not seem that we are prepared to analyze it in a general way at the moment.

Conclusion

We have reviewed several behavioral and ecological perspectives on search behavior. These include simple descriptions of types of search behavior (e.g., area-restricted search), statistical descriptions of movement, and strategic models of group search. Clearly this represents a wide-ranging and somewhat disconnected set of issues. We argue, however, that this correctly reflects the state of the art. The phenomenon of search makes connections to nearly every corner of animal biology, from mating behavior to decision making, yet it does not seem central to any of them. As a consequence, each subtopic of animal biology seems to have something to say about search, yet together these disparate threads fall short of a coherent perspective.

What can be done about this? Broadly, we have two options. One could argue that search reflects a simple reality, so we do not need a coherent treatment of search behavior. Accordingly, the importance of search varies from one biological situation to the next, and thus the current patchwork of ideas about search biology is precisely what we need. Alternatively, one could argue that in accepting this argument we are doomed to have the subdisciplines of animal biology reinvent the wheel, since they each come to the analysis of search behavior de novo. Perhaps worse, we are likely missing a common conceptual framework that would help us see biological connections that are now obscure. A key issue for the future is to address how a common conceptual framework for the analysis of search behavior can be constructed.

First column (top to bottom): Iain Couzin, Frederic Méry, Reuven Dukas, David W. Stephens, Melissa Bateson, Iain Couzin
Second column: David W. Stephens, Luc-Alain Giraldeau, Frederic Méry, Thomas T. Hills, Thomas T. Hills in discussion, Bruce Winterhalder
Third column: Reuven Dukas, Melissa Bateson, Thomas T. Hills, Bruce Winterhalder, Luc-Alain Giraldeau, John M. C. Hutchinson

4

Searching for Fundamentals and Commonalities of Search

John M. C. Hutchinson, David W. Stephens,
Melissa Bateson, Iain Couzin, Reuven Dukas,
Luc-Alain Giraldeau, Thomas T. Hills,
Frederic Méry, and Bruce Winterhalder

Abstract

This chapter reports the discussion of a group of mostly behavioral biologists, who attempt to put research on search from their own discipline into a framework that might help identify parallels with cognitive search. Essential components of search are a functional goal, uncertainty about goal location, the adaptive varying of position, and often a stopping rule. The chapter considers a diversity of cases where search is in domains other than spatial and lists other important dimensions in which search problems differ. One dimension examined in detail is social interactions between searchers and searchers, targets and targets, and targets and searchers. The producer-scrounger game is presented as an example; despite the extensive empirical and theoretical work on the equilibrium between the strategies, it is largely an open problem how animals decide when to adopt each strategy, and thus how real equilibria are attained. Another dimension that explains some of the diversity of search behavior is the modality of the information utilized (e.g., visual, auditory, olfactory). The chapter concludes by highlighting further parallels between search in the external environment and cognitive search. These suggest some novel avenues of research.

Evolutionary Biology of Search

To begin, it may be useful to say something about the perspective we bring to the study of search. Our group is predominantly whole-organism biologists who investigate the mechanisms and adaptive significance of behavior. In doing this, behavioral ecologists commonly appeal to optimality or game-theoretical models, and these models, along with knowledge about animal genetics, physiology, neurobiology, phylogeny and development, have guided our thinking about search.

For example, a classic optimality model considers when a foraging animal should stop feeding in a patch being depleted of prey and switch to a new patch, despite the cost of moving (Charnov 1976). The prediction most often tested is that increasing the travel time between patches should increase the time spent in each patch. This prediction has generally been confirmed, but less successful have been predictions about the absolute time spent in a patch (Nonacs 2001) and what cues to attend to so as to decide when to leave a patch (e.g., Roche et al. 1998; Hutchinson et al. 2008). Failures like this lead biologists to change or elaborate the basic model, for instance by incorporating additional aspects of the environment or by invoking some informational or cognitive constraint (e.g., Nonacs 2001; Hills and Adler 2002). Ideally, predictions are tested by manipulating the environment of an individual in the hope of a real-time response, but alternatives are to utilize variation among species or natural variation among individuals of a single species.

If what follows manages to say anything novel of interest to workers on cognitive search, we suspect that it will be because of, not despite, this perspective of the adaptation of behavior. Our biological perspective also brings to the table a greater diversity of search problems faced by different animals, and plants too (de Kroon and Mommer 2006), than by humans and our machines.

The Essence of Search

How would you define search? It is all too easy for a definition to use a near synonym like "locate," which does not gain us much, or unintentionally to exclude phenomena such as searching internally for a solution to an anagram. Seeking a definition moved us beyond sterile questions of semantics, because it enabled us to recognize the essence of the search process that makes it distinct. We agreed that it would not be useful to define the term so broadly that it covered all adaptive processes.

Luc-Alain Giraldeau provided the initial insight. He proposed that for something to qualify as search there must first be a defined goal, such as food, mates, or particular information. The search itself then consists of acting to vary position according to some scheme that facilitates finding the goal. We definitely do not mean to restrict "vary position" to moving in space; rather, we include movement in other dimensions, such as sampling at different times of day or shifting attention somehow in one's brain. It seems an important component of the definition that the varying of the position is adapted toward efficient location of the goal, hence the importance of defining the goal first. Thus we would not consider as search the process by which sand grains get deposited by the wind on the lee side of a dune. Nor is it search if animals explore and learn about the environment incidentally, ahead of starting to seek a goal (latent learning: Thistlethwaite 1951). Our opinion is that search does not start until that goal seeking starts.

The goal that we invoke here is the function of the behavior. Without getting into philosophical debates about teleology, biologists are happy to say that a character has a particular ultimate function if design considerations suggest that natural selection has adapted it for that purpose. We are not talking about the proximate goal that one must identify to understand the *mechanism* of a control problem such as search. In this perhaps we differ from some other groups in this volume. To bring out the distinction, consider the princess and monster game, a classic example from the theory of search games (Isaacs 1965). A princess and a monster are free to move around in a darkened room or other space. The monster's goal, in the sense we intend, is to catch the princess; but, since neither can detect the other until they collide, its proximate goal cannot be capture but merely to move in particular prespecified directions.

Formally there may be an additional part of the search process: the application of a stopping rule to decide when the goal has been attained. Some valid sorts of search may lack a stopping rule. For instance, one can imagine a chemotactic bacterium following a gradient to the source; when it reaches the source it need not apply a stopping rule but oscillate around the source, its goal seeking continuing. If there is a stopping rule, its application is itself part of the search process. Note that a stopping rule may test the environment repeatedly during a search even though it triggers stopping of the task only once.

One important aspect of search is that there is some uncertainty in the location of the goal. If you can see the target and then walk straight toward it, that does not seem like search, although others coined the phrase "nonexploratory search" to cover situations where there is no uncertainty. Compare leafing through a book to find a particular passage with using the subject index: the former represents search with uncertainty, whereas an index is like a lookup table in computer programming, which is constructed to avoid repeated search or calculation. What about a blind organism that can apply a deterministic algorithm to locate a target reliably, say by chemotaxis? If it is absolutely always able to find the target, this behavior seems analogous to walking straight toward a visible target. Now consider the ability of some ants to return straight to their nests using solely path integration of their wiggly outward route (Müller and Wehner 1988). That does not initially sound like search, but actually their method of path integration is a clever approximation rather than exact (Müller and Wehner 1988), and they routinely must apply backup search mechanisms (Wehner 2003; Merkle and Wehner 2010). So, if we define search as involving uncertainty, recognizing a phenomenon as search may require us to know about the proximate mechanism and its performance.

We wondered whether a characteristic of search is that uncertainty tends to be reduced, or at least not to increase, at each step. One exception is the case when the search is for a mobile target known to be initially within some distance but able to move away (Foreman 1977), although perhaps search still tends to delay the increase of uncertainty compared to random movement by the searcher. Real searches for a particular mobile prey can often fail, but this should not stop us considering the strategy that maximizes the probability of capture as a search.

Another aspect of most search is that it is sequential. By this we do not mean to exclude cases of multiple agents working in parallel and maybe sharing information; still each agent individually is searching sequentially. By "sequential" we intend to capture the idea that several steps must be taken to reach the target; a single-step process of selection between options is not search. The options change at each step and information gained from earlier phases should inform the choices made at later steps. A revealing example in this context is the secretary problem (Freeman 1983), the archetypal case of sequential search, which has been applied to model mate choice. Candidates of different qualities appear in random order one at a time; the object is to select a candidate of good quality, and each of a sequence of decisions is whether to accept the current candidate or continue inspecting further candidates. In this case, the only scope for varying "position" is the gain in information from inspecting the next candidate, but the crucial aspect is that information on the qualities of candidates inspected at earlier steps should determine whether search is terminated at later steps.

We tried, but failed, to agree on a single-sentence definition of search, preferring instead to list the key components: a functional goal, uncertainty about goal location, the adaptive varying of position, and often a stopping rule.

Nonspatial Search

The term search is most directly associated with seeking items in space, for instance, searching for your keys. But the term is also used in nonspatial contexts, and we thought it worth constructing a list of these in the hope of recognizing novel analogies between different domains.

Information

Many of the examples below fit into the larger category of information search. Searching for information is an implicit component of most search models, because finding the right target requires first acquiring relevant information (Vergassola et al. 2007). But sometimes we might consider that finding particular information is a goal in itself (Inglis et al. 2001). For instance, an explanation for why animals will work to explore suboptimal food sources (contrafreeloading) is that they gain the knowledge to utilize these sources if the currently better source disappears (e.g., Bean et al. 1999). Models from foraging for food have been reapplied to searching for information both on the Web and in our brains (Pirolli 2007; Wilke et al. 2009).

Quality

Selecting between mates is an example of a search over items of different qualities. In real life, candidates may well be distributed in space, but idealized models such as the secretary problem ignore this spatial component: the only decision is whether to continue search, not where to move, and it depends only on the qualities and number of earlier items, not on their positions. An interval between the inspection of successive items may represent a travel cost of moving between them, but the spatial aspect only makes a qualitative difference if there were some correlation of quality with position or if, for instance, checking one shop rather than another is more attractive because a third shop is closer to the first. Speed dating and comparison shopping on the Internet provide examples where a spatial component seems largely lacking. Nevertheless the money that advertisers pay to appear at the top of a Google search suggests that even slight spatial differences may be prominent to us.

Time

Animals may have to learn when during the day events are likely to occur (e.g., Biebach et al. 1994) or how long a resource takes to renew after the last visit (e.g., Henderson et al. 2006). Sampling over time so as to predict when an event will reoccur in the future is a search process. For instance, many of us will have learned from trial and error what times of day we will be best able to find a parking space near work. When bees start to learn when a food source is available, their sampling is biased earlier in the day than when they had first experienced the reward on previous days, which is adaptive in searching for the "opening time" of the source (Moore and Doherty 2009). Resampling a patch more intensely immediately after it depletes may also represent an adaptive search strategy in time (by analogy with area-restricted search: Gibson et al. 2006).

Correlation Structure and Learning

Just as there may be an association between a time of day and the occurrence of an event, other events or conditions might be associated with each other. Many forms of learning have been designed by natural selection for detecting this correlational structure in the world and responding to it adaptively. Habituation, which occurs following repeated exposure to the same meaningless stimulus, enables organisms to identify and ignore irrelevant events that do not predict meaningful events. Similarly, classical conditioning, which occurs when a previously neutral stimulus is temporally correlated with a meaningful event, enables organisms to identify and respond appropriately to events that predict meaningful events.

We debated extensively whether these types of learning should qualify as search. Although they share the goal of reducing uncertainty about the consequences of events, it is not clear that they involve any adaptive alteration of "position," as required by our definition of search. Indeed, they appear to be passive processes that occur all the time with no clearly defined start or end, similar to latent learning.

Operant conditioning or trial-and-error learning, in which an animal learns the association between its actions and the occurrence of meaningful events, enables animals both to predict and to control these events. In addition to having the goal of reducing uncertainty about the consequences of actions, this form of learning additionally has the feature that an animal can actively explore the correlational structure of the world during acquisition by varying the circumstances in which it tries out actions. Therefore, we conclude that this form of learning has all the features that we have defined as characteristic of search. It is unclear whether operant conditioning always has a stopping rule.

Memory

Many kinds of memory retrieval are also search processes, involving cued activation of knowledge representations acquired from prior experience (Pachur et al., this volume). Importantly, memory retrieval also shares a parallel with spatial search in that similar items are retrieved near one another in time. Thus, in a free recall task where a person is asked to name as many different animals as possible, items remembered successively tend to lie in similar subcategories; for instance, first we might list pets, then birds, then animals from the Antarctic (Bousfield 1953).

Puzzle Solutions

Other sorts of search are solutions to puzzles, such as algebra or chess. We would be interested to learn how our minds organize the set of possible solutions, how we search through this landscape, and whether one could identify naturally occurring analogues to these sorts of problems for nonhuman animals.

Morphology and Physiology

All organisms are themselves the product of natural selection. We hesitate to call genetic evolution search because it involves neither a searcher nor a well-defined goal. However, analogous genetic algorithms have been constructed by humans to optimize the design of complex machinery such as turbine blades (Gen and Cheng 1997). This is a search process: the program is written so as to converge toward a specified goal. Similarly, Sherlock Holme's search method for the truth, by eliminating all alternatives, has echoes in how our immune system selects out all immune cells sensitive to self, thus enabling it subsequently to recognize non-self (the clonal selection theory). Animals may use other search heuristics to improve the design of aspects of their external phenotype-like burrows and tools. Thus spiders adjust the spacing between the lines of their web in response to the size of prey caught (Schneider and Vollrath 1998). Going beyond morphology, any homeostatic mechanism has the property of directing the state toward the neutral or set point. When there is imprecision, lags, or overshoot in the process, this seems like search, but something like a mechanical thermostat may lack the aspect of uncertainty required to fit our definition.

A Taxonomy of Search

Already we have mentioned a diversity of search problems. To recognize structural similarities between search in different domains, it helps to consider in what fundamental ways the problem of search can vary. This might also facilitate understanding why different methods of search are used in different search problems.

A distinction is often made between searching for one particular item (e.g., the dropped key to your house or a missing offspring) and searching for a class of items. Contrast the birdwatcher who goes out to a sewage farm on the off chance that something interesting will be there with the serious twitcher who flies out to Fair Isle specifically to see the rare American vagrant that was reported on Birdline. In practice, it is usually possible to recognize a continuum between these extremes: the twitcher would be satisfied by an even rarer species that turned up while he was there. Models of optimal search when the target is a specific individual known to lie within a specified area predict rather different behaviors (e.g., systematic searching, randomized strategies; Alpern and Gal 2003) than when any individual in a population will suffice (Hutchinson and Waser 2007).

Some searches, archetypally for a male mate or for a nest site, are one-shot processes: once you make your choice, you stop searching. In contrast, once a bird finds one worm, it immediately starts searching for another, so the problem is iterated. The iteration seems important mainly in affecting the opportunity costs; one reason that the bird is less fussy about the quality of a worm than of its mate is because spending more time searching for one food item detracts from time searching for the next food item. In this respect there is no fundamental difference from the effect of other costs of search, such as mortality risk and locomotion costs. There may also be external time constraints, such as the ending of the breeding season (e.g., Backwell and Passmore 1996).

Another aspect is the dimensionality and topology of the problem. Contrast one-dimensional searching for flotsam along a river bank (or between a succession of secretaries knocking at your door) with the extra freedom of movement in search of two- or three-dimensional space: somewhere in between are ants exploring a tree or foragers relying on tracks through thick scrub; they face a network of restricted moves that creates a topologically very different search space than the almost unrestricted search of a shark in the ocean. Just as important as the topology are the movement rules allowed in this landscape (e.g., in the secretary problem whether recall of candidates inspected earlier is allowed).

In some searches the animal can be guided only by its past experience in the patch, as in area-restricted search for buried prey (e.g., Nolet and Mooij 2002). In other cases there are external cues, such as a pheromone plume, that assist in locating the target and perhaps in indicating target density (e.g., Waage 1978). Mueller and Fagan (2008) make a similar distinction. The experimental and theoretical analysis of how animals utilize cues such as gradients and landmarks is well developed (e.g., Fraenkel and Gunn 1961; Schöne 1984; Dusenbery 2001).

In the absence of external cues, the autocorrelation of items and their qualities in space and time provides the only information that the searcher uses. Autocorrelation in space is an integral part of models of area-restricted search (Benhamou 1992), but in other cases modelers have instead invoked discrete recognizable patches of items in a sea of absence (e.g., Charnov 1976). Which is more appropriate depends both on the actual distribution of targets and on the ability of the searcher to recognize the edge of the patch at a glance (Bond 1980). Autocorrelation in time involves the processes of depletion, disturbance, and renewal. Analyses of data derived from modern tracking technologies demonstrate the importance of considering autocorrelation in space and time at multiple scales simultaneously (e.g., Fauchald and Tveraa 2006; Amano and Katayama 2009).

An unduly neglected aspect of search is social interactions among searchers and targets. We devote the next two sections to considering how social interactions can transform the problem.

Social Interactions

Search is not always a single individual seeking an inanimate target that is indifferent to being located. There can be positive (mutualistic, +), negative (competitive, –), or indifferent (neutral, 0) relationships, to varying degrees, among social searchers, among social targets, or between searchers and targets, whether social or solitary (summarized in Figure 4.1). Interactions may be infrequent or nearly continuous. Once atune to these social possibilities, one can recognize a large set of possibilities that may shape the evolution of search behavior.

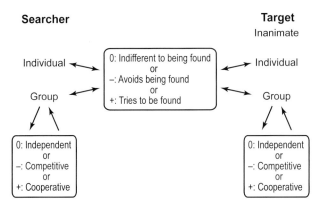

Figure 4.1   A schematic summary of the possible social interactions of searchers with other searchers, of searchers with their targets, and of targets with other targets.

Searchers

Normally we expect competition between foragers. Think of searching for a parking space as near as you can to a cinema: we probably suppose that the closest spots will tend to be occupied already, which makes us use different search strategies than if we expected randomly distributed spaces (Hutchinson et al. 2012). Because the strategies used by others determine the distribution of spaces, the situation is game theoretic. The converse case of cooperation or sharing of information among searchers also affects the effectiveness and appropriate choice of different search tactics. In some central-place foragers (social insects, camp-based hunter-gatherers), it is deliberate sharing of information that allows improvement in the locating of resources. But even if individuals do not deliberately signal to others, they may coordinate by copying processes, resulting in emergent search properties of collections of individuals in contact with one another (see Box 4.1).

Searcher-Target Interactions

Some sorts of targets want to be found (e.g., mates, +), some do their best to avoid being found (e.g., prey, –), and some are indifferent (e.g., a water source, 0). Mates may signal their presence to potential suitors; prey may adopt cryptic or evasive tactics. Each thereby may change what strategies are effective for the searcher. The brain presumably locates information for storage in a manner to facilitate its being found: memories in some sense want to be located. Similarly, we expect food-storing birds to hide their caches at a pattern of sites that facilitate rediscovery by themselves, but with the complication that the cues should not make it easy for competitors to pilfer (Cheng and Sherry 1992; Barnea and Nottebohm 1995; Briggs and Vander Wall 2004). Plants may distribute their flowers on an inflorescence so as to benefit from the search rules

Box 4.1   Collective Search

Generally speaking, adaptive search strategies act to match individual behavior to the relevant statistical properties of the environment. In terms of sensing, separating a relevant signal from environmental noise is often a challenge. At the level of individuals, sensory adaptation and simultaneous use of multiple modes of sensory information can allow individuals to respond dynamically to maximize the signal-to-noise ratio. When searching as a collective, however, strategies may be implemented both at the individual and group level. An illustrative example of collective search is to consider each individual as a sensing agent capable of detecting and responding to relevant environmental features, such as the estimated direction of a local resource gradient, but also to other individuals. If the environment has simple structure, such as a linear gradient and low noise, taxis up the gradient is relatively straightforward. In more complex environments, such as where local noise inhibits taxis or where simple gradient climbing can result in entrapment in local optima, collective strategies can facilitate much more effective search.

Modeling such behavior, Torney et al. (2009) considered the case of locating the source of a chemoattractant within a stochastically fluctuating advective flow; think of how blood from an injured swimmer might drift offshore toward a patrolling shark. This is a ubiquitous behavior important to the lives of many aquatic animals and observed over a wide range of scales. In this situation, individual-level search is particularly ineffective since the filamentous and turbulent structure of the plume confuses local search strategies, resulting in individuals following local optima and seldom being able to find the source itself. Similar problems apply when considering any spatially heterogeneous gradient of resource (including gradients of discrete resources). A highly effective strategy under such circumstances is for multiple individuals to reconcile their goal-oriented taxis with social interactions (i.e., affiliating or aligning with others). The central principle is that if organisms dynamically adjust how much they are influenced by social interactions based on their confidence in their own environmental assessment, they can, as a collective, find global optima. Thus, in the model of Torney et al. (2009), if an individual perceives an increasing local concentration of odor, it decreases the weight it places on social interactions. When concentrations are unpredictable or declining, individuals may instead place more weight on social interactions. This strategy does not require organisms to know the informational state of others explicitly but nevertheless can spontaneously create a time-varying spatial leadership structure in which individuals with low confidence follow spontaneously those who are obtaining relevant information from the environment. Thus individuals continuously adapt to the changing physical and social structure of their environment, giving them the capacity to respond to structural information over length scales much larger than their own range of perception.

Evidence that animals can, and do, adjust their sensitivity to the behavior of others comes from studies of schooling fish. For example, the context dependence of interaction ranges can explain the group-size distribution of schooling killifish (Hoare et al. 2004), and stickleback fish have been shown to restrict their schooling tendency when they can gather direct reliable information from the environment, but increase their tendency to group with others when this information is perceived to be unreliable or scarce (van Bergen et al. 2004).

of pollinators, but not necessarily in the very best interest of the pollinators (Jordan and Harder 2006).

A special case is when both searcher and target are mobile and can search for each other (technically, models of rendezvous: Alpern and Gal 2003). For instance, both sexes of some butterfly species fly to the tops of hills (hill-topping) to facilitate encounter there (Alcock 1987). In contrast, had they not evolved to utilize such an asymmetry in the environment, the optimal policy to maximize encounter is for both sexes to move as fast as possible in straight lines (Hutchinson and Waser 2007). A similar situation of symmetrical roles for searcher and target is mutual mate choice, which has been modeled both with and without competition between searchers through depletion (e.g., Collins and McNamara 1993; Johnstone 1997).

Targets

Targets, if they are living, have their own internal relationships that affect search. Many animals create exclusive home ranges to avoid competition with neighbors, and their consequent overdispersion should affect the search rules used by predators (Iwasa et al. 1981). Conversely, in the selfish herd model individuals hide behind neighbors so as to minimize their own chance of being selected by a predator, incidentally creating herds (Hamilton 1971), which may facilitate the search of the predator (Treisman 1975).

Open Questions

Behavioral ecologists have models for many of the behaviors mentioned above. The application of game theory can predict rather different outcomes than models that ignore the social interactions we have considered here (e.g., Johnstone 1997; Hamblin et al. 2010). But do animals, including humans in everyday life, also know to shift their search methods in social situations? For instance, if a traplining hummingbird tries to adjust its revisit rate to a particular flower, it is crucial for it to judge whether nectar supply has declined because of competition (when it should revisit sooner) or because the flower is producing at a slower rate (when it should revisit later; Garrison and Gass 1999). A different sort of question is whether models of social foraging may be relevant to cognitive search processes that involve parallel processing. For some more open questions, we now address in more detail the game-theoretic analysis of the well-studied producer-scrounger paradigm.

The Peculiar Social Dynamics of Selfish Parallel Search

When several selfish animals search in parallel for some resource—be it mates, nesting material, food, or information itself—they have an option that is never available in an individual search process: they can either search for the resource themselves or search for other individuals that have already uncovered a resource item. For instance, when a group of pigeons search the ground for hidden seeds, only some do the actual searching whereas almost all of the group will gather at any one individual's discovery. The decision of whether to invest in one or the other search mode is modeled as an economic decision using a game-theoretic approach: the producer-scrounger (PS) game, where producer is the strategy of searching directly for the resource and scrounger is the alternative of searching for individuals that have uncovered the resource (Barnard and Sibly 1981). Very similar scenarios have received other names, such as tolerated theft in anthropology or free-loading in economics. Essentially the dynamics are always the same. The PS game has been modeled in many different ways (see Giraldeau and Caraco 2000; Arbilly et al. 2010) and has given rise to an extensive experimental research program (Giraldeau and Dubois 2008; Katsnelson et al. 2011). In all cases, the question is directed at predicting what fraction of the selfish parallel searchers searches directly for items.

All PS models predict that the strong frequency dependence of the scrounger strategy's payoffs leads to an equilibrium frequency of producers and scroungers characterized by equal payoffs for each strategy. In behavioral ecology, the usual account of how this equilibrium is attained involves invoking a mutant scrounger strategist originating within a population of pure producers. The rare mutant outperforms the producers and so the strategy spreads in the population over generations. As the scrounger strategy becomes more common, its fitness declines and eventually reaches the fitness of the producer strategy. At that point, no further evolution occurs because both strategies have equal payoffs. This equilibrium point is referred to as an evolutionarily stable strategy (ESS) because no other combination of strategies can do better within this population (Maynard Smith 1982).

However, in almost every situation in which the predictions of the PS game have been studied experimentally, the equilibrium is reached quickly within a generation, not over evolutionary time. Moreover, individuals rarely search only as scroungers or as producers. Instead usually individuals alternate, sometimes rather quickly, between the two strategies. The process through which the population of parallel searchers reaches the equilibrium therefore involves selfish agents using a decision rule adapted to maximize their individual benefits but leading the group to an equilibrium point that is not an evolutionary equilibrium in the sense above, but rather a Nash equilibrium that is behaviorally stable. The optimal decision rule specifies the probability of playing scrounger given how often it is played in the population. In the case of two-person games, we know that such a decision rule can yield different equilibria than the ESS described earlier (McNamara et al. 1999).

The form of the optimal decision rule that evolves depends on the payoffs of playing each strategy as encountered over evolutionary time. But the assumption of the model is that the players themselves simply apply the hardwired rule that has evolved, and thus respond not to the payoffs but only to the proportions of the strategies. In real life, however, given the diversity of foods and environments encountered each day and the differing payoffs of the two strategies in each, what might evolve instead is a rule that does try to sample the current payoff of each strategy and shift the probabilities of playing each accordingly. A number of early studies proposed learning rules that allow individuals to adjust their search strategy based on their experienced payoffs (e.g., Harley 1981). These learning rules must contend with the nontrivial problem of estimating the value of searching as a producer or as a scrounger while these payoffs keep changing as a result of other players also switching policy to learn both payoffs. How animals might discover their best policy remains a gap in our knowledge about the parallel search of groups of selfish agents.

When trying to derive lessons from this collective search to problems of cognitive search, one must first determine whether cognitive search might be represented as a collective of selfish agents. If it can, then no doubt the dynamics of the PS game will emerge. However, even if the collective search involves cooperating rather than selfish cognitive search agents, scrounging will likely remain an option. In such cases, research has shown that cooperative solutions to the PS game dynamics can often lead to cooperative producers extending their assistance to all other searching agents, which means more scrounging in cooperative systems compared to selfish ones (Mathot and Giraldeau 2010). It would be important, therefore, to investigate the extent to which cognitive search can be represented as a group of agents searching in parallel (cf. Minsky 1986).

Multiple Modalities and Search Cues in the External Environment

Within the animal kingdom, a wide variety of senses are known. In addition to the obvious senses of vision, hearing, chemosensitivity (olfaction, taste) and touch (somatosensitivity), animals may be sensitive to magnetic and electric fields, gravity, acceleration, time of day, the configuration of their own bodies (proprioception), and to the sensation of internal states, such as the fullness of the gut (visceral senses). Potentially any of these could be used to guide search. Which senses provide the most suitable cues to guide particular search problems is partly a function of the laws of physics and chemistry. For instance, in dense forest sound carries better than light; in turbulent wind, airborne pheromones will not allow precise location of a target. Even within each modality, selection of the signal allows some tuning of the physical properties; thus frequency affects sound transmission, and pheromones differing in their half lives are used in an adaptive way by ants to mark their trails with different permanences (Dussutour et al. 2009). Sensitivity to a particular modality depends not only on the physical properties of the cue but on the sense organs and brain of the searcher, which are constrained by their costs of construction and maintenance.

The physical differences between modalities can explain some of the variation of search strategy used by different organisms or the same organism in different contexts. Thus a moth can use its eyes to fly straight to a bright flower or use the moon as a distant navigational beacon (keeping it at a constant angle). And when searching for a mate releasing a pheromone it follows another distinctive search strategy, flying crosswind when not sensing the odor, and flying upwind when within the odor plume (Sotthibandhu and Baker 1979; Kennedy 1983).

Physical aspects may also explain both what modalities a species has evolved to use for search and which of these modalities it uses in particular circumstances. For instance, a pigeon may use a sun compass in clear weather but switch to a magnetic compass when the sun is obscured (Walcott 2005). Shine et al. (2005) consider why male garter snakes at low densities rely on following olfactory trails to find females (olfaction is accurate in distinguishing sex), whereas at high densities they switch to visual tracking (vision is not disrupted by the trails of rivals and greater speed is valuable in the more competitive situation). A common pattern is that searching animals switch between modalities sequentially as they approach the target and each sense gets into range. For instance, the digger wasp *Philanthus triagulum* hunting prey is first attracted visually by a smallish and moving object, then approaches closer downwind to check its scent, jumps on it, and can then use tactile or taste cues (Tinbergen 1958). Analogously, female sage grouse first assess males gathered in a lek on the basis of their calls and then visit only those passing this test for a closer inspection of display rate (Gibson 1996). Similar winnowing of options by one cue at a time is mirrored in strategies humans used in Internet shopping (Fasolo et al. 2005).

Sequential application of each cue, one at a time, is one way in which cues of multiple modalities may be combined in search, but there are many other possibilities and many patterns have been observed (Candolin 2003; Hutchinson and Gigerenzer 2005). There is also a rich literature in human decision making on how we combine information from different cues when comparing two items (Payne et al. 1993; Gigerenzer et al. 1999; Bröder and Newell 2008). It seems that often we do apply one cue at a time, even for information already in memory, particularly if the information was not originally presented as a single image (Bröder and Schiffer 2003); a single image seems unlikely if the information comes from several modalities and appears at separate times.

We observe that one aspect of search shows a striking commonality across modalities. When searching for cryptic prey visually, humans and other animals tend to pick a characteristic feature and focus on that, filtering out other information (e.g., Dukas 2002). Such so-called search images improve performance at spotting the target prey and other objects sharing the feature, but decrease our ability to detect other dissimilar prey items (Dukas and Kamil

2001). Analogues of search images have been found in the auditory (Fritz et al. 2007) and olfactory domains (Cross and Jackson 2010). Even bacteria can tune their sensitivity to particular chemicals in their environment (Muller-Hill 1996), so it may be a rather general feature of search in the external world. The following might be an analogue in memory search: when people have to decide whether a sequence of sounds is a valid word, they recognize "robin" as a valid word more quickly if they have been warned that any valid word presented is likely to be the name of a bird (Neely 1977).

Humans form different neuroanatomical representations of memories depending on the sensory modalities they use to encode those memories (Markowitsch 2000). Do we also search for things in memory differently depending on the modality with which the memory was encoded? For instance, whereas it is straightforward to order colors and sounds along simple axes such as wavelength or loudness, with tastes there are no such obvious dimensions because of the physical basis of chemosensitivity. And even though most real visual stimuli are complex patterns which also cannot be readily ranked along a single dimension, the poverty of our language to describe tastes points to a difference in our ability to classify them. Does this mean that we store and access memories for tastes differently than we do for memories of visual objects? Is the process by which a wine expert deduces the origin and vintage of a wine from its taste different from how an expert attributes a painting?

Further Connections between Search in Behavioral Ecology and Cognitive Psychology

As our discussion above reveals, external search problems (often the domain of ecology) and internal or more abstract search problems (often the domain of psychology) are perhaps not as unrelated as they may at first appear. Here we explore some more of the potential connections between ecological and psychological perspectives by considering specific problems in cognitive psychology about which insights from ecological research offer new questions.

Interindividual Variation in External Information Search

For a grazing animal, exploration for new resources often goes on simultaneously with the exploitation of those resources. In other cases, for instance, when an animal or human is searching for a new home, an exploration phase precedes the exploitation. In the exploration phase, the search is only for information in the external environment.

One task that captures this distinction between exploration and exploitation is called the sampling paradigm (Hills and Hertwig 2010). In the sampling paradigm, a person is asked to make a decision between two options (Option A and Option B). The person is allowed to sample freely from these two options, without receiving any direct reward, gaining only information that will later be useful. The options themselves are associated with specific payoff distributions (e.g., Option A pays $3 with certainty, Option B pays $32 10% of the time, and $0 otherwise). So, for example, a person might sample from Option A several times and witness potential payoffs (e.g., $3, $3, $3) and then sample from Option B (e.g., $0, $0, $30). After some amount of sampling, the person makes a final consequential choice between the two options, and only then actually receives one payoff.

Studies of the sampling patterns in this information-search task reveal a bimodal distribution in the frequency with which individuals switch back and forth between Options A and B (Hills and Hertwig 2010). Some participants sample repeatedly from Option A, then they switch to sample repeatedly from Option B, and then they make a final decision. Others participants switch frequently between Option A and Option B. People who frequently switch tend to take fewer samples overall than those who switch less frequently. People who frequently switch are also more likely to make a decision consistent with a roundwise decision policy, one based on the number of times a sample from one option beats the preceding sample from the other option. People who switch infrequently are more like to choose the option associated with the higher expected value overall.

Individual differences in search behavior are not restricted to humans. In the fruit fly *Drosophila*, natural allelic variation in a protein kinase gene results in the "rover" and "sitter" dimorphism (Osborne et al. 1997). Rovers leave food patches more readily, visit more food patches, and revisit food patches less compared to sitters, which are more sedentary and aggregate within food patches (Nagle and Bell 1987; Pereira and Sokolowski 1993; Stamps et al. 2005). The same gene has been implicated in learning and memory traits in *Drosophila* larvae and adults (Méry et al. 2007; Reaume et al. 2011), and orthologues are involved in regulating food-related and social behaviors in a variety of other animals (Reaume and Sokolowski 2009). Do similar genetic differences underlie the variation in human search patterns? Moreover, might these differences in search behavior reflect differences in cognitive processing that influence a wide range of tasks involving cognitive search, including learning?

Memory Search

Memory search can be characterized as search through information topologies stored in the brain (Davelaar and Raaijmakers, this volume; Hills and Dukas, this volume). What is the structure of these topologies? In the semantic fluency task, people are asked to recall as many items as they can from a specific category (e.g., "say all the animals you can think of"). In this task, humans often produce items as if they were retrieving them from memory clusters (Bousfield 1953). Some data suggests that semantic memory may reflect a clumpy or patch-like structure (Steyvers and Tenenbaum 2005). This suggests that human memory search could follow similar foraging policies as described for animals foraging on spatial patches of prey (Hutchinson et al. 2008; Hills et al. 2009).

However, memory representations differ in potentially important ways from space. Understanding the nature of these potentially dynamic topologies may be critical to our understanding of how memory search works. For example, an item in memory can belong to different representations simultaneously: the word "cat" can belong to the category of "pets" as well as to the category of "predators." The representation need not be based solely on semantic similarity but also, for instance, on phonological similarity ("cat" and "bat"). Thus words could potentially belong to more than one patch. Studies of memory search should ask what is the patch structure of memory and how are these patches used. For example, do the patch-like subcategories (e.g., pets) really reflect some special organizational linking of items in memory, or are items in memory evenly spread and the apparent patches simply the behavioral outcomes of individuals moving in memory from one item to a nearby item, what Pollio et al. (1968) called an "associative" search? Studies of memory search can potentially explore the cognitive mechanisms guiding search in similar ways to those used to study animal foraging. For example, increasing the costs necessary to switch between patches leads animals to stay in patches for longer periods of time (Nonacs 2001). The analogous manipulation in a memory-recall experiment could be accomplished by imposing external costs, for instance, by increasing the time it takes to be presented with a new category for free recall (if subjects are paid in terms of recalled items per unit time; cf. Wilke et al. 2009). One could also look at recall patterns from more or less sparse semantic domains: foods are highly semantically similar; occupations may be less so. Recent models of semantic space allow the objective computation of similarity between words based on large corpora of text, using word co-occurrence (Jones and Mewhort 2007). This offers innovative ways to represent the landscape over which memory searches.

Do nonhuman animals also search memory as if it had a patchy structure? One experiment that we considered involved training a pigeon to peck at several categories of images (e.g., cats, trees, and human faces). These could then be presented on a grid with numerous distractors (i.e., images not belonging to the target categories). After extensive training, the pigeons could then be asked to recall the locations of these targets on an unlabeled grid. Would they recall the items by category (e.g., first all the cats, then all the trees), as if the information were stored in semantic patches or in some other way such as spatial proximity?

Some animals possess cognitive maps which allow them to take novel routes between spatial locations. Might information in memory be stored as a cognitive map, allowing humans and nonhuman animals to link previously unlinked information adaptively?

Problem Solving

Another form of internal cognitive search involves manipulating the arrangement of information in working memory in such a way that it provides a solution to a problem. Chess players search for potential solutions to a chess problem, even if they have never before seen this particular arrangement of chess pieces (De Groot 1965). A similar kind of problem involving a search through arrangements is the Tower of London problem, involving the lawful rearrangement of colored balls on sticks to match a final target pattern (Shallice 1982). A novice player cannot solve such a problem by recalling the answer; it requires the active construction of a new solution, by cognitively simulating and searching through the possibilities.

Some nonhuman animals appear capable of this kind of problem solving. Jumping spiders plan paths before moving (Tarsitano and Andrew 1999). Some individual ravens faced with food suspended on a string discovered how to lift it up using beak and feet without trial-and-error learning of the process (Heinrich 1995). Emery and Clayton (2004) discuss other examples of such insight.

These kinds of planning associated with problem solving might be productively thought of as forms of route planning, similar to the way rats have been demonstrated to simulate exploration of space actively in so-called episodic future thinking (Redish, this volume). Are searches through configural solution spaces governed by similar kinds of strategies, as found in spatial search?

Language Acquisition

Is learning language also a kind of search process? Social animals may have as a developmental goal the acquisition of effective communication strategies. Human children learn language, learning both word meaning and grammar, and they do so in predictable ways. However, the process of language acquisition is still not well understood. Could it represent a search process? Goldstein et al. (2003) suggest this possibility by noting that human children share a phase of exploratory linguistic babbling similar to that found in birds; in both cases, the babbling appears to be "shaped" by interactions with adults. Analogously, male brown-headed cowbirds (West and King 1988) and satin bowerbirds (Patricelli et al. 2002) rely on feedback from females they court to refine their courtship behavior. Even *Drosophila* males show plasticity in the courtship dance, which is learned through successive interactions with females (Polejack and Tidon 2007). Though the question is rather broad, could goal-directed exploration characterize the learning of these various forms of communication?

Tailpiece

This chapter is not a comprehensive review of search, but rather reflects the esoteric choice of topics that matched our interests and expertise and that we had time to discuss. The topic seems endless because search is such a widespread phenomenon and research on it so multifarious. By thinking carefully about what is fundamental to search, and by recognizing some commonalities between research in different disciplines, we hope to have introduced a little more structure into the topic. There may never be a single overarching theory of search, but some imposed structure is helpful in recognizing how our own research relates to existing work, and in drawing attention to relevant gaps in our knowledge that require investigation.

Search, Goals, and the Brain

5

Executive Control of Cognitive Search

Joshua W. Brown and Derek E. Nee

Abstract

At a basic level, cognitive search involves several parameters: Under what circumstances should a search be initiated, and how should the goal be specified? What are the criteria by which the search is judged a success or failure? How are corrective actions implemented when search strategies are judged insufficient?

Studies of cognitive control have the potential to address each of these questions. In this chapter, a number of issues related to executive control of search are discussed, including the way in which hierarchical search goals are monitored and updated. A new theory of cognitive control is proposed to begin to answer these questions, and open questions that remain are highlighted for future enquiry.

Initiating and Maintaining Searches

Initiation of Search

Searches are generally initiated on the basis of a goal and a lack of certainty about how best to achieve it. Goals may be anything, from finding a shape in a visual scene to remembering where the car keys are to finding a mate. Goals, and how to achieve them in an ever-changing environment, are the raison d'être of cognitive control. At the neural level, active goals are represented, in part, as a pattern of sustained activity across the dorsolateral prefrontal cortex (dlPFC) (Miller and Cohen 2001) and other regions, such as the intraparietal sulcus (IPS) (Chafee and Goldman-Rakic 2000). According to the biased competition model (Miller and Cohen 2001), sustained activity in dlPFC represents goals and working memory. Goal-related dlPFC activity interacts with posterior cortical regions to bias the flow of information across competing networks, much like a switch yard at a railroad station (Rogers and Monsell 1995), thereby enhancing activity in posterior regions that represent relevant information (Egner and Hirsch 2005). Hence, activation in the dlPFC primes the cognitive system to encode and maintain information relevant to goals.

Goal Maintenance

Goals are thought to be maintained in the dlPFC via sustained patterns of activity. This activity is modulated by neuromodulators, such as dopamine and norepinephrine, which influence the persistence of these goal representations and, in turn, influences how readily an animal will change goals as opposed to perseverate. In particular, a lower barrier to switching goals implies a lower barrier to either beginning or abandoning a search. Dopamine has been studied extensively as a principal mediator of reinforcement (Schultz 1998), but it also influences the stability of sustained activity patterns in dlPFC. Either too much or too little dopamine can reduce the stability of activity, thus making it easier for new working memory and goal representations to become active (Muly et al. 1998). The neural mechanisms underlying this "sweet spot" of stability have been modeled computationally (Brunel and Wang 2001; Durstewitz et al. 1999, 2000; Redish et al. 2007). Essentially, the optimal level of dopamine seems to deepen the attractor basins of the network state, which requires a stronger input to cause a change in the pattern of which units are active and inactive. At the behavioral level, as dopamine levels increase towards optimal stability, animals may perseverate on their current goal.

Perseveration on a goal constitutes the "exploitation" end of a spectrum between exploration and exploitation (Kaelbling et al. 1996). At the other end of the spectrum, a lack of stability in goal representations may lead to constant switching, which constitutes a process resembling a search except that it never terminates to allow consumption of what was found. This link among tonic dopamine levels, search, and the exploration/exploitation trade-off has been treated previously, and it appears that dopamine may bias behavior toward exploitation (Hills 2006). With regard to drug abuse, addictive substances typically cause a lasting release of dopamine (Grace 2000), which is associated with the recurring drug-taking behavior that characterizes addiction.

Norepinephrine has also been implicated in cognitive flexibility, although the neural mechanisms are somewhat less studied than those of dopamine. As discussed more fully by Cools (this volume), greater tonic norepinephrine seems to reduce cognitive flexibility, which corresponds with increased gain in the responsiveness of neurons to both excitation and inhibition (Hasselmo et al. 1997).

Internal versus External Search

Searches may target internal cognitive processes in addition to the external environment. There is good evidence that many of the same neural mechanisms involved in searching the external environment are also recruited for searching information in the mind held in working memory (Awh et al. 2006). For example, Nobre and colleagues (2004) demonstrated common recruitment of the IPS and the frontal eye fields when subjects either directed attention to an external location or to a location held in working memory. Nee and Jonides (2009) replicated this effect with more complex searches of external visual and internal memory information and demonstrated additional common dlPFC activation for both types of searches, presumably in the service of maintaining goals during search. Behaviorally, it has been demonstrated that attention is captured by externally presented objects that match objects held in working memory, indicating interactions between attentional and working memory systems (Downing 2000; Pashler and Shiu 1999). Moreover, holding information in working memory reduces filtering of distraction, consistent with the idea that both selective attention and working memory draw upon the same attentional resources (de Fockert et al. 2001). Taken together, attentional mechanisms that search the external world also appear to be necessary for searches of memory.

Despite strong commonalities between external search and working memory, one consistent finding is that internal searches recruit ventrolateral prefrontal cortex (vlPFC)[1] to a greater degree, particularly in the left hemisphere (LaBar et al. 1999; Mayer et al. 2007; Nee and Jonides 2009; Nobre et al. 2004). Although the left vlPFC is often associated with the maintenance and manipulation of verbal information, one study has reported greater left vlPFC activation when selecting a spatial location from memory compared to selecting a spatial location in perception (Nobre et al. 2004). Moreover, left vlPFC involvement in memory search extends beyond working memory and includes searches of long-term memory as well (Cabeza et al. 2002). Hence, the left vlPFC may be generally involved in searching internal memory space (Zhang et al. 2004) in a way that is distinct from external searches.

Criteria for Search Success or Failure

Searches end either in success or failure, but a key underlying question is: What criteria determine success versus failure? Suppose an animal is foraging for food, but finds only a little food and is still hungry. Should the search be considered a success or a failure? The answer to this question depends on prior expectation. If food is very scarce, then the expectation may be that virtually no food will usually be found, in which case finding even a little food may be considered a success. On the other hand, if food is typically plentiful, then

---

[1] We use the term "ventrolateral" prefrontal cortex (vlPFC) to distinguish these activations from the dorsolateral prefrontal cortex (dlPFC). Activations from the cited studies typically fall in and around pars triangularis (BA 45), which is the dorsal most aspect of the inferior frontal gyrus, and often also extends into the inferior frontal sulcus. Although there is some ambiguity as to where vlPFC ends and dlPFC begins, the activations reported here are ventral to activations we refer to as within dlPFC, which are on the middle frontal gyrus (BA 9 and 46).

finding only a little food may be considered a failure. This example illustrates two basic principles of evaluating search success or failure: (a) expectations are key to the evaluation and (b) expectations are formed on the basis of prior experience or information. Nonetheless, there is often no explicit environmental cue that a search has failed, so the evidence of absence must be inferred from the absence of evidence (Sagan 1996:213). The monitoring and evaluation functions required to infer search success or failure is a central concern of cognitive control.

Models of cognitive control typically have two main components: one for monitoring and one for control. For example, one model (Botvinick et al. 2001) casts the monitor as a response conflict detector, while the controller implements attentional focus or increased caution. Response conflict occurs when cues in the environment are associated with two different responses that are mutually incompatible. Computationally, response conflict can be detected by multiplying the activities associated with the mutually incompatible responses (Botvinick et al. 2001). While conflict models predominate (Yeung et al. 2004, 2005; Yeung and Nieuwenhuis 2009), others have cast the monitor as detecting errors; that is, a failure to achieve a desired goal (Holroyd and Coles 2002) or the likelihood of errors (Brown and Braver 2005, 2007). There is ongoing debate on whether such dedicated monitoring and control pathways are necessary to account for cognitive control phenomena. Some argue for the existence of such mechanisms (Monsell 2003; Rogers and Monsell 1995), while others argue that simpler mechanisms (e.g., priming) are sufficient (Altmann 2003; Altmann and Gray 2002; Mayr et al. 2003). With respect to this debate, we propose that dedicated control structures can provide useful contributions to the control of search processes.

The Predicted Response–Outcome Model

Recently, we proposed a new model of performance monitoring and cognitive control functions in the medial prefrontal cortex (mPFC, including anterior cingulate cortex), which we refer to as the predicted response–outcome (PRO) model (Alexander and Brown 2011). The PRO model can detect when searches fail, and provides a monitoring and evaluation function with two interacting components (Figure 5.1). The first component, the predictor, generates a prediction of the expected outcomes of an action, which in the context of search would correspond to successfully finding the object (and in the expected quantities). The neural activity representing this expected outcome increases as time elapses, such that if the object of the search is available, then it ought to be found within a certain time frame. In other words, not finding sufficient quantities early on would not be considered failure, but failure will be signaled if sufficient quantities are not found after a longer period of time. This kind of representation can be thought of as qualitatively similar to a hazard function of the probability of finding the searched-for object, given that it exists (Ghose and

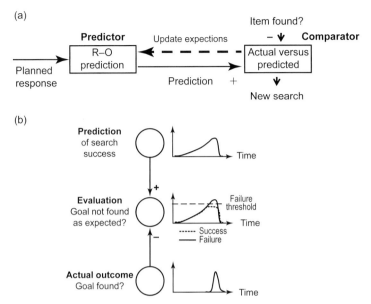

Figure 5.1 Predicted response–outcome (PRO) model: (a) Planned searches activate learned response–outcome (R–O) predictions. These predicted outcome signals indicate the expected findings of the search. (b) The Comparator unit receives a timed prediction from the Predictor unit that signals when the search should yield a finding. The actual findings (the outcome) are compared against the expected findings, and failure to find the searched-for item leads to both an update of the search outcome predictions and a possible initiation of a new search.

Maunsell 2002). The second component, the comparator, subtracts the actual outcome from the expected outcome. The net result is that when a searched-for object is found, a signal of the actual finding suppresses the expectation activity in the comparator. Conversely, when the object of the search is not found, the predictor activity increases unopposed and signals search failure in the comparator. Of note, failure can be detected at any point in time, whenever the difference of the prediction activity minus the actual success outcome exceeds a specified threshold. In addition, finding greater than expected amounts of the goal, or finding it sooner than expected, would not be evaluated as a failure, although other aspects of the PRO model not discussed here would signal it as a surprising event. Neurophysiological findings in monkey mPFC are consistent with the PRO model, as described below.

The PRO model differs from existing models of mPFC in that it does not compute response conflict, as do some other models (Botvinick et al. 2001). Our simulations suggest that the PRO model can simulate virtually all of the known effects in mPFC such as error, response conflict, and error likelihood, among others (Alexander and Brown 2011). The PRO model derives from our error likelihood model (Brown and Braver 2005), but it differs in two ways. First, the PRO model predicts various outcomes, including possible rewards, and is not restricted to predicting only errors. These prediction signals may be formed by mechanisms within mPFC, or they may instead be formed elsewhere and sent to the mPFC. We are actively investigating this question. Second, the PRO model adds a mechanism that signals any discrepancies between the outcome predictions and the actual outcomes. These discrepancy signals resemble a dopaminergic temporal difference signal that has been proposed as an alternative account in the earlier RL–ERN models (Holroyd and Coles 2002; Holroyd et al. 2005). Nonetheless, the PRO model posits different mechanisms to account for the signals. In one earlier model, the dopaminergic error signal from the midbrain disinhibits the mPFC (Holroyd and Coles 2002). In contrast, the PRO model suggests that such error signals are computed internally by the mPFC. In another model, the dopamine signals train mPFC to recognize conjunctions of events that constitute errors (Holroyd et al. 2005). In contrast, the PRO model signals not conjunctions but comparisons of actual versus expected events. Furthermore, while the PRO model may influence dopaminergic signaling, it does not depend on external dopamine signals to function per se.

With this different approach, the PRO model can account for data that other models cannot. For example, whereas the response conflict model of the anterior cingulate cortex (ACC) may account for greater activity during search, it cannot account for feedback-related ACC responses (Holroyd et al. 2004). The PRO model accounts for activation at the time of feedback as a discrepancy between actual and expected outcomes. Of note, when a search is expected to fail or is rarely successful, then the PRO model would predict that activity related to search failure should be weaker. In fact, weaker error signals have been found when errors are more likely (Brown and Braver 2005), and error signals even reverse when success occurs unexpectedly (Jessup et al. 2010). Such reverse reward effects are difficult to reconcile with dopamine-based models of the ACC that compute signed differences in reward expectation (Holroyd and Coles 2002; Holroyd et al. 2005). By contrast, the PRO model interprets this latter finding with complementary mechanisms that detect surprising occurrences as well as surprising nonoccurrences.

With the PRO model framework, the threshold at which a search failure is signaled is a product of two parameters. The first parameter is the strength of the prediction. Prediction strength in the PRO model is proportional to the previously experienced probability of finding the searched-for object and the quantity of the searched-for object that is expected to be found (Amiez et al. 2005). The second parameter is the strength of what was found. The greater the quantity found, the greater the suppression of the expectation signal in the comparator and the less likely it is that a failure will be signaled.

Predictions about the success of a search are learned from past experience. When a searched-for object is not found, the resulting error signal from the comparator drives learning in the predictor unit to reduce the predictions of success in similar searches in the future. This is tantamount to raising the threshold for signaling failure. In this way, predictions about what constitutes success for a given search are dynamically updated in nonstationary environments. The greater the nonstationarity, the greater the ongoing discrepancy signals and resulting mPFC activity, as has been found with fMRI results in humans (Behrens et al. 2007).

Certain kinds of task-switching tasks can be thought of as cognitive searches, similar to foraging. For example, some tasks require subjects to choose a certain option or strategy to gain reward, but after some trials, the reward is depleted. The subjects must then detect the depletion and search for a new strategy that yields reward, similar to patch-leaving in animal foraging. Tasks of this kind include the Wisconsin card sort task (Grant and Berg 1948) as well as searches for a correct sequence of button presses (Bush et al. 2002; Procyk et al. 2000) or lever manipulations (Shima and Tanji 1998). Notably, these tasks differ somewhat from much of the traditional task-switching literature, which involve either explicit cues or unambiguous patterns that cue a task switch (Altmann and Gray 2002; Rogers and Monsell 1995). In cases where the new task is explicitly cued, searching for the appropriate task is not required. In contrast, task switches due to the absence (or surprising reduction) of an expected reward may involve different neural mechanisms. When reward is reduced, ACC is active prior to a switch, but it is not active for explicitly cued switches (Bush et al. 2002; Shima and Tanji 1998). Thus the task switches cued implicitly by reduced or absent reward can be thought of as a disconfirmation of the current strategy, which may in turn lead to renewed or continued searches for a more effective strategy. In a broader sense, task switches due to reward omission and exploration of the environment (as opposed to exploitation) may be thought of as two sides of the same coin: reduced reward may be a cue to switch or a current reward level may still be deemed insufficient if a possibly greater reward may be found elsewhere. The common question is: What constitutes a sufficient level of reward, below which a search for better reward will be initiated?

The PRO model framework, as applied to cognitive search, can account for a variety of findings regarding implicit task-switching paradigms. The Wisconsin card sort task (Grant and Berg 1948) yields activation in the mPFC for negative feedback that leads to a search for the new correct strategy (Monchi et al. 2001). In monkeys, negative feedback also leads to greater activity in ACC during search (Procyk et al. 2000; Shima and Tanji 1998), as is also the case in humans (Bush et al. 2002). Similarly, ACC is more active when monkeys are actively searching than when behavior is routine (Procyk et al. 2000). More broadly, monkey supplementary eye fields in the mPFC have distinct subpopulations of cells with activity profiles that apparently anticipate the outcome of actions and shut off when expected outcomes occur, and other subpopulations of cells that signal the actual occurrence of an expected outcome, such as a reward (Amador et al. 2000; Ito et al. 2003).

Controlling and Correcting Search Strategies

Searches can fail for many reasons. A primary concern of cognitive control is to minimize the possibility of failure, while at the same time detecting failure when it does occur and driving corrective action. A central question then is: How are these functions accomplished? First, a signal is needed to indicate when failure is likely. Such a prediction signal can, in turn, drive greater attention and effort to maximize the chance of success with the existing strategy, or it can drive a change in strategy to find another search tactic that is more likely to succeed. Previous models cast the prediction of an error as driving increased caution by slowing down response processes (Botvinick et al. 2001; Brown and Braver 2005) or by increasing attentional focus (Botvinick et al. 2001; MacDonald et al. 2000; Posner and DiGirolamo 1998). In this case, slower and more careful processing of the environment may lead to detection of the searched-for object when environmental cues are otherwise weak and easy to miss (Clark and Dukas 2003). A second issue involves how failures are detected and corrected. There is evidence that the mPFC is involved in error avoidance (Magno et al. 2006) as well as error correction (Modirrousta and Fellows 2008).

The PRO model yields two relevant signals in this regard from the predictor and comparator components (Figure 5.1). The predictor provides a prediction of what will be the outcome of a search, including possible failure. These prediction signals would be sufficient to provide a greater level of control toward the goal of avoiding failure, whether by searching more carefully or by trying a different strategy, according to the predicted outcome. For example, if the model predicts a likely failure to detect some event in a certain situation, then an increase in attention is most likely to lead to reward and consequent reinforcement. If instead the model predicts that the resources are likely depleted such that no amount of greater attention will succeed, then a change in strategy is most likely to be rewarded. In the PRO model, a second control signal derives from the comparator. As described above, this signals when a failure has in fact occurred, in that the searched-for object has not been found. This signal is exactly what is needed to drive a change in strategy, which is essentially a task switch that is cued implicitly by reduced reward, as described above.

Hierarchies of Strategy

In a foraging task, the appropriate change in strategy may involve giving up exploiting the current patch or environment and returning to an exploratory set to search for new resources. Of note, this foraging example highlights the hierarchical nature of search goals. At the lowest level of the hierarchy, foraging in a given part of an environment may involve searching a limited region for a particular resource, and many individual resources may be found. In this case, a visual search may be conducted, and if the searched-for object is not found in the fovea, then the search "fails" at the lowest level and a new location is searched in the immediate vicinity. We have suggested that the mPFC may yield evaluations of failure in general, but it is an open question as to whether the mPFC may detect failure of lower-level visual search.

As resources are depleted and become scarcer, more careful and attentive processing may be needed to find the resources, expressed as greater attentional focus and longer processing times (Botvinick et al. 2001; Brown et al. 2007b). When resources are depleted beyond a certain level, this modulation of the lower-level strategy is no longer sufficient. In such a case, it is time to change the higher-level strategy and switch from exploiting the current location and instead explore for a new location. The PRO model comparator would provide the signal necessary to drive the change in strategy. This proposal is consistent with ACC activation due to reduced available reward in both humans and monkeys (Bush et al. 2002; Shima and Tanji 1998).

The hierarchical nature of search leads to a credit assignment problem, which may be seen in an expanded variant of the explore versus exploit foraging task. We may suppose, for example, that foraging strategies may be for a more- versus less-preferred food and that there is a choice of continuing to forage versus waiting and conserving energy until more resources become available. In this scenario, we might suppose that an animal will search for a preferred food in a limited region until the preferred food is depleted in that region. As food becomes scarcer, the animal might implement increased attentional control to find less salient food items. Once the local region is depleted, the animal will qualitatively switch control strategies from greater attention in the current region to exploration of a different region for the preferred food instead. Once the preferred food is depleted, the animal might again switch strategies to forage for nonpreferred food, subsequently switching strategies between exploration versus exploitation for the nonpreferred food. Once even the nonpreferred food is depleted, the animal may switch strategies between foraging and resting or waiting for more resources. This example of a hierarchical goal structure for search leads to an important question: If a failure occurs, at which level of the goal hierarchy should failure be ascribed? For example, when a food item is not found, does this mean the animal should pay more attention to the local region and look in another nearby location (lowest-level search failure)? Or does it mean that the animal should explore for new regions (mid-level search failure)? Or does it mean that the animal should switch to foraging for another, less-preferred food (higher-level failure)? Or does it mean that the animal should give up searching entirely and conserve energy until new resources arrive (highest-level failure)?

The PRO model suggests an answer to the hierarchical goal credit assignment problem. The answer begins with the assumption that just as there are multiple levels of goals, there are also multiple levels of outcome predictions. At the lowest level, a visual search may involve the expectation of a particular object in the fovea. This is not to suggest that the evaluation of the visual scene is necessarily carried out in the ACC. Instead, there is evidence that visual cortex may carry similar temporally structured expectation signals in anticipation of particular visual cues, which appear as attentional signals (Ghose and Maunsell 2002).

At the next level, the ACC evaluates reward, or the lack thereof, and may drive a corresponding change in mid-level strategy aimed at successfully searching for the same reward (Bush et al. 2002; Procyk and Joseph 2001; Shima and Tanji 1998). Exploration-related activity in cognitive search is also associated with anterior prefrontal activation (Daw et al. 2006). When the searched-for reward is not found, then, in the framework of the PRO model, it may be that a prediction signal of finding a certain quantity of reward over a longer timescale (many trials) eventually goes unmet by a longer-term measure of actual successful trials, and this could lead to a higher-level switch in strategy to search for other kinds of reward. In the same way, an even longer timescale prediction of total reward aggregated across multiple reward types may develop, and if it is not met by successful search across a variety of reward types, then a highest-level switch in strategy may be made to give up the search and switch to a strategy of waiting until new resources become available.

The key point, and the proposed solution to the hierarchical credit assignment problem, is that outcome predictions are associated with a corresponding action. If a low-level visual foveation action fails to yield the searched-for object in the fovea within a few hundred milliseconds, then the failure violates the expectation of the eye movement foveating an object within a short time. It does not necessarily violate the higher-level expectation associated with the overall search strategy, which is that the object will eventually be found, perhaps after some longer time period of minutes. The PRO model's ability to specify not only the nature of expected outcomes but also their timing allows for a short-term failure to be signaled without necessarily signaling the failure of a higher-level goal that is expected to take more time to achieve.

The template of hierarchical goals in search is ubiquitous, with examples ranging from animals' search for food to cognitive search of memory to humans searching for employment or mates. In the end, the hierarchical monitoring and control of search goals may be carried out by a corresponding hierarchical structure of evaluating shorter and longer timescale predictions about the outcomes of one's own actions.

Conclusion and Open Questions

Our aim in this chapter has been as much to raise questions as to propose answers. In the course of exploring the topic of cognitive control in search, several potentially controversial or at least unresolved issues may be highlighted. First is the question of whether and to what extent there are distinct structures in the brain that provide executive control of search. We have outlined the PRO model as a possible mechanism of executive control, but undoubtedly there are other possibilities. It may be that what appear to be effects of executive function are in fact properties that derive from the nature of regions that drive the search, so that no additional control structures are necessary. This question parallels the debate over whether executive control is necessary to account for effects associated with explicitly cued task switching.

If there are indeed neural mechanisms dedicated to executive control of search, then the next question is what distinct brain regions are involved in monitoring and evaluating the different kinds and hierarchical levels of search, and whether or to what extent there is overlap. There is evidence that mPFC monitors the outcome of actions and drives changes in at least higher-level strategies, but it is less clear whether these same regions are involved in lower levels of search (e.g., visual search). This leaves open the question of what possible distinct brain regions are involved in detecting failure at different levels in the hierarchy of search goals, and whether those distinct regions share nevertheless a common neural architecture related to prediction and evaluation.

Correspondingly, there is a question of how and where in the brain the search goals are represented. We have generally referred to working memory and goal representation in the dlPFC, but this is a relatively large region. Some have argued that the hierarchy of lower- to higher-level goals is represented along a posterior-to-anterior gradient within the lateral PFC (Koechlin et al. 2003; Kouneiher et al. 2009). This leaves open the possibility that a similar gradient exists in the medial PFC that interacts with lateral PFC, although this has yet to be explored.

Another open question is the degree to which search has memory or not. There is evidence that visual search has no memory (Horowitz and Wolfe 1998), but it is not clear how this finding can be reconciled with effects showing inhibition of return (Klein and MacInnes 1999), which would imply memory. With respect to higher levels of cognitive search, monkeys seem to have a strong memory and ability to infer which search spaces remain as plausible resources, as they show near optimally short and successful searches at the cognitive level (Procyk and Joseph 1996). If higher cognitive search has memory, then the interaction between dlPFC and mPFC may be reciprocal. More specifically, mPFC may drive changes in the strategy represented by dlPFC and IPS, but dlPFC may, in turn, constrain how error signals are generated in mPFC and what kinds of new strategies may be implemented in response to search failure. The effect of working memory context on performance monitoring is suggested by recent studies of individuals with schizophrenia (Krawitz et al. 2011).

Acknowledgments

This work was supported by R01 DA026457.

6

Search Processes and Hippocampus

A. David Redish

Abstract

Deliberation entails the sequential, serial search through possible options. This means that deliberation requires a mechanism to represent the structure of the world, from which predictions can be generated concerning these options and the expectations of the consequences of taking those options. Deliberation requires a mechanism to move mentally through those predictions as well as a mechanism to evaluate and compare those predictions. Neural signals for each of these factors have been found in the rat.

Introduction

The concept of the cognitive map introduced by Tolman (1938, 1939, 1948) fundamentally entails representations of the structure of the world. In fact, Tolman's original formulation of the "cognitive map" was more "cognitive" than "map." Tolman did not necessarily envision the cognitive map as spatial (for a discussion, see Johnson and Crowe 2009). Nevertheless, the translation of the cognitive map into modern neuroscience (primarily through O'Keefe and Nadel 1978) was fundamentally a spatial vision. Over the subsequent several decades, the concept of the cognitive map was more about whether the hippocampus encoded an actual "map" than about how the map was used (Nadel 1991; Eichenbaum et al. 1992; O'Keefe 1999; Eichenbaum 2000; Redish 2001). Examining the information and computational processes that the cognitive map would provide to the rat allowed an integration of the memory and spatial results into a unified theoretical picture (Redish 1999). In this chapter, I will return to the question of Tolman's original concept: in order to predict, one needs representations of the structure of the world.

Place Cells and the Structure of the World

The spatial tuning of place cells is known to be derived from internal dead-reckoning representations: representations of spatial location and orientation maintained through self-motion information (Redish 1999). Those dead-reckoning systems appear to lie in the medial entorhinal cortex utilizing the grid-cell representations now known to lie therein (Fyhn et al. 2004; Hafting et al. 2005). These internal coordinate systems are then associated in hippocampus proper with external sensory signals, providing information about spatial position (Knierim et al. 1998; Redish 1999). The hippocampus can, in turn, use these learned associations between representations of external landmarks and internal representations of position to reset the internal coordinate system when the animal becomes lost (Redish and Touretzky 1997; Touretzky and Redish 1996) and to prevent drift during navigation (Samsonovich and McNaughton 1997; Redish et al. 2000). Although hippocampal lesions disrupt the spatial reliability of the grid-cell tuning, they do not seem to disrupt the internal coherence of grid cells (Bonnevie et al. 2010). In contrast, the internal coherence of grid cells depends on theta rhythmicity interactions arising from septal nucleus (Brandon et al. 2010; Koenig et al. 2010). This implies that the grid cells use septal signals to integrate dead-reckoning information and can continue to do so without hippocampus, but that the hippocampus is necessary to prevent drift.

In a variety of conditions, however, place cells also show reliable nonspatial tuning (Redish 1999; Pastalkova et al. 2008). Unlike spatial tuning, which appears to be ubiquitous in hippocampal representations, nonspatial tuning can appear, or not, in an environment depending on the specific path distribution (McNaughton et al. 1983; Muller et al. 1994), task and goal distribution (Markus et al. 1995; Olypher et al. 2002; Jackson and Redish 2007; Ainge et al. 2011), and training within that environment (Wood et al. 2000; Bower et al. 2005). This led several authors to conclude that the nonspatial information was represented as different maps (reference frames: Touretzky and Redish 1996; Redish and Touretzky 1997; Redish 1999; charts: McNaughton et al. 1996; Samsonovich and McNaughton 1997). A more nuanced description may be that the nonspatial representations depend, as proposed by Tolman in his original formulation of the cognitive map, on the structure of the world (Johnson and Crowe 2009).

Several recent experiments have found that hippocampal "place" cells will represent sequences of nonspatial information (Fortin et al. 2002; Agster et al. 2002) and distance (Pastalkova et al. 2008; Takahashi et al. 2009a; Gill et al. 2011) through a waiting period, as originally proposed by Levy (1996; see also Levy et al. 2005). Even on spatial experiments, cells can differentiate overlapping paths that originate from and proceed to different locations (Wood et al. 2000; Ferbinteanu and Shapiro 2003; Ainge et al. 2011). For example, Wood et al. (2000) found that when rats alternate on a simple T-choice with returns, hippocampal place cells encode the two overlapping paths on the central track depending on whether the journey is a left-to-right or right-to-left occurrence. However, Bower et al. (2005) found that such a differentiation occurred only if the rat was initially trained with a separation between directions. Both Griffin et al. (2007) and Ainge et al. (2007) found that even when rats were trained identically to those in Wood et al. (2000), if a delay was imposed (thus making the task hippocampally dependent), the differentiation seen by Wood et al. (2000) vanished.

This difference likely depends on how animals are bridging the "gaps" in the task (Redish 2001). There are three ways to bridge a temporal or spatial gap: (a) priming, which is likely dependent on changes in sensory cortices, requiring the repetition of a cue for memory; (b) active maintenance of information and rehearsal, likely dependent on working memory and recurrent circuits in the prefrontal cortex; and (c) recall, dependent on storage and recall of episodic memory situations.

Open Questions:

- When do hippocampal place cells encode nonspatial information and when do they not?
- How does the structure of the world impact those representations?

Episodic Future Thinking and Episodic Past Thinking

Memory is only evolutionarily useful if it affects future actions. An important question, therefore, is: How does episodic memory affect future decision making? Four not necessarily mutually exclusive hypotheses include (a) recognition of individual past events for single-trial learning (Zilli and Hasselmo 2008; Lengyal and Dayan 2007), (b) training up other systems (Marr 1971; Alvarez and Squire 1994; Sutherland and McNaughton 2000), (c) reevaluation of the past (Loftus and Palmer 1974; Schacter 2001; Schacter and Addis 2007; Buckner and Carroll 2007), and (d) episodic future thinking (Buckner and Carroll 2007; Schacter et al. 2008).

The hippocampus has long been identified as a means of "bridging a gap" in tasks that require recognition of individual trials (Rawlins 1985; Redish 1999, 2001). For example, in T-maze alternation, the hippocampus is only necessary if a delay is imposed between the trials (Dember and Richman 1989; Ainge et al. 2007). In an explicit model of this, Zilli and Hasselmo (2008) showed that a one-trial learning memory capable of recognizing past individual events can bridge gaps in hippocampal-dependent tasks. Differentiating between recognition memory, in which one recognizes the familiarity of a situation, and recollection memory, in which one recalls an earlier situation and compares the memory with one's current observations, Eichenbaum et al. (2007) suggest that the hippocampus is necessary for recollection, but not recognition. In spatial tasks, one might identify this as including a "self-localization" process in which the animal identifies the situation it is in and differentiates it from other similar situations (Redish and Touretzky 1997; Redish 1999; Fuhs and Touretzky 2007). In general, recollection will depend on a reconstruction process through which past experiences will need to be rebuilt for comparison with present circumstances (Buckner and Carroll 2007; Schacter et al. 2007).

Open Question: Does the phenomenon of self-localization that is seen in rodents correspond to this more general process in humans?

From almost the very beginning of the place-cell literature, it was noted that place cells fired outside their place fields during nonattentive rest states (Pavlides and Winson 1989; O'Keefe and Nadel 1978). From the first ensemble recordings, it was noted that the ensembles reactivated during sleep states after a task more than before a task (Wilson and McNaughton 1994; Kudrimoti et al. 1999). Bringing these results in line with observations of a limited length retrograde amnesia after hippocampal damage, Squire and colleagues (Squire 1987; Reed and Squire 1998; Squire and Alvarez 1995; cf. Nadel and Moscovitch 1997; Sutherland et al. 2001, 2011) suggest that the hippocampus might be training up other systems during off-line sleep states (Marr 1971; Alvarez and Squire 1994; Redish et al. 1998; Hoffmann and McNaughton 2002; Ji and Wilson 2007; Euston et al. 2007). Although there is good evidence that both the hippocampus and cortex replay representations during sleep that had been experienced during previous wake states (Pavlides and Winson 1989; Buzsáki 1989; Hasselmo 1993), it is still not clear how veridical those replays are. Although there is good evidence that hippocampus plays a role in bridging gaps, particularly contextual ones, it has been well-established that conscious human recall of past events is not veridical. Past memory is "constructed" (Loftus and Palmer 1974; Schacter 2001). The other two hypotheses for the role of hippocampal memory attempt to explain this lack of veridicality.

The hypothesis that the role of hippocampus is to reevaluate the past suggests that the primary effect of hippocampus on decision making will occur during off-line processes. Presumably, this reevaluation will occur during replay, which suggests that the replay events may include search processes (Samsonovich and Ascoli 2005). It has recently been established that replay is useful for learning (Jackson et al. 2009; Ego-Stengel and Wilson 2010; Wilson et al. 2010), as suggested by early computational models (Buzsáki 1989; Hasselmo 1993). There is evidence that the hippocampus may provide search-like off-line mechanisms during replay in awake states (Gupta et al. 2010; for additional discussion, see Derdikman and Moser 2010); however, whether these same search-like processes occur during sleep states is still unknown.

The three hypotheses above suggest that hippocampus plays no immediate (online) role in decision making, only a supportive (off-line) role. As discussed above, if one has a representation of the structure of the world (a cognitive map), then one could use it to "search through the future" to predict outcomes. This would be particularly useful for one-off critical decisions, like deciding where to go to graduate school or which job to take. In practice, this would become an imagination of what a future would be like: it would be episodic future thinking (Buckner and Carroll 2007; Schacter et al. 2008). Humans with hippocampal damage are severely impaired in the ability to construct imagined situations, including potential future situations (Hassabis et al. 2007). When rats come to choice points, they search through (at least the immediately available) future options (Johnson and Redish 2007) and evaluate them (van der Meer and Redish 2009). A role for the hippocampus in episodic future thinking suggests an explanation for the lack of veridicality of past declarative memories: the brain is using the same episodic imagination process it evolved to imagine future representations to construct past memories (Buckner and Carroll 2007; Schacter and Addis 2007). In a sense, episodic memory may not be memory after all, but rather "episodic past thinking" reconstructed from partial memories stored in cortical systems.

Finally, it is important to remember that the hippocampal activity, at a moment in time, is (usually) a relatively accurate representation of the animal's location within a context. From hippocampal neural ensembles during behavior, it is possible to decode position to an accuracy of better than 1 cm (Wilson and McNaughton 1993) and to decode time within a gap to an accuracy of better than 0.5 second (Itskov et al. 2011). These signals could potentially be used to signal contextual information for conditioning (Holland and Bouton 1999; Rudy 2009) or navigation (Burgess et al. 1994; Redish 1999; Foster et al. 2000).

Of course, all of these hypotheses are potentially viable; they do not necessarily conflict with each other. To determine whether they are incompatible with each other or not, one must first address the question of how they would be implemented computationally in the brain. Computational models have shown that one can, for example, bridge gaps, self-localize spatially, and replay memories all within the same network without interference between them (e.g., Redish et al. 1998; Redish 1999).

Open Questions:

- To what extent does the phenomenon in which place cells represent other places and other experiences correspond to the phenomena of episodic future thinking and recollection (episodic past thinking) seen in humans?
- What role does the hippocampus play in decision making? Does it play an active role online, or only an off-line monitoring role?

Replay

Because place cells carry information about the spatial location of the rat, it is possible to decode spatial location from a population of cells (Wilson and

McNaughton 1993; Brown et al. 1998; Zhang et al. 1998). Because place cells also fire spikes outside of their place fields, even decoding attempts based on the tautology of taking both training and test sets from the same data set occasionally decode to a different location from that of the rat (Jensen and Lisman 2000). Because these representations are self-consistent (Johnson et al. 2008), we interpret these as representations of other locations or other times (Johnson et al. 2009).

Replay has historically been interpreted as being related to consolidation of memory from hippocampal (episodic) representations to cortical (semantic) representations (Wilson and McNaughton 1994; Alvarez and Squire 1994; Nadel and Moscovitch 1997; Hoffmann and McNaughton 2002; Euston et al. 2007). However, replay might also support training (Foster and Wilson 2006; Johnson and Redish 2005), exploration (Samsonovich and Ascoli 2005; O'Neill et al. 2008; Csicsvari et al. 2007), or planning (Diba and Buzsáki 2007; Johnson et al. 2008; Singer and Frank 2009).

Replay during sleep states has been reported to be primarily forward in its sequence (Skaggs and McNaughton 1996; Nádasdy et al. 1999), but studies of replay during awake states have found a more complex story emerging. For example, replay during awake states can be reversed (Foster and Wilson 2006), even of remote locations not recently experienced (Davidson et al. 2009; Gupta et al. 2010), and even when animals never experienced that backward sequence (Gupta et al. 2010). Gupta et al. (2010) discovered that one can even find sequences played out during awake sharp waves that the rat has never experienced in either a forward or a backward direction, thus supporting the possibility that the hippocampus is searching through potential paths in the environment (Samsonovich and Ascoli 2005). These these shortcuts were a key component of the original cognitive map proposal (Tolman 1948; O'Keefe and Nadel 1978; Redish 1999).

Although early studies suggested that the amount of time experienced within an environment drove the amount of replay (Kudrimoti et al. 1999; Jackson et al. 2006; O'Neill et al. 2006), more recent studies, which looked at the specifics of what is replayed, find a more complex story. Looking directly at the information played out during awake sharp waves, Gupta et al. (2010) found that it was not the most recent experience that was being played out. On a figure-eight, T-choice maze, Gupta et al. (2010) ran a task that included three reward contingencies: selecting the left side for reward, selecting the right side for reward, or alternating sides for reward. During the critical probe days, the contingency switched halfway through the 40-minute session. In these three reward conditions, the recency with which rats experience the two sides can vary greatly. Gupta et al. (2010) found that rats replayed remote locations (the opposite side of the maze) more often when they had not been recently experienced. This suggests that replay during awake states may also serve to counteract the effect of repeated experiences which could overemphasize certain parts of the map because they were more recently experienced (Gupta et al. 2010;

Derdikman and Moser 2010). This would be critical to maintaining an accurate representation of the structure of the world. It is also possible that non-historical, but spatially valid replay (e.g., as seen by Gupta et al. 2010) could aid in training a more generalized semantic memory and may explain why semantic memory is less autobiographically concrete than episodic memory (Tulving 1983).

Sweeps and Phase Precession

When animals are running, the hippocampal local field potential shows a strong 7 Hz rhythm called "theta" (Vanderwolf 1971; O'Keefe and Nadel 1978). The phase of the spike fired by a given place cell relative to this theta rhythm precesses from late in the theta cycle, when the animal first enters the place field, to earlier and earlier in the cycle, as the animal runs through the place field (Maurer and McNaughton 2007). This is most cleanly seen on linear tracks, where place fields are directional and a simple plot of the phase versus position of spikes fired by a given cell will show a definitive precession (O'Keefe and Recce 1993; Skaggs et al. 1996). However, it is also seen in other tasks in which rats reliably run through place fields, including on open fields (Skaggs et al. 1996; Huxter et al. 2008). It can even be seen during pauses when hippocampal firing divides up those pause times (Pastalkova et al. 2008; Takahashi et al. 2009a; Macdonald et al. 2010).

It is important to recognize that there are two ways to view "phase precession": as a change in the phase of the cell as an animal runs through the field or as a sequence of firing of cells within a single theta cycle. Although the early studies of phase precession recognized this duality (Skaggs et al. 1996), it was often thought that the purpose of the internally generated phase precession was to construct this internal sequence to allow learning of asymmetric connections for replay (Skaggs et al. 1996; Mehta et al. 1997; Redish and Touretzky 1998). Alternative theories proposed that asymmetric connections drove the internal sequence, producing phase precession (e.g., Tsodyks et al. 1996; Jensen and Lisman 1996). However, an alternate hypothesis is that the sequence of firing is primary and phase precession is an epiphenomenon of a hippocampal generation of the sequence within the theta cycle combined with progress toward a goal (Lisman and Redish 2009). Support for this hypothesis comes from evidence that the sequence of firing within a theta cycle is more stable than the phase of a given cell's firing (Dragoi and Buzsáki 2006).

Phase precession was first seen on linear tracks where place fields are directional. Skaggs et al. (1996) noted that the phase of spiking provides additional information capable of subdividing a place field (Jensen and Lisman 2000). This means that if phase precession could be seen in nondirectional cells, three observations were possible:

1. The phase could match at the start of the place field, indicating that cells reflected past history.
2. The phase could match at the peak of the place field, indicating that phase simply reflected firing rate.
3. Or, the phase could match at the end of the place field, indicating that the cells reflected a prediction of the future.

Studies of bidirectional cells on cue-rich linear tracks (Battaglia et al. 2004) and in two-dimensional tasks (Huxter et al. 2008) found definitively that place fields show the third condition, indicating that place fields are representing prediction toward a goal (Lisman and Redish 2009).

Further support for this hypothesis has come from examinations of hippo-campal "place" cells during nonspatial running. Hirase et al. (1999) had rats run on a running wheel within a given cell's place field. They found that cells did not show phase precession; instead, cells fired at constant phase. Pastalkova et al. (2008) trained rats to run on a running wheel for a given time and found (as predicted by Levy et al. 2005) that cells divided up the time on the running wheel. In contrast to Hirase et al. (1999), Pastalkova et al. (2008) found that their cells showed phase precession—the difference is that Pastalkova et al.'s rats had a goal toward which they were running.

When rats come to difficult decision points on spatial tracks, they pause and look back and forth. This behavioral observation has been termed "vi-carious trial and error" (Muenzinger and Gentry 1931; Muenzinger 1938; Tolman 1938). During these attentive-pausing behaviors, rats remain in theta (Vanderwolf 1971). Decoding neural ensembles during these decision pro-cesses revealed theta phase-coupled sweeps of representation far ahead of the animal (Johnson and Redish 2007). Like phase precession, these sweeps were initiated from the location of the animal or slightly behind it, and they pro-ceeded ahead of the animal within a single theta cycle. However, the sweeps proceeded much farther ahead than the sequential firing within a theta cycle typically seen on simple tasks. In addition, sweeps occurred first in one direc-tion and then in the other, changing direction completely on each theta cycle.

These far-reaching sweeps occurred only on passes through the decision point during which animals showed vicarious trial and error. On the tasks used by Johnson and Redish (2007), animals eventually learned to run through the decision point without stopping, having made their decision earlier or hav-ing transferred the decision-making processes into a different nonhippocampal system (Schmitzer-Torbert and Redish 2002; van der Meer et al. 2010). As the behavior changed, decoded hippocampal representations first swept in both directions, then in only one direction; then they became indistinguishable from phase precession, only going a short distance ahead of the rat (Johnson and Redish 2007). The suggestion that phase precession is actually an epiphenom-enon of the within-theta cycle sequence (Dragoi and Buzsáki 2006) and prog-ress toward a goal (Lisman and Redish 2009) suggests that phase precession and the sweeps of representation seen by Johnson and Redish (2007) may reflect a single process of prediction.

Open Questions:

- Is phase precession a special case of sweeps?
- What is the relationship between preplay before movement that is reported as occurring during sharp waves (e.g., Diba and Buzsáki 2007; Singer and Frank 2009) and sweeps that are reported as occurring during theta (e.g., Johnson and Redish 2007)?

Evaluation and Action Selection

The purpose of cognitive search is to identify the best action to take in a given situation. Thus, when performing a cognitive search, it is not enough to predict the future, one must also evaluate those future expectations to determine their relative value to one's goals and then select between them. These evaluation processes have been suggested to exist within the ventral striatum or nucleus accumbens. Even as far back as the 1980s, it was suggested that the ventral striatum may serve as the "interface between the limbic system and actions" (Mogenson et al. 1980). In part, this was because manipulations of ventral striatum were known to affect actions, but it was not clear whether they were affecting the action-selection process itself (Mogenson 1984) or the evaluation process (Berridge 1996, 2007), which would lead to action-selection changes (Atallah et al. 2007).

The hippocampal system projects to the ventral striatum through the CA1 and subiculum regions (Groenewegen et al. 1987; Voorn et al. 2004). Functionally, hippocampal firing and ventral striatal firing are correlationally coupled (Martin 2001). For example, sharp waves in the hippocampus (during which replay occurs) precede the firing of ventral striatal cells (Pennartz et al. 2004). In fact, the reactivated sequence in the hippocampus leads to specific reactivated reward-related firing in the ventral striatum (Lansink et al. 2008, 2009).

Ventral striatal medium spiny neurons show a variety of responses on tasks. Some cells show "ramps" or "anticipatory" activity, increasing their activity as the animal approaches a reward, usually spatially (Lavoie and Mizumori 1994; Miyazaki et al. 1998; Mulder et al. 1999; van der Meer and Redish 2009, 2011; but also temporally, Carelli and Deadwyler 1994; Nicola et al. 2004a). Other cells show responses that reflect value-related motor actions (Mulder et al. 2004; Roesch et al. 2009; Nicola 2010) and cues that signal impending reward (Carelli and Deadwyler 1994; Nicola et al. 2004a; Roitman et al. 2005; van der Meer and Redish 2009). Finally, some cells show firing in response to reward-receipt (Carelli and Deadwyler 1994; Lavoie and Mizumori 1994; Miyazaki et al. 1998; Nicola et al. 2004b; van der Meer and Redish 2009).

At task points in which sweeps are known to occur, ventral striatal reward-related cells show excess activity, such that a decoding algorithm applied to the data decodes to times of reward-receipt rather than to the location of the animal (Carelli and Deadwyler 1994; Lavoie and Mizumori 1994; Miyazaki et al. 1998; Nicola et al. 2004b; van der Meer and Redish 2009). Although not explicitly studied this way, reward-related cells fire just before movement toward a goal (German and Fields 2007; Nicola 2010), when hippocampal ensembles show a pre-play representation of expected future paths (Diba and Buzsáki 2007; Singer and Frank 2009). The obvious hypothesis is that these cells represent a covert expectation or evaluation of reward (Johnson et al. 2009; van der Meer and Redish 2009, 2010). Importantly, they occur before an animal turns around when correcting the final decision in a vicarious trial and error (VTE) event (van der Meer and Redish 2009).

Recently, we found that ventral striatal anticipatory "ramp" cells phase precess relative to the hippocampal theta rhythm (van der Meer and Redish 2011). It has long been suggested that these cells could play a role related to value representations (Daw 2003), because they increase activity as they approach the goal; upon reaching the goal, firing drops dramatically. In the cognitive map literature, these predicted cell types have been referred to as "goal" cells because they encode distance to a goal (Burgess et al. 1993). If phase precession in hippocampus actually reflects the combination of a sweep-like sequence within a given theta cycle and progress toward a goal, then phase of a ventral striatal distance-to-goal or value-of-the-current-situation cell may reflect the evaluative step of this sweep-like sequence.

Other structures have also been identified as being involved in search, planning, and evaluation, including both the prefrontal cortex (Jones and Wilson 2005; Hyman et al. 2010; Peters and Büchel 2010; DeVito and Eichenbaum 2011) and the orbitofrontal cortex (Gallagher et al. 1999; Tremblay and Schultz 1999; Padoa-Schioppa and Assad 2006). In particular, the hippocampal-prefrontal interaction coupling identified by cellular and local field potential interactions improves during successful search-based tasks, but not during task failures (Jones and Wilson 2005; Hyman et al. 2010). Representations preceding expected outcomes in the orbitofrontal cortex depend on hippocampal integrity (Ramus et al. 2007).

We have recently found that orbitofrontal cortex reward-related neurons also show excess activity during the same VTE events as hippocampal sweeps and ventral striatal covert-reward activity (Steiner and Redish 2010). These orbitofrontal representations, however, occur after the turn around when correcting the final decision in a VTE event, which suggests that the orbitofrontal cortex is not part of the evaluation step in the decision-making process. This is consistent with recently hypothesized roles of the orbitofrontal cortex in signaling information about expectancies more than evaluation (Schoenbaum and Roesch 2005; Murray et al. 2007; Takahashi et al. 2010; Wilson et al. 2010; McDannald et al. 2011).

Open Questions:

- What role does ventral striatum play in action selection? Is it only evaluative? Or does it include action-selection components?
- What is the function of phase precession in ventral striatal ramp cells?
- How does the relationship between the hippocampus and the prefrontal cortex change during cognitive search-based processes?
- What role does the orbitofrontal cortex play in action selection? Is it evaluative or does it only encode expectations?

Automaticity

In situations with repeated, reliable reward contingencies, rats automate behaviors, switching from deliberative, flexible map-based decision systems to habit-based, inflexible, situation-response decision systems (Restle 1957; O'Keefe and Nadel 1978; Packard and McGaugh 1996; Balleine and Dickinson 1998a; Killcross and Coutureau 2003; Redish et al. 2008). Although the mechanism of these habit-based decision systems is beyond the scope of this chapter, theoretical suggestions differentiate deliberative from habit-based decisions by their search processes (Daw et al. 2005) and their representations of future expected outcomes (Balleine and Dickinson 1998a; Niv et al. 2006; van der Meer and Redish 2010).

These theories suggest that the flexible, map-based decision system includes a model of the state-transition structure of the world (Daw et al. 2005), allowing a prediction of the outcomes of actions (Daw et al. 2005; Johnson et al. 2007) and an online evaluation of the outcomes (Balleine and Dickinson 1998a; Niv et al. 2006; van der Meer and Redish 2010), whereas the habit-based processes simply associate a value with a situation-action pair (Daw et al. 2005; Sutton and Barto 1998). Unfortunately, the names that seem to have stuck are "model-based" and "model-free" because the former requires knowledge of the transition structure of the world (Daw et al. 2005; Niv et al. 2006). However, the latter also requires categorizing situations, entailing some knowledge of the state structure of the world (Redish and Johnson 2007; Gershman et al. 2010).

These theories suggest that deliberation-based systems will learn to recognize situation-situation and situation-action-situation transitions and use those to provide a "cognitive map," consistent with hippocampal learning on hippocampal-dependent tasks (Hirsh et al. 1978; O'Keefe and Nadel 1978; Tse et al. 2007) and the increased hippocampal-prefrontal coupling on these tasks (Jones and Wilson 2005; Hyman et al. 2010; Peters and Büchel 2010; DeVito and Eichenbaum 2011). This "cognitive map" learning will be ubiquitous, and cells will show reliable contextual (spatial) representations on any task, regardless of whether the task is hippocampally dependent or not. Consistent with this hypothesis, place cells are observed on both hippocampally dependent and independent tasks (for a review, see Redish 1999).

In contrast, habit-based systems will learn to associate stimuli (situation/state representations) with actions only in contexts in which those stimuli (situation/state representations) reliably produce reward. This is the whole point of reinforcement learning, which is solving the credit-assignment problem (Sutton and Barto 1998). Lesion studies suggest that the dorsal striatum is likely a key structure in the habit learning system (Packard and McGaugh 1996; Graybiel 1990, 1998). Consistent with these hypotheses, dorsal striatal cells develop representations of key components of the task (Jog et al. 1999; Barnes et al. 2005, 2011; Thorn et al. 2010; van der Meer et al. 2010). These cells only represent information when that information is reliably rewarded (Schmitzer-Torbert and Redish 2008; Berke and Eichenbaum 2009).

Upon explicit examination of dorsal striatal neural ensembles on the same task in which hippocampal sweeps and ventral striatal covert representations of reward were seen, van der Meer et al. (2010) found that dorsal striatal ensembles showed neither effect. Even though dorsal striatum eventually developed representations of spatial location more reliably than the hippocampus on this task (for this task, space carries information about appropriate action selection; Schmitzer-Torbert and Redish 2004, 2008), those dorsal striatal representations never represented the future over the past. Similarly, although dorsal striatum contained reward-related cells (Schmitzer-Torbert and Redish 2004), those reward-related cells never showed covert reactivations. These data strongly support the view that the difference between the deliberative ("model-based") and habit-based ("model-free") systems is the presence of search and expectancy processes in the deliberative system and the lack of such processes in the habit-based system.

Open Questions:

- What controls which system to drive behavior?
- Is this related to the role of the prefrontal cortex in deliberation and evaluation?

Computational Pathologies

The fact that the decision-making process is a mechanical and algorithmic process (even if a complex one) implies that there are potential vulnerabilities or failure modes that can occur within the process which will lead to mismade decisions (Redish et al. 2008). Several potential vulnerabilities can be identified within the deliberative search-and-evaluate process discussed above. The first two errors reviewed below entail errors in the results of the search. The final two errors entail errors in the process itself.

Errors in Expectations

The simplest error in prediction-based decision-making systems is that the system may predict the wrong outcome, either through misrecognition of situations, through mislearning of outcomes, or through misinformation. Gamblers, for example, are often cited as falling victim to the illusion of control, in which they believe that their own actions can control random effects (Wagenaar 1988; Langer and Roth 1975; Ladouceur and Sévigny 2005). Similarly, a person who believes in the positive effects of alcohol is more likely to drink than someone with a negative belief, independent of the actual effect of alcohol on the subject in question (Goldman et al. 1987; Jones et al. 2001).

Misevaluation

Even if the expectation leads to the correct answer, the evaluation process may misvalue the outcome. In the deliberative system, valuation is a dynamic process that depends on a combination of motivational, prediction, and memory processes (Balleine 2001; Niv et al. 2006). Several addiction theories are based on the misevaluation of expected outcomes (e.g., Robinson and Berridge 2001, 2003). These valuation processes depend on emotional processes (Damasio 1994) and lead to observable irrationalities (Andrade and Ariely 2009). The valuation process itself is a complex calculation, depending on memory (Balleine 2001), set points (Kahneman et al. 1982; Koob and Le Moal 2006), differences in risk sensitivity to gains and losses (Kahneman and Tversky 1979; Glimcher et al. 2008), and framing effects (Kahneman and Tversky 2000), including incompatibilities in valuation as a function of how these values are measured (Ahmed 2010). For example, rats will work harder for self-administered cocaine or for heroin than for sweetened water, but will prefer sweetened water when given the choice (Cantin et al. 2009, 2010). Similarly, addicts are highly inelastic when faced with small increases in drug costs (Carroll 1993; Grossman and Chaloupka 1998; Bickel and Marsch 2001), but will remain drug-free for very small, but tangible rewards (Higgins et al. 2002).

Obsession

The hypothesis that deliberation entails an actual search through potential future possibilities opens up the possibility that the search may repeat itself. The search process is a memory process (Johnson et al. 2007), and thus retrieving a potential path through the structure of the world entails recall and reconstruction of past episodic memories (Buckner and Carroll 2007). If the representation of the structure of the world is not balanced, the agent may be more likely to retrieve one potential path over others. A memory process that repeatedly retrieves a single path through potential futures may be clinically identifiable as a form of obsession (Redish and Johnson 2007).

Craving

The hypothesis that deliberation entails a representation of future outcomes for evaluation (Balleine and Dickinson 1998a; Niv et al. 2006; van der Meer and Redish 2010) implies a potential model for craving (Redish and Johnson 2007). Craving is an explicit, intense desire for a specific thing (Halikas 1997; Tiffany 1999). This implies that craving must include an expectation of that specific thing, whether it be as a goal to be achieved (Tiffany 1990) or an identification of a potential path to that thing (Goldman et al. 1987). Craving should not appear in habit-based relapse (Tiffany and Wray 2009; Redish 2009), where paths to drug use are reliable and often nonconscious (Tiffany 1990; Robbins and Everitt 1999; Altman et al. 1996; Sayette et al. 2000; Oei and Baldwin 2002; Everitt and Robbins 2005; Dickerson and O'Connor 2006; Redish et al. 2008). As one example, craving appears in alcoholics only when the path to a goal is thwarted (Sinha and O'Malley 1999; Addolorato et al. 2005), presumably leading to a switch from habit-based to deliberative systems (Redish et al. 2008).

Open Questions:

- How repetitive can search be? Is this related to obsession?
- How is the evaluation actually accomplished? Can we explain the irrationalities mechanistically?
- How do the search and evaluation processes interact? How do these interactions change in pharmacological and behavioral addictions?

Summary

The hippocampus represents the spatial and contextual information necessary for decision making (O'Keefe and Nadel 1978; Cohen and Eichenbaum 1993; Redish 1999). In particular, it is critical for the successful integration of those cues in terms of the construction of future expectations (Hassabis et al. 2007; Buckner and Carroll 2007), presumably due to its auto-associative properties (McNaughton and Nadel 1990). Under the hypothesis that decision making is separable into search-based processes and automated or cached processes, the hippocampus is implicated in search-based processes, particularly in the construction of future expectations (Johnson and Redish 2007), and can be contrasted with dorsal striatum, which is implicated in the development of lookup tables for cached-action (non-search-based) decisions (van der Meer et al. 2010). Open questions remain, however, as to the specific role played by the hippocampus in active (search-based) decision making, the hippocampal relation to structures usually associated with evaluation process (such as ventral striatum and orbitofrontal cortex), and the role played by the hippocampus in clinical search failures (such as errors in expectations and craving).

Acknowledgments

This work was supported by NIH grants R01 MH080318 and DA024080.

7

Neural Bases of Actions and Habits

John P. O'Doherty and Bernard W. Balleine

Abstract

Considerable evidence suggests that the behavioral mechanisms for instrumental action selection are mediated by two distinct learning processes: a goal-directed process whereby actions are selected with reference to the incentive value and causal relationship between actions and associated outcomes, and a more reflexive habitual process in which actions are elicited by antecedent stimuli without any consideration of the associated outcome. This chapter reviews evidence from experiments in both rodents and humans which suggests that the behavioral dichotomy between these two modes of action selection are also reflected at the neural level, involving at least partly dissociable regions: a circuit involving the medial prefrontal cortex and dorsomedial striatum is implicated in goal-directed learning, whereas a region of posterior lateral dorsal striatum is implicated in habitual learning. Building on the arguments put forward by Winstanley et al. (this volume), it can be concluded that the specific neural circuits identified as contributing to goal-directed learning, but not those involved in habit learning, are a constituent element of the neural systems underlying cognitive search.

Introduction

Historically, the basal ganglia were thought to exert bottom-up modulatory control of motor output via the control of feedback from the pallidum and thalamus to motor and premotor cortices. Recently, interest has turned to its role in the top-down or executive control of motor movement (Miller 2008). This interest has largely been fueled by new behavioral findings in various species together with more detailed models of the neuroanatomy, which have linked feedforward inputs via the corticostriatal circuit with these feedback functions through a network of partially closed corticobasal ganglia loops (Alexander and Crutcher 1990; Nambu 2008). In this chapter we review some of this evidence coming from experiments in rodents and humans and point to what appears to be a striking similarity in both the behavioral and neural bases of action control in these species. In particular, we will argue that evidence for the existence of distinct behavioral mechanisms for action selection is also reflected at the neural level within corticostriatal circuits in both species. Furthermore, we will propose that only a subset of these circuits are likely to contribute to the action planning and selection phase of cognitive search, as defined by Winstanley et al. (this volume).

Multiple Sources of Action Control in Rodents and Humans: Goals and Habits

There is now considerable evidence from experiments on both rats and humans to suggest that the performance of reward-related actions reflects the interaction of two learning processes: one that controls the acquisition of goal-directed actions, and the other the acquisition of habits. On an associative level, in the goal-directed case, action selection is suggested to be mediated via an association between the response representation and the representation of the outcome engendered by those actions (R–O), whereas in the case of habit learning, action selection is suggested to be controlled through learned stimulus-response associations (S–R) without any associative link to the outcome. As such, the performance of actions under goal-directed control reflects their relationship to and the value of their consequences, whereas those under habitual control, being more reflexive and elicited by antecedent stimuli rather than their consequences, do not. It can, therefore, be established whether any action is controlled by the goal-directed or the habit-learning process by evaluating the effect on the performance of an action produced by (a) changes in the value of its associated outcome and (b) changes in the causal relationship between the action and the outcome. Two kinds of experimental tests have been developed to establish these differences, referred to as outcome devaluation and contingency degradation, respectively.

Outcome Devaluation

In the outcome devaluation test, animals are typically trained to press a lever for a specific outcome after which the incentive value of that outcome is changed; for example, by pairing the consumption of that outcome with illness (induced by an injection of lithium chloride), or by feeding the animal to satiety on that outcome to induce specific satiety. In the test, the animal is given the opportunity to respond again on the action in extinction (i.e., in the absence of any feedback from outcome delivery), so as to establish the extent to which performance depends on the encoded relationship between action and outcome and the current value of that outcome.

After a moderate amount of training, animals typically decrease performance of the action associated with the devalued outcome relative to actions associated with outcomes that are not devalued (Adams 1981; Colwill and Rescorla 1985; for a review, see Dickinson and Balleine 1995). This sensitivity of behavior to the value of the outcome indicates that that action is goal-directed. However, if animals are given more extensive training, behavior at the extinction test is markedly different. Instead of showing a reduced response to the action associated with the devalued outcome, the animals typically continue to respond as if the outcome has not changed value (Adams and Dickinson 1981; for a review, see Dickinson and Balleine 1995). This suggests that after extensive training, actions are no longer goal-directed; they no longer depend on the action-outcome association and have instead become habitual.

Although the behavioral studies described above were all performed in rodents, importantly, very similar effects have recently been found in human subjects. Tricomi et al. (2009) trained human subjects to press different buttons to gain access to symbols that corresponded to small quantities of two different snack foods, one of which they were given to eat at the end of the session. When allowed to eat a particular snack food until satiated, thereby selectively devaluing that snack food, undertrained subjects subsequently reduced their performance of the action associated with the devalued snack food compared to that of an action associated with a nondevalued snack food in an extinction test. In contrast, after overtraining, performance was no longer sensitive to snack food devaluation, and subjects responded similarly on both the action associated with the devalued outcome and the action associated with the nondevalued outcome, indicating that in humans as well as in rodents behavior transitions to habitual control after extensive training.

Contingency Degradation

In addition to differences in associative structure demonstrated by differential sensitivity to devaluation, the goal-directed and habitual learning processes also appear to be driven by different learning mechanisms in that they are differentially sensitive to changes in the action-outcome contingency. Contingency pertains to the differential probability of obtaining an outcome if an action is performed compared to when an action is not performed. If, following performance of a given action, the probability of an outcome is high compared to when that action is not performed, then there is a highly contingent relationship, whereas if the probability of obtaining an outcome is similar when an action is performed compared to when it is not, then despite the continued contiguity of action and outcome, the contingency is low for that action-outcome relationship. Goal-directed actions are highly sensitive to changes in contingency. In the classic demonstration of this by (Hammond 1980), animals were trained on a highly contingent action-outcome schedule. Following this, the contingency was degraded by introducing noncontingent outcomes so that the probability of obtaining the outcome at a given point in time was now similar whether or not the action was produced. Rats' behavior was sensitive to this contingency degradation in that response rates decreased markedly following the contingency degradation. This finding has been replicated in a number of better-controlled demonstrations (Balleine and Dickinson 1998b; Colwill and Rescorla 1986; Dickinson and Mulatero 1989; Williams 1989). However, as with outcome devaluation, sensitivity to contingency degradation appears to depend on the degree of training. Dickinson et al. (1998) showed that after animals have been extensively trained on a contingent schedule, they were markedly less sensitive to contingency degradation: animals maintained responding on the degraded action compared to an undertrained group.

Although the influence of overtraining on contingency sensitivity has not been assessed in human subjects, there is considerable evidence that human causal judgments exhibit a comparable sensitivity to the degradation of the action-outcome contingency produced by the delivery of unpaired outcomes (Shanks and Dickinson 1991; Wasserman et al. 1983).

It is important to note that in contingency degradation, the contiguity between an action and its outcome is maintained; the only change to the schedule is the introduction of additional noncontiguous outcomes. These findings suggest, therefore, that habitual S–R behavior, in contrast to goal-directed behavior, is not driven by contingency but instead is likely driven by a much simpler learning rule—one that pertains merely to the contiguous relationship between actions and outcomes.

Role of the Corticostriatal Network in Goal-Directed and Habitual Learning in Rats and Humans

One might anticipate that these distinct learning and behavioral processes have distinct neural determinants, and recent research has confirmed this prediction. In the following section we review evidence suggesting that homologous regions of the cortical-dorsal striatal network are involved in these learning processes in rats and humans, findings that have been established using many of the same behavioral tests described above.

Neural Substrates of Goal-Directed Learning

In rats, two components of the corticostriatal circuit have, in particular, been implicated in goal-directed learning: the prelimbic region of prefrontal cortex (see Figure 7.1a) and the area of dorsal striatum to which this region of cortex projects, the dorsomedial striatum (Figure 7.1d) (Groenewegen et al. 1990; McGeorge and Faull 1989; Nauta 1989). Lesions of either of these regions prevents the acquisition of goal-directed learning, rendering performance habitual even during the early stages of training as assessed using either outcome devaluation or contingency degradation tests (Balleine and Dickinson 1998a; Corbit and Balleine 2003; Yin et al. 2005). Importantly, prelimbic cortex, although

Rodent   Human

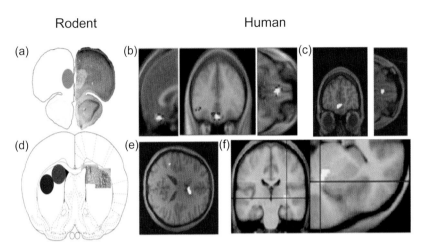

Figure 7.1   (a) Photomicrograph of an NMDA-induced cell body lesion of prelimbic prefrontal cortex (right hemisphere) and approximate region of lesion-induced damage (orange oval; left hemisphere) found to abolish the acquisition of goal-directed action in rats (cf. Balleine and Dickinson 1998a; Corbit and Balleine 2003; Ostlund and Balleine 2005). (b) Region of human ventromedial prefrontal cortex (vmPFC) (here, medial orbitalfrontal cortext, mOFC) exhibiting a response profile consistent with the goal-directed system. Activity in this region during action selection for a liquid food reward was sensitive to the current incentive value of the outcome, decreasing in activity during the selection of an action leading to a food reward devalued through selective satiation compared to an action leading to a nondevalued food reward (after Valentin et al. 2007). (c) Regions of human vmPFC (mPFC and mOFC) exhibit sensitivity to instrumental contingency and thereby exhibit response properties consistent with the goal-directed system. Activation plots show areas with increased activity during sessions with a high contingency between responses and rewards compared to sessions with low contingency (after Tanaka et al. 2008). (d) Photo-micrographs of NMDA-induced cell-body lesions of dorsomedial and dorsolateral striatum (right hemisphere) with the approximate region of lesion-induced damage illustrated using red and purple circles, respectively (left hemisphere). This lesion of dorsomedial striatum has been found to abolish acquisition and retention of goal-directed learning (cf. Yin et al. 2005) as well as to abolish the acquisition of habit learning (Yin et al. 2004). (e) Region of human anterior dorsomedial striatum exhibiting sensitivity to instrumental contingency from the same study described in (c). (f) Region of posterior lateral striatum (posterior putamen) exhibiting a response profile consistent with the behavioral development of habits in humans (after Tricomi et al. 2009).

necessary for initial acquisition, does not appear to be necessary for the expression of goal-directed behavior; lesions of this area do not impair goal-directed behavior if they are given after initial training (Ostlund and Balleine 2005). However, dorsomedial striatum does appear to be critical for both the learning and expression of goal-directed behavior; lesions of this area impair such behavior if made either before or after training (Yin et al. 2005).

The finding that parts of rat prefrontal cortex contribute to action-outcome learning raises the question of whether there exists a homologous region of

the primate prefrontal cortex that contributes to similar functions. A number
of fMRI studies in humans have found evidence that a part of the ventromedial prefrontal cortex (vmPFC) is involved in encoding the expected reward
attributable to chosen actions, which might suggest this region as a candidate
area for a possible homologue (Daw et al. 2006; Hampton et al. 2006; Kim et
al. 2006; Tanaka et al. 2004). These findings suggest that human vmPFC is
involved in encoding value signals relevant for reward-based action selection;
however, the above studies did not deploy the behavioral assays necessary to
determine whether such value signals are goal-directed or habitual. To address
this issue, Valentin et al. (2007) had subjects learn to select instrumental actions to obtain one of two distinct food outcomes (tomato juice or chocolate
milk) while in an fMRI scanner. Following this, one of the foods was devalued
by feeding the participant to satiety, and the volunteers were tested again in
extinction just as in the previously described rodent paradigms (Figure 7.1b).
By testing for regions of the brain which show a change in activity during
selection of a devalued action compared to that elicited during selection of
a valued action from pre- to post-satiety, it was possible to isolate areas that
show sensitivity to the learned action-outcome associations. The regions found
to show such a response profile were medial OFC as well as an additional part
of central OFC.

Further evidence of a role for human vmPFC in contributing to goal-directed learning, and in encoding action-outcome based value signals specifically,
has come from a study by Tanaka et al. (2008; see Figure 7.1c). In this study,
rather than using outcome devaluation, areas exhibiting sensitivity to the contingency between actions and outcomes were assessed. As described earlier,
sensitivity to action-outcome contingency is another key feature (i.e., besides
sensitivity to changes in outcome value) that distinguishes goal-directed learning from its habitual counterpart. To study this process in humans, Tanaka et al.
abandoned the traditional trial-based approach typically used in experiments
using humans and nonhuman primates, in which subjects are cued to respond
at particular times in a trial, for the unsignaled, self-paced approach more often used in studies of associative learning in rodents, in which subjects themselves choose when to respond. Subjects were scanned with fMRI; while in
different sessions they responded on four different free operant reinforcement
schedules which varied in the degree of contingency between responses made
and rewards obtained. Consistent with the findings from outcome devaluation
(Valentin et al. 2007), activity in two subregions of vmPFC (medial OFC and
medial prefrontal cortex), as well as one of the target areas of these structures
in the human striatum, the anterior caudate nucleus (Haber et al. 2006; Ongür
and Price 2000) was elevated on average across a session when subjects were
performing on a high contingency schedule compared to when they were performing on a low contingency schedule; see Figure 7.1e. Moreover, in the subregion of vmPFC identified on the medial wall, activity was found to vary not
only with the overall contingency averaged across a schedule, but also with a

locally computed estimate of the contingency between action and outcome that tracked rapid changes in contingency over time within a session, implicating this specific subregion of medial prefrontal cortex in the on-line computation of contingency between actions and outcomes. Finally, activation of medial prefrontal cortex also tracked a measure of subjective contingency; that is, the ratings of the subjects regarding the causal efficacy of their actions. This rating, taken after each trial block, positively correlated (approximately 0.6) with measures of objective contingency, suggesting that the medial vmPFC-caudate network may interact directly with medial prefrontal cortex to influence causal knowledge.

Neural Substrates of Habit Learning

The finding that medial prefrontal cortex and its striatal efferents contribute to goal-directed learning in both rats and humans, raises the question as to where in the corticostriatal network habitual processes are implemented. Considerable prior, although behaviorally indirect, evidence from studies using tasks that are nominally procedural and could potentially involve stimulus-response learning (largely simple skill learning in humans or maze learning in rats) has implicated a region of dorsal striatum lateral to the caudate nucleus—referred to as dorsolateral striatum in rat or putamen in primates—in habit learning. More direct evidence, was provided in a study by Yin et al. (2004). Rats with lesions to a region of dorsolateral striatum were found to remain goal directed even after extensive training which, in sham-lesioned controls, led to clear habitization; that is, whereas actions in lesioned rats remained sensitive to outcome devaluation, those of sham controls did not. This increased sensitivity to the consequences of actions was observed both with outcome devaluation and contingency degradation procedures; in the latter case, overtrained rats were unable to adjust their performance of an action when responding caused the omission of reward delivery whereas inactivation of dorsolateral striatum rendered rats sensitive to this omission contingency (Yin et al. 2005). This finding suggests that this region of dorsolateral striatum plays a critical role in the habitual control of behavior in rodents (see Figure 7.1d).

To establish whether a similar area of striatum also contributes to such a process in humans, Tricomi et al. (2009) scanned subjects with fMRI while they performed on a variable interval schedule for food rewards; one group of subjects was over-trained in order to induce behavioral habitization. In the group that was given this procedure, activity in a region of lateral striatum (caudoventral putamen), was found to show increased activation on the third day of training when an outcome devaluation test revealed subjects' responding to be habitual, compared to the first day of training when responding in undertrained subjects was shown to be goal directed (see Figure 7.1f). These findings provide evidence to suggest that this region of posterolateral putamen in humans may correspond functionally to the area of striatum found to be critical for habitual control in rodents. Additional hints of a role for human caudoventral striatum in habitual control can be gleaned from fMRI studies of "procedural" sequence learning (Jueptner et al. 1997; Lehéricy et al. 2005). Such studies have reported a transfer of activity within striatum from anterior striatum to posterior striatum as a function of training. While these earlier studies did not formally assess whether behavior was habitual by the time that activity in posterolateral striatum had emerged, they did show that, by this time, sequence generation was insensitive to dual task interference, a behavioral manipulation potentially consistent with habitization.

Other Neural Signals Related to Reward-Based Action Selection

Now that we have reviewed the behavioral and neuroanatomical characteristics of goal-directed and habitual processes, we turn to other types of processes that play a role in directing or otherwise influencing action selection.

Outcome Values

As alluded to above, central to the goal-directed system is the selection of actions with reference to the current incentive value (or experienced utility) of outcomes. It stands to reason, therefore, that the implementation of goal-directed action selection will depend on mechanisms for evaluating and representing the experienced utility of these outcomes. Current theories suggest that outcome values are established by associating the specific sensory features of outcomes with emotional feedback (Balleine 2001; Dickinson and Balleine 2002) and, given these theories, one might anticipate that neural structures implicated in associations of this kind would play a critical role in goal-directed action. The amygdala, particularly its basolateral region (BLA), has long been argued to mediate sensory-emotional associations, and recent research has established the involvement of this area in goal-directed action in rodents. The BLA has itself been heavily implicated in a variety of learning paradigms that have an incentive component (Balleine and Killcross 2006); indeed, in several recent series of experiments, clear evidence has emerged for the involvement of the BLA in incentive learning. In one series, we found that lesions of the BLA rendered the instrumental performance of rats insensitive to outcome devaluation, apparently because they were no longer able to associate the sensory features of the instrumental outcome with its incentive value (Balleine et al. 2003; Corbit and Balleine 2005). This suggestion was confirmed using post-training infusions of the protein synthesis inhibitor anisomycin after exposure to an outcome following a shift in primary motivation. In this study, evidence was found to suggest that the anisomycin infusion blocked both the consolidation and the reconsolidation of the stimulus-affect association underlying incentive learning (Wang et al. 2005).

In humans, the evidence on the role of the amygdala in outcome valuation is somewhat ambiguous though broadly compatible with the aforementioned evidence from the rodent literature. While some studies have reported amygdala activation in response to the receipt of rewarding outcomes such as pleasant tastes or monetary reward (Elliott et al. 2003; O'Doherty et al. 2001a, 2001b, 2003), other studies have suggested that the amygdala is more sensitive to the intensity of a stimulus rather than its value (Anderson et al. 2003; Small et al. 2003) as the amygdala responds equally to both positive- and negative-valenced stimuli matched for intensity. These latter findings could suggest a more general role for the amygdala in arousal rather than valuation per se. Alternatively, the findings are also compatible with the possibility that both positive and negative outcome valuation signals are present in the amygdala (correlating both positively and negatively with outcome values, respectively), and that such signals are spatially intermixed at the single neuron level (Paton et al. 2006). Indeed, in a follow-up fMRI study by Winston et al. (2005), BOLD responses in amygdala were found to be driven best by an interaction between valence and intensity (i.e., by stimulus of high intensity and with high valence), rather than by one or other dimension alone. This suggests a role for this region in the overall value assigned to an outcome, which would be a product of its intensity (or magnitude) and its valence.

Even clearer evidence for the presence of outcome valuation signals has been found in human vmPFC (particularly the medial orbitofrontal cortex) and the adjacent central orbitofrontal cortex. Specifically, activity in the medial orbitofrontal cortex correlates with the magnitude of monetary outcome received (O'Doherty et al. 2001a), and medial along with central orbitofrontal cortex correlates with the pleasantness of the flavor or odor of a food stimulus (Kringelbach et al. 2003; Rolls et al. 2003). Furthermore, activity in these regions decreases as the hedonic value of that stimulus decreases when subjects become sated (Kringelbach et al. 2003; O'Doherty et al. 2000; Small et al. 2003). De Araujo et al. (2003) found that activity in caudal orbitofrontal cortex correlated with the subjective pleasantness of water in thirsty subjects and, moreover, that insular cortex was active during the receipt of water when subjects were thirsty compared to when they were sated. This suggests the additional possible involvement of at least a part of insular cortex in some features of outcome valuation in humans. Further evidence of a role for medial orbitofrontal cortex in encoding the values of goals has come from a study by Plassman et al. (2007), who used an economic auction mechanism to elicit subjects' subjective monetary valuations for different goal objects—pictures of food items, one of which subjects would later have the opportunity to consume depending on their assigned valuations. Activity in medial orbitofrontal cortex was found to correlate with subjective valuations for the different food items. Consistent with the idea that outcome values are computed with reference to associations between sensory features and affective responses, a number of studies have shown that is possible to modulate outcome value representations in vmPFC in humans by leveraging extrinsic influences. Examples of such influences are the provision of price information, whereby neural responses to outcome value differ to the flavor of an identical wine, depending on whether that wine is perceived as being either expensive or cheap (Plassmann et al. 2008), or merely by the use of different semantic labels, such as by referring to the same "cheesy" odor as pertaining to a gourmet cheese or a sweaty armpit (de Araujo et al. 2005). Thus, experienced outcome values are labile and can be influenced not only by changes in internal motivational states, but also by other extrinsic factors that may act on affective evaluation.

Pavlovian Values

Pavlovian value signals pertain to the encoding of a predictive relationship between stimuli and outcomes that are acquired following the repeated pairing of that stimulus with a particular outcome. Subsequent presentation of the stimulus elicits a predictive representation of the associated outcome. Unlike the habitual and goal-directed mechanisms described earlier, this form of prediction is purely stimulus-outcome based and does not contain any representation of a response in the associative structure. However, Pavlovian values can exert strong modulatory influences and biasing effects on action selection.

The clearest evidence for this effect comes from demonstrations of the outcome-specific form of Pavlovian-instrumental transfer (Colwill and Rescorla 1988; Corbit and Balleine 2005; Corbit et al. 2001, 2007; Holland 2004; Rescorla 1994). In outcome-specific transfer, an animal's choice between multiple simultaneously available instrumental responses leading to different outcomes can be biased by the presentation of a Pavlovian cue that is previously associated with one of those outcomes, such that the animal will tend to favor the instrumental action corresponding to the particular outcome with which that cue has been associated. Outcome-specific transfer effects are evident, for example, in the impact that in-store advertisements and other marketing strategies have on consumer behavior (Smeets and Barnes-Holmes 2003), as well as in addictive behavior (Hogarth et al. 2007).

Lesion studies in rodents indicate that the ventral striatum contributes to the outcome-specific influence of Pavlovian values on action selection, especially the nucleus accumbens shell (Corbit et al. 2001), the dorsolateral striatum (Corbit and Janak 2007), and structures afferent to these regions, including the mediolateral orbitofrontal cortex (Ostlund and Balleine 2007) and basolateral amygdala (Corbit and Balleine 2005). Outcome-specific transfer can be differentiated from another form of Pavlovian-instrumental interaction called general transfer, in which a Pavlovian cue exerts a nonspecific energizing effect on instrumental behavior by increasing the vigor of instrumental responses (Corbit and Balleine 2005; Holland 2004). General transfer seems to depend on circuitry involving the ventral striatum and amygdala that is clearly dissociable from that involved in the outcome-specific transfer effect: lesions of the nucleus accumbens core and amygdala central nucleus affect general transfer but leave specific transfer intact, whereas lesions in the nucleus accumbens shell and basolateral amygdala have the converse effect (Corbit and Balleine 2005; Corbit et al. 2001).

In humans, Talmi et al. (2008) reported that BOLD activity in the central nucleus accumbens (perhaps analogous to the core region in rodents) was engaged when subjects were presented with a reward-predicting Pavlovian cue while performing an instrumental response; this led to an increase in the vigor of responding, consistent with the effects of general Pavlovian to instrumental transfer. In a study of outcome-specific Pavlovian-instrumental transfer in humans using fMRI, Bray et al. (2008) trained subjects on instrumental actions, each leading to one of four different unique outcomes. In a separate Pavlovian session, subjects were previously trained to associate different visual stimuli with the subsequent delivery of one of these outcomes. Specific transfer was then assessed by inviting subjects to choose between pairs of instrumental actions which, in training, were associated with the different outcomes in the presence of a Pavlovian visual cue that predicted one of those outcomes. Consistent with the effects of specific transfer, subjects were biased in their choice toward the action leading to the outcome consistent with that predicted by the Pavlovian stimulus. In contrast to the region of accumbens activated in the general transfer design of Talmi et al. (2008), specific transfer produced BOLD activity in a region of ventrolateral putamen: this region was less active on trials where subjects chose the action incompatible with the Pavlovian cue, compared to trials where they choose the compatible action, or indeed other trials in which a Pavlovian stimulus paired with neither outcome was presented. These findings could suggest a role for this ventrolateral putamen region in linking specific outcome-response associations with Pavlovian cues and could indicate that on occasions when an incompatible action is chosen, activity in this region may be inhibited. Given the role of this more lateral aspect of the ventral part of the striatum in humans in specific Pavlovian-instrumental transfer, it might be tempting to draw parallels between the functions of this area in humans with that of the shell of the accumbens implicated in specific transfer in rodents. At the moment, such suggestions must remain speculative until more fine-grained studies of this effect are conducted in humans, perhaps making use of higher resolution imaging protocols to differentiate better between different ventral striatal (and indeed amygdala) subregions.

Summary and Conclusions

Relationship to Cognitive Search

As discussed by Winstanley et al. (this volume), the term cognitive search can be considered to be relevant to only a subset of behavioral patterns that might look "search-like." In particular, they argue that cognitive search is applicable to behavior that would fit into the category described here as goal-directed and is not applicable to behavior elicited by the habitual system, or for that matter the Pavlovian one. In this chapter, we have highlighted a specific neural circuit involving a medial prefrontal and medial dorsal striatum which, in both humans and rodents, appears to be involved in goal-directed learning; thus this specific circuit is likely to play a key role in cognitive search as defined by Winstanley et al. Furthermore, cognitive search was broken down into a number of distinct subprocesses (Winstanley et al., this volume). The behavioral analyses and neural evidence that we have described here is perhaps most easily accommodated under the subprocesses identified by Winstanley et al. as "action planning" and "action selection." To plan which actions to select, we argue that the animal will retrieve the outcome values associated with those actions and that in order to do so, the circuitry identified here for goal-directed learning is likely to be involved.

Human and Rodent Homology

Although there are numerous unanswered questions, we have shown that there is likely to be a great deal of commonality in the way the corticobasal ganglia network functions to control adaptive behavior, and therefore contributes to cognitive search, in mammalian species. We have described evidence for a functional similarity between the prelimbic area and its dorsomedial striatal target in rodents, and the vmPFC and its target in anterior caudate nucleus in humans. These networks appear to be involved in goal-directed behavioral control in rodents and humans respectively and are therefore a contributing component of the neural implementation of cognitive search. We also describe commonalities in the network that mediates habit learning, with a part of the posterior striatum being implicated in both rodents and humans, although such a system is unlikely to participate specifically in cognitive search.

The findings presented here further illuminate ongoing debates in the literature about the extent to which human and rodent brain systems can be equated. While the homology between the rodent dorsomedial striatum and human caudate nucleus is relatively well established (Balleine et al. 2007), there has been considerably more controversy as to whether the rat possesses similar prefrontal cortical regions to humans and other primates (Preuss 1995). Nevertheless, growing evidence based on connectivity and density of connections, neurotransmitter types, embryological development, cytoarchitectonic characteristics, and (last but obviously not least, from our perspective) functional similarity indicates that rodent prelimbic-medial orbital cortex region is analogous to human ventromedial prefrontal-medial orbital cortex (see Brown and Bowman 2002; Uylings et al. 2003).

Relationship between Lesion and fMRI Data

While considering functional homology, it should be noted that the findings in the two species also arise predominantly from two distinct techniques: lesions in rodents versus fMRI in humans. It is important to bear in mind that these methods assess very different aspects of the functioning of these circuits. While lesion studies identify the critical causal role of these areas in the particular processes, fMRI studies are correlative in nature and agnostic as to causality between a given activation and behavior. However, fMRI methods do allow measurement of changes in neural activity as learning occurs, thereby providing insight into the dynamics of neural activity associated with each of these learning processes. An important area for further research will be to attempt to integrate the findings better across the two species; for example, by using neuroimaging methods to identify neural activity changes in these networks in rodents, or by studying the effects of discrete lesions or disease-related impairment of these circuits on goal-directed and habitual behavior in humans.

We have not reviewed evidence from studies using single or multiunit neurophysiological recording techniques to record from these areas in rodents or in nonhuman primates (Barnes et al. 2005; Hikosaka 2007; Pasupathy and Miller 2005). This, in part, reflects space constraints; however, we also note that such studies have arguably not successfully delineated between neurons involved in goal-directed and habitual processing as yet, because the critical behavioral assays have typically not been included. Nevertheless, such a method, if coupled with appropriate behavioral assays, is clearly likely to play an increasingly important role in enabling a more detailed characterization of the dynamics of neural activity in these structures.

Interactions between the Systems

We have presented evidence in favor of a dichotomy between goal-directed and habitual processes but recognize that in practice, these forms of learning most likely interact. Under some situations, they may cooperate while in others they may inhibit or interfere with one another. As discussed herein, it is clear that under some circumstances they do indeed interact at all: goal-directed and habitual control of performance often appears to be all or none, rather than some mixture of the two. In other situations, these processes appear to be temporally related to one another and to function in synergy during the selection, evaluation, and implementation of actions. This constitutes a critical problem that must be resolved if we are to formulate accurate models of real-life decision making within the overall framework of cognitive search, as proposed by Winstanley et al. (this volume).

8

Chemical Neuromodulation of Goal-Directed Behavior

Roshan Cools

Abstract

Directing our behavior adequately to current goals requires a trade-off between cognitive flexibility and cognitive stability. In this chapter, empirical data and theories are reviewed which show that this trade-off depends on optimal modulation of frontostriatal circuitry by the major ascending neuromodulatory systems of dopamine, noradrenaline, and acetylcholine. Highlighted are the roles of dopamine in (a) the prefrontal cortex in the stabilization of goal-relevant representations and (b) in the basal ganglia in the flexible updating of those representations. The cognitive neurochemistry of cognitive flexibility is, however, complex, with different forms of flexibility implicating subcortical and/or cortical dopamine, noradrenaline, and/or acetylcholine. The review concludes with a number of open questions raised by attempts to reconcile the different, complementary theories about the neurochemistry of the flexibility-stability trade-off.

Introduction

Our environment changes constantly. The ability to adapt flexibly to these constant changes is unique in humans. We can persist with current behavioral strategies as long as these seem optimal for goal achievement, yet we can also update our strategies flexibly when the need for change becomes sufficiently salient. How do our minds achieve this flexibility? This is not a straightforward issue, because only some of the changes around us are relevant and require cognitive flexibility. Most other changes are irrelevant (i.e., they represent noise) and should be ignored. In the latter case, adaptive behavior depends on cognitive stability rather than cognitive flexibility. What we need is an ability to regulate dynamically the balance between cognitive flexibility and cognitive stability depending on current task demands.

The trade-off between cognitive flexibility and stability is related to that between divided and focused attention (Hasselmo and Sarter 2011) as well as exploration and exploitation (Daw et al. 2006). With regard to the latter trade-off, exploration generally refers to active cognitive search for new, potentially better alternatives, whereas exploitation generally refers to the pursuit of what is currently known to be the best option (Daw et al. 2006). Exploration or cognitive search has been proposed to be triggered by changes in overall utility; that is, reductions in the overall perceived costs and benefits of ongoing behavior (Aston-Jones and Cohen 2005b). However, it might also be elicited by a salient, novel, or unexpected stimulus, an effect that has been captured by the concept of an "exploration bonus" assigned to such stimuli. For instance, imagine sitting at your desk, engaged in an e-conversation with a colleague, when a fire breaks out in your building. How do our minds decide when the environmental change is sufficiently salient to trigger flexible attention shifting? And how do we make sure that we do not respond to every little distracting sensory event in our office? Setting the threshold adequately for such attention shifting (to external events in the environment or internal events in working memory) is critical for optimal goal-directed behavior and requires cognitive control.

The brain region that has been associated most commonly with cognitive control is the prefrontal cortex (PFC). We know that this region does not act in isolation to bias cognitive control, but rather interacts with a set of deep brain subcortical structures, in particular the striatum, in so-called frontostriatal circuits. Processing in these circuits is extremely sensitive to modulation by the major ascending neuromodulators—dopamine, noradrenaline, acetylcholine, and serotonin—which is not surprising given diffuse ascending inputs from the brainstem to both the PFC and various subcortical structures. The widely distributed and diffuse nature of these neuromodulatory projections has led many investigators to assume that they serve relatively nonspecific functions, such as arousal and sleep-wake cycle regulation. In this chapter, I review some current ideas about the role of these neuromodulators, in particular dopamine and to a lesser degree noradrenaline and acetylcholine, in cognitive flexibility and stability, which suggest that they serve more specific functions in goal-directed behavior. I begin by highlighting the role of dopamine in the PFC in the stabilization of goal-relevant representations. Then I describe evidence for a role of dopamine in the basal ganglia (BG) in a functionally opponent component process (i.e., the flexible updating of goal-relevant representations). Critically, I end by pointing out that this distinction is likely oversimplified, and that a full understanding of the neurochemistry of cognitive flexibility requires us to take into account the degree to which such flexible updating of goal-relevant representation involves top-down, goal-directed search, associated with the PFC, versus habitual control mechanisms, associated with the BG.

Neurochemical Modulation of the Prefrontal Cortex and the Stabilization of Goal-Relevant Representations

The neurochemical mechanisms of the stability component of the flexibility-stability trade-off are potentially somewhat better understood than are those of the flexibility component. Indeed, one of the best known functions of the PFC is the active stabilization of goal-relevant representations, an important component process of working memory (Baddeley 1986; Fuster 1989; Goldman-Rakic 1995). The importance of the PFC for working memory was first demonstrated by Jacobsen (1936), who showed that monkeys with frontal lobe lesions were impaired on the well-known delayed response task. Electrophysiological work with monkeys supported the primate lesion work by demonstrating that the firing of PFC neurons persists throughout the delay of delayed response tasks (Fuster and Alexander 1971), even in the face of distraction. Further, functional magnetic resonance imaging (fMRI) studies with human volunteers have revealed similarly persisting responses in the human PFC during delayed response tasks (Curtis and D'Esposito 2003). According to current ideas, these persistent responses during working memory tasks might correspond to the influence of excitatory top-down signals in the PFC, which bias the competition among brain regions in posterior sensory cortex. These PFC signals may increase the activity of brain regions processing goal-relevant representations and, by virtue of mutual inhibition, suppress activity of brain regions processing irrelevant representations (Miller and Cohen 2001).

In keeping with the pronounced sensitivity of the PFC to modulation by dopamine, there is extensive empirical support for an important role of dopamine, in particular D1 receptor (D1R) stimulation, in the PFC in these aspects of working memory (Goldman-Rakic 1995). Administration of the dopamine receptor agonist bromocriptine to healthy volunteers altered signal change in the PFC during distractor resistance in a working memory task (Cools et al. 2007b) (Figure 8.1). This paralleled effects of global dopamine depletion in the nonhuman primate PFC on task performance, which was more susceptible to distraction than that of control monkeys (Crofts et al. 2001). Although the actual mechanism by which dopamine alters stabilization of working memory representations requires further empirical study, hypotheses have been put forward based on *in vitro* electrophysiological and computational modeling work. Specifically, effects of D1R stimulation on cognitive stabilization might reflect dopamine-induced increases in the signal-to-noise ratio of neuronal firing in the PFC (Servan-Schreiber et al. 1990), leading to increased robustness of these representations in the face of intervening distractors (Durstewitz and Seamans 2008). For instance, recent neurophysiological data from monkeys (Vijayraghavan et al. 2007) have shown that D1 receptor stimulation in the nonhuman primate PFC improves the spatial tuning of cells during the performance of a spatial delayed response task by blocking task-irrelevant firing. The finding that dopamine-induced improvements of spatial tuning are

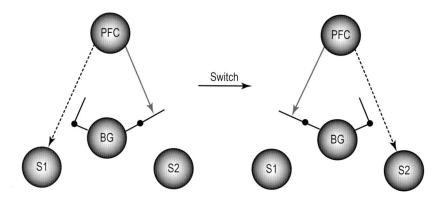

Figure 8.1   Schematic illustration of the working hypothesis that the basal ganglia (BG) control attention shifting by regulating top-down projections from prefrontal cortex (PFC) to posterior sensory areas. The PFC biases information processing in favor of posterior sensory regions that support currently goal-relevant representations (e.g., S1) away from regions that support currently goal-irrelevant representations (e.g., S2). In the model, this top-down control mechanism mediated by the PFC is in turn regulated by the BG, which implement a shift in attention (e.g., in response to novel salient stimuli) by closing the gate to one region (e.g., S1) while simultaneously opening the gate to another region (e.g., S2). Redrawn, with permission, after van Schouwenburg, Aarts, and Cools (2010a).

accompanied by suppressive effects on the firing of PFC cells concurs with the general observation from human neuroimaging that working memory improvement after dopamine-enhancing drug administration is accompanied by reductions in PFC activity.

Research indicates that the stabilization of goal-relevant representations depends not only on dopamine, but also on noradrenaline and acetylcholine transmission, possibly via modulation of attention (Arnsten 2009) and uncertainty signals (Yu and Dayan 2005), respectively. In the case of noradrenaline, for example, Arnsten (2009) has shown that the ability of a network of neurons to maintain firing over a delay period is strengthened by noradrenergic α2A receptor stimulation. According to her recent proposal (Arnsten 2009), dopamine and noradrenaline might subserve complementary roles in cognitive stabilization with α2A receptor stimulation enhancing network firing for shared inputs, thus increasing "signal," and D1 receptor stimulation sculpting neuronal firing by decreasing firing to nonpreferred inputs, thus decreasing "noise." In the case of acetylcholine, several cellular effects could contribute to the cholinergic enhancement of the stabilization of goal-relevant representations, including muscarinic receptor stimulation-induced persistence of spiking activity of PFC cells (Hasselmo and Sarter 2011).

Role of Dopamine in the Basal Ganglia in Cognitive Updating of Goal-Relevant Representations

The previous section highlighted the importance of dopamine, in particular, in the PFC for the stabilization of goal-relevant representations as well as for the filtering of new input that might be irrelevant to ongoing processing. One could say that the net effect of dopamine in the PFC is an elevation of the threshold for a new representation to be selected. Of course, this is adaptive when new input is irrelevant. However, it is maladaptive when new input is relevant. In this case, existing goal-relevant representations need to be flexibly updated rather than protected. Accumulating evidence indicates that dopamine is also implicated in this complementary updating aspect of cognitive control. Current theorizing suggests, however, that these effects of dopamine on updating might implicate not only the PFC but also, at least in some conditions, the BG (Frank 2005).

The proposal that dopamine in the BG subserves the flexible updating of goal-relevant representations fits with the traditional view of the BG as a selection or threshold-setting device, gating task-relevant representations to the PFC via the direct Go pathway, while simultaneously inhibiting competing task-irrelevant representations via the indirect NoGo pathway (Frank 2005; Mink 1996). Interestingly, dopamine has opposite effects on these two pathways, increasing activity in the direct BG pathway while suppressing activity in the indirect BG pathway. The net effect is a lowering of the threshold for a representation to be selected. This hypothesis is in line with suggestions that dopamine signals mediate the switching of attention to unexpected, behaviorally relevant stimuli (Redgrave et al. 1999) and more generally concurs with a rapidly growing body of data which shows BG involvement during updating of working memory representations (e.g., Dahlin et al. 2008). Furthermore, it is also consistent with empirical data that reveal effects of BG dopamine manipulations on set shifting (Haluk and Floresco 2009; Kellendonk et al. 2006). Furthermore, administration of the dopamine D2 receptor agonist bromocriptine to healthy volunteers altered signals related to set shifting in the BG, but not in the PFC (Cools et al. 2007b) (Figure 8.1). This finding paralleled later findings that behavioral effects of bromocriptine on set shifting could be predicted from baseline levels of dopamine in the BG (Cools et al. 2009) as well as selective set-shifting deficits in patients with BG dysfunction (Cools 2006).

As in the case of the modulation of the stabilization of working memory representations, the mechanism by which dopamine alters set shifting requires further empirical study. However, integration of ideas about the role of the PFC in top-down attention biasing and of the BG in selective gating raises the possibility that the BG facilitate set shifting by gating interactions between the PFC and posterior sensory cortex, thus controlling the top-down biasing of competition between goal-relevant and goal-irrelevant representations (Figure 8.2). This hypothesis is reminiscent of ideas that the (attentional or motor) output

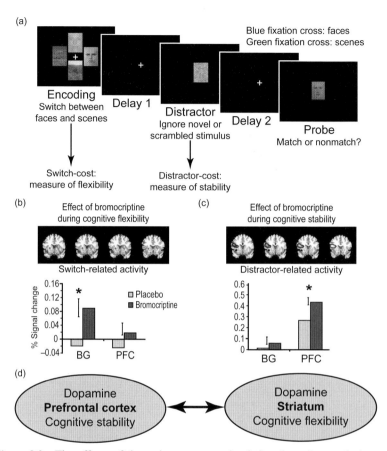

Figure 8.2 The effects of dopamine receptor stimulation depend on task demands and the neural site of modulation. (a) A delayed match-to-sample (DMS) task was used that provided a measure of cognitive flexibility (attention shifting during encoding) as well as a measure of cognitive stability (distractor resistance during the delay). Subjects memorized faces or scenes, depending on the color of the fixation cross. If the cross was blue, then subjects memorized the faces; if it was green, then they memorized the scenes. Subjects occasionally shifted during encoding between attending to faces and scenes. A distractor was presented during a delay. Subjects were instructed to ignore this distractor. (b) Top panel: effects of bromocriptine on basal ganglia (BG) activity during shifting, as a function of trait impulsivity. Whole-brain contrast values (>25) are overlaid on four coronal slices from the Montreal Neurological Institute high-resolution single-subject magnetic resonance image. Bottom panel: effects of bromocriptine on shift-related activity in the BG and left prefrontal cortex (PFC) in high-impulsive subjects only. (c) Top panel: effects of bromocriptine on PFC activity during distraction as a function of trait impulsivity (all contrast values >25 shown). Bottom panel: effects of bromocriptine on distractor-related activity in the BG and left PFC in high-impulsive subjects only. (d) Schematic representation of the hypothesis that dopamine modulates cognitive flexibility by acting at the level of the BG while modulating cognitive stability by acting at the level of the PFC. Reprinted with permission from Cools and D'Esposito (2011).

of the PFC can be gated by dopamine-dependent activity in the striatum (Hazy et al. 2007). Evidence for such output gating by dopamine in the BG came from a recent fMRI study, in which subjects shifted attention between the faces and the scenes of overlapping face/scene stimuli (van Schouwenburg et al. 2010b). The attention shifts were accompanied by potentiation of goal-relevant representations relative to goal-irrelevant representations in stimulus-specific posterior visual cortex (fusiform face area and parahippcampal place area), presumably reflecting top-down biases from the PFC. Effective connectivity analyses revealed that the BG indeed played a critical role in regulating these attention shifts by gating the top-down bias from the PFC on stimulus-specific posterior cortex. Dopamine could alter such top-down biasing of competition between goal-relevant and goal-irrelevant representations via stimulation of dopamine receptors on neurons in the BG, altering the balance between activity in the Go and NoGo pathways of the BG and lowering the threshold for gating top-down influences. Preliminary evidence concurs with this hypothesis, and showed that dopamine receptor stimulation with a dopamine receptor agonist in humans modulates activity in the BG, but not the PFC during attention shifting in this paradigm (van Schouwenburg et al., unpublished data). These data suggest that dopamine might modulate set shifting at the level of the BG (e.g., by modulating flow through frontostriatal circuits), and generally concur with empirical evidence from genetic and neurochemical imaging work, which reveals that variation in striatal dopamine function is associated with altered neural efficiency (Crofts et al. 2001) in the PFC and associated working memory updating and attention switching (Kellendonk et al. 2006; Landau et al. 2009; Nyberg et al. 2009; Stelzel et al. 2010).

Dopamine is not the only neuromodulator that modulates attention shifting. For example, drug-induced enhancement of noradrenaline activity has also been shown to potentiate attention shifting to motivationally significant stimuli in a manner fairly similar to dopamine (Sara 2009). Salient events are known to elicit both phasic noradrenaline and dopamine responses. As with dopamine, this orienting of attention to salient stimuli has also been compared with a temporary lowering of a decision threshold. Furthermore very similar ideas have been put forward to account for effects of acetylcholine on Posner target detection tasks (Hasselmo and Sarter 2011). Specifically, it has been argued that a salient target, which has been found to evoke phasic acetylcholine release in the PFC, may elicit an attentional shift akin to Posner's attentional orienting response, in order to align attention with a source of sensory input. Acetylcholine could do this by enhancing sensory input from the thalamus to the PFC and, at the same time, shutting down top-down suppression from the PFC. Interestingly, regions in the ventral parts of the BG that are strongly innervated by dopamine can selectively influence cholinergic modulation of thalamic sensory inputs to the PFC. Thus another mechanism by which BG dopamine might facilitate attention shifting is by gating acetylcholine-dependent interactions between the PFC, the thalamus, and stimulus-specific sensory areas in posterior cortex.

Trading off Flexibility and Stability

Cognitive flexibility and stability might be conceptualized as representing functionally opposing processes. If we update too readily, then we are likely to get distracted, rendering our behavior unstable. Conversely, if our representations are overly persistent or stable, then there is a danger of inflexibility and unresponsiveness to new information. Empirical data support the hypothesis that these two opponent processes might be subserved by dopamine in the BG and the PFC, respectively. Roberts and colleagues (Robbins and Roberts 2007) injected the neurotoxin 6-OHDA into the BG or PFC of nonhuman primates and showed that, while dopamine lesions in the PFC *improved flexibility* (attentional set shifting), dopamine lesions in the BG actually *impaired flexibility* (attentional set shifting). Subsequent work showed that this modulation of flexibility during attentional set shifting may have resulted from effects on performance during the preceding set-maintenance stages of the task (Crofts et al. 2001). Specifically, that subsequent study revealed that dopamine lesions in the PFC led to *enhanced distractibility* (poor attentional set maintenance), whereas dopamine lesions in the BG actually *reduced distractibility* (enhanced attentional set maintenance). Thus the contrasting effects on set maintenance may well underlie the contrasting changes measured in the subsequent attentional set-shifting stages of the task. Interestingly, an analogous observation was recently made in Parkinson's disease patients, who exhibit relatively selective dopamine depletion in the BG. These patients exhibit not only impaired set shifting on a variety of tasks but also enhanced distractor resistance (Cools et al. 2010a). Overall, the opposing effects of BG and frontal dopamine lesions suggest that a dynamic balance between cognitive stability and flexibility may depend on precisely balanced dopamine transmission within the PFC and the BG, respectively. The functional opponency between stability and flexibility maps well onto the neurochemical reciprocity between dopamine in the PFC and the BG. Increases and decreases in PFC dopamine lead to decreases and increases in BG dopamine, respectively (Kellendonk et al. 2006; Pycock et al. 1980).

This working hypothesis is reminiscent of the dual-state theory put forward recently by Durstewitz and Seamans (2008), which is grounded in *in vitro* neurophysiology, biophysically realistic computational modeling work, as well as empirical pharmacological work (Floresco et al. 2006). According to this theory, PFC networks can be either in a D1-dominated state, which is characterized by a high-energy barrier that favors robust stabilization of representations, or in a D2-dominated state, characterized by a low-energy barrier favoring fast, flexible shifting between representations. This alternative receptor-based theory is not necessarily inconsistent with the presented working hypothesis, according to which dopamine in the BG and the PFC subserve the distinct roles of flexibility and stability, respectively, particularly given the observation that D2 receptors are more abundant in the BG than in the PFC, which contains fewer D2 than D1 receptors.

Neurochemical Modulation of Cognitive
Flexibility and Exploration

At first glance, the hypothesis that dopamine modulates certain forms of set shifting by acting at the level of the BG rather than the PFC is perhaps incompatible with traditional notions that effects of dopamine on high-level cognitive control are mediated by the PFC. In fact, not all forms of set shifting depend on dopamine in the BG. For example, although several studies have observed sensitivity of the set-shifting deficit in Parkinson's patients to withdrawal of dopaminergic medication (Cools 2006), other studies have failed to reveal such dependency on dopamine in the BG (Kehagia et al. 2010). Similarly, while a range of pharmacological neuroimaging studies has revealed selective modulation of BG signals by dopamine during set shifting, several other pharmacological studies have revealed effects of dopamine in the PFC during set shifting.

One possible explanation is that the extent to which flexible behavior implicates (neuromodulation of) the BG or the PFC depends on the degree of exploration, or cognitive search, required for the type of set shifting assessed. This observation concurs with recent evidence which indicates that the catecholamine-*O*-transferase gene, which primarily controls dopamine in the PFC, affects exploratory decisions during a learning task (Frank et al. 2009). Furthermore, a recent microdialysis study (van der Meulen et al. 2007) demonstrated increased catecholamine release in the PFC during serial reversal learning, an effect that was particularly pronounced in the early stages of the task, when reversals presumably required a relatively greater degree of exploration than during the late stages of the task. Conversely, a task that is disproportionally sensitive to dopaminergic medication in Parkinson's disease, associated with BG dopamine depletion, is the task-switching paradigm, where switches are externally cued, thus requiring little to no cognitive search. Demands for cognitive search are particularly low in some versions of this paradigm (e.g., those requiring switches to naming the direction of the arrow of an arrow/word stimulus), in which task sets are well established. It is these "habitual" shifts that are sensitive to dopaminergic medication in Parkinson's disease. The same medication in Parkinson's disease, however, has no effect on other versions of this paradigm, such as those requiring switches to poorly established task sets (e.g., classifying digits as odd or even, versus high or low), when demands for cognitive search might be enhanced (Kehagia et al. 2010). A similar argument might be put forward when considering the insensitivity to BG dopamine of performance on Wisconson card sort-like tasks, such as extra-dimension-al set shifting (EDS), which requires cognitive search for a newly rewarded stimulus according to changes in the relevance of stimulus dimensions. Both dopaminergic medication in Parkinson's disease and BG dopamine lesions in nonhuman primates leave unaffected performance on an initial EDS (Lewis et al. 2005). By contrast, a subsequent EDS back to the originally relevant at-tentional set is severely impaired by dopamine lesions in the BG (Collins et al. 2000), consistent with the dopamine-dependent deficit seen in Parkinson's patients during task switching between well-established sets. Another form of set shifting that seems to critically involve dopamine in the BG is reversal learning (Clatworthy et al. 2009; Cools et al. 2007a, 2009). In the traditional version of this task, a negative prediction error encountered upon contingency reversal, due to choice of the previously rewarded stimulus, also implies that the nonchosen stimulus is now rewarded. Accordingly, demands for explo-ration, or search, in traditional tasks of reversal learning are relatively low. Instead, adequate reversal learning depends on the optimal pursuit of what is currently known, based on experience, to be the best option (i.e., exploitation).

The hypothesis that BG dopamine is concerned with forms of set shifting that do not involve exploration or cognitive search, but rather only exploitation of learned information, concurs with the well-known implication of dopamine and the BG in "model-free" reinforcement learning (i.e., trial-and-error learn-ing to maximize rewards). Conversely, the hypothesis that the PFC (and its neuromodulation) is concerned with forms of set shifting that implicate explo-ration concurs with empirical neuroimaging data (Daw et al. 2006) as well as with current theories about the role of prefrontal neuromodulation in explora-tion (Aston-Jones and Cohen 2005b). In particular, Aston-Jones and Cohen have invoked the adaptive gain theory, according to which different modes of noradrenaline transmission regulate the trade-off between exploitation and exploration. In this model, a high phasic mode promotes exploitative behavior and focused attention by facilitating processing of task-relevant information, whereas a low tonic noradrenaline mode ensures that irrelevant stimuli are filtered. Increasing the tonic mode promotes behavioral disengagement and divided attention, thus allowing potentially new and more rewarding behaviors to be explored. The transition from the phasic to the tonic noradrenaline mode is controlled by specific regions in the PFC (i.e., the orbitofrontal cortex and the anterior cingulate cortex), which in turn control the firing of noradrenaline neurons in the brainstem in a top-down manner.

The notion that (tonic) cortical noradrenaline is particularly important for explorative modes of behavior concurs with empirical findings from work with experimental animals as well as humans, which show that EDS is sensitive to manipulation of (tonic) noradrenaline transmission (Robbins and Roberts 2007). This series of findings also raises the possibility that the effect of non-specific catecholamine modulation of EDS reflects modulation by noradrena-line rather than dopamine. Furthermore, the dopamine-insensitive EDS deficit in Parkinson's patients, which is restricted to conditions that require shifting to a dimension that is not very salient (thus maximizing demands for cognitive search; Cools et al. 2010b), might also be mediated by frontoparietal cortical abnormalities in catecholamine (e.g., noradrenaline) neurotransmitter systems rather than BG dopamine dysfunction.

The adaptive gain theory emphasizes the importance of noradrenaline for exploration and is complementary to a different influential proposal that tonic noradrenaline activity serves a neural interrupt or network reset function, thus enabling the interruption of ongoing activity, or revision of internal representations, based on new sensory input (Yu and Dayan 2005). A unique feature of the model by Yu and Dayan is that it predicts noradrenaline to be involved predominantly when changes in the environment are unexpected (as opposed to expected). In their conceptualization, unexpected uncertainty is induced by gross changes in the environment that produce sensory observations strongly violating top-down expectations, as in the case of EDS. This is contrasted with expected uncertainty, which arises from known unreliability of predictive relationships within a familiar environment (Yu and Dayan 2005). Critically, they argue that expected uncertainty is signaled by acetylcholine, a stance that is consistent with observations, mentioned earlier, that cholinergic changes are associated with attentional shifts in Posner-like attention-orienting paradigms where subjects are aware of cue invalidity (Hasselmo and Sarter 2011). By contrast, cholinergic manipulations generally leave EDS unaffected. Thus according to these ideas, both increases in (tonic) noradrenaline and acetylcholine align attention with a source of sensory input, by enhancing sensory input from the thalamus to the PFC and by shutting down top-down internal models held online by the PFC. However, the signals that trigger this noradrenaline- and acetylcholine-mediated flexibility might differ. The theory is generally consistent with observed sensitivity of EDS to noradrenaline, but not acetylcholine. Furthermore, it also concurs with observed sensitivity to acetylcholine, but not noradrenaline, of (late but not early) reversal learning (Chamberlain et al. 2006; Robbins and Roberts 2007).

Conclusion and Open Questions

The empirical data and theories reviewed in this chapter indicate that the balance between cognitive flexibility and stability depends critically on modulation by the major ascending neuromodulatory systems. I have focused on the roles of dopamine, but also mentioned those of noradrenaline and acetylcholine. While cognitive stabilization is well established to depend critically on D1R stimulation in the PFC, the literature on the cognitive neurochemistry of cognitive flexibility is more complex, with striatal dopamine, and frontal noradrenaline and acetylcholine being important for different forms of shifting. An understanding of these apparent discrepancies requires us to recognize that cognitive flexibility is not a unitary phenomenon, with distinct forms of flexibility implicating different cortical and subcortical neurochemical mechanisms.

One factor that might be taken into account when assessing the neurochemical mechanisms of flexibility is the degree of exploration, or search, for new, potentially better alternatives as opposed to the exploitative pursuit of what is currently known to be the best option. Explorative forms of shifting that involve cognitive search, such as EDS, seem more sensitive to catecholaminergic modulation of the PFC, in particular by noradrenaline, whereas exploitative (or habitual) forms of shifting that do not involve cognitive search (e.g., certain forms of task switching and reversal learning) seem more sensitive to dopaminergic modulation of the BG. Future work should address the further question of whether, and if so how, issues of unexpected versus expected uncertainty relate to issues of explorative versus exploitative shifting. For instance, the disproportionate sensitivity to cholinergic manipulations of late versus early reversals (Robbins and Roberts 2007) might be interpreted to reflect the reduced degree of exploration required for late versus early reversals. However, it might also reflect the fact that late reversals are more expected than are early reversals. Similarly, the disproportionate catecholamine release in the PFC during early versus late reversals (van der Meulen et al. 2007) might reflect the greater degree of exploration required for early versus late reversals, but it might also reflect the fact that early shifts are less expected than are late reversals. Finally, along the same lines, one might also raise the question whether "habitual" shifting, such as task-set switching and repeated EDSs, are disproportionately sensitive to dopamine in the BG due to the fact that such paradigms involve relatively little cognitive search, or rather because the uncertainty that triggers these "habitual" shifts is more expected than unexpected.

A further factor that should be taken into account in future cognitive neurochemical work concerns the hierarchical nature of cognitive search. Search goals can be defined at different levels of abstraction, something that is well illustrated by the difference between intra-dimensional shifting (IDS) and EDS. Both types of shift have relatively high demands for cognitive search and both are triggered by relatively unexpected uncertainty. However, IDS involves changes within a stimulus dimension (novel exemplars, e.g., yellow or blue), whereas EDS involves changes between stimulus dimensions (e.g., shape or color). This factor of hierarchy may become relevant when considering findings that (tonic) noradrenaline manipulations affect EDS, but not exploration of changes along one and the same stimulus dimension in a four-arm bandit task (Jepma et al. 2010).

More generally, it is clear from the above that cognitive approaches to neurochemistry have revealed that dopamine, noradrenaline and acetylcholine likely serve more specific functions in goal-directed behavior than has been traditionally assumed. This specificity arises in part from the different computations that are carried by the targeted regions, which differ in receptor distribution, but also reflects most likely a number of other factors that were not addressed explicitly in this chapter. These factors include the computations carried out by brain structures that control the ascending systems in a top-down manner, the baseline dependency of the neuromodulatory effects, and the (phasic versus tonic) timescale of neurotransmitter effects. The particular importance of considering the timescale of neuromodulatory effects is illustrated by the adaptive gain theory of Aston-Jones and Cohen (2005b), which attributes distinct exploratory and exploitative functions to the tonic and phasic modes of noradrenaline transmission. However, the timescale of neurotransmission also plays a central role in current thinking about dopamine (Niv et al. 2007), acetylcholine as well as serotonin (Cools et al. 2011). These modes may serve partly antagonistic and partly synergistic roles, the latter possibly realized by synaptic overflow from phasic events followed by slower reuptake. For example, the reward-and-punishment prediction error signals that reinforcement learning theories hypothesize to be carried by phasic dopamine and serotonin responses, respectively, might also contribute, when averaged slowly over time, to response vigor or action threshold setting by measuring average reward and punishment rate (Cools et al. 2011). Clearly, it will be crucial to obtain better insights in the degree to which commonly used neurochemical manipulations affect phasic versus tonic transmission.

In conclusion, future work will benefit from adopting a cognitive mechanistic approach to neurochemistry, to allow us to move beyond apparent discrepancies between theories of dopamine, noradrenaline and acetylcholine in terms of cognitive control, attention, working memory, or learning. This is pertinent given the implication of most neuromodulators in all of these processes and will help us further define the computational nature of the flexibility-stability paradox.

Acknowledgments

Supported by the Netherlands Organization for Scientific Research (Vidi grant 016.095.340), the Dutch Brain Foundation, a Hersenstiching fellowship F2008(1)-01), the National Institute of Health (R01 DA020600), and the Human Frontiers Science Program (RGP0036/2009-C).

First column (top to bottom): Trevor W. Robbins, Roshan Cools, A. David Redish, Cyriel M. A. Pennartz, John P. O'Doherty, Christian Büchel
Second column: Cyriel M. A. Pennartz, Trevor W. Robbins, A. David Redish, Jeremy K. Seamans, Daniel Durstewitz, Joshua W. Brown, Catharine A. Winstanley
Third column: Catharine A. Winstanley, Bernard W. Balleine, Trevor W. Robbins, Bernard W. Balleine, Joshua W. Brown, Roshan Cools, Jeremy K. Seamans

9

Search, Goals, and the Brain

Catharine A. Winstanley, Trevor W. Robbins,
Bernard W. Balleine, Joshua W. Brown, Christian Büchel,
Roshan Cools, Daniel Durstewitz, John P. O'Doherty,
Cyriel M. A. Pennartz, A. David Redish, and Jeremy K. Seamans

Abstract

The process of cognitive search invokes a purposeful and iterative process by which an organism considers information of a potentially diverse nature and selects a particular option that best matches the appropriate criteria. This chapter focuses on the neurobiological basis of such a goal-directed search by parsing the process into its main components, suggested here as initiation, identification of search space, deliberation, action selection, and evaluation and search termination. Unexpected uncertainty is suggested as a key trigger for the onset of the search process. Current data posit that this is represented in the anterior cingulate, parietal, and inferior frontal cortices, suggesting these areas could be particularly important in search initiation. A change in motivational state, likely signaled by a wide range of brain regions including the amygdala, can also play a role at this stage. The neural structures which represent the set of to-be-searched options may vary depending on the search domain (e.g., spatial, visual, linguistic). During deliberation, predictions regarding the consequences of selecting these options are generated and compared, implicating areas of frontal cortex as well as the hippocampus and striatum, which are known to play a role in different aspects of outcome evaluation. Action planning and selection likely involve an interplay between the prefrontal cortex and basal ganglia, whereas search termination could involve the specific neural networks implicated in response inhibition. The influence exerted over the search process by the major ascending neuromodulators (dopamine, norepinephrine/noradrenaline, serotonin, and acetylcholine) is also considered, and a particularly critical role suggested for dopamine and noradrenaline, given their ability to influence cognitive flexibility and arousal. Finally, pathologies of search processes are discussed, both with respect to brain damage and psychiatric illness.

Introduction and Overview

Search is defined as "movement in pursuit of a resource at an unknown location" (Hills and Dukas, this volume). This very general definition allows search to be applied quite broadly from protozoa to humans. While laudable, this breadth could also motivate comparisons in process that are less desirable. The focus on superficial aspects of search, particularly the movements that collectively define the search response, provides a ready means of identifying search. However, it also implies that identity in response means identity in mechanism, and this may be problematic. It is tempting to argue that the occurrence of an organized set of responses associated with exploration (such as orienting, locomoting, pausing, turning, returning, and so on) always reflects a deliberated, goal-directed search process under cognitive control, whether nascent or explicit. Nevertheless, care should be taken with such assumptions. Considerable research has established that seemingly indistinguishable behavioral responses can, at different times and under different constraints, be controlled by quite distinct determinants. Take the case of lever pressing in rats as an example (see O'Doherty and Balleine, this volume). The behavior in which rats press a lever for food appears to be a quintessential goal-directed response mediated by both its relation to a goal (the specific food) and by the value of that goal; a movement in pursuit of a resource certainly qualifies as a search response. However, it is now well known that when the action is overtrained or goal access is placed under certain temporal constraints, the determinants of this response can change: it is no longer a flexible, deliberate goal-directed action; it becomes more routine, automatic, inflexible or habitual. Although it would still satisfy the broad behavioral definition of a search, such an automated process entails a reflexive movement elicited by antecedent stimuli, rather than its consequences. Hence, if we believe search to be essentially a goal-directed behavior, most exploratory behavior only looks like a search response; it utilizes different brain structures and depends on different computations within the mammalian brain. This leads us to reject it as a true cognitive search response.

As a consequence, it is necessary in all situations to establish whether a putative search response satisfies two conditions:

1. The performance of the search response is determined by the organism as being causal with respect to some specific resource or goal.
2. Its performance is sensitive to changes in the value of the goal.

There are, in fact, at least three kinds of search response which, by this definition, do not qualify as cognitive search. These responses reflect the operation of three different motivational constraints and can be referred to as "evaluative processes," "Pavlovian processes," and "habitual processes." Note first that sensory processing is common to each and is assumed to be more or less constant across all forms of search or search-like responses. In a novel or changing environment, sampling the sensory environment is critical, and search in this domain is likely to be general, constrained by a bottom-up attentional process sensitive to physical salience, regulated by motivational arousal, and subject to simple learning processes such as habituation.

Evaluative Processes

The first motivational constraint on search is the learning process by which stimuli become associated with specific, innate motivational processes, thereby conferring value on sensory events (e.g., contact with stimuli that provoke nutrient activity produces an association between those stimuli and the nutrient system resulting in what might be called the "representation of a specific food"). Increases in nutrient deprivation have long been reported to elicit an immediate increase in activity and orienting; food deprivation, for example, increases orienting to foods, as well as an increase in the production of vacuous consummatory/defensive reactions appropriate to those processes (e.g., food events will provoke consummatory responses—salivation, chewing, gastric motility, etc.). Thus although these appear to reflect search, they are actually reflexes elicited by internal states and not by their relationship to a specific resource (Changizi and Hall 2001).

Pavlovian Processes

A second motivational constraint is provided by the tendency of sensory events, or event representations, to become associated when they are paired in a manner that allows the activation of one representation to activate the other. Importantly, events that predict those sensory events that have been subject to evaluative conditioning provoke what is typically called Pavlovian conditioning. As a consequence, the former event (i.e., the "conditioning stimulus") can produce (a) conditioned consummatory/defensive reactions and (b) conditioned preparatory reactions, such as behavioral approach/withdrawal. Whereas consummatory reactions are produced by activation of the specific sensory features of evaluative incentives, the preparatory reactions are produced by activation of either specific motivational states or affective states (e.g., appetitive and aversive states productive of general activity, and other conditioned responses like approach and withdrawal). As is well known, these responses are not determined by their relationship to the goal (or "unconditioned stimulus"; see Holland 1979; Holland and Straub 1979).

Habitual Processes

The third motivational constraint reflects the ability of environmental cues to become associated with responses and, under invariant conditions and by prolonged training, to elicit those responses irrespective of the value of the goal or the relationship between response and procuring the goal. These habit processes can transition between environmental states, like goal-directed search, but are not based on any knowledge of the structure of the environment. Instead, they are based on state-response associations. In the parlance of reinforcement learning models, they are "model-free" rather than "model-based" responses (cf. Daw, this volume).

Goal-Directed Search

Now that we have considered processes that would *not* conform to cognitive search, let us consider the processes within the goal-directed system that would be considered representative of this class of search. Within this domain, search might be initiated to obtain information related to a number of different processes underpinning the goal-directed system: the perceptual level, the level of causal structure, the level of goal selection and the level of action selection. At the perceptual level, goal-directed search could be initiated over the perceptual environment in a deliberative sense to find and locate relevant stimuli for goal-directed action (such as visual search; see Wolfe, this volume). At the causal structure level, search might also be initiated through a set of internal hypothesis spaces to elucidate the likely causal structure of the decision problem (i.e., the rules governing the representation of states and transitions between states). This is necessary so that the appropriate decision structure is represented from which options can be selected. At the goal-selection level, search needs to be initiated to determine which goal from the multiple possiblities the animal wants to pursue. The final type of search is over the space of possible actions that might be selected to obtain a particular outcome.

We argue that the primary computational signal underpinning search in a motivated animal is the need to minimize uncertainty in the animal's representation of information pertaining to each level of the goal-directed decision process. This uncertainty should be computed separately for each of the different component processes underpinning the goal-directed system.

The domains of cognitive search in Table 9.1 are those that we consider to be particularly amenable to an analysis in terms of brain mechanisms. From the outset, it should be made clear that it is unlikely that search can be reduced to a single process operating within a single neural system. Rather, searches may engage the articulation of different neural systems working in a combinatorial fashion, both in series and in parallel. However, it is also necessary to parse search processes further to investigate candidate neuronal mechanisms and to identify large-scale neural systems through which search is implemented. These neural systems may, for example, include regions in which relevant representations are held that may be accessed by other systems, for example, in a "top-down" manner. They may further be subject to modulation by ascending, diffuse neurochemical systems (e.g., the monoamines, dopamine, norepinephrine, and serotonin) mediating states of arousal, stress, and general motivation, which influence the fidelity of representations as well as the efficiency of search processes. It is highly likely that the search process itself utilizes some fundamental neuronal mechanisms common to many behavioral processes, such as prediction errors and outcome expectancies, though the exact

Table 9.1   Types of search process.

Non-goal-directed, search-like responses

1. Sensory/perceptual feature processes
   - Sensitive to levels of general arousal
   - Composed of reflexive orienting responses
   - Subject to habituation
2. Evaluative processes
   - Elicited by motivationally salient cues (stimuli associated with primary motivational states)
   - Composed of reflexive-orienting responses
   - Productive of arousal
   - Stimulus–motivation (S–M) associative structure
3. Pavlovian processes
   - Elicited by stimuli associated with evaluative incentives
   - Composed of consummatory/defensive reflexes (e.g., lick, chew, blink, freeze)
   - Preparatory responses (e.g., approach, withdrawal, restless activity)
   - Stimulus–stimulus (S–S) associative structure
4. Habitual processes
   - Elicited by antecedent stimuli with which the response has become associated through reinforcement
   - Model free
   - Stimulus–response (S–R) associative structure

Goal-directed search processes

1. Perceptual search: gathering information from the world
2. Search over causal models: to identify (hidden) structures of environmental contingencies and define the search space; requires inference as well as perception
3. Search over goals: internal, based on current motivational states and needs
4. Searching over actions, exploring action–outcome (A–O) relationships
5. Model based

---

mechanism by which these are integrated into the search structure is an open question, as theorized in the next section.

To undertake a neural analysis of search, it is therefore necessary to identify its main components, and the following key elements are proposed:

1. Initiation of search
2. Identification of the set of to-be-searched options
3. Deliberation, including evaluation of the value of possible options and predicted outcomes
4. Action selection
5. Search termination, including evaluation of search success

The different subprocesses of cognitive search are now considered in turn, with their associated possible neural correlates. In general, we note that relevant neuroscientific investigations have generally relied on a rather limited number of species; namely rodents, nonhuman primates and humans, studied individually in rather artificial, laboratory-based environments. Nevertheless, we hope that at least some of what will be described has more general application to the situations and themes considered by this Forum. Some of the utility of this analysis will be considered in the context of various pathologies. For example, stress can have significant effects on aspects of the search process. Behavioral evidence of "search deficits" is also considered in human patients with discrete brain damage, or within functional cognitive deficits arising through neurological or neuropsychiatric disorders.

Components

Search Initiation

Search initiation can be thought of as a two-stage process, driven by both the onset of a motivational state (e.g., hunger, thirst, need for information) and an uncertainty regarding how to satisfy that need. There may well be competing goals to pursue, in which case there is also uncertainty as to which goal state should take precedence, and also a fundamental uncertainty about which action will best serve the organism in achieving its aim.

Prediction Errors

One key signal capable of triggering a search would be the occurrence of an unexpected event (i.e., if what is observed is inconsistent with what is expected). This process would also be key in other evaluative stages of the search process. Once organisms have become familiar with their environment and have learned about cues or subspaces that were previously associated with rewards, this knowledge can be used to generate predictions about the consequences of cues, events and actions. Computationally, the operation by which actual outcomes are compared to expectancies is cast as a calculation of prediction error. In basic form, a prediction error is computed by subtracting the expected outcome from the actual, observed outcome (Rescorla and Wagner 1972). Recent behavioral and neurophysiological studies have shed light on the neural systems involved in these computations. An important discovery (Schultz et al. 1992, 1997) was that the firing of dopaminergic neurons in the primate brain obeys a response pattern predicted by models of reinforcement learning based on temporal prediction errors (Sutton and Barto 1998). Before task acquisition, dopamine neurons transiently fire to rewards that are delivered unexpectedly, and also when rewards are preceded by a sensory cue (conditioned stimulus). After the animal has learned that the reward is reliably preceded by a conditioned stimulus, dopamine neurons no longer increase firing when receiving a reward. In contrast, they still fire to reward delivery when this is unpredicted to the animal (i.e., when the sensory cue is omitted). When an expected reward is omitted, the firing rate of dopamine neurons transiently decreases. Overall, phasic increments in firing occur whenever a positive prediction error occurs (receiving more reward than predicted at that moment), and a decrement occurs when the error is negative (receiving less reward than expected). Importantly, once the animal is trained on a conditioning task and dopaminergic neurons stop firing in response to the now predicted reward, they will fire in response to stimuli or contexts that reliably predict reward in time. This backwards referral process transfers the dopaminergic signals from the end result (reward) to the environmental elements acting as the earliest predictors of reward.

In the context of search initiation, however, it is important to emphasize that dopamine probably serves more functions than just mediating an error in reward prediction. Dopamine neurons can also respond to novel stimuli as well as to generally salient stimuli, which may contribute to an animal's motivation to search novel spaces. Moreover, the tonic (sustained) component of dopaminergic signaling appears to be related to other processes, such as opportunity costs (Daw et al. 2006), vigor (Niv et al. 2007; Robbins and Everitt 1992), stability of representations (Durstewitz et al. 2000; Redish et al. 2007; Seamans and Yang 2004), uncertainty about future reward (Fiorillo et al. 2003), as well as to basic abilities of initiating motor actions and maintaining flexible posture and rhythmic movements, as is dramatically illustrated by Parkinson's disease. Salient, noxious stimuli and stress have also been described to enhance dopamine release (e.g., Matsumoto and Hikosaka 2009; Goto et al. 2007), and this may likewise have implications for search initiation and cessation. Finally, other brain systems have been shown to generate error- and surprise-related information; for example, the orbitofrontal cortex (Sul et al. 2010; van Duuren et al. 2009), anterior cingulate cortex (Gehring and Fencsik 2001), and habenula (Bromberg-Martin et al. 2010c). A more thorough consideration of the neurochemical regulation of search is provided later (see section on Deliberation and Evaluation).

The Nature and Importance of Uncertainty in the Initiation of the Search Process

Given the importance we have placed on prediction errors in mediating the search process, it follows that a guiding principle in the initiation and subsequent termination of search pertains to the degree of uncertainty present regarding aspects of the world. According to this idea, one of the main computational principles driving the search process is to minimize uncertainty in both the representation of relevant features of the environment and concerning the nature of the interaction with that world. Building on the ideas outlined above, that there may be multiple components of search which differ in terms of the types of information being considered, it follows that there may be different types of uncertainty concerning information at different levels of the inference hierarchy, from perceptual features to action–outcome (A–O) relationships.

One useful way of thinking about the representation of these features and the consequent computation of uncertainty is through a Bayesian framework. Bayesian models are a class of simple models that build probabilistic representations that capture beliefs about the state of the world. Mathematically they use Bayes's theorem to update those belief representations (called priors), based on the difference between the actual observed outcomes and the expected representations (prediction errors). These models can represent inference processes about different features of the environment so that, for example, one inference process might encode beliefs about the perceptual environment (which stimuli are present), whereas another might capture beliefs about the hidden causal structure in the environment (e.g., which rules are in place, the context of the agent), and another inference process might compute beliefs about the relationship between particular actions and associated outcomes. Thus, the goal of minimizing uncertainty can operate for different types of inference process and motivate different goal-directed search strategies to minimize uncertainty for each type of inference process where necessary. Another feature of these types of models is that the inference structures can sometimes be arranged in a hierarchy where beliefs at one level of the hierarchy are used to inform and update beliefs at higher and lower levels. In this context, it may be useful to consider that inference over causal structure and inference over A–O relationships can usefully be considered to be part of a hierarchy, with causal structure at the higher level and A–O representations at the lower level; information about which action is currently rewarded (as computed at the lower level) will also be propagated up the causal structure hierarchy and used to update beliefs at that level (in Bayesian terminology the inferred A–O relationships can be used to construct the posterior beliefs). This is a bidirectional process because beliefs about causal structure can also inform priors about which action is currently rewarded.

Within each type of inference process, uncertainty can also be broken down into different components, only some of which are relevant to search. One proposal (Yu and Dayan 2005) is that there are at least two different types of uncertainty. The first is termed *expected uncertainty* and corresponds to the known variance in the world; for example, if an action gives reward only 50% of the time, compared to an action yielding reward 100% of the time, these actions would have different expected uncertainties over reward distributions. In the context of A–O relationships, this form of uncertainty corresponds to what is called risk in economics. Crucially, this form of uncertainty should *not* in principle instigate search, as it corresponds to intrinsic irreducible uncertainty in the properties of the A–O contingencies; hence there is no way to minimize this through search.

The second type of uncertainty is *unexpected uncertainty*, which is proposed to correspond to features of the world that are unknown. For example, if a given action gives reward 80% of the time, and suddenly and unexpectedly shifts so that the probability of getting reward on that action is now only 20% of the time, this is a form of unexpected uncertainty. Unexpected uncertainty is likely to motivate search, because once an unexpected change is detected, the agent may need to resample the environment to update knowledge about its properties.

A third form of uncertainty described recently (Payzan-LeNestour and Bossaerts 2011) is *estimation uncertainty*. This form refers to the uncertainty in beliefs based on the fact that estimates of the true state of the world are noisy; if we have only sampled an A–O relationship a few times, we might have very high levels of estimation uncertainty about that A–O relationship, whereas if we sample that A–O relationship many times, our beliefs about that outcome will become more precise and our estimation uncertainty will be reduced. Estimation uncertainty is perhaps the most fundamental type of uncertainty that underpins search, as minimization of this kind of uncertainty is necessary to build an accurate picture of the decision problem for all types of representation (whether involving perceptual information, causal structure, or A–O structure). There is a complex relationship between estimation uncertainty and unexpected uncertainty; clearly, if there is a high level of volatility in the environment, unexpected uncertainty will be high and estimation uncertainty will also be high because the agent will constantly need to change its estimations as a function of the change in the underlying contingencies.

Given that the goal of this chapter is to focus on the neural correlates of search processes, we must consider *where* uncertainty is represented in the brain, particularly with respect to unexpected and estimation uncertainty, as these brain regions will be important in the initiation and termination of cognitive search according to the theoretical framework advanced here. In the economic literature, unexpected uncertainty is often described as "ambiguity," and it has been studied in experimental situations where the precise odds of obtaining a reward outcome are hidden from the participant. Activity in parietal and inferior frontal cortex has been observed when participants are making choices over conditions of high ambiguity (when the probabilities are unknown) compared to low (when the probabilities are known) (Huettel et al. 2006). Other evidence for the representation of uncertainty in the brain comes from an fMRI study in which human subjects performed a simple bandit decision task (Behrens et al. 2007). Behrens et al. varied the "volatility" or rate of change of the reward contingencies at different times in the experiment; at some points, the probability of being rewarded on a particular action changed rapidly over time, whereas at other points the probability of being rewarded changed less rapidly. They used a Bayesian model that computed a representation of uncertainty and correlated this with the fMRI data. They found that activity in the anterior cingulate cortex correlated with their uncertainty representation. Crucially, in their modeling, they did not distinguish between unexpected and estimation uncertainty, so it is unclear which of these signals is encoded in the anterior cingulate cortex.

Neural measures of uncertainty will be manifested either in direct measures of increased firing patterns with uncertainty or through measuring the internal self-consistency of neural representations. An important paradigm capturing changes in uncertainty in perception and decision making is the "diffusion model" of accumulating neural evidence, expressed by changes in firing rate (Churchland et al. 2008). As concerns self-consistency, representations are distributed across multiple cells, and the activity of a population of cells can either "agree" or "disagree" on a representation (Jackson and Redish 2003). These measures can be quantitatively identified through a three-step process from neural ensemble recordings, in which tuning curves are first derived from neural activity and behavior, then represented values are decoded from neural activity and those tuning curves, and finally, through a derivation of expected neural activity, from tuning curves and the decoded behavior (Johnson et al. 2009; Zhang et al. 1998). An important question is whether fMRI signals which correlate with uncertainty reflect the computation of uncertainty per se, or downstream processes associated with uncertainty, such as neural signals that reflect the generation or perception of increased autonomic arousal (i.e., changes in respiration and cardiovascular activity), or even direct effects on blood flow arising from such changes (Birn et al. 2006). The answer to this question remains to be empirically determined.

Comparators

We can identify comparison operations at three different stages of the search process. At initiation, a comparison needs to determine if there is unexpected uncertainty, hence leading to exploration and initiation of search. During the search, a continuing comparison process needs to continue to check whether or not the search has found the goal. Finally, after termination of the search, an evaluation process needs to compare the observed outcome from the expected outcomes; that is, did the search accomplish what was expected?

The identification of an environment as being novel can play an important role in the search process and is one of the most obvious examples of a huge rise in unexpected uncertainty. When rats are faced with a novel environment, their first priority is safety, and they run to a location within the environment that has some protection from potential predators (Chance and Mead 1955). This location forms what is called a "home base," from which they then explore in small journeys with a distinctive pattern: rats leave the home base, exploring with a slowly variable path, until they suddenly turn toward the home base and run directly home (Chance and Mead 1955; Eilam and Golani 1989;

Redish 1999; Whishaw and Brooks 1999). The outbound journey and the return journey have very different behavioral characteristics; the outbound journey is slow and meandering, whereas the return journey is ballistic (Drai and Golani 2001). The length of subsequent outbound journeys increases with experience, suggesting that rats are exploring increasingly more of the environment. Following from the hypothesis laid out here that search entails the reduction of uncertainty, we can identify these outbound journeys as searches that reduce the uncertainty in the environment. Whether this termination of the exploration path occurs due to reaching a threshold of novelty stress or fear (Crusio 2001; Pardon et al. 2002) or due to recognition of unreliability in the spatial representation as a result of drift in dead-reckoning systems (Redish 1999) is as yet untested. It is possible that drift in dead-reckoning systems (measurable to the animal as uncertainty in its position) can drive stress and fear, leading to a threshold at which the rat decides that it must return to the home base to reset its dead-reckoning information from a known position (Redish 1999).

Hippocampal comparators. A number of researchers have suggested that the CA1 region of the hippocampus serves as a comparator (Vinogradova 2001), particularly for the detection of novelty (Lisman and Grace 2005; Lisman and Otmakhova 2001). These hypotheses were based, in part, on anatomical and neurophysiological studies of convergent inputs from entorhinal cortex and CA3 on individual CA1 neurons (Groenewegen et al. 1987; Witter and Amaral 1991) under the assumption that the recurrent connections in CA3 could provide a delay. While it is true that hippocampal lesions significantly reduce spatial exploration (Archer and Birke 1983; O'Keefe and Nadel 1978; Redish 1999), particularly through a reduction in recognition of changes in the environment (Clark et al. 2000; Thinus-Blanc 1996; Zola et al. 2000), single cellular activity purely reflecting novelty has not been found in hippocampus. However, mismatch-like signals have been found in this region when rats were swimming in an annular maze and searching around the location where they expected a hidden platform (Fyhn et al. 2002). Changes in novelty are also reflected in population activity within the hippocampus, in that more cells are active in novel environments due to a reduction in inhibitory activity (Wilson and McNaughton 1993). Place cells generally show activity in their place fields from the first experience through the field (Hill 1978); nevertheless, they change their activity over the course of several hours (Cheng and Frank 2008), through an NMDA-receptor-dependent mechanism (Austin et al. 1993; Kentros et al. 1998). This suggests that while the firing of individual CA1 cells primarily reflects information about the world, differences in activity—even correlations between cell firing patterns—can be used to provide additional signals such as novelty. While cross-trial reliability can be interpreted as reflecting uncertainty (Fenton and Muller 1998; Kelemen and Fenton 2010), it can also reflect unaccounted-for parameters, external or internal (Johnson et al. 2009). As animals familiarize themselves with an environment, the decoded position from the neural population becomes more accurate due, in large part, to the stabilization of place fields with experience (Austin et al. 1993; Wilson and McNaughton 1993).

Anterior cingulate comparators. In terms of evaluating whether a search has successfully achieved the specified goal, the anterior cingulate cortex has been found to respond to errors (Gemba et al. 1986), and it was originally conceived of as a comparator between actual and intended outcomes (Falkenstein et al. 1991; Gehring and Fencsik 2001). Although some work has cast anterior cingulate cortex as a conflict detector (Carter et al. 1998), there is now evidence that the anterior cingulate cortex compares actual versus expected outcomes (Ito et al. 2003; Jessup et al. 2010), as distinct from actual versus intended outcomes. The anterior cingulate cortex is especially active when a search is initiated, and it shuts off once the object of the search has been found (Shima and Tanji 1998; Bush et al. 2002), or even once the uncertainty about the object of the search has been eliminated (Procyk et al. 2000). This suggests that the anterior cingulate cortex is active during search to compare expected findings (including, but not limited to, the object of the search) against the actual findings. As the anticipated successful completion of the search becomes nearer in space and time, the anterior cingulate cortex cells become progressively more active (Shidara and Richmond 2002). Overall, the anterior cingulate cortex may monitor an ongoing search in two ways: (a) it may continually anticipate the outcome of a search and (b) it may become active when a comparison between actual and expected outcomes yields a discrepancy, which in turn requires corrective action (Modirrousta and Fellows 2008). In this way, the anterior cingulate cortex may monitor and contribute to effective search.

Identification of the Set of To-Be-Searched Options

From an ethological perspective, search is usually seen in terms of progress through space to reach a goal; however, cognitive search can occur in both "spatial spaces" (e.g., a rat trying to find a food source in a maze) and "nonspatial spaces" (e.g., selection among different goals or among different actions available to the animal). An important issue, therefore, is whether search processes that occur within different domains are processed by different brain structures. It seems plausible that searches involving various types of information will involve different neural structures which specifically encode, retrieve, or store that type of information. Neural systems of imagination and planning often utilize the sensory systems involved in their sensory processing; thus, for example, visual imagination involves primary and secondary visual cortex (Kosslyn et al. 2001), and a similar pattern of activation holds for the auditory cortices during imagination of sounds (Daselaar et al. 2010; Zatorre and Halpern 2005).

*Neural Representations Specific to the Domain
of Information To-Be-Searched*

Searching for semantic information. Retrieving information in verbal fluency (and naming) tasks can be understood as a mental search through an internal representation ("lexicon"). Whereas category fluency (e.g., naming all animals that come to mind) and letter fluency (e.g., naming all words that come to mind that begin with the letter "L") both share the necessity to initiate and control search, they differ with respect to the information that is retrieved: category fluency requires access to semantic information, whereas letter fluency is related to orthographical and phonological information. Early functional neuroimaging studies implicated areas of the prefrontal, parietal, and temporal cortices in this task (Friston et al. 1991; Frith et al. 1991b). Subsequent studies have attempted to dissociate the functional roles of these structures with respect to specific subcomponents of the task, such as accessing semantic information. This was mainly inspired by the notion that objects are characterized by a variety of features and associations in multiple sensory domains (e.g., smell, taste, color, shape, sound) but also in the action domain (e.g., associated movement patterns). This led to the hypothesis that diverse attributes of an object are represented in cortical areas that are involved in processing each particular type of information.

This hypothesis has been investigated by asking volunteers to retrieve specific semantic associations of objects. For instance, if the color of an object was relevant to the search, this led to an activation of the ventral occipito-temporal junction, an area that is also activated in the context of color perception (Chao and Martin 1999). Certain objects are well characterized by their use. This implies that in the representation of tools, motor areas might play a role. In agreement with this notion, activation in the left ventral premotor cortex has been observed in tasks involving the retrieval of semantic information pertaining to tools, such as their names (Chao and Martin 2000; Martin and Chao 2001). All the examples mentioned above used univariate tests, in essence showing increased activation for certain object categories. This was then complemented by observations indicating that even distributed information in cortical areas can be "decoded" using multivariate pattern classification techniques of fMRI data (Haxby et al. 2001; Polyn et al. 2005).

Searching through space. The hippocampus has been long identified as a key component of spatial navigation (Morris et al. 1982; O'Keefe and Nadel 1978; Olton and Papas 1979; Redish 1999), particularly in the context of spatial search processes (Johnson and Redish 2007; Morris 1981; Tse et al. 2007). There is also ample evidence to suggest that the hippocampus encodes more than just spatial representations, but may likewise be important for complex temporal information (Fortin et al. 2002). Recently, hippocampal cells have been shown to divide up temporal sequences when animals must run on a treadmill during a delay to a goal (Macdonald et al. 2010; Pastalkova et al. 2008; Takahashi et al. 2009a). These firing patterns appear to act much like spatially encoding place cells, each of which fires only in a small portion of an environment, or along a small portion of a repeated journey (Levy 1996). Amnesic patients with medial temporal lobe lesions have been observed to be impaired in trace eyeblink conditioning, in which a temporal gap is introduced between the conditioned and unconditioned stimuli (Clark and Squire 1998; McGlinchey-Berroth et al. 1997). fMRI studies have also revealed activation of the hippocampus in Pavlovian trace conditioning (Buchel et al. 1999) that was not seen in a similar cue conditioning paradigm (Buchel et al. 1998; LaBar et al. 1998).

Contextual conditioning probes the association of a large set of multisensory stimulus features, including spatial information. Such learning has been shown to involve the hippocampus in rodents (Bouton 2004; Kim and Fanselow 1992) and humans (Cohen and Eichenbaum 1993), particularly in the face of contextual changes (Rawlins 1985; Redish 1999). Similar observations have been made in human functional neuroimaging, showing activation in the hippocampus in contextual fear conditioning (Lang et al. 2009; Marschner et al. 2008). Although many fMRI studies have highlighted the role of the hippocampus in establishing "maps" that include the dimensions of space and time, it is important to note that current functional imaging cannot provide enough detail about the underlying mechanisms of how the hippocampus integrates these features into such a map.

The hippocampus is not necessary, however, for simple one-step representations of causal structure in the world: hippocampal lesions do not interfere with either acquisition or performance of a lever press for food task (Corbit and Balleine 2000); animals with hippocampal lesions remain sensitive to devaluation, indicating that even without a hippocampus, animals remain knowledgeable about the consequences of their actions. Whether the hippocampus is necessary for deeper searches through causal structure is still unknown. Even in spatial tasks, the hippocampus is primarily necessary for the development of a world schema (cognitive map) on which expected outcomes can be placed; once the schema is learned, even new outcomes can be learned in the environment. Lesion data suggest the existence of nonhippocampal representations of such schematic, causal structure (Tse et al. 2007).

Nevertheless, as noted above, hippocampal lesions have profound effects on exploration and on the ability to use knowledge about the spatial world to find goals and targets, particularly when there is uncertainty (Kesner and Rogers 2004; Morris 1981; Redish 1999; Sutherland et al. 2011). As a classic example, the hippocampus is necessary to learn the location of a platform within a cloudy pool of water (the "Morris water maze"; Morris 1981; Sutherland et al. 2011), particularly when animals are started from many locations within the pool (e.g., with uncertainty in the starting point), and during early learning (e.g., with uncertainty in the location of the platform). The hippocampus is no longer necessary if animals have a single cue they can approach (Eichenbaum et al. 1990), or if they are overtrained (Day et al. 1999), both of which reduce the uncertainty in the location of the platform. In these cases, other nonhippocampal systems are capable of guiding the rat to the platform, including systems for stimulus–response (S–R)-based, egocentric navigation (McDonald and White 1993; Packard and McGaugh 1992).

Neural Representations Independent of the Domain
of Information To-Be-Searched

In humans, the anterior cingulate cortex is activated across a wide array of seemingly unrelated cognitive tasks involving very different cues and responses (Duncan and Owen 2000). In rats, anterior cingulate cortex and medial prefrontal cortex neurons appear to encode virtually all relevant aspects of any task the animal is required to perform, including cues and choices as well as reward magnitude, reward probability, action sequences, and abstract task rules (Hyman et al. 2005; Jung et al. 1998; Lapish et al. 2008; Narayanan and Laubach 2009). Furthermore, if the rules of a task change, there is a tightly correlated change in the way the same stimuli and responses are represented by the anterior cingulate cortex, both at the level of single neurons and ensembles (Durstewitz et al. 2010; Jung et al. 1998; Rich and Shapiro 2009). Therefore, the anterior cingulate cortex represents actions and stimuli with reference to the task being performed (Hoshi et al. 2005). Accordingly, it has been proposed that the anterior cingulate cortex, forming a continuum with adjacent medial prefrontal areas, is an integral part of a network that formulates task sets; that is, the dynamic configuration of perceptual, attentional, mnemonic, and motor processes necessary to accomplish a particular task (Dosenbach et al. 2006; Sakai 2008; Weissman et al. 2005).

As reviewed by Ridderinkoff and Harsay (this volume), the idea that the anterior cingulate cortex formulates task sets has been expanded to suggest a more general role of the region as part of a salience network that tracks all homeostatically relevant (salient) stimuli and events. In support of this idea, it has recently been observed that in the absence of an overt task situation, ensembles of anterior cingulate neurons formed highly distinct representations of novel environments which became less distinct as the environments became more familiar. However, the manner in which anterior cingulate cortex ensembles represented environments changed when tasks were performed. For instance, if rats had learned to perform a specific action in a specific environment, the action and the corresponding environment was represented by similar activity state patterns. In contrast, when rats were required to perform the same task continuously across different environments, the ensembles consistently represented only the task elements, and the representation of the environment was much less evident. While these data support the idea that the anterior cingulate cortex represents whatever is currently salient, they suggest that tasks are the key factor in organizing these representations. Therefore, once a goal has been selected, the anterior cingulate cortex may formulate a task set or a representation of the set of stimuli and actions that are relevant to attaining the goal. It then tracks the progress of the animal within the task space (Lapish et al. 2008; Shidara et al. 2005).

Deliberation and Evaluation

Evaluation of stimuli and outcomes is important to the selection of intermediate or final targets of search and is equally important for computing prediction errors (discussed above). The assessment of outcome can occur in many ways, and we need to distinguish various modalities in the representation of outcomes: by value (understood with reference to homeostatic brain mechanisms defining the animal's needs) as well as by sensory properties defining the identity and quality of the outcome. For instance, a monkey searching for bananas can be said to have successfully completed its search once it finds a banana; however, in some cases this outcome is more valuable than in others. In the case of sensory-specific satiety (where the monkey has had its fill of a particular food, in this case bananas), the banana will be less valuable than if the monkey had not encountered a banana in some time. The specific taste and consistency of the banana define qualities other than its reward value. For example, an apple may be equal in reward value as compared to the banana, but yet have a different behavioral significance to the animal, potentially affecting its future search. Therefore, an important aspect of search is the determination of stimuli for which to search.

Whereas the gustatory cortex codes specific tastes of food rewards, the orbitofrontal cortex is important because it represents the value of outcomes (Padoa-Schioppa 2009) and it contains neurons that code the expected value of stimuli and actions (Baxter et al. 2000; Schoenbaum et al. 1998). Orbitofrontal neurons are activated by both primary rewards and conditioned reinforcers and may become activated before, during, or after a reward delivery. Neurons in this region can also discriminate between different rewards, largely irrespective of the actual features of reward-predicting stimuli or the responses used to obtain them (Padoa-Schioppa and Assad 2006). Neurons in rat orbitofrontal cortex are sensitive to different parameters of reward outcome (e.g., magnitude and probability of an upcoming reward; van Duuren et al. 2007, 2009). Perhaps most importantly, the responses of orbitofrontal neurons discriminate rewards based on their relative preference or value to the animal (Tremblay and Schultz 1999). Accordingly, the neural coding of food reward is subject to satiety (Rolls et al. 1999), confirming that neuronal activity is related to value coding. In addition, however, signaling within the orbitofrontal region also appears to reflect the sensory-specific qualities of the outcome regardless of value (e.g., a banana versus an apple, when valued equally; McDannald et al. 2011). Furthermore, orbitofrontal neurons also respond to aversively predicting stimuli; here the response is again related to the relative preference of one aversive outcome versus another (Hosokawa et al. 2007; Morrison and Salzman 2009). Therefore, orbitofrontal neurons and networks might weigh the relative preference of different rewards as well as factor in whether the search for reward is offset by the potential harms involved.

The results of these calculations might then bias striatal activity so as to guide the appropriate actions to be taken (Simmons et al. 2007). Although the rodent ventral striatum receives little direct input from the orbitofrontal cortex (Schilman et al. 2008), it has also been strongly implicated in coding the value of outcomes as well as expected values. This structure receives strong inputs from the hippocampal formation and basolateral amygdala, which are important in forming stimulus–outcome (S–O) associations and relaying these to downstream areas, such as the ventral pallidum, to affect motor behavior (Parkinson et al. 2000). Many ventral striatal cells generate "ramps" in firing rate when animals are expecting a reward, with the firing becoming more intense as the animal gets temporally or spatially closer to reward delivery (Lansink et al. 2008; Lavoie and Mizumori 1994; Schultz et al. 1992; van der Meer and Redish 2011). Distinct subsets of ventral striatal cells code expected value at different task phases in advance of reward, or distinctly respond upon reward delivery. A possible difference between orbitofrontal and ventral striatal coding may reflect differences in representation of value and identity: while the ventral striatum is necessary for rodents to recognize any change in value, whether it be due to changes in amount of food delivered or in identity of food delivered, the orbitofrontal cortex was only necessary for rodents to recognize changes in identity (McDannald et al. 2011).

The coding of outcome value by ventral striatal cells may have two important functions. First, given the strong projection from the ventral striatum to the ventral tegmentum (the primary source of dopaminergic projections to cortical and limbic regions), the ventral striatum may provide expectancy and/or outcome signals that are used in the computation of prediction errors at the level of the dopamine cells. However, which brain areas are needed to compute dopamine error signals is not precisely known. Recent discoveries characterized the firing of habenula cells as an inverse signal, with high firing during disappointment (unexpected losses) and decreases in firing during surprising rewards (unexpected gains) (Bromberg-Martin et al. 2010a; Matsumoto and Hikosaka 2009). The habenula has an inhibitory influence on the dopamine cells through an inhibitory nucleus called the tail of the ventral tegmental area (VTA) (AKA rmTG) (Jhou et al. 2009). In addition to the contribution made by a ventral striatum to VTA projection, the orbitofrontal cortex may have an important role because contralateral orbitofrontal cortex–VTA inactivations have been reported to disrupt learning from unexpected outcomes (Takahashi et al. 2009b). Second, the ventral striatum projects to downstream structures, such as the ventral pallidum, and from there on to lower downstream structures in the brain stem, or up to the thalamus to complete an anatomical loop back to prefrontal cortex. These output pathways are thought to convey motivational influences on patterns of motor behavior and cognitive processing.

Regarding the evaluation of different options in the spatial realm, hippo-campal representations have been found to reflect future paths ahead of the rat, both during foraging behavior on mazes and in open situations (Lisman and Redish 2009), and specifically during decision making when rats are faced with explicit choices (Johnson and Redish 2007). During normal navigation, some hippocampal neurons fire when the animal is located in a particular place. These place cells fire at specific phases relative to an internal 7–10 Hz hippocampal local field potential called "theta" (Maurer and McNaughton 2007; O'Keefe and Recce 1993; Skaggs et al. 1996). It has been suggested that these phase precession phenomena represent a prediction of future paths that could be taken by the animal (Jensen and Lisman 1996). The discovery that the phases of firing in bidirectional place fields only converge in the two directions at the end of the field suggests that these place fields are, in fact, representing distance to a goal (Lisman and Redish 2009; Battaglia et al. 2004; Huxter et al. 2008). When rats are forced to make explicit choices, they sometimes pause and look back and forth between options, as if confused (or searching) between those options (Tolman 1938). During this pause-and-look behavior, termed "vicarious trial and error" (Muenzinger and Gentry 1931), hippocampal rep-resentations in area CA3 serially represent the potential options ahead of the rat (Johnson and Redish 2007). In downstream evaluative structures, such as ventral striatum and orbitofrontal cortex, cells that normally respond to reward also respond during these vicarious trial-and-error events (Steiner and Redish 2010; van der Meer and Redish 2009), suggesting a covert search-and-eval-uation process (van der Meer and Redish 2010). These forward sweeps may represent cued memory retrieval, given the functions attributed to CA3 in this process (Marr 1971; McNaughton and Morris 1987; O'Reilly and McClelland 1994; Redish 1999), and may subserve prospective search.

One of the unsolved questions in this field concerns how the various evalu-ation systems interact. It is important to note that the orbitofrontal cortex most densely projects to the dorsomedial striatum (Price 2007; Schilman et al. 2008). Given that this striatal sector has been implied in mediating A–O associations (Yin et al. 2005), it is reasonable to hypothesize that orbitofrontal cortex may provide information about the outcome component of this associative process. However, caution should be exercised in this context; recent anatomical stud-ies suggest five divisions of orbital cortex, from medial to lateral, with only the medial orbital and the most medial portion of ventral orbital projecting to medial striatum (Schilman et al. 2008). In fact, more lateral regions proj-ect largely to lateral and ventral regions of striatum and appear to play a role in stimulus-based rather than action-based predictions of outcomes (Ostlund and Balleine 2007). Certainly, as noted above, the ventral striatal system has generally been strongly implicated in mediating the motivational effects of Pavlovian cues and contexts on behavior. Finally, it should be emphasized that there are many more brain structures where information about outcome expectancy is expressed. For instance, areas implied in visual processing, visuospatial behavior, and visual search express reward value information (parietal cortex: Platt and Glimcher 1999; visual cortex: Shuler and Bear 2006). These data reveal how widespread the effects of reward expectancy are across the brain, whereas the causal generation of evaluative signals driving action selection is likely to be primarily restricted to frontal-basal ganglia circuitry.

Working memory is also critical at this stage for strategy development as it allows the organism to consider multiple options online. The effect of strategy representations in working memory is essentially to narrow down the initial pool of candidate actions that may be employed in the search. There is general agreement that working memory involves the network interactions among lateral prefrontal cortex and parietal cortex (Chafee and Goldman-Rakic 2000), although subcortical regions such as the striatum and hippocampus can also contribute. Overlapping regions of ventrolateral prefrontal cortex may therefore provide top-down cognitive control of cognitive search from this perspective (Nobre et al. 2004).

Action Selection

At the conclusion of this deliberation and evaluative stage, it can be presumed that an action is needed to test the predictions of the search and obtain the goal in question. This is true regardless of whether the goal was abstract, such as information (a test of the individual's newly updated representation of the world), or physically substantive, such as food reward. There are times when this will involve complex action planning, thereby requiring almost a separate subsearch in which a set of possible actions must be identified and evaluated, versus simpler engagement of a well-known motor movement.

Analyses of action systems in human or animal subjects usually depend on experimentally highly constrained situations, such as voluntary, as distinct from stimulus-elicited, limb or eye movements receiving rewarding feedback. In functional imaging tasks in humans, these engage regions of the prefrontal cortex, including dorsolateral regions, as well as the premotor and supplementary motor cortex, which project into the so-called parallel loops of the cortico-striatal systems (Alexander et al. 1990; Berendse et al. 1992; Voorn et al. 2004; Zahm and Brog 1992). Again, it is important to realize that these activations can also be produced (generally to a lesser degree of activation) by instructions to imagine a given action, such as serving the ball in tennis, or even thinking of the meaning of a hammer (Martin and Chao 2001). The human functional imaging observations have been paralleled by experimental observations from electrophysiological recordings in nonhuman primates. Thus, there is a cortical representation of many voluntary actions in premotor regions that may also be sensitive to observations of others performing similar actions (so-called mirror neurons: Cattaneo and Rizzolatti 2009; Rizzolatti et al. 2009). It has been presumed that such "ideo-motor" representations may be important in inferring intentions in social situations. Electrophysiological observations linking action representations and outcome representations in nonhuman primates suggest that there is a distribution of reward-related activity throughout the entire prefrontal cortex but that it is only in certain regions coincident with representations of action information (Kennerley and Wallis 2009; Wallis and Miller 2003); this notably includes the anterior cingulate cortex. Furthermore, human neuroimaging and nonhuman primate lesion data highlight an important role for this region in representing A–O information (Walton et al. 2005).

Role of Prefrontal Cortex in Action Planning

Action planning is likely to involve the prefrontal cortex and supplementary/premotor areas. For instance, in rodents and nonhuman primates, the medial prefrontal cortex contains a large fraction of neurons sensitive to the setting of task rules (Birrell and Brown 2000; Durstewitz and Seamans 2002; Mulder et al. 2003; Peyrache et al. 2009; Rich and Shapiro 2009; Wallis et al. 2001). Upon a switch of strategy and adoption of another task rule, subsets of prefrontal cortex ensembles that were previously active now become inactive, and previously silent ensembles are activated. Further evidence from primates has implied prefrontal and premotor/supplementary motor area structures in planning and executing complex action sequences (Averbeck et al. 2006; Wise et al. 1996), and the most rostral components of prefrontal cortex appear to be involved in the hierarchical organization of behavior and of complex cognitive operations (Koechlin et al. 2000, 2003). It is not yet known whether the rapid alterations in the temporal organization of frontal activity correspond to internal, generative search processes themselves or to the execution of planned actions and application of task rules. However, if we assume that the information retrieved during forward sweeps in the hippocampus is of a generative nature (see earlier section on Deliberation and Evaluation), and that it is coupled in time to similar processes in connected brain areas, then it is straightforward to hypothesize that internal search for future actions involves medial prefrontal cortex—which receives strong hippocampal input (Jay and Witter 1991) that produces firing time-locked to the hippocampal theta rhythm, particularly during decision making and attentive tasks (Hyman et al. 2010; Jones and Wilson 2005)—and related structures for planning and action selection.

Passingham (1993) has reviewed evidence that the medial premotor cortex is required to retrieve the appropriate movement in the absence of external cues or prompts. However, he also concludes that the dorsolateral prefrontal cortex is required for self-directed sequences of actions that often make up goal-directed behavior. Damage to Brodmann area 46 impairs self-ordered visual search behavior in monkeys (Passingham 1985); analogous results have been found following dorsolateral prefrontal lesions in humans (Manes et al.

2002; Owen et al. 1990). It is, however, not yet clear whether the deficits arise from working memory or response selection impairments (or both). Frith and colleagues have provided evidence that self-generated sequences (of "willed action") activate areas 9/46 within the dorsolateral prefrontal cortex, when there is no obvious working memory component (Frith et al. 1991a).

Action planning has also been studied in humans in terms of the Tower of London problems, which involve sequencing a set of actions to obtain a single specified goal (Shallice 1982). Note that this sequence can also be an imagined sequence (Owen et al. 1995). To solve such tasks, subjects have to search through a number of possible sequences in a finite problem space, a process that may correspond to "deliberation." These sequences can include various key "intermediate positions," or subgoals, which can serve as aids to a solution when it begins to exceed working memory capacity. Performance on such tasks is known to depend on a fronto-parietal-striatal system (Baker et al. 1996; Owen et al. 1990; Shallice 1982), notably involving the dorsolateral and dorsomedial prefrontal cortex. The presumption is that the anterior cingulate cortex may represent the general task set, as reviewed above, whereas the set of visuospatial options may be encoded by the parietal cortex and the execution of the selected sequence in the basal ganglia. Finally, the dorsolateral prefrontal cortex may be especially involved in response selection (Frith et al. 1991a).

Solution of the Tower of London problems is not conventionally related to reward outcomes unless a specific payoff matrix is devised, in which case these action sequences are more likely to engage reward representations in the neural systems encoding value, such as within the orbitofrontal cortex (Wallis et al. 2001). In the conventional task, however, a successful outcome is symbolized simply by correct feedback for the solution. For this reason, such tasks are often labeled as exemplifying "cold" cognitive processes. Planning can, however, involve more complex A–O searches, for example, in selecting actions that anticipate future long-term motivational needs. In addition, planning can involve the scheduling of actions to obtain multiple goals (as in shopping), a task exemplified by the so-called "six elements test," which is especially sensitive to damage of the anterior frontal prefrontal cortex (Burgess et al. 2000).

Action Planning within the Basal Ganglia

Although areas of prefrontal cortex are no doubt involved in action planning, action selection itself is thought to depend critically on activity within the basal ganglia. Action selection initiates a process of action evaluation through the response–outcome (R–O) association; that is, the value of the action is estimated on the basis of the predicted reward value of the outcome which is contingent on that action. Finally, the action selection and evaluation processes combine to initiate an action (see also Balleine and Ostlund 2007). Of the current theories of how this is achieved, perhaps the most plausible is the associative-cybernetic model, which posits that action selection is largely controlled by stimulus(outcome)–response learning, S(O)–R, and hence by outcome retrieval (Dickinson and Balleine 1993). Although the learning of A–O associations has been associated with discrete structures (prelimbic cortex) within the rat medial prefrontal cortex, such A–O learning also implicates the dorsomedial striatum, to which this region of the rodent frontal cortex projects (see O'Doherty and Balleine, this volume). Unlike the prelimbic cortex, the dorsomedial striatum is also apparently necessary for the expression of goal-directed actions, and so the dorsomedial striatum is presumably responsible for response selection in situations where search is required between different established options. Other regions of the basal ganglia, such as the dorsal putamen (or dorsolateral striatum in rodents), are implicated in the learning and expression of S–R habits where no outcome or goal is represented and which therefore is not considered to require a cognitive search.

The fact that the dorsomedial region of the striatum mediates the encoding of R–O associations, whereas the dorsolateral region mediates S–R learning, poses some problems for the associative-cybernetic model: the critical associative and S–R memory systems that contribute to instrumental performance course through corticostriatal circuits localized to adjacent regions of the dorsal striatum, but it is unclear how these two pathways interact to permit the formation of S(O)–R associations identified as critical for action selection. The generally accepted architecture of the basal ganglia emphasizes the operation of functionally distinct, closed parallel loops connecting prefrontal cortex, dorsal striatum, pallidum/substantial nigra, thalamus, and feeding back onto the originating area of prefrontal cortex (Alexander et al. 1986). According to this view, there is considerable vertical integration within loops but less clearly lateral integration across loops. As a consequence, various theories have had to be developed to account for lateral integration: the split loop (Joel and Weiner 2000) or spiraling midbrain-striatal integration (Haber et al. 2000; Haruno and Kawato 2006). These models have not yet found wide acceptance. In contrast, older theories of striato-pallido-nigral integration proposed that, rather than being discrete, corticostriatal connections converge onto common target regions particularly in the globus pallidus—a view that allows naturally for integration between various corticostriatal circuits (Bar-Gad et al. 2003). Although anatomical studies challenge this view, recent evidence has emerged supporting a hybrid version; in addition to the segregated loops, there may also be integration through collateral projections from caudate (or dorsomedial striatum) converging with projections from the putamen (or dorsolateral striatum) onto common regions in both the internal and external globus pallidus (Nadjar et al. 2006). Whether these converging projections underlie the integration of the O–R and R–O associations, which the associative-cybernetic model identifies as critical for the initiation of instrumental performance, remains an open question.

Search Termination

Once a particular search action has been executed, the outcome of the action must be evaluated in terms of whether or not it led to successfully achieving the anticipated goal of the search. As outlined earlier in our discussion, this process involves comparator operations which likely take place within the anterior cingulate cortex. If the comparator output indicates a discrepancy between the actual versus expected outcome, this signals two items of information. The first is that a corrective action may need to be taken (Modirrousta and Fellows 2008). In the case of search, the corrective action is to terminate the current strategy and initiate a new search. There is evidence from monkey neurophysiology that anterior cingulate cortex is active especially during the time of a search; that is, from the time when an unsuccessful strategy is rejected until a new strategy is found (Procyk et al. 2000; Shima and Tanji 1998). In experienced animals, such searches may not be random but instead near optimal (Procyk and Joseph 1996), such that at least in certain tasks, experienced animals do not often try an unsuccessful option twice during a search. This suggests a kind of inhibition of return in higher-level cognitive search, similar to that found in lower-level visual search (Wolfe 2003). A second piece of information signaled by discrepancies is that the A–O prediction was potentially incorrect and should therefore be updated (Matsumoto et al. 2007). When the environment is nonstationary or highly volatile, such predictions will be continually out of date and will therefore yield ongoing discrepancy with the actual outcomes, as has been observed with fMRI studies (Behrens et al. 2007).

Hence, just as search is initiated by rising uncertainty or enhanced motivational drive, search termination can be triggered by a reduction in uncertainty or the recognition that the uncertainty is irreducible, implying that the uncertainty is expected, rather than being a form of unexpected or estimation uncertainty. As discussed above, detection of changes in uncertainty will again involve comparators. Search termination may also result from a shift in motivational state, either appetitive or aversive. For example, in the aversive case, termination of open space exploration in rodents might be triggered by increases in anxiety and stress upon departure from the home base, as indexed, for example, by increases in heart rate variability (Aubert et al. 1999; Behrens et al. 2007). Increases in danger signs (e.g., suddenly bright lights or the addition of predator odor) will send an exploring rat scurrying back to its home base. Brain regions involved in aversion-induced processes include the amygdala and the prefrontal cortex, suggesting that they may well play a role in search termination. Similarly, parts of the frontal cortex are also likely to play a role in the case of shifts in appetitive motivation (e.g., through detection of satiety signals). Thus, the orbitofrontal cortex may play a central role as evidenced by the existence of satiety-responsive neurons in the medial orbitofrontal cortex of the macaque (see section on Deliberation and Evaluation).

This observation highlights a role for reductions in hedonic value in search termination (Pritchard et al. 2008).

The final stage of search termination is the process of action stopping or response inhibition, which involves fronto-basal ganglia networks (Eagle and Baunez 2010). Two forms may be distinguished, with nonselective stopping (or "clamping") of already initiated actions recruiting primarily a network connecting the inferior frontal cortex with the supplementary motor area and the subthalamic nucleus (Aron et al. 2007; Schall et al. 2002; Stuphorn 2006; Stuphorn and Schall 2006). However, a form of stopping that might have wider validity in the context of search is selective stopping, which involves a plan to stop only a select set of actions (Aron 2010). This latter, more proactive form of inhibitory control is generated according to the goals of the subject rather than by an external signal, and has hypothetically been claimed to involve the striatum and its modulation by dopamine.

Neurochemical Regulation of Search

The major ascending neuromodulatory systems, dopamine, norepinephrine (noradrenaline), serotonin, and acetylcholine, play a critical role in many, if not all, of the subcomponent processes of search that we have outlined above (see also Cools et al., this volume). Dopamine, for example, is well known to alter performance on high-level cognitive tasks, such as the Tower of London forward planning test, probabilistic reversal learning, and self-ordered search in spatial working memory (Robbins 2007; Cools 2006). Although much work has highlighted the role of dopamine in reinforcement-based habit learning associated with the dorsolateral striatum, these high-level cognitive effects likely reflect modulation of goal-directed search processes associated with the prefrontal cortex and dorsomedial parts of the striatum (Cools et al., this volume). These dopamine-sensitive processes may include search initiation, option identification, search evaluation, option selection, or search termination. To illustrate the importance of neurochemical modulation in search, we highlight in this section some data evidencing its implication in search initiation.

Dopamine likely contributes to search initiation by signaling a reward prediction error (Schultz 2007). However, it also contributes to search initiation via mediating changes in the motivational state. For example, increases in anxiety and stress are known to be accompanied by changes in neurochemical state, such as supra-optimal increases in dopamine, norepinephrine, and corticosteroids (Arnsten 2009), which in turn have been demonstrated to disrupt the optimal functioning of the prefrontal cortex (Seamans and Yang 2004). Accordingly, anxiety or stress might mediate search termination by inducing supra-optimal levels of dopamine and norepinephrine in the prefrontal cortex. The importance of neurochemical state changes are also likely to play a role in the case of appetitive motivational shifts, such as satiety, which involves

modulation of the orbitofrontal cortex and the striatum by the mesolimbic dopamine system (and its interactions with the hypothalamus) and appetite-reg-
ulating hormonal systems (Farooqi et al. 2007; Kringelbach and Stein 2010).
Search initiation might also depend on noradrenergic activity, which has long
been known to affect attention, particularly in the face of different levels of
uncertainty (Robbins 1997). Thus elevated tonic norepinephrine levels, arising from activity within the locus coeruleus, might play an important role in
initiating search by serving a network reset function; such a function enables
the interruption of ongoing activity (Sara 2009) and the revision of internal
representations based on new sensory input (Aston-Jones and Cohen 2005b;
Yu and Dayan 2005). Specifically, it has been suggested that norepinephrine
is particularly crucial when changes in the environment are unexpected (as
opposed to expected; Yu and Dayan 2005). Consistent with this hypothesis
are observations that manipulations of norepinephrine affect performance on
paradigms in which behavioral change is driven by unexpected uncertainty,
such as those measuring extra-dimensional set shifting (Robbins and Roberts
2007). Extra-dimensional set shifting requires subjects to shift attention from
one dimension of multidimensional stimuli (e.g., shape) to another (e.g., col-
or), and might be particularly appropriate for modeling search processes due to
the requirement to identify and evaluate different response strategies based on
alternate sets of stimulus features.

Conversely, it has been argued that behavioral change signaled by expected
uncertainty is mediated by acetylcholine, a hypothesis that is consistent with
observations that cholinergic changes are associated with attentional shifts in
Posner-like attention-orienting paradigms where subjects are aware of cue invalidity (Hasselmo and Sarter 2011). In contrast, cholinergic manipulations
generally leave extra-dimensional set shifting unaffected. This general distinction between the norepinephrine and acetylcholine systems fits with observations on intra-dimensional reversal learning in response to changes in
reward contingencies: late, but not early, reversal learning (i.e., when changes
are expected) is sensitive to acetylcholine, but not norepinephrine (Robbins
and Roberts 2007). Accordingly, both increases in (tonic) norepinephrine and
acetylcholine may align attention with a source of sensory input, perhaps by
enhancing sensory thalamic input to the prefrontal cortex and by shutting
down current top-down internal models held online by the prefrontal cortex
(Hasselmo and Sarter 2011; Chamberlain et al. 2006; Yu and Dayan 2005).
However, the signals that trigger this norepinephrine- and acetylcholine-mediated shifting might differ, with only the former type of shifting (i.e., that
triggered by unexpected uncertainty) being relevant for search as defined here.

In addition to dopamine and norepinephrine, serotonin is also critical for
search initiation, as evidenced by its implication in behavioral extinction
(Walker et al. 2009), which depends on behavioral change in response to unexpected uncertainty. Specifically, Walker et al (2009) have shown that depletion of both dopamine and serotonin in the orbitofrontal cortex of nonhuman

primates (marmosets) impaired extinction of previously rewarded behaviors, albeit in different ways, with serotonin depletion specifically suppressing the exploration of the never-rewarded option, though allowing overall extinction to proceed normally. By contrast, depletion of orbitofrontal dopamine allowed normal exploration of alternatives to occur but greatly retarded extinction.

Finally, we note that the relationship between effects of neurotransmitters and search is complex and nonlinear. In the case of dopamine, it is well established that there is an inverted U-shaped relationship between levels of dopamine receptor stimulation and performance on working memory tasks, whereby both too little and too much dopamine are associated with poor performance (Arnsten 1998). The implication of this observation is that increases in dopamine (e.g., through administration of dopamine-enhancing drugs) will improve performance of individuals with suboptimal baseline levels of dopamine, while impairing performance of individuals with already optimized baseline levels of dopamine. Similar nonlinear functions have been established for Tower of London planning (Williams-Gray et al. 2008), cognitive switching (Cools and D'Esposito 2011), and probabilistic reversal learning (Clatworthy et al. 2009), all involving cognitive search. Furthermore, there are multiple inverted U-shaped functions, so that effects of dopamine depend not only on the baseline neurochemical state of the system, but also on task demands (Cools and D'Esposito 2011; Cools and Robbins 2004). Thus, administration of dopaminergic drugs have been shown to improve performance on one type of cognitive search (i.e., probabilistic reversal learning), while simultaneously impairing performance on another type of cognitive search (i.e., spatial working memory), even within the same individual (Clatworthy et al. 2009; Cools et al. 2001).

Interim Summary

To summarize, we suggest that cognitive search is a goal-directed behavior that can exist across multiple domains (spatial, causal structure, goals, actions) and that a fundamental aim of a cognitive search is to reduce the unexpected (or estimation) uncertainty present at any of these levels. The search process itself can be compartmentalized into five general stages: initiation; outlining of the to-be-searched options; deliberation and evaluation; action planning/selection; termination. A theoretical depiction of how search could be structured based on what we know of neural function and specialization, is outlined in Figures 9.1 and 9.2.

A rise in unexpected uncertainty, represented in the brain within the anterior cingulate, parietal and inferior frontal cortices, can provide the trigger for search initiation. Comparator computations, such as those performed within the hippocampus and anterior cingulate, may make a critical contribution in terms of detecting outcomes which deviate from what was expected. Dopamine

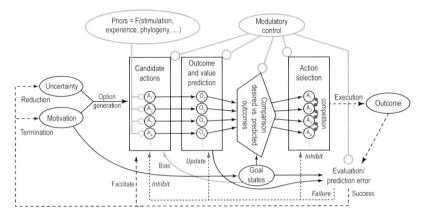

Figure 9.1 Functional circuit for cognitive search. The search process is initiated by a basic motivation or need, such as hunger, combined with an uncertainty about how to attain this goal. This leads to the generation of a number of candidate strategies for how to resolve this situation. The candidate options generated depend on the currently present sensory input, prior experience, biological biases, etc. A prediction for the outcome and value attained by choosing any particular option is generated, which is then compared to the desired goal state. This will narrow down the pool of candidate options. In a competitive process, the option is selected that is most strongly favored by biases, prior experience, proximity of predicted outcome to the goal, etc. The selection of the appropriate actions and thereby the execution of this option will lead to an actual outcome, which is then evaluated with respect to the desired goal state, yielding a prediction error signal. Depending on the sign of this signal, action, value, and outcome representations will be updated. In case of failure, the action will be inhibited for subsequent selection, whereas in the event of success, uncertainty will be reduced and the need may be resolved. At any stage, these processes may be modulated to widen or narrow, for example, the scope of the search.

signals, which are thought to carry prediction error information, can likewise play an important role at this stage. Motivational states, such as hunger or fear, can also stimulate an environmental search, and these are signaled by a broad range of brain systems, including the amygdala. The set of to-be-searched options is identified, and the neural structures involved may vary by the type of information under scrutiny; the hippocampus, for example, is involved in representing searchable spatial or temporal representations. However, the anterior cingulate may play a relatively unique role at this stage in that it appears to represent diverse sets of information that are relevant for the task at hand.

During the deliberation phase, predictions regarding the outcomes and values of these options are generated and evaluated in terms of whether they are likely to meet the goals of the search. Key areas of frontal cortex, such as the dorsolateral and orbitofrontal cortex as well as the hippocampus, ventral striatum and caudate putamen, play distinct roles in this process. Again, the anterior cingulate is implemented due to its involvement in conflict and prediction error monitoring. Once the most promising option has been identified, the

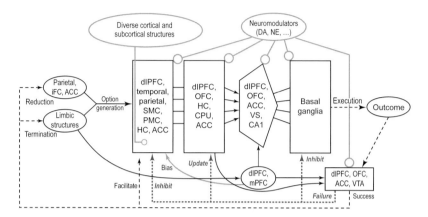

Figure 9.2 Anatomical circuit for cognitive search. This schema illustrates how the functional processes described in Figure 9.1 may map onto anatomical structures. ACC: anterior cingulate cortex; CA1: region of hippocampus; CPU: caudate putamen; DA: dopamine; dlPFC: dorsolateral prefrontal cortex; HC: hippocampus; iFC: inferior frontal cortex; mPFC: medial prefrontal cortex; NE: norepinephrine; OFC: orbitofrontal cortex; PMC: premotor cortex; SMC: supplementary motor cortex; VS: ventral striatum; VTA: ventral tegmental area.

actions required to execute this strategy are determined largely through competition within the basal ganglia, but also via input from the dorsolateral frontal cortices, as well as premotor and supplementary motor cortex, if the motor sequence is complex. The final outcome of the search is then evaluated, a phase which recruits similar regions involved in comparison processes at other stages of the search, and the search process terminated if either the motivational state is resolved or uncertainty reduced. The neuromodulators dopamine and norepinephrine may be particularly important in multiple aspects of the search process due to their ability to influence cognitive flexibility and arousal, but other neurotransmitters such as serotonin may also play a role. Optimal levels of these neurotransmitters may vary for different types of search depending on the precise cognitive processes involved.

Pathologies of Search Processes

Examination of deficits in patients with focal lesions (e.g., in the prefrontal cortex) begins to inform us about the mediation of specific neural components of the search process. In general, patients with prefrontal cortex lesions are impaired in search-like situations that benefit from the application of strategy or structure to the problem, such as the Tower of London (Shallice 1982). For example, impairments in the application of strategy in a self-ordered spatial search task have been observed in patients with focal lesions in the lateral prefrontal cortex, but not in temporal lobe lesion patients (who nevertheless exhibit mnemonic deficits on the task; Owen et al. 1990). Further examples of the role of the prefrontal cortex in search focus on retrieval or generation strategies as exemplified by verbal fluency and alternate use (divergent-thinking) tasks (Eslinger and Grattan 1993). Frontal patients are impaired in imposing a strategy on category and letter retrieval, even though their semantic lexicon is relatively intact (Baldo et al. 2006). Moreover, functional neuroimaging studies have strongly implicated the lateral prefrontal cortex in memory retrieval processes involving recall and/or selection of either verbal or nonverbal material (Badre and Wagner 2002; Cabeza and Nyberg 2000; Thompson-Schill et al. 1997). Frontal patients have difficulty not only with searching the past, but also with "searching the future," and the left frontal cortex is thought to underlie such "mental time travel" (Nyberg et al. 2010).

By contrast, patients with brain damage in the parietal cortex can exhibit deficits in search-like processes ("neglect"), not because of a problem with imposing structure or strategy, but rather because of a basic spatial representational deficit, leading to a restricted set of options available for search (Vossel et al. 2010). Moreover, some patients with predominantly posterior cortical lesions in the left hemisphere experience forms of apraxia that may resemble search deficits, but can be understood in terms of difficulty with retrieving semantic representations of actions.

Patients with medial temporal lobe lesions exhibit difficulties in cognitive search (Hassabis et al. 2007) and tend to use action-selection systems that do not depend on search processes. Some have suggested that this deficit occurs due to deficits in stored memory representations (Squire 1987; Buckner and Carroll 2007). Others have suggested that this deficit arises from a problem in the construction of novel conjunctions of representations, particularly of episodic representations of the potential future options (Hassabis et al. 2007; Buckner and Carroll 2007). Both suggestions are controversial (Atance and O'Neill 2001; Sutherland et al. 2011; Holland and Smulders 2011; Nadel and Moscovitch 1997).

Problems with search-like processes also surface in a wide variety of neuropsychiatric and neurological disorders, which are characterized by a more diffuse pattern of neuropathology but striking functional deficits. For example, certain symptoms of obsessive-compulsive disorder, depression, Parkinson's disease, schizophrenia, addiction, and attention deficit hyperactivity disorder can be interpreted within the current theoretical framework. In the case of depression, for example, the search space might be restricted as a result of negative and affective biases that limit the capacity to recall information or generate future options (Beck et al. 1979; Sutherland et al. 2011; Lloyd and Lishman 1975; Murphy et al. 1999). By contrast, such affective biases may be required for normal socio-emotional decision making (Damasio 1994), including moral judgments. These may go awry in proactive aggressive disorders, like psychopathy (Blair 2008; Blair and Mitchell 2009). Thus psychopaths may search an abnormally wide range of options in a way that is not constrained by social rules of affective biases, such as disgust, empathy, and fear.

Obsessive-compulsive disorder provides some particularly interesting potential applications of the current framework. On one hand, obsessive-compulsive disorder can be characterized as a failure to complete a search, particularly in the domain of obsessions, leading to excessive checking or monitoring behavior and "worrying," possibly as a consequence of anterior cingulate dysfunction (Schlosser et al. 2010). On the other, there is some evidence that the normal balance between A–O knowledge and habitual knowledge is biased toward the latter (Gillan et al. 2011), likely reflecting the known orbitofrontal-striatal dysfunction present in obsessive-compulsive disorder (Menzies et al. 2008).

Addiction can also be characterized in terms of a narrowing of effective goal states. Thus the search for drugs occludes that for other goals that drive adaptive behavior, such as food and social interaction (Hyman and Malenka 2001). Whether this is due to motivational deficits, search process deficits, or other problems is still unknown and controversial (Altman et al. 1996; Redish et al. 2008). Finally, delusional symptoms in psychosis, including schizophrenia, can also be cast in terms of the current framework. Specifically, these symptoms of "abnormal beliefs" have been argued to reflect a search-like disturbance in constructing causal models of the world, which can lead to inappropriate "jumps to conclusions" (Fletcher and Frith 2009). The anterior cingulate cortex shows reduced error signaling in schizophrenia (Carter et al. 2001), and subsequent work showed that these reduced error effects stem from an underlying deficit in the ability to predict the consequences of an action in schizophrenia (Krawitz et al. 2011).

Concluding Remarks

Our aim was to consider cognitive search in such a way that would allow some hypotheses to be generated regarding its underlying neural and neurochemical bases. As is often seen, when evaluating the contribution of behavioral neuroscience to the larger field of psychology, consideration of the biological underpinnings of search helped to critically inform the discussion as to the nature of the search process itself. At the outset of this discussion, we defined search as a goal-directed behavior which could be parsed into five key stages. Although few studies have addressed the biological basis of cognitive search per se, careful consideration of the psychological constructs implicated at each stage has allowed for the creation of a model that reflects the neural circuitry so far identified in mediating these subprocesses.

When exploring the rationale for this model, data were considered from a range of experimental paradigms, including human imaging studies, neuropsychological assessment of brain-damaged patients, lesions, and electrophysiological studies in animals. The evidence from these disparate fields largely overlapped in pinpointing which brain areas may be responsible for performing the specialized functions we identified as inherent in the search process. The ability of researchers to record ongoing neural activity while animals are performing certain goal-directed behaviors clearly allows advances to be made in determining how particular computational functions (such as the calculation of prediction errors or the generation of comparisons) may be accomplished at a neuronal level. Computational modeling theories continue to evolve, and their ability to approximate, decode, and predict both single cell, network, and population activity is constantly improving. Our understanding of how our brains are capable of implementing complex processes, such as a cognitive search, will certainly benefit from this growing field.

While the anterior cingulate cortex appears to be crucial to so many of the stages of search identified here, particularly with respect to evaluation of ongoing behavior, questions still remain as to how expectancies are generated and interpreted within this and other brain regions. Although it seems fairly well established that dopaminergic firing can signal prediction errors, which area(s) provide(s) the critical inputs that drive those predictions? How does neuronal activity within the anterior cingulate shape the prediction error signal, or change as a result of its detection? If the anterior cingulate is already crucial for many phases of search, what are the additional functions of the striatum?

Current data also suggests that the dopamine system does much more than carry prediction errors, yet this signal has proved particularly amenable to investigation at both the neuronal and behavioral levels of analysis. Understanding how drugs and chemicals can influence, and are influenced by, neuronal and cognitive function remains an important goal of neuroscience research, particularly with regards to improving treatment options for psychiatric illness. Models which capture how neuronal circuits are modified by the tonic and phasic firing patterns generated not just by dopamine neurons, but by neurons that produce norepinephrine and serotonin and other neurotransmitters, may be heuristically useful in guiding experimental design in this field. Such models depend on continuing evaluation of drug effects on behavior and brain function, experiments which are highly informative in their own right.

We have been proscriptive in specifying how cognitive search might operate in the mammalian brain; namely, in the context of goal-directed action. We have indeed eschewed what might turn out to be only superficial comparisons with behavior in many species that is ostensibly goal-directed, but which has not been subjected to rigorous experimental tests of its goal-directed nature. It is nevertheless possible that the physical basis of search processes postulated here as contributing to goal-directed search might be related to more general biological processes. Only very high-level descriptions of what search processes entail will ultimately be able to address this issue. In the interim, a useful strategy will be to compare the nature of the search processes for the various components we have defined as contributing to goal-directed search, most of which depend on distinct neural networks. Such comparisons will determine whether similar neurocomputational principles are implicated, and hence whether there are fundamental aspects of search mechanisms in the brain held in common.

Mechanisms and Processes
of Cognitive Search

10

Visual Search

Jeremy M. Wolfe

Abstract

This chapter considers the range of visual search tasks, from those involving very brief-ly presented stimuli to those involving search processes that extend over many days. Most of the discussion centers on "classic" visual search tasks, as studied in the lab. Here, observers look for targets in displays of varying numbers of distractor items. The efficiency of these search tasks is driven by how effectively attention can be guided toward target items. Guidance, in classic search, is based on *preattentive* processing of a limited set of attributes (e.g., color, size). Thus, if the target is known to be red, attention can be guided to red items. If it is known to be big and red, both features can guide attention. Some of the rules of the human visual search engine are described and consideration is given to how these rules apply or change when moving from "classic" search tasks to real-world search tasks. Connections to other search literatures, includ-ing foraging and memory search, are highlighted.

Introduction

> Now, said Sir Gawaine, I will make here avow, that tomorrow morn, without longer abiding, I shall labour in the quest of the Holy Grail, that I shall hold me out a twelvemonth and a day, or more if need be, and never shall I return again unto the court till I have seen it more openly than it hath been seen here; and if I may not speed I shall return again. —modestly edited from Malory (1470/1998, Book 13, Chapter 7)

Now that is a visual search! A target item, the Holy Grail, has been shown to the observer before the trial. The search will prove to have plenty of distractor items including shields, tombs, and a castle of maidens. It has an estimate of a response time on the order of a year and a somewhat ambiguous stopping rule (based on success—"speed"—or lack thereof). This somewhat fanciful example stakes out one end of a continuum of visual search, as illustrated in Figure 10.1.

The continuum is laid out on a coarsely logarithmic timescale that covers everything from stimuli flashed for a fraction of a second to tasks that might

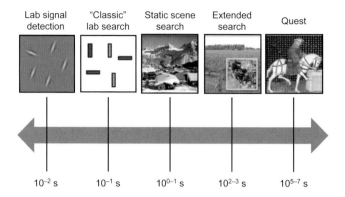

Figure 10.1 The temporal continuum of visual search tasks.

extend over many days. In this chapter, the bulk of specific details will come from the realm of "classic" visual search tasks. These are tasks where observers search for a target among some number of distractor items, usually distributed more-or-less randomly on a computer screen. This is the source of most of the details for the simple reason that it is not practical to collect thousands of instances of searches that last for days or even for minutes. However, the real-world behavior that we are trying to understand often operates at these longer timescales. After reviewing classic visual search, I will turn to issues that arise when we try to scale up from classic laboratory tasks. When we try to scale up, we will find important connections with other aspects of search covered in this volume.

Classic Visual Search

In classic visual search experiments, observers search for a target among some number of distractors. Typically, the target is present on 50% of trials. In some cases, targets might be present on all trials. In these cases, observers might be asked to localize the target or identify some mark on it. The measures of greatest interest are usually the response time (RT) and the slope of the RT versus set size function. Error rates are important but are typically considered as contaminants of the pattern of RTs. Ideally, error rates are relatively low in these experiments. RTs and slopes are of interest because they vary systematically with the search task. Figure 10.2 shows three search tasks and some corresponding data. The first column shows a version of a *feature search*, where the target is defined by the presence of a sufficiently salient basic feature (here color). It does not matter how many "trees" are in the display and it does not matter much if the target is present or not. RT will be nearly independent of set size, so the slopes will be near zero for both target-present and target-absent

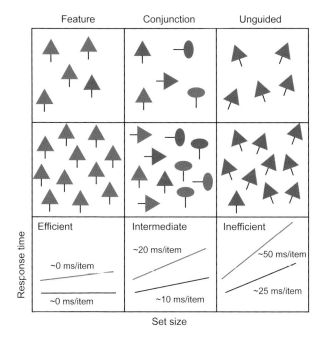

Figure 10.2 Three search tasks. In each case, the target is a vertical, brown "coni-fer." The top two rows show examples with smaller and larger set sizes. The bottom row shows cartoon versions of corresponding data. In the Feature column, the target is defined by a single, unique feature (brown). In the Conjunction column, the target is the only item that is brown, vertical, and triangular. In the Unguided column, the target is defined by the basic feature, vertical orientation, but identifying this is made difficult through the presence of distractor orientations tilted to the left and right of the vertical target.

trials. The general interpretation, held for many years (Donderi and Zelnicker 1969; Egeth et al. 1972; Neisser 1963) is that these features can be processed in parallel. *Parallel processing* is a theoretical claim. A theory-neutral approach to the description of the data is to label these results as "efficient."

In other search tasks, RT increases roughly linearly with the number of items. The most straightforward version of such a search is perhaps one in which it is necessary to fixate each item before it can be identified; for ex-ample, a search for one particular small letter among others. Since the eyes can fixate on only three to four items per second, this imposes a slope of ~125 ms/item for target-present trials and ~250 ms/item for target-absent attempts. These slope predictions are based on an assumption that this search would be (a) serial, (b) self-terminating (so target-present search would stop when the target was found, on average after looking at half the letters), and (c) would assume that the letters were sampled without replacement (i.e., no refixation on rejected distractors). This third assumption will be discussed later. If the letters are made large enough so that fixation of each item is not a limiting step, then the data in a letter search will look something like the bottom-right cartoon graph in Figure 10.2. There is a wide range of "inefficient" search tasks, where target-present slopes will be in the vicinity of 25 ms/item and target-absent slopes will be roughly twice that.

This pattern has been proposed to reflect serial, self-terminating deployments of attention, most influentially by Anne Treisman in her *feature integration theory* (FIT) (Treisman and Gelade 1980). She argued that a limited set of basic features could be processed in parallel, but that binding those features together required attention and was limited to one act of binding at a time. These binding operations could take place at a rate of about 20 per second or 50 ms/item. Thus, if the target was not defined by a single basic feature, the result in Treisman's original formulation would be a serial, self-terminating search with slopes of about 25 ms/item in target-present and 50 ms/item for target-absent trials.

A critical type of search for this theory is *conjunction search*, an example of which is found in the middle column of Figure 10.2. Here, the target is the same brown "conifer" as in the feature search. However, in the conjunction search, it is not enough to know that it is brown. The example in Figure 10.2 utilizes a "triple conjunction" (Dehaene 1989; Quinlan and Humphreys 1987) in which the target is brown, triangular, and vertical among distractors which share one or two, but not all three, of those features. More typical in the literature are studies of conjunctions of two features: observers might be asked to find the red vertical among green vertical and red horizontal distractors. Regardless of the order of the conjunction, FIT held that conjunctions required binding, and binding required the serial deployment of attention, one item at a time. Other theories challenged FIT's serial/parallel dichotomy (Kinchla 1974; Bundesen 1990, 1996; Palmer 1995; Palmer et al. 2000; Duncan and Humphreys 1989), and the pattern of RTs is far from definitive proof of serial search (Atkinson et al. 1969; Townsend 1971; Townsend and Wenger 2004; Thornton 2002). Indeed, it is the persistence of the serial/parallel debate that led to the proposal to describe slopes with theory-neutral terms on an "efficient"–"inefficient" scale (Wolfe 1998). Calling a set of slopes "parallel" might get you into a fight; calling the same slopes "efficient" should be merely descriptive.

A major empirical challenge to FIT was that many conjunction search tasks produce slopes that are too efficient to be considered as serial and self-terminating (McLeod et al. 1988; Nakayama and Silverman 1986; Wolfe et al. 1989). Insight into the reason for this efficiency can be found in a study by Howard Egeth et al. (1984). They had observers look for a red *O* among black *O*s and red Ns. They found that observers could restrict their attention to the red subset and did not need to search randomly among all the items, even if identifying a red *O* did require an attention-demanding binding operation. In retrospect, this seems commonsensical. If you are looking for your cat in the living room, you do not deploy attention at random even if no unique basic feature defines the cat. You somehow restrict your attention to items with cat-like size, color, etc.

This is the core idea behind the *guided search theory* (Wolfe 1994, 2001; Wolfe et al. 1989, 2011). It has been refined several times, but the core model is a simple modification of FIT. Initial visual processing takes place in parallel across the visual field. Binding and object recognition are strongly capacity-limited: one or maybe a very few items can be bound and recognized at one time. Attention is used to select items for binding or recognition in an essentially serial manner. A limited set of attributes extracted from the early processing can be used to guide attention so that selection is not random.

Top-Down and Bottom-Up Guidance

Guidance of attention exists in two forms: *bottom-up guidance* refers to guidance that is stimulus-driven whereas *top-down guidance* refers to guidance that is observer-driven (i.e., the product of the observer's goals). The feature search in Figure 10.2 (first column) shows an example of bottom-up guidance. When this figure was first presented, I did not bother to mention the identity of the target because it was not necessary. Attention is summoned to an item that is different from its neighbors. In this case, there is only one so the target "pops out." Salience models of visual attention can be considered to be models of the bottom-up component (Itti et al. 1998; Koch and Ullman 1985; Nothdurft 2000; Parkhurst et al. 2002).

Bottom-up guidance is not sufficient for all searches. In the conjunction example of Figure 10.2 (middle column), all of the items differ from their neighbors, making bottom-up "salience" largely useless. However, if you are asked to find horizontal, green conifers, you can somehow configure your visual search engine to guide you to "green," "horizontal," and "triangle." This is top-down guidance. This will allow you to find the target quite efficiently, as indicated by the intermediate slopes of the corresponding RT versus set size functions in the figure. Conjunction search can, in fact, be as efficient as any feature search if the right stimuli are chosen (Theeuwes and Kooi 1994). More recent versions of salience models incorporate top-down guidance (Navalpakkam and Itti 2005).

The distinction between bottom-up and top-down is not entirely unambiguous. Suppose you are searching for any odd-man-out stimulus; for example, the sole red stimulus among green objects, vertical among horizontal objects, etc. When a target happens to repeat in another trial, RT will be a little bit faster for the second "primed" trial. Thus, RT for a red target on trial N will be a bit faster than the RT for a red target on trial $N-1$ (Kristjansson and Driver 2008; Krummenacher et al. 2010; Maljkovic 1994; Wolfe et al. 2003). Does this make it bottom-up (driven by the last stimulus) or top-down (driven by the change in the internal state of the observer produced by the prior stimulus)?

In the context of this Forum, it is interesting to note that the role of guidance in visual search is a lot like the role of retrieval cues in memory search. In both cases, the role is to reduce the search space to a set of items with the correct attributes.

Limits on Guidance

In visual search, effective guidance is very constrained and governed by rules. To begin, as Treisman recognized in FIT, the set of attributes that can be processed in parallel is limited. This is not the place to review that literature fully, but there are probably between one dozen and two dozen guiding attributes (Wolfe and Horowitz 2004). No one questions attributes such as color or orientation. However, debate persists about candidate attributes like faces and emotional expression (e.g., Hershler and Hochstein 2005, 2006; VanRullen 2006).

Of equal interest, guidance, even by an uncontroversial feature, is different to the perception of that feature. Consider the unguided search (third column) of Figure 10.2. The target is the same vertical, brown conifer; when present, it is the only vertical item. It is easy to tell the difference between a vertical tree and one tilted to the left or right by 20 degrees. However, the search for a vertical target among ±20° distractors will be reliably inefficient (Wolfe et al. 1992). The rule is that search is hard when the distractors flank the target in the feature space (e.g., reddish orange targets among red and orange distractors [Bauer et al. 1996; D'Zmura 1991] or medium targets among big and small). An exception to that rule comes when targets are categorically unique. A target that is the only "steep" orientation or the only "left-tilted" orientation will be relatively easy to find (Wolfe et al. 1992), and similar effects occur in color (Daoutis et al. 2006).

Perceptual "salience" is not the same as guiding salience. Figure 10.3 is a colormetrically uncontrolled demonstration of a very carefully colormetrically controlled experiment (Lindsey et al. 2010). Look for the five desaturated targets of different colors. In the experiments, desaturated targets were perceptually exactly between their white and saturated distractors. Moreover, the perceptual differences between red and its desaturated pink were made to be equal to the differences between blue and light blue, green and light green, and so forth. With everything carefully equated, it turns out to be much easier to find the desaturated red and orange items than any other colors. It is interesting that the best colors are "skin" colors and the very best seem to be blushing skin (Changizi et al. 2006), but that could be mere coincidence. For present purposes, the important point is that you cannot infer the guiding properties of stimuli, simply by looking at them. A pale blue and a pale red may each lie exactly in between white and a saturated version of the blue or red. However, in a search task, the pale red will be much easier to find than the pale blue. Similarly, your mother's face may be a very salient stimulus for you, but it will not pop out in an array of other faces.

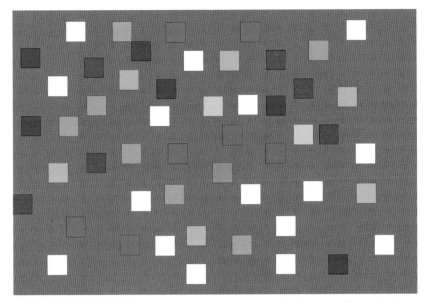

Figure 10.3 Look for the desaturated targets. Even with these uncalibrated colors, you may find that it is easier to find desaturated red and orange than blue, green, or purple.

Other constraints speak to the structure of objects or the "proto-objects" (Rensink 2000b) that exist "preattentively." Consider the field of "tents" in Figure 10.4. These are all color × color conjunctions. If you look for the tents that are half-red and half-yellow among red-blue and blue-yellow distractors, that search turns out to be quite inefficient. Apparently, you can only specify one value for each object attribute at a time: one color, one orientation, etc. (Wolfe et al. 1990). However, you can break this rule if your object has subordinate and superordinate parts. Thus, the red tent with the yellow door is quite easy to find (Wolfe et al. 1994). The tent that has blown over by 90° stands out, but the tent that is upside down (180° rotation) is less obvious. Preattentive proto-objects do not seem to represent the "top" and "bottom" of oriented objects very well, even when, like these tents, they have a top and bottom. Thus, for purposes of visual search, a 90° rotation is "bigger" and more salient than 180° (Wolfe et al. 1999).

The parts of preattentive objects hang together tenaciously, but the bindings of features to those parts are not available until you attend to the object. Thus, in Figure 10.5, we have two very basic search tasks: (a) find the long green bit among medium and short bits and (b) find the green horizontals among green verticals and purple horizontals. The problem with the second task, the simple conjunction, is that you cannot guide attention to "green" and "horizontal" because *every* item contains a green and purple as well as vertical and horizontal feature in the displayed "plus" shapes. Before attention arrives, the plusses

Figure 10.4 Targets defined by conjunctions of two colors. It is easier to spot a red tent with a yellow door, than to find a red and yellow tent.

have been put together, but you do not know how the colors bind to the component orientations (Wolfe and Bennett 1997; Treisman and Schmidt 1982). The problem with the first simple size search is that your search engine refuses to see the component segments of the lower left cross. It contains the long green segment. Preattentive processing has connected two green segments into the same green bar in each plus. The original segments are lost to the search engine (Rensink and Enns 1998).

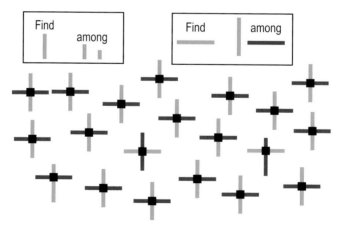

Figure 10.5 Before attention arrives, features are bundled into proto-objects. Thus, it is hard to find a green horizontal element because each object contains green, purple, vertical, and horizontal features.

Thus, when I tell my visual search engine to look for a peach in the fruit bowl, the search engine translates "peach" into a set of guiding instructions which I, the observer, might barely recognize as peach-like. These instructions will be coarser, more categorical, and simply different than the verbal description I might offer for the same object. Moreover, guidance will operate over a set of proto-objects with rules of their own. Returning to the memory retrieval cues analogy, one might wonder if the internal guidance of that search engine has any similarities to visual guidance. In any case, it is worth noting that we do not have any very clear idea about what it means to turn "peach" into guiding instructions. In *guided search* (Wolfe 1994), this is modeled by assuming that the coarse, categorical guiding properties are channels (or receptive fields) whose tunings are coarse and categorical. However, that does not explain how we translate the desire to find "peach" or "cat" into the activation of the correct guiding channels.

Memory in Classic Search

Memory and memory retrieval have multiple roles in classic visual search. One of these is seen if one models "inefficient" searches as serial self-terminating searches. Such a model typically implies that rejected distractors must be tagged and remembered so that the observer can quit when the set of all items is exhausted. *Inhibition of return* (IOR) was proposed as the mechanism for this (Klein 1988, 2000). In typical IOR experiments, attention is first directed toward a location or object. If attention is then diverted, it is found to be more difficult to get attention or the eyes back to that location than if attention had not visited there in the first place—an inhibition that can be seen at the neuronal level in some cases (Bichot and Schall 2002).

Horowitz and Wolfe (1998) did an experiment in which items in an inefficient search task were randomly replotted every 100 ms, rendering useless IOR or any other memory for rejected distractors. This dynamic condition would have forced observers to "sample with replacement" from the display. The control condition, static serial self-terminating search, should have been sampling without replacement. Search efficiencies were essentially the same for the static and dynamic cases, though the efficiency of sampling with and without replacement should differ by a factor of two. They concluded that, far from having perfect memory for rejected distractors, "visual search has no memory" (Horowitz and Wolfe 1998). A certain amount of argument ensued (Horowitz and Wolfe 2003; Peterson et al. 2001; Shore and Klein 2000) and the issue has not yet been entirely resolved. However, proponents of IOR now argue that it serves as something like a *foraging facilitator* (Klein and MacInnes 1999), which keeps search biased toward new items. Almost no one argues for perfect memory for rejected distractors.

Stopping Rules

This raises the very vexing question of stopping rules in search: When does an observer abandon an unsuccessful visual search? Readers of this volume will find that this is a ubiquitous problem in a wide range of search tasks. In visual search, the results of the debate over memory for rejected distractors effectively eliminated the idea that search ends when every item has been examined. That was never a good model. It had nothing to say about the slopes of target-absent trials for more efficient search tasks (e.g., conjunction or feature search) where exhaustive searches on target-absent trials were clearly not occurring. Simple versions of exhaustive stopping rules would predict lower RT variance on absent trials (always quit after N steps) than on present trials (quit after randomly sampling the target in a serial search). This, however, is not the case: RT variance is almost always higher on absent trials (Ward and McClelland 1989).

Much more plausibly, observers will have to set some sort of quitting threshold, and that threshold will need to be based on the observers' experience with the task. What should be thresholded? In the Chun and Wolfe (1996) model, the internal search engine monitored the quality of remaining items. Once the *activation value* of the best remaining item fell below threshold, it was time to stop. A straightforward version of this model assumes memory for rejected distractors. Wolfe and Van Wert's (2010) model assumes a time threshold. A diffusion process of some sort (Ratcliff 1978; Brown and Heathcote 2008) accumulates toward a boundary, and if that boundary is hit before a target is found, the observer stops with a "no" response. Timing models are made more difficult by variation in set size. Absent trials with small set sizes will end before large set size trials. The threshold (or the rate of diffusion, or the starting point) needs to be tied to an estimate of set size. This is not trivial in classic search once the number of items gets above the subitizing limit of about four items. It is very hard to implement for search in real-world scenes where the concept of set size may not be well defined. Zenger and Fahle's (1997) threshold was based on the observers' willingness to accept a distractor as a target—"imperfect rather than incomplete search"—but this is largely a model of errors, not RT.

The *stopping rule problem* in visual search is very clearly related to the same question in memory search where there is also a diversity of candidates; for instance, Davelaar and Raaijmakers (this volume) list (a) total time spent retrieving, (b) time since last retrieved item, (c) decrease in retrieval rate, and (d) number of retrieval failures.

The *patch-leaving problem* in the foraging literature has similar concerns: When is it time to quit this patch and move on to the next? (For a discussion, see McNamara and Fawcett, this volume; Bond 1981; DeVries et al. 1989; Pyke et al. 1977; Wajnberg et al. 2000.) Turning from the field back to the computer, a Google search will generate a deep stack of links. How far down the list should the searcher go (see Fu, this volume)?

In many of these domains, the setting of the stopping rule is based on the searcher's experience with the task. In visual search, evidence for this dependency comes from examination of the sequence of RTs. Especially when observers get reliable feedback, target-absent RTs decrease modestly after correct responses and increase more markedly after errors (Chun and Wolfe 1996). Note that this does not explain what is being adjusted internally but rather makes it clear that stopping rules are being adjusted in a dynamic manner.

Prevalence Effects and Classic Search at the Airport

The classic lab visual search task is, of course, very artificial. We like to think that it probes basic processes used in many real-world search tasks but, most of the time, the real world is not presented in discrete, independent trials of a second or two in length. There are exceptions, and airport baggage screening is one of the more interesting examples. Airport screeners look for threats using X-ray images of bags that contain a variable number of objects. A decision has to be made about a bag in a few seconds. There are important differences between airport screening and classic lab search. Obviously, the stakes are much higher at the airport, and the task is much more difficult than the average lab task. The observers are trained experts, but perfectly reliable feedback is not given. Finally, the targets are very rare. True threats occur on a vanishingly small proportion of trials (fortunately!). Threats do appear because they are electronically inserted into the image at a low rate as a form of quality control (the exact rate is not specified for security reasons).

What is the effect of low prevalence on search behavior? In early work, it markedly increased miss errors in the lab (Wolfe et al. 2005). This could be a speed-accuracy trade-off brought about by the mechanics of the stopping rule. With targets being very rare, you can successfully say "no" very quickly without making many errors. Indeed, some of the errors might simply have been pre-potent motor responses (Fleck and Mitroff 2007). A speed-accuracy trade-off would appear as a decline in signal detection measures of performance like D'. However, in subsequent work with harder tasks, D' proved to be quite stable with changes in prevalence. The effect of prevalence appeared as a criterion shift. As targets became rare, missed errors increased but false alarm errors decreased (Wolfe et al. 2007). Basically, observers are less likely to identify an ambiguous stimulus as a target if targets are very rare. Thus, two aspects of observers' behavior are changed by feedback from the search task (see Figure 10.6).

When attention is used to select an item, that item becomes the stimulus for a two-alternative forced-choice (2AFC) decision. Is it a target or is it not? In many, if not most, classic search tasks, this is a trivial decision, but if the stimuli are ambiguous, as in baggage screening, this is a signal detection task where the balance of miss and false alarm errors is set by a criterion. If the 2AFC answer is yes, an overall "yes, target is present" response can be generated;

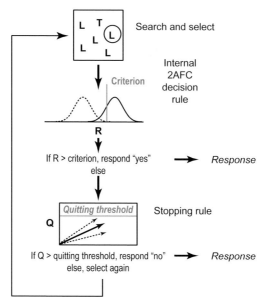

Figure 10.6 A flowchart model showing two types of decision in visual search tasks: a two-alternative forced-choice (2AFC) decision about the identity of each selected item and a stopping rule. Here R represents the internal response to a target (the signal distribution on the right) or distractor (the noise distribution on the left); Q measures an internal quitting signal that diffuses toward a threshold. Search is terminated when the value of Q exceeds that threshold.

otherwise, a second decision must be made about stopping. As noted above, this can be modeled as accumulation of a signal toward a quitting threshold. If the accumulator hits the bound, an overall "no" response can be generated; otherwise, the process cycles. Prevalence and other factors, such as reward structure (Healy and Kubovy 1981), influence both the 2AFC decision criterion and the quitting threshold (Wolfe and Van Wert 2010).

Signal Detection Search Tasks

The presence of an embedded 2AFC signal detection process inside the standard, classic search task provides a link between classic search tasks and a substantial body of work that typically involves search stimuli presented for a fraction of a second, rather than being visible until a response is made (the leftmost category on the continuum of Figure 10.1, lab detection signal). In these experiments, the measures of interest are usually accuracy and derived measures like D', rather than RT. Moreover, the theoretical perspective of this work generally considers the entire display as one signal detection problem (Palmer et al. 2000; Verghese 2001). Consider search for a target of one orientation among distractors of other orientations: Why does accuracy decline as set size increases, which it will when target-distractor orientation differences are not too large and displays are brief? If a single item is presented briefly, then this is a classic 2AFC signal detection task. If multiple items are present, then each item distractor will generate some noise. If response is based on the sum of signal and noise across the display (SUM rule), then more distractors means a poorer signal-to-noise ratio. If the response is based on a decision made about the item producing the biggest internal activation, more distractors mean a greater a chance that the largest activation comes from a distractor or, on a blank trial, that a distractor produces an activation above the criterion for a "present" response. These and other possibilities can be teased apart through careful psychophysical experimentation. Similar methods can be used to assess the sources of noise in the search process (Dosher et al. 2010) or the fine-grain effects of attention within the visual system (Carrasco and McElree 2001).

Returning to Figure 10.6, the signal detection approach to search may be telling us about the details of the first steps in a more extended, classic search. The entire stimulus is processed in parallel to make the selection that is the subject of that first 2AFC decision in Figure 10.6. If the process is truncated at that point and a decision is demanded, it might be a decision about the field of signals that were about to guide selection, or it could be a decision about that selection. Those working in this tradition do not generally put much stock in covert deployments of attention. They would replace the covert "selection" step in Figure 10.6 with an overt eye movement step and might conceive of the signal detection step as a decision about the current fixation (e.g., Najemnik and Geisler 2005, 2008). Indeed, an emphasis on the importance of eye movements can also be seen in some work within the classic lab search paradigm (Zelinsky 2008).

Interim Summary

Signal detection methods are the atom-smasher experiments of the visual search enterprise. They are not very similar to the search task that might occur in the world outside the lab, but they can reveal the inner workings of the process. Combined with classic search experiments (and a great deal of neurophysiology, not touched upon here; see Itti et al. 2005) a general picture emerges:

1. There is too much information to process fully at one time. Thus, through selection by covert deployments of attention (or overt eye movements), only a small part of the input is passed to object recognition processes at any one moment.
2. The "small part" is probably an object or proto-object (Goldsmith 1998), and the system can most likely handle 20–30 of these per second.

3. A limited set of basic attributes, processed in parallel across the field, can be used to guide selection so that those 20–30 items can be picked intelligently if useful basic feature information is present.
4. Search is an iterative process of deciding about the status of each selected item and selecting again if the item is a distractor.
5. The process need not be a strict set of steps. Items could be selected while other items are bound and recognized. The whole process could be more like a "car wash" or "pipeline" (Murdock et al. 1977; Wolfe 2003). That being the case, the distinction between "serial" and "parallel" accounts of search is, at best, blurred.
6. Finally, there must be a stopping rule of some sort, responsive to the pressure to get the job done, but not to make too many mistakes.

It is possible to make simulation-style models that can capture a wide range of basic search results (Wolfe 2003, 2007), though it should be noted that the stopping rules never seem to work quite right.

From Screens to Scenes

This is all very good, but our goal is not to explain search for isolated items on computer screens. We want to understand search in the real world. Can we generalize from the principles learned in work represented in the two leftmost boxes of Figure 10.1 (lab signal detection and classic lab search) to the wider world? When we move to the middle box of Figure 10.1 (static scene), we move from the world of isolated objects to the world of continuous scenes. This introduces some problems. Consider Figure 10.7: What is the set size? Let us look for "people" in the figure. It is easy to find the man on the path (even though he is represented by rather few pixels). How do you do that? A simple extension of the discussion from the previous sections would say that you "tell" your search engine to find "people." The search engine then defines people in terms of the dozen or two basic features and, because of the diversity of items in a real scene, only very few people-like items are visited by attention. If this were true, then finding someone in this scene should be about the same as finding someone in a random array of diverse real-world objects. However, it turns out that search for objects in arbitrary sets—even for very specific objects—is quite inefficient whereas search in scenes appears to be much more efficient, although it is hard to estimate "efficiency" in scenes due to the impossibility of measuring set size.

Scenes introduce forms of guidance not available in classic search. One way of viewing this is to consider the boxes in Figure 10.8. Which one of these boxes could *just* hide a person? All the boxes are the same, so in the absence of the scene, the question would produce a random answer. Here, however, Box 2 is too big and Box 3 is too small because the 3D layout of the scene provides

Figure 10.7 It is surprisingly easy to find the person in this scene. How is this accomplished?

what we can call *depth guidance*. Even without identifying the object, most objects can be ruled out as targets because they are the wrong size. Box 4 can be ruled out because people do not float. This is guidance by scene syntax, the structural constraints imposed by the scene. Alternatively, if you imagine Box 4 as lodged in the tree, it is still probably not a human because humans are unlikely to be in the tree, even if it is physically possible. This is semantic guidance, the meaning of the scene (Vo and Henderson 2009).

Of course, in this case memory tells you that the target is hidden behind Box 1 (Hollingworth 2006). If asked to find a human again, however, you might

Figure 10.8 Which of these boxes could just hide a human, and why?

perform a visual search again, rather than relying on memory, because the costs of searching memory may be greater than the cost of simply performing the visual search again (Kunar et al. 2008).

If airport baggage screeners are professionals performing classic visual search, radiologists might be considered to be the professionals performing scene search (Krupinski 2010). Here, unlike in baggage, the structure of the scene is now critical. Again the targets may be very rare; however, multiple targets can often appear in the same image and it is probably important to find all of them, complicating the stopping rules.

From Looking at Scenes to Searching in Scenes

Work on scene search usually involves search for a target in a static scene, followed by another search in another scene. However, as we move to the fourth box in Figure 10.1 (extended search), consider tasks where the searcher inhabits the same scene for an extended period. Foraging tasks are a good example. A search for clues in a crime scene might be another. Here the main interest may be the stopping rule (or, in foraging terms, the patch-leaving rule). In a foraging task, the observer can collect target after target but at some point, it is time to move to the next patch. The marginal value theorem says that you should leave when your rate of return drops below the average for the task as a whole (Hills and Dukas, this volume). This will depend on the depletion of resource in the current patch as well as on the time required to get to the next patch. There is a substantial animal literature on foraging but very little in the human visual search domain. This is an area of rich potential. Are humans optimal foragers in particular domains? If they are, is this a good thing when they find themselves in other "foraging" tasks with unusual demands? For example, consider intelligence community image analysts, surveying some vast region of the Earth's surface. They must forage in one patch or area and then move to others if they are to ever get through the task, but they may also be under instructions to find "everything" of interest. How does pressure to maintain the rate of return in foraging interact with the demand to be exhaustive? Problems of this sort will touch on many of the search domains represented in this volume.

Finally, as we move to the fifth box in Figure 10.1 (quest), this need for a multidisciplinary approach to studying the search problem only grows. Here we imagine searches that are prolonged over hours, days, or more. Fluctuations in motivation and alertness become issues. Now the searcher is moving through the environment, even more than in a simple foraging example. Various forms of memory become critical: memory for the layout of the world, memory for previous states of the world, and memory for a possibly complex target or set of targets.

We have reached the boundary of scientific inquiry in visual search. It is probably too much to imagine that there will be vast progress in the study of "quests" in the near future. However, search in scenes is already a very active field, building on the work with classic search tasks, and extended search (e.g., foraging) seems ripe for progress. Even if we are not ready to find the Holy Grail, there are applied search domains from airport security to radiology to satellite image analysis that would benefit from clearer understanding of the fundamental principles of visual search.

11

Human Memory Search

Eddy J. Davelaar and Jeroen G. W. Raaijmakers

Abstract

The importance of understanding human memory search is hard to exaggerate: we build and live our lives based on what we remember. This chapter explores the characteristics of memory search, with special emphasis on the use of retrieval cues. We introduce the dependent measures that are obtained during memory search, such as accuracy and search time, and discuss how these have contributed to our understanding of human memory search. The three phases of memory search (initiation, progression, and termination) are discussed in relation to the strategies employed by the human retriever. Finally, the experimental paradigms used in the memory literature are compared to examples of animal foraging behavior to identify points of contact for developing a general cross-domain understanding of search processes.

Introduction

In the cognitive sciences, human memory holds a special place. The ancient Greeks debated the origins and phenomenology of memory well before psychology existed as a recognized discipline. Within psychology, memory has a checkered past: it has been strongly connected to consciousness, been actively ignored during the behaviorist era, and has subsequently been reinstated as a bona fide topic of investigation. Despite the long history of research in human memory, many questions still remain and others have become more refined based on scientific advancements. In this chapter, we provide an overview of the cognitive components of human memory search.

The importance of understanding human memory search is hard to exaggerate. In everyday lives, people talk with each other about past events. During such conversations, information needs to be retrieved as quickly as possible and preferably be an accurate description of those events. The accuracy of retrieved memories is a critical aspect in legal court cases where prosecution of the defendant depends on eyewitness testimonies. These types of memories are referred to as episodes and episodic memory retrieval and will be addressed in this chapter. Retrieval from semantic memory (i.e., memory for facts and encyclopedic knowledge), such as conducted by a medical doctor when making a diagnosis based on observed medical test results, will also be addressed. These test results will trigger a search through semantic memory for their possible causes. Understanding semantic memory retrieval will lead to an understanding of how medical doctors derive with their list of candidate diagnoses. The speed and accuracy of episodic and semantic memory retrieval has secondary effects on processes that depend on them with potential life-altering or life-threatening consequences.

In the research laboratory, human memory is investigated using a range of memory tasks in a variety of paradigms. These tasks can be roughly categorized as single- versus multi-item recall, free-ordered versus serially ordered recall, and recognition. Episodic recall tasks involve reporting a single or multiple item(s) from a recently experienced event, such as words on a list. Semantic recall tasks involve reporting information from the long-term knowledge base, such as the exemplars of the category *animal*. The type of task used constrains the types of dependent measures that can be obtained. Common dependent measures used in research are memory accuracy, various indicators of retrieval time, confidence, and various derived measures related to memory organization. Here, we focus mainly on free recall paradigms, where information needs to be retrieved from episodic memory. This choice for episodic free recall is primarily due to its nature of allowing the participant maximal freedom to deploy search strategies. Where relevant, we contrast the search strategies with the more constrained semantic recall tasks.

We eschew the discussions on short-term or working memory and the comparisons of competing memory theories. Instead, we highlight the common views on memory search and point to productive areas for further research. We discuss characteristics of memory search and retrieval cues, which are hints that help memory retrieval, and focus on dependent measures that are obtained during memory search, such as accuracy and search time. The termination of an open-ended memory search constitutes our focus in the penultimate section, after which we address other approaches to human memory search that take inspiration especially from the animal foraging literature.

General Characteristics of Human Memory Search

To make our discussion of the general characteristics of memory search more concrete, we offer the following example: Suppose you are in a conversation and someone (let us call him Bob) mentions the film *Enemy of the State*. Bob tries to recall the name of the leading actor but is unable to do so. Let us now assume that you have not seen that particular movie. Bob mentions that the leading role is played by a black actor who is quite famous. You suggest "Denzel Washington" but Bob says no. After a while, you think of the city of Washington, D.C. and other U.S. cities, including Los Angeles. You suddenly remember a TV series about a black family in Bel Air, which prompts you to say: "Oh, it must be Will Smith."

We have all experienced such a situation many times. It represents a prototypical situation of memory search and also reveals some of the key characteristics of memory search processes. First, what is retrieved from memory at a given moment is determined by the cues that are available. Second, through the use of such cues we have some control over what is retrieved from memory. Third, retrieval of the information that we are seeking may be hampered by other similar information in memory (in this example, the name Denzel Washington). Finally, although not in our example, we may give up at some point and decide that further search is useless.

The above example represents a semantic-cued recall task, in which hints (black actor, famous, not Denzel Washington) are given, while you jog your memory. Cues are not always provided by the environment in this manner, and people may generate their own cues (Los Angeles). In contrast, the prototypical paradigm used in the research laboratory is the (episodic) list-learning paradigm, in which a series of items (pictures, words, letters) are presented one at a time to the participant for memorization. After presentation of this list, the participant is asked to report all items that were memorized: the larger the number of items on the list, the lower the probability of recalling each item (e.g., Murdock 1962). Interestingly, the order in which the items are reported and the retrieval latencies reveal much about the search strategies employed by the participant on this task. Generally, memory search is characterized by the use of retrieval cues, the three stages of memory retrieval, and by its sequential, self-terminating nature, which we now discuss in turn.

The Cue-Dependent Nature of Memory Search

Tulving and Madigan (1970) once characterized memory retrieval using the Latin proverb: *Ex nihilo nihil fit* (nothing comes from nothing). This saying points nicely to the critical importance of *retrieval cues*. It is a common assumption in human memory research that when something comes to mind, there is always a triggering stimulus. This may be an external event, such as a question that is asked or a specific remark, but it may also be an internally generated event, such as a particular thought. Over the past thirty years or so, memory researchers have especially emphasized the importance of *context* as a retrieval cue. Thus, being in the same environmental context as during the original event or being in the same physiological state helps the retrieval of information stored in that context. This has been called the *encoding-specificity principle*, which states that successful retrieval is a function of the overlap between the information present at retrieval and the information stored in memory (Tulving and Thomson 1973).

The importance of retrieval cues may be understood if one assumes that what gets stored in a memory trace is a sample of the information that was present in the mind's eye at the time of the original event. Hence, the memory trace includes not just the target event but also any fleeting thoughts and feelings that happen to be present. It is generally assumed that the features present in the retrieval cues determine what is activated from memory. Hence, retrieval cues have two (related) properties: they determine which memory traces are activated (i.e., determine which traces are in the search set) and how strongly a trace within the search set is activated. It is often assumed that the higher the overlap in the features present in the retrieval cues and the stored trace, the more that trace will be activated (Tulving and Thomson 1973); in some recent models, activation is a function of both the number of overlapping and nonoverlapping features (see Shiffrin and Steyvers 1997).

Strategic and Automatic Aspects of Memory Retrieval

Generally, memory search consists of three phases: initiation, progression, and termination. Given a specific set of retrieval cues, the retrieval process is completely automatic in that the activation of memory traces, given a specific set of cues, is an automatic process that is determined by the associative strengths from the cues to the memory traces. This does not mean, however, that we have no control over what is retrieved from memory. Each of the three phases is under strategic control. For example, we have some strategic control over what is retrieved through the choice of retrieval cues. When we are trying to recall a specific name, we may resort to an alphabetic strategy, simply trying the successive letters of the alphabet to see whether one "works" (see Gronlund and Shiffrin 1986). In addition to the choice of retrieval cues, which affects the progression of memory search, there are additional aspects where there is some strategic control, two of which have been discussed in the literature (Raaijmakers and Shiffrin 1981). First, before the actual search process, there is the decision to search or not to search. We may decide on the basis of the information given that a memory search is unlikely to lead to a successful answer and decide not to even make an attempt. It is usually assumed that such a choice is based on a quick evaluation of the amount of activation generated by the available cue information. If this falls below some criterion, we may quickly decide that the answer is unlikely to be found so that a search process would be futile. Second, after an unsuccessful search attempt, we have a choice to either give up or continue the search. If we continue searching, we may decide to change the set of probe cues used (e.g., by including information retrieved on prior search attempts) or maintain the same set of cues.

Memory Search as a Sequential, Self-Terminating Process

Many models for recall are formulated in such a way that the probability of successful recall is given by some analytic formula (some function of, e.g., the study time, the retention interval, and/or the strength of competing memory traces). However, analyses of retrieval latencies (discussed further below) reveal that recall memory is well captured by the assumption that recall is based on a sequential process (Diller et al. 2001; Nobel and Shiffrin 2001). Thus, in theoretical models of recall memory (Raaijmakers and Shiffrin 1981), it is assumed that the retrieval process consists of a series of retrieval attempts. Each retrieval attempt may end with either successful recall, a decision to stop (give up), or a decision to continue the search process. Importantly, the decision to terminate the search process is based on the unfolding of the search itself. In other words, there are typically no external criteria, such as a fixed time limit for retrieval, by which search is terminated. In unlimited time, memory search in recall tasks is self-terminating. We will come back to how terminating decisions are reached later.

Characteristics of Retrieval Cues

Types of Retrieval Cues

As mentioned earlier, retrieval cues consist not just of the test item as presented to the subject, but also of various other types of information. In our example of naming the leading actor in *Enemy of the State*, the additional retrieval cues can be the thoughts generated during the memory search (e.g., "Denzel Washington," "Los Angeles"). Within the list-learning paradigm, these other types of information may further include other items that were presented in close temporal proximity to the target item (e.g., another item on the list), items that have a preexperimental association to the target item (e.g., extralist cues), things the subject thought about while encoding the item (e.g., a mental image formed to connect the list items), the internal physiological state (e.g., if the subject was under the influence of a particular drug during encoding), and the external context (e.g., the room in which the encoding took place).

Each of these types of cues has been shown to affect the probability of retrieving the target item. In list free recall, recalled items are most likely to be followed by recalling other items from neighboring serial positions (Howard and Kahana 1999; Kahana 1996), indicating that one item can cue another nearby in the list. Performance in recall tasks is higher when the physiological state corresponds to the state the subject was in during encoding (Eich 1977, 1980). This has been shown for both emotional states as well as for drug-induced states, even when drugs by themselves have a negative effect on memory. For example, even though alcohol by itself has a negative effect on memory, recall performance is better after (moderate) consumption of alcohol if the encoding also took place while being under the influence of alcohol (Goodwin et al. 1969). Similarly, testing in the same environmental context has a positive effect on recall (Godden and Baddeley 1975). This even holds if the testing is done in a different context but the subject is reminded of the encoding context (e.g., by giving a photograph of the original context; Smith 1979).

Effectiveness of Retrieval Cues

Whether or not a specific retrieval cue is effective depends on a number of factors. The two most important ones are (a) the strength with which the cue is associated to the target item, and (b) the number of other terms that are also associated with the cue.

The first factor corresponds to what is often termed "memory strength" and is considered to be a function of the number of matching features between the cue and the memory trace, and possibly the number of mismatching features (see the REM model; Shiffrin and Steyvers 1997). The second factor has been termed the size of the search set. The search set can be defined as the set of retrieval candidates that are activated in response to retrieval cues. An effective retrieval cue will be one that limits the search set to a few memory traces (including, of course, the target trace). The opposite happens when cues activate a large set of distracting traces (Anderson 1974; Watkins and Watkins 1976). There also appears to be a general rule such that if a cue does not lead to additional focusing of the search (decreasing the size of the search set) that cue will not lead to an increase in memory performance.

Cue Combination

Given specific values for the associative strengths of a cue to the memory traces, memory models specify some kind of rule to translate these strengths into a predicted probability of recall. This could be some negative exponential function (as in the ACT model; Anderson 1983) in which absolute strength is transformed into a probability of retrieval, or a relative strength calculation in which the absolute strength is divided by the total strength of all competing memory traces (e.g., Raaijmakers and Shiffrin 1981). A separate issue, however, concerns what the relation should be when two (or more) cues are combined. Should the search set consist of all traces associated to either of the cues, or only those traces associated to both cues? An empirical answer to this question was obtained by Humphreys et al. (1991). In a semantic memory task, they showed that when two cues were given in combination, the search set (the number of items compatible with both cues) was limited to exactly one and the probability of retrieving the answer was very high; when either cue was given by itself, retrieval probably was much lower. Nairne (2002) points out that to be effective, the additional cues should have more overlap with the target item than with distracting information.

From these findings we may conclude that the search set should be more or less equal to the intersection of the search sets evoked by each cue separately. Such a mechanism explains why the probability of finding an answer increases as we are given more relevant (and diagnostic) information (more retrieval cues). Formal models of memory, such as the *search of associative memory* or SAM (Raaijmakers and Shiffrin 1980, 1981), have incorporated such a mechanism through the assumption that the activation of a trace, when multiple cues are given, is a function of the (weighted) product of the associative strengths to each cue separately.

Cue Switching/Updating

Although in some search models it has been assumed that the cues are determined at the start of the search process, a more realistic assumption is that information that is retrieved during the search process may subsequently be used as an additional cue or may replace one of the cues used thus far. In the SAM model for free recall, for example, it was assumed that an item recovered during the search would then be used as an additional cue to make it easier to retrieve items that had been associated to the recovered item during the initial study. Similarly, in the models proposed by Kahana and his associates (see Howard and Kahana 1999), it is assumed that contextual information retrieved during the search is used to update the contextual retrieval cue used in subsequent searches. In many models of serial recall, contextual cues represent the list position and are updated during the retrieval process (Brown et al. 2000; Burgess and Hitch 1999; Henson 1998). Therefore, these models assume that the unfolding of context information during retrieval is independent of the retrieved items. Contemporary models that tackle both serial and free recall tasks (Anderson et al. 1998; Brown et al. 2007a) have yet to resolve this distinction.

The updating of cues based on retrieved information leads to clustering across recalled items. For example, in episodic free recall tasks, in which list words are drawn from multiple semantic categories, participants tend to use the category label (which they generate internally as recall proceeds) as a retrieval cue to recall list items in clusters, first from one category, then another, and so on (Patterson et al. 1971; Tulving and Pearlstone 1966). This pattern is also seen in the semantic fluency task, in which participants are asked to report as many animal names as possible in a given time (Bousfield et al. 1954; Bousfield and Sedgewick 1944). Participants tend to cluster the animals by subcategories, such as zoo animals, pets, and aquatic animals. Thus, cue updating/switching seems to be present in searching for multiple items in both episodic and semantic memory. This search behavior is what Hills and Dukas (this volume) refer to as area-restricted search in internal environments (see also Stephens et al., this volume).

The three phases of memory search (initiation, progression, and termination) apply to each retrieval cue, making the entire memory search consist of a hierarchy of cue-related retrieval. Both levels of the hierarchy have a signature in memory accuracy and retrieval time to which we turn next.

Memory Accuracy

From the beginning of experimental investigation into human memory search, the focus has predominantly been on the accuracy (and its derived measures) of memory search, possibly due to the easier method of collecting such data for accuracy than for latencies. Despite the wealth of data of memory accuracy, questions and debates exist regarding the processes that underlie the data. Here we highlight three such findings for the list-learning paradigms.

First, when participants are instructed to report any items that come to mind, in addition to retrieving items from the list, participants may (a) retrieve items from previous lists, (b) report items related semantically or phonologically to target items, and (c) repeat items that were already reported. With normal instructions, these errors are relatively rare. Evidence for this view comes from studies (Kahana et al. 2005; Unsworth et al. 2010) in which participants reported anything that comes to mind during the retrieval period. In those studies, large numbers of intrusions are produced that are related to the items from the list. Thus, without the explicit instruction to report everything that comes to mind, a filtering process occurs after generation of the items. Despite its importance, this filtering process has yet to be unraveled. Initial attempts involve using existing processes, such as recovery in the SAM model, as the locus for memory filtering (Kimball et al. 2007; Sirotin et al. 2005).

Second, memory accuracy can be conditionalized as a function of the input list position, leading to serial position profiles with increased accuracy of free recall for items from the beginning and end of the list (primacy and recency effects, respectively). The common view is that primacy effects are due to extra rehearsal of the early items (but see Tan and Ward 2000). A long-standing debate questions whether recency effects in immediate free recall reflects retrieval from a short-term store. Formal models that argue against the existence of a short-term store (Brown et al. 2007a; Howard and Kahana 2002) attribute all recency effects to the encoding-retrieval match combined with changing episodic context. Because the context gradually changes during encoding of the list items, recent items are encoded in a context that is more similar to the context at retrieval than are earlier items, and this gradient of contextual similarity underlies the recency effect. Models that also include a short-term store (Atkinson and Shiffrin 1968; Davelaar et al. 2005; Raaijmakers and Shiffrin 1980, 1981) attribute recency effects in immediate free recall to a more accurate readout from the short-term store. The debate centers around the need to postulate a short-term store to account for data (for reviews, see Davelaar et al. 2005; Sederberg et al. 2008).

Third, memory accuracy can be conditionalized against the distance between the serial positions of the previously retrieved item and the current item. A robust finding in free recall is the observation that successively reported items were presented in close proximity during encoding (Kahana 1996). In other words, when retrieving a word from list position n, the next word that is retrieved is more likely to be from position $n + 1$ or $n - 1$ than $n + 2$ or $n - 2$. This supports models that include a changing context representation (Estes 1955; Howard and Kahana 2002; Mensink and Raaijmakers 1988). In addition, this so-called lag-recency effect is asymmetric with the forward transitions (e.g., $n + 1$) being more likely than backward transitions (e.g., $n - 1$). This asymmetry has been explained in terms of preexperimental context being retrieved and incorporated in the ongoing changing context during encoding and retrieval (Howard and Kahana 2002). Detailed predictions from these assumptions are still heavily debated using formal modeling (Farrell and Lewandowsky 2008).

Memory Retrieval Time

Memory search takes time, and the profile of memory search latencies have been used to address a number of questions regarding the dynamics of retrieval. Here, we review some temporal variables and their impact on theorizing.

Cumulative Retrieval Functions

As early as the 1940s, researchers focused on the cumulative recall function (Bousfield and Sedgewick 1944). This function sets the total number of items retrieved so far against the time spent in memory search. This function is shown to be well described by a cumulative exponential:

$$N(t) = N_{asy}^{*}\left[1 - \exp(t / \tau)\right], \tag{11.1}$$

with recall asymptote N_{asy} and mean latency τ (Bousfield and Sedgewick 1944). Researchers theorize that this good fit of a cumulative exponential is indicative of a system in which items are sampled with replacement, tested, and reported if they have not already been retrieved (Indow and Togano 1970). If there is a finite-sized pool of retrieval candidates, sampling-with-replacement leads to a diminishing rate of sampling-yet-unretrieved items.

The sampling-with-replacement process has become a critical element in theories of human memory search. The important assumption is that to obtain an exponential cumulative retrieval function, retrieved items should be independent of each other, which is not the case when, for example, retrieved items are clustered. Deviations from exponential functions have been observed and discussed in terms of the dependence among retrieved items, both in semantic retrieval tasks (Bousfield et al. 1954) and episodic retrieval tasks (Patterson et al. 1971). In addition, deviations from exponential functions are also observed when participants employ specific strategies within cued categories (Gronlund and Shiffrin 1986; Indow and Togano 1970).

The actual process by which resampling can occur is still unclear. Three options can be discerned in the literature. First, the sampled item remains activated to the full extent given the retrieval cue (Davelaar 2007; Indow and Togano 1970). Second, the sampled item receives a decreased sampling probability that is still above some baseline level. This approach features in models of serial recall, which use a competitive queuing process (for a review and comparison, see Davelaar 2007) that is employed to produce sequential output. Third, the sampled item is increased in strength, making it more likely to be resampled. This increment is explicitly modeled in SAM, as a free parameter, allowing SAM to hover between the first and third options. Related to the third option is the proposal that a sampled item is re-encoded in memory, but in a separate trace (Laming 2009; Nadel and Moscovitch 1997). As retrieval continues, this sampled item has an increased opportunity to be resampled, even though the strength of each trace is unaltered. The different options do make different predictions with regard to retrieval latencies, which future research may elucidate.

Interresponse Times

In addition to a global cumulative retrieval function, the time between successive retrievals is a further temporal variable of great importance in studies of memory search. Several studies have analyzed the intricacies of interresponse times (IRTs) (Murdock and Okada 1970; Patterson et al. 1971; Rohrer and Wixted 1994; Wixted and Rohrer 1993, 1994). The main finding is that in episodic retrieval, the IRTs increase with more items retrieved. Rohrer and Wixted (1994; see also Rohrer 1996) presented evidence to suggest that the IRTs follow a pure-death hyperbola, in which the mean ith IRT equals the mean retrieval latency τ (across all items) divided by a number of items still in the finite-sized search set. This inevitably implies that at any given time the size of the search set can be estimated by the size of the IRT.

The validity of estimating search set size from IRTs was initially tested by manipulating list length, presentation duration, and proactive interference (Rohrer 1996; Rohrer and Wixted 1994; Wixted and Rohrer 1993). The method was subsequently applied to verify the loss of memory traces in patients with Alzheimer's disease (Rohrer et al. 1995) and the decreased rate of retrieval in patients with Huntington's disease (Rohrer et al. 1999). IRTs have been found to be sensitive to whether items are retrieved from episodic or semantic memory (Rohrer 2002), suggesting that the relations among items need to be considered in deriving conclusions based on IRTs. This is most prominently demonstrated in the categorized recall task (Patterson et al. 1971) mentioned earlier, in which within-cluster IRTs are much faster than between-cluster IRTs.

Total Time and Exit Latency

Apart from the temporal microdynamics, two further measures of retrieval time have been utilized in recent years. Dougherty and Harbison (2007) modified the standard free recall paradigm to allow participants to indicate when they have finished memory search. The instructions were given before the experiment, allowing participants to calibrate their internal system for the task. This slight modification produces a measure of total search time (i.e., the time from the start of the recall phase to the time of stopping) and the exit latency (i.e., the time between the onset of the last retrieved item and the time of stopping). The total time increases while the exit latency decreases with the number of items retrieved. These two additional measures have proven to be vital in our understanding of how memory search terminates, as we describe next.

Memory Search Termination

After a series of retrieval events, a person may decide to terminate memory search. In list recall tasks in the laboratory, participants may have various reasons to stop searching memory, such as wanting to receive the experiment payment for minimal effort, a lack of desire to help out in research, or a genuine feeling that further memory search will not lead to retrieving any more list items. When decisions, such as making a medical diagnosis, depend on short-listing potential candidates, prematurely terminating the memory search for those candidates may have dire consequences (but so may searching too long in time-critical cases). Finding out how a person decides that further memory retrieval is futile relies on new paradigms and analyses, and may involve incorporating ideas from related areas, such as decision making.

Stopping Rules in Memory Search and Decision Making

In research on decision making, stopping rules are seen as an important factor in deciding effectively. Essentially, a stopping rule is needed to terminate an ongoing process (e.g., searching for information) so that a response can be generated. Here lies the important difference between the vast literature on stopping rules in decision making and the limited literature on stopping rules in memory search.

Browne and Pitts (2004) make a distinction between choice problems and design problems. Choice problems are characterized by the goal of choosing one out of several candidates. When the process stops, a single response is registered. Design problems are characterized by the goal of producing as many new responses as possible. When the process stops, the retriever has decided that further search will not produce any new responses. Problems studied in the decision-making literature are often of the first type, although there is considerable research on decisions made in what could be considered a hybrid fashion, first involving searching for one or more cues, with stopping rules indicating when enough cues have been found to select a single option (Gigerenzer et al. 2012). Memory paradigms such as recognition memory, which require a single yes/no response, are also categorized as choice problems. This is in contrast with the recall paradigms discussed above which involve the generation of multiple responses and can thus be categorized as design problems.

Sophisticated methods exist to investigate the type of stopping rules used in memory tasks that require a single response, such as the *systems factorial technology* (Fific et al. 2008; Townsend and Nozawa 1995; Townsend and Wenger 2004). These methods have yet to be further developed to deal with stopping rules in memory paradigms that require multiple responses. In those tasks, participants employ a stopping rule aimed at producing as many items as possible. When memory search is terminated, the retrieved information may be used in a second step that involves selection among the retrieved items. Thus in a medical decision-making task, the medical doctor will employ two separate stopping rules: one for memory search to maximize the number of candidate diagnoses retrieved (a design problem) and one for selection to maximize the accuracy of final diagnosis (a choice problem).

Optimal Stopping

To understand the problem faced by the human retriever, it is useful to set memory search for multiple items against a wider set of related stopping problems that may inform optimal rules for design problems. The first is the rank-based sequential decision-making task, commonly known as the "secretary problem." In this task, a person interviews and ranks secretaries, one at a time. After each interview the person has to decide whether to hire the just-interviewed secretary or continue to the next one. Once a decision to continue is made, this secretary is taken off the list of candidates. The stopping rule aims to maximize the probability of hiring the best secretary out of those interviewed. As stopping results in a decision, the problem is a choice problem (for a review, see Freeman 1983). Even though people might use a satisficing (aspiration-level-based) stopping rule for both memory search and rank-based sequential decision making, the structural similarity between the problems is low. The best secretary may be anywhere in the sequence of interviewees, whereas the memory item that best matches the cue(s) will be activated most strongly and thus retrieved first.

The second stopping problem comes up in the capture-recapture approach to estimating the size of a population. Here, an animal is captured from a finite-sized population, marked and returned to the population (sampling-with-replacement), and the probability of recapturing the marked animal can be used to estimate the population size. The most useful rule for deciding when to stop capturing the animals weighs minimizing the cost of capturing animals against the benefit of having a better estimation (for a review, see Nichols 1992). A related capture problem occurs in a debugging procedure in computer science (e.g., Chao et al. 1993; Forman and Singpurwalla 1977). Though such capture problems are similar to memory search in focusing on the yield of found versus unfound items, the details and aims of these problems make them choice problems (a decision about number of animals or remaining bugs is made) rather than design problems. Furthermore, in the bug capture problem, the important difference from memory search is the low probability of occurrence of bugs and the need to take the bug out of the pool of program code (sampling-without-replacement). Nevertheless, the requirement of capture problems to estimate the number of yet-to-be-captured targets may also be important in memory search, though new studies are needed to determine whether people actually make such estimates when retrieving items from memory.

These related stopping problems serve to emphasize the importance of explicitly defining the problem that humans face when retrieving information from memory. The assumptions drawn from the memory literature are that the retrieval process in list-learning paradigms and semantic fluency tasks involves sampling-with-replacement and the aim is to maximize the number of items retrieved while minimizing costs, both violated by the stopping problems just presented. On the other hand, the problems of rank-based sequential decision making and capture-recapture assume that individual candidates are independent of other candidates. For memory search this is an untenable assumption, given the episodic contextual association in all episodic recall tasks and semantic associations in all semantic recall tasks. The influence of the associative structure on stopping rules is a topic for future investigation.

Evaluating Stopping Rules in Human Memory Search

Four stopping rules commonly used in models of free recall were addressed by Harbison et al. (2009). These rules involved thresholds on:

1. total time spent retrieving (Davelaar et al. 2005);
2. time since last retrieved item (Rundus 1973);
3. decrease in retrieval rate (Young 2004); and
4. number of retrieval failures (Raaijmakers and Shiffrin 1980).

To test these stopping rules, Harbison et al. (2009) implemented these rules in the SAM memory model framework and quantitatively fitted the resulting models to data on total retrieval time and exit latency obtained from an open-ended free recall paradigm. The first three rules did not provide qualitative fits to the data. The number-of-failures rule captured the data qualitatively and also provided a strong quantitative fit.

The computational work by Harbison et al. (2009) showed that many computational theories use an implausible stopping rule for free recall. This is not to say that Rule 4 is the true stopping rule. Instead, in the absence of alternative rules that provide such quantitative fits, the number-of-failures rule is the best rule we currently have to describe how humans terminate their memory search. This can be compared with similar evaluative studies (e.g., Wilke et al. 2009) of stopping rules for cognitive search (as opposed to list recall). The deployment of Rule 4 in large-scale models of decision making, such as HyGene (Thomas et al. 2008), also gives better fits to human data on medical decision-making tasks.

An interesting observation is that toward the end of a recall protocol, participants tend to repeat already-reported items (Unsworth et al. 2010). Although this finding is striking, some (Laming 2009) hold that the participant's realization that the same word has already been retrieved triggers the decision to terminate memory search. Further empirical and computational work is needed to address the true causal relationships underlying increased repetitions and search termination.

Other Approaches to Human Memory Search

Our discussion in the preceding sections focused mainly on the mechanisms involved in memory search. These approaches use detailed analyses of memory accuracy and retrieval times. Alternative approaches provide powerful metaphors and analytic tools to further research in mechanisms of human memory search.

Keyword-Based Search Analogy

Human memory search is often likened to how information is retrieved from a database using a search engine with search terms combined by Boolean logic (e.g., *AND* and *OR*). There are, of course, many technical differences regarding the storage and retrieval of information; more informative differences between human memory search and keyword-based search are in terms of the use of cues and keywords. Typically in a search engine, typing keywords *A AND B* will produce information that is associated with both *A* and *B*. Humans, however, may still report *A-notB* items and *B-notA* items. Whereas these intrusions may seem to reveal limitations of the human memory search process, they crucially highlight the utilization of cues. For example, humans seem to interpret *A AND B* as *A OR B*, with a greater weight for *A-and-B* items. In sampling models (e.g., Raaijmakers and Shiffrin 1981), cues are combined multiplicatively, but it is not inconceivable to use an additive rule in which cues are differentially weighted. This would allow modeling the intrusions seen in humans together with the ability to select items that are associated with both cues.

Rational Analysis of Memory Search

A rational approach to human memory can be applied in ways that are similar to what has been done in the decision-making literature. One prominent example is the work by John R. Anderson and colleagues (Anderson and Milson 1989; Anderson and Schooler 1991). In their work, the retrieval of a memory trace is governed by two main factors: a history factor, which describes the pattern of prior use of the memory trace, and a context factor, which underlies the cue-dependency of memory retrieval. These two factors are multiplied to obtain the odds that the particular item is needed and thus will be retrieved. Human memory search is assumed to terminate when the need odds fall below a cost-benefit ratio. Thus far, the theory has been applied to the macrodynamics of memory retrieval, but a full rational analysis that includes temporal microdynamics is yet to be developed.

Animal Foraging

In recent years, researchers have compared search through the cognitive system with animal foraging behavior (Hills 2006; Hills et al. 2009; Hutchinson et al. 2008; Metcalfe and Jacobs 2010; Wilke et al. 2009). This is a very useful comparison and has allowed the wide literature on optimal animal foraging behavior to be integrated with cognitive search. To appreciate the similarities and differences, we recast two memory paradigms in terms of an animal foraging paradigm. The reader is invited to compare these examples with the chapters in this volume by Stephens et al. and by McNamara and Fawcett.

Cued recall memory paradigms could either involve one or multiple cues that result in one or more target items being retrieved. In human memory search, a cue demarcates the search set from which items are retrieved. Therefore, the search set can be compared to a patch of food, with the food items being analogous to the memory items. A task such as semantic fluency (naming as many animal names as possible) can be recast as foraging in a patch of *pets*, then a patch of *zoo animals*, then a patch of *aquatic animals*, and so on (see Hills et al. 2009). In our movie example presented earlier, the cues (black actor, famous) initially pointed to a wrong target item (Denzel Washington). This incorrect item changed the cognitive landscape (via U.S. cities) and opened up a path to the correct patch (a TV series set in Los Angeles) which involves the target item (Will Smith). Given such examples, one can address the question of whether patch-leaving behavior of animals is similar to cue-switching behavior in memory search. Hills et al. (2009) did exactly this and successfully applied a model of patch-leaving behavior to search through semantic memory.

Episodic recall tasks in lab settings typically require an initial step of learning a sequence of patches. These patches may contain a single item or a number of items. The size of the patches is determined during encoding, where strategies, such as rehearsal, lead to larger patches. These patches are connected by episodic links that are expected to follow a contextual similarity gradient. Assuming that all items are not semantically related, the paths among all learned items are only of an episodic nature. At retrieval, a searcher "forages" for the list items using the episodic paths. In free recall, the searcher forages through patches in any order; however, in serial recall, the searcher essentially exhibits trail following along the similarity gradient. Animals that use trail following, such as ants, leave behind chemical traces that gradually fade with time. The memory literature shows that the longer the list of items, the less likely the participant reports the items in serial order, and instead starts retrieval with more recent items (Ward et al. 2010). Therefore, to make the trail-following analogy of episodic recall work, one can hypothesize that episodic traces fade with time (though this raises the question of what to do if the trail fades away completely). However, this is inconsistent with work showing that the contextual gradients remain for a very long time (Howard and Kahana 1999). This example highlights limits to how widely ideas from the animal foraging literature can be applied to human memory search.

Apart from these aspects of the traces that link patches, an obvious distinction between animal foraging and human memory search is that in the latter, all the items have been experienced at least once, whereas animals may search for never-experienced food patches. Therefore, human memory search may be better compared to exploitation behavior in animals. Of course, not all human memory phenomena will be usefully comparable with animal foraging. For example, recognition memory involves a single yes/no response to a probe based on an overall sense of familiarity. This does not appear to involve a search process (Diller et al. 2001; Nobel and Shiffrin 2001) and thus cannot be reasonably compared with animal search behavior.

Information Foraging Approach

An approach to searching for information that is directly inspired by the animal foraging literature and attracts wide attention is information foraging theory (Pirolli 2007; Pirolli and Card 1999). According to this theory, a forager enters a patch of information and stays within that patch until the benefit of staying within that patch (in terms of the rate of gain of valuable information per unit time) falls below the benefit of searching elsewhere. The information foraging approach can be applied to memory search by assuming that each patch represents a subsearch set that is delineated by a retrieval cue. Recent work (Hills et al. 2009; Rhodes and Turvey 2007) suggests that this approach is useful in accounting for the clustering behavior seen in semantic memory retrieval that is known to defy the strict cumulative exponential retrieval function (Bousfield et al. 1954). Applying information foraging theory to more fine-grained temporal dynamics is one of the challenges for the near future.

Concluding Remarks

Over the last 100 years we have seen a remarkable increase in our understanding of how humans search for and retrieve information from memory. We are able to infer, based on profiles of memory accuracy and retrieval times, how the information is organized in the cognitive system and how it is found again. This increased understanding has helped in applications ranging from verifying claims about memory structure in patients with brain damage to shedding light on what makes individuals differ in their memory abilities. It has also fueled healthy debates on the precise interpretations of findings, which in turn has led to a deeper insight in the boundary conditions of particular theories. It is fair to say that without inspiration from considering the diversity of search strategies seen in humans and animals, the study of human memory search would have settled on a single cumulative exponential function of retrieval. The cognition is in the details.

12

Model-Based Reinforcement Learning as Cognitive Search

Neurocomputational Theories

Nathaniel D. Daw

Abstract

One oft-envisioned function of search is planning actions (e.g., by exploring routes through a cognitive map). Yet, among the most prominent and quantitatively successful neuroscentific theories of the brain's systems for action choice is the temporal-difference account of the phasic dopamine response. Surprisingly, this theory envisions that action sequences are learned without any search at all, but instead wholly through a process of reinforcement and chaining.

This chapter considers recent proposals that a related family of algorithms, called model-based reinforcement learning, may provide a similarly quantitative account for action choice by cognitive search. It reviews behavioral phenomena demonstrating the insufficiency of temporal-difference-like mechanisms alone, then details the many questions that arise in considering how model-based action valuation might be implemented in the brain and in what respects it differs from other ideas about search for planning.

Introduction

Theories from reinforcement learning (Sutton and Barto 1998)—the branch of artificial intelligence devoted to trial-and-error decision making—have enjoyed prominent success in behavioral neuroscience. In particular, temporal-difference learning algorithms such as the actor-critic are well known for characterizing the phasic responses of dopamine neurons and their apparent, though nonexclusive, role in reinforcing, or "stamping-in" successful actions so that they may be repeated in the future (Schultz et al. 1997). Because these theories provide a crisp quantitative characterization of the variables learned by these algorithms and the learning rules that should update them, they have proved directly useful in the laboratory, where they have been used to analyze and interpret trial-by-trial time series of behavioral and neurophysiological data (Daw and Doya 2006).

Indeed, these computational characterizations are so precise that they have been repeatedly falsified in experiments (Hampton et al. 2006, 2008; Tolman 1948; Dickinson and Balleine 2002; Daw 2011; Li and Daw 2011; Bromberg-Martin et al. 2010b). The problem may be less that the theories are incorrect where they are applicable, and more that they have a limited scope of application. Anatomically, dopamine neurons project widely throughout a number of areas of the brain, where dopaminergic signaling likely subserves different roles; the temporal-difference theories speak chiefly to its action at only two such targets, dorsolateral and ventral striatum. Functionally, psychologists studying animal conditioning have long distinguished two subtypes of instrumental learning (for full review of relevant psychological and neuroscientific data, see Balleine and O'Doherty chapter, this volume). Temporal-difference theories are closely related to one type: *habitual* learning of automatized responses, which is also associated with the dorsolateral striatum. However, the same theories are unable to explain behavioral phenomena associated with a dissociable but easily confused type of instrumental learning: *goal-directed* learning (Dickinson and Balleine 2002; Balleine et al. 2008). Since goal-directed behaviors are thought to involve evaluating actions via traversing a sort of associative chain, they are also much more relevant to cognitive search.

Recent work has suggested that goal-directed instrumental learning also has a formal counterpart in reinforcement learning, in a family of algorithms known as *model-based* reinforcement learning (Daw et al. 2005; Balleine et al. 2008; Redish et al. 2008; Rangel et al. 2008; Doya 1999). These algorithms are distinguished by learning a "model" of a task's structure (e.g., for a spatial task, a map) and using it to evaluate candidate actions (e.g., by searching through it to simulate potential spatial trajectories). In contrast, temporal-difference algorithms associated with the nigrostriatal dopamine system are *model-free* in that they employ no such map or model, and instead work directly by manipulating summary representations such as a *policy*, a list of which actions to favor.

The promise of model-based reinforcement learning theories, then, is that they might do for goal-directed behavior, cognitive search, and planning what the temporal-difference theories did for reinforcement: provide a quantitative framework and definitions that could help to shed light on the brain's mechanisms for these functions. At present, this project is at an extremely early stage. In particular, while there have been reports of neural correlates in some way related to model-based reinforcement learning throughout a large network (van der Meer et al. 2010; Hampton et al. 2006, 2008; Valentin et al. 2007; Gläscher et al. 2010; Daw et al. 2011; Simon and Daw 2011; Bromberg-Martin et al. 2010b), there is not yet a clear picture of how, mechanistically, these computations are instantiated in brain tissue. Indeed, model-based reinforcement learning is a family of algorithms, including many potentially relevant variants. In this chapter, I will attempt to catalog some of the possibilities by (a) defining the framework and how its components might map to common laboratory tasks and psychological theories, and (b) identifying some of the important dimensions of variation within the family of model-based algorithms, framed as questions or hypotheses about their putative neural instantiation.

Reinforcement Learning and Behavioral Psychology

Goal-Directed and Habitual Behaviors

Psychologists have used both behavioral and neural manipulations to dissociate two distinct types of instrumental behavior, which appear to rely on representations of different sorts of information about the task. Consider a canonical instrumental task, in which a rat presses a lever for some specific rewarding outcome (say, cheese). For this behavior to be truly goal-directed, it has been argued, it should reflect two distinct pieces of information: a representation of the action-outcome contingency (that pressing the lever produces cheese), together with the knowledge that the outcome is a desirable goal (Dickinson and Balleine 2002). Then the choice whether to lever press, or instead to do something else, would rely on a simple, two-step associative search or evaluation: determining that the lever press is worthwhile via its association with cheese.

However, behavior need not be produced this way. An alternative theory with a long history in psychology is the *stimulus-response habit*. Here, the rat's brain might simply represent that in the presence of the lever, an appropriate response is to press it. One advantage of such a simple, switchboard mechanism of choice (i.e., that stimuli are simply wired to responses) is that it follows a very straightforward learning rule, which Thorndike (1911) called the *Law of Effect:* if a response in the presence of some stimulus is followed by reward, then strengthen the link from the stimulus to the response.

Such a simple reinforcement-based mechanism can accomplish a lot; indeed, an elaborated version of it continues to be influential since it lies at the core of the actor-critic and other popular temporal-difference models of the nigrostriatal dopamine system (Maia 2010). The disadvantage of this method is that since "choices" are hardwired by reinforcement and are thereafter not derived from any representation of the actual goals, they are inflexible. Thus, such a theory predicts that at least under certain carefully controlled circumstances, rats will work on a lever for food that they do not presently want (e.g., because they are not hungry).

Although this rather unintuitive prediction is upheld in some situations (e.g., in rats who have been overtrained to lever press, hence the term *habit*), reward devaluation procedures of this sort have also been used to demonstrate that in other situations, rats do demonstrably employ knowledge of the action-outcome contingency in deciding whether to lever press. That is, they exhibit truly *goal-directed* behavior *in addition to* mere habits (Dickinson and Balleine 2002; Dickinson 1985; for a fuller review, see Balleine and O'Doherty, this volume). This research on the associative structures that support instrumental lever pressing offers a more refined and carefully controlled development of an earlier critique of habits, which had been based on rodent spatial navigation behavior. There, Tolman (1948) argued that animals' flexibility in planning novel routes, when old ones were blockaded, new shortcuts were opened, or new goals were introduced, could not be explained on the basis of stimulus-response habits but instead demonstrated that animals planned trajectories relying on a learned "cognitive map" of the maze.

Here, we consider computational accounts of these behaviors from reinforcement learning, focusing mainly on goal-directed action. The standard psychological theory is that these behaviors are driven by particular associations, either between stimuli and responses or between actions and outcomes. Although the reinforcement learning models employ closely related representations, it is useful to keep in mind that operational phenomena—lever pressing may be differentially sensitive to reward devaluation, rats may adopt novel routes in mazes that were not previously reinforced—are distinct from the theoretical claims about precisely what sorts of associations underlie them.

Reinforcement Learning and the Markov Decision Process

In computer science, reinforcement learning is the study of learned optimal decision making; that is, how optimally to choose actions in some task and, moreover, how to learn to do so by trial and error (Sutton and Barto 1998). To motivate subsequent discussion, the framework is laid out here in moderate mathematical detail; for a more detailed presentation see Balleine et al. (2008).

The class of task most often considered, called the Markov decision process (MDP), is a formal, stylized description of tasks which captures two key aspects of real-world decisions. First, behaviors are sequential (like in a maze or chess): their consequences may take many steps to play out and may depend, jointly, on the cumulative actions of each step. Second, the contingencies are stochastic (like steering an airplane through unpredictable wind, or playing a slot machine or a game involving rolls of dice). The problem solved by reinforcement learning algorithms is given an *unknown* MDP—like a rat dropped in a new box—to learn, by trial and error, how best to behave.

Formally, at each time step, t, the task takes on some state, s_t, and the agent receives some reward, r_t, and chooses some action, a_t. States are situations: they play the role of stimuli (e.g., in a lever-pressing task) and of locations (e.g., in a navigation task). Actions (like turning left or right or pushing a lever) influence the state's evolution, according to the *transition function,*

$$T(s,a,s') = P(s_{t+1} = s' | s_t = s, a_t = a), \qquad (12.1)$$

which specifies the probability distribution over the new state, s_{t+1}, given the preceding state-action pair. In a spatial task, the transition function characterizes the layout of a maze; in an instrumental task, it characterizes the contingencies by which lever presses lead to events like food delivery.

By influencing the state, the agent tries to maximize rewards. The reward, r_t, measures the utility of any rewarding outcome that the subject receives on trial t. Rewards depend stochastically on the state, s_t; averaging out this randomness, we define the *reward function* as the average reward in a state:

$$R(s) = E[r_t | s_t = s].$$ (12.2)

For instance, in a lever-pressing task for a hungry rat, the reward would be positive in states where cheese is consumed; in chess, it is positive for winning board positions. Together, the reward and transition functions define an MDP.

MDPs characterize a reasonably broad and rich class of tasks; the main simplifying assumption is the "Markov property" for which they are named: future events can depend on past states and actions only via their influence on the current state. (Formally, the functions R and T are conditioned only on the current state and action.) This is a crucial assumption for the efficient solution of the problems, though there is work on extending reinforcement learning accounts to tasks that violate it (Dayan and Daw 2008).

The Value Function

The difficulty of decision making in an MDP is the complex sequential interactions between multiple actions and states in producing rewards. (Think of a series of moves in a chess game.) Formally, we define the agent's goal as choosing actions so as to maximize his future reward prospects, *summed* over future states, in *expectation* over stochasticity in the state transitions, and *discounted* (by some decay factor $\gamma < 1$) for delay. Choosing according to this long-term quantity requires predicting future rewards; that is, evaluating (and learning) the complex, tree-like distribution of possible state trajectories which may follow some candidate action.

Formally, expected value over these trajectories is defined by the state-action value function:

$$Q^\pi(s,a) = R(s) +$$
$$\gamma \sum_{s'} T(s,a,s') \left\{ R(s') + \gamma \sum_{s''} T[s', \pi(s'), s''][R(s'') + \ldots] \right\}.$$ (12.3)

It measures the value of taking action a in state s by a series of future rewards R summed along a series of states, s, s', s'', ..., and averaged over different trajectories according to the state transition probabilities T.

Note that the value of taking action *a* in state *s* also depends on the choices made at future states; thus the function depends on a choice *policy* π (a mapping from states to actions: like a set of stimulus → response associations, one for each state) that will be followed thereafter.

The value definition may be written in a simpler, recursive form, which underlies many algorithms for solving it:

$$Q^{\pi}(s,a) = R(s) + \gamma \sum_{s'} T(s,a,s') Q^{\pi}[s', \pi(s')]. \tag{12.4}$$

Since Q^{π} measures value with respect to a policy π, it can be used to evaluate actions at a state (conditional on π being followed thereafter) or to evaluate *policies* themselves to try to find the best one; a process called policy iteration. Alternatively, a variant of Equation 12.4 defines Q^*, the future values of the *optimal* policy—optimal because actions are chosen so as to maximize the term on the righthand side:

$$Q^*(s,a) = R(s) + \gamma \sum_{s'} T(s,a,s') \max_{a'} Q^*(s',a'). \tag{12.5}$$

Having computed or learned $Q^*(s, a)$, it is possible to choose the best action at any state *s* simply by comparing its values for each action at a state.

Evaluating Q(s, a)

Broadly, there are two families of approaches to reinforcement learning. Most work in psychology and neuroscience focuses on model-free reinforcement learning algorithms such as temporal-difference learning; these algorithms are the ones associated with the action of dopamine in parts of striatum, mainly because they learn using an error-driven update rule based on a prediction error signal that strikingly resembles the phasic responses of dopamine neurons. Briefly, these algorithms work by directly learning a value function (e.g., *Q*) and/or a policy π from experience with rewards, chaining together observed rewards into long-run expectations by making use of the recursive nature of Equations 12.4 and 12.5. (Since the relationship between temporal-difference algorithms and the brain has been well studied, further discussion will not be given here; for details, see Balleine et al. 2008.)

Temporal-difference algorithms are called *model-free* because they do not learn or make use of any representation of the MDP itself (i.e., the one-step transition and reward functions *T* and *R*). The second family of approaches, *model-based* reinforcement learning, focuses on learning to estimate these functions (a relatively straightforward exercise), which together form a complete description of the MDP. Given these, the value function $Q^*(s, a)$ can be computed as needed, albeit via the laborious iterative expansion of Equation 12.4 or 12.5 into a long, tree-structured sum like Equation 12.3, and then actions chosen to maximize it. (As discussed below, the Markov property helps make this evaluation more tractable, at least if the number of states is small.)

Models and Goals

The model-based versus model-free distinction echoes that between goal-directed and habitual instrumental behaviors (Daw et al. 2005). A model-based agent chooses actions by computing values, making use of a representation of the transition structure, T, of the world (including which actions in which states lead to which outcomes) and the reward function, R, or what these outcomes are currently worth. Because they are grounded in these representations, these choices will adjust automatically to changes in this information via devaluations, contingency degradations, shortcuts, and so on: all of the operational hallmarks of goal-directed behavior.

Conversely, model-free reinforcement learning lacks such a representation: it chooses either directly from a learned policy π, or from a learned representation of the aggregated value function $Q^*(s, a)$. Neither of these objects represents the actual outcomes or contingencies in the task: they simply summarize net value or preferred actions. Thus, like stimulus-response habits, they cannot directly be adjusted following a change in goals.

All of this led to the proposals that the two categories of instrumental behavior are implemented in the brain using parallel circuits for model-based and model-free reinforcement learning (Daw et al. 2005; Balleine et al. 2008; Redish et al. 2008; Rangel et al. 2008). My focus here is on the nature of the less well-understood, model-based part of this architecture.

World Models versus Action-Outcome Associations

In psychological theories, habitual behavior is envisioned to arise from stimulus-response habits. This is directly analogous to reinforcement learning's state-action policy. Goal-directed behavior is thought instead to arise from the combination of action-outcome and outcome-goal value associations. These two constructions roughly parallel the transition and reward functions used by model-based reinforcement learning. However, the transition function generalizes the action-outcome association to a broader class of multistep tasks (i.e., MDPs) in which there are generally no simple one-to-one mappings between actions and outcomes; instead, whole series of actions jointly give rise to a whole series of outcomes, and the goal of the decision maker is to optimize their aggregate value.

In this setting, the action-outcome association is replaced by the one-step transition model $T(s, a, s')$, which describes how likely action a in state s will lead to state s'. Here, s' is playing the role both of an (immediate) outcome, with value $r(s')$ given by the reward model, and also a state in which further actions might lead to further states and outcomes. (It is merely a notational convention that these two aspects of the state are not more explicitly dissociated.)

Thus, many of the richer consequences of model-based choice in an MDP (e.g., flexible planning over multistep paths such as in adopting novel routes in a spatial maze) are not well captured in the context of basic instrumental conditioning. Spatial navigation tasks exercise more of this complexity; indeed, stylized spatial tasks called "gridworlds" are standard test beds for reinforcement learning software in computer science (Sutton and Barto 1998). In this respect, model-based reinforcement learning serves to generalize the careful theoretical developments from instrumental conditioning back into the richer experimental settings where researchers, such as Tolman (1948), first birthed many of the concepts. That said, the action-outcome association as a unit plays a quite literal role in many theories of instrumental choice. For instance, its salience determines the relative strength of goal-directed and habitual actions in Dickinson's (1985) influential theory, and it can often be unclear how to extend these ideas beyond instrumental tasks involving simple action-outcome contingencies.

A more general point is that numerous sorts of behaviors (e.g., instrumental lever pressing, route planning, and explicit planning tasks from human neuropsychology, such as the Tower of London test) can all be characterized in terms of model-based reinforcement learning. However, all such tasks may not exercise entirely the same psychological and neural mechanisms: there may not be a single "model-based" system. Indeed, as detailed in the remainder of this chapter, there are numerous variants of model-based reinforcement learning, and different such mechanisms may contribute to different domains.

Model-Based Valuation

To simplify choice, model-free reinforcement learning solves a rather complex learning problem: estimating long-run aggregate, expected rewards directly from experience. Conversely, the *learning* problem in model-based reinforcement learning is quite straightforward (Gläscher et al. 2010), because it does not attempt to detect long-run dependencies; instead, it just tracks immediate rewards and the one-step transition contingencies. At choice time, these one-step estimates must be, in a sense, strung together to compute long-run reward expectations for different candidate actions.

Thus, the major question for neural instantiations of model-based reinforcement learning—and the one most relevant to cognitive search—is not learning but evaluation: How does the brain make use of the learned model to compute action values? Below, different aspects of this question will be considered.

Parallel or Serial

An obvious approach to model-based evaluation is to start at the current state and compute the values of different actions by iteratively searching along different potential paths in the tree of future consequences, aggregating expected rewards (Figure 12.1). This corresponds to working progressively through the branching set of nested sums in Equation 12.3. But need it work this way?

Equation 12.4 suggests an alternative to this: a straightforward *parallel* neural instantiation (Sutton and Pinette 1985; Suri 2001). This is because it defines the actions' values *collectively* in terms of their relationships with one another and reveals that evaluating any one of them effectively involves evaluating them all together.

Notably, if Equation 12.4 is viewed as defining a linear dynamical system, one in which, over repeated steps, the values on the left side are updated in terms of the expression on the right side, then the true values Q^π are its unique attractor. In reinforcement learning, this is an instance of the value iteration equation, many variants of which are proved to converge. It is reasonably simple to set up a neural network that relaxes quickly to this attractor (e.g., one with neurons corresponding to each state-action pair, connected to one another with strengths weighted by the transition probability, and with additional inputs for the rewards r_s). The addition of the *max* nonlinearity in Equation 12.5 complicates the wiring somewhat, but not the basic dynamical attractor story.

Although this approach may make sense for tasks with moderately sized state spaces, it is clearly not directly applicable to denser domains like chess:

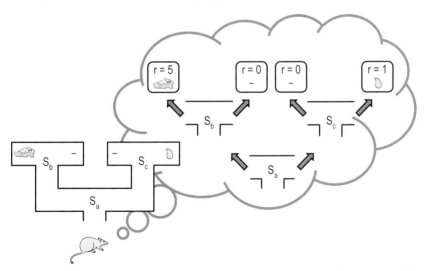

Figure 12.1   Depiction of tree search (after Niv et al. 2006): a rat faces a maze, in which different turns lead to states and rewards. This model-based reinforcement learning method for evaluating different candidate trajectories involves enumerating paths and their consequences through a "tree" of future states and rewards.

it would be impossible, for example, to devote one neuron to each state (i.e., board position). Indeed, the efficient solution of Equation 12.5 by dynamic programming methods (like value iteration) depends on the number of states being bounded so that the size of the tree being explored does not grow exponentially with search depth. Formally, the Markov property ensures that the same n states' values are updated at every iteration, since the path leading into a state is irrelevant for its future conseqences. Hence, the "tree" is thus not really a tree in the graph theoretic sense: it has cycles. By bounding the explosion of the search tree, this property allows for search time to be linear in n and in depth.

When the number of states is too large to allow this sort of global view, selectivity in contemplating states, and probably some degree of serial processing, appears inevitable. In this case, values would presumably be computed for actions at the current state, in terms of its local "neighbors" in the search over trajectories. In neuroscience, at least in spatial tasks, both the behavioral phenomenon of vicarious trial and error (Tolman 1948), whereby rats look back and forth at decision points as though contemplating the alternatives serially, and findings of apparent neural representations of individual prospective trajectories and their rewards (van der Meer et al. 2010) suggest that candidate future routes are contemplated serially, starting from the current position.

Searching and Summing

We may consider the evaluation of Equation 12.5 by a serial search through a "tree" of potential future states, summing rewards over trajectories and averaging them with respect to stochastic transitions to compute action values. Psychologically, controlling such a search and keeping track of the various intermediate quantities that arise clearly implicates multiple aspects of working memory and executive control. In humans, this is consistent with the neuropsychological basis of planning tasks, such as the Tower of London (Robbins 1996).

Notably, for better or worse, the reinforcement learning perspective on search is somewhat different than in other parts of psychology and artificial intelligence. First, the focus in Equation 12.5 is on accumulating rewards over different potential trajectories, so as to choose the action that *optimizes* reward expectancy, rather than on the needle-in-a-haystack search problem of seeking a path to a single, predefined goal, as in planning. The latter perspective has its own merits: it enables interesting possibilities like backward search from a goal, which is not usually an option in reinforcement learning since there is no single target to back up from. The idea of outcomes influencing choice, as by a backward search, may have some psychological validity even in reward-based decision situations. For instance, shifts in behavior mediated by focus on a particular goal are suggested by the phenomenon of cue-induced craving in drug abusers and by related laboratory phenomena such as outcome-specific Pavlovian-instrumental transfer, where a cue associated with (noncontingent availability of) some particular reward potentiates actions that produce it.

Since they do not actually impact actions' values, as defined in Equations 12.3–12.5, simple "reminders" of this sort would not be expected to have any effect if choices were determined by a full model-based evaluation. One way to reconcile these phenomena with the reinforcement learning perspective is: if the full tree is not completely evaluated, then cues may affect choices by influencing which states are investigated.

Indeed, work on search in classical artificial intelligence (such as on systematically exploring game trees) focuses on the order in which states are visited (e.g., depth- or breadth-first, and how branches are heuristically prioritized) and conversely in determining what parts of the tree may be "pruned" or not explored. These issues have received relatively little attention in reinforcement learning. One idea that is potentially relevant to neuroscience is that of multistep "macro" actions, called *options*, which are (roughly speaking) useful, extended sequences of behavior, "chunked" together and treated as a unit. Though they are often used in model-free reinforcement learning, in the context of model-based evaluation, options can in effect guide searches down particular paths—following an entire chunk at once—and in this way bias model-based valuation and potentially make it more efficient (Botvinick et al. 2009). Other search prioritization heuristics use Bayesian analyses of the value of the information obtained, a cognitive counterpart to analyses of the explore-exploit dilemma for action choice (Baum and Smith 1997).

Averaging and Sampling

An equally important aspect of the reinforcement learning perspective on valuation, which is less prominent in other sorts of search, is that transitions are stochastic, and values are thus computed in expectation over this randomness (Equation 12.5). Going back even to early analyses of gambling (Bernoulli 1738/1954), this sort of valuation by averaging over different possible outcomes according to their probabilities is a crucial aspect of decision making under uncertainty and risk of numerous sorts. It is also one aspect of the MDP formalism that is not well examined in spatial navigation tasks, where the results of actions are typically deterministic.

The need for such averaging to cope with stochasticity or uncertainty may have important consequences for the neural mechanisms of model-based evaluation. In machine learning and statistics (though not so much, specifically, in reinforcement learning), problems involving expectations are now routinely solved approximately by schemes in which random *samples* are drawn from the distribution in question and averaged, rather than explicitly and systematically computing the weighted average over each element of the full distribution (MacKay 2003).

Such sampling procedures now also play a major role in many areas of computational neuroscience (Fiser et al. 2010), though again, not yet so much in reinforcement learning theories. Notably, Bayesian sequential sampling models have provided an influential account of how the brain may analyze noisy sensory stimuli, such as judging whether a fuzzy visual stimulus is moving left or right (Gold and Shadlen 2002; Ratcliff 1978). These theories account for both behavior (reaction times and percent correct) and neural responses (ramping responses in neurons in posterior parietal cortex) during noisy sensory judgments by asserting that subjects are accumulating evidence about the stimulus by sequentially averaging over many noisy samples.

Intriguingly, the success of such models appears not to be limited to situations in which there is objective noise or stochasticity in the stimulus, but instead also extends to similar behavior on more affective valuation tasks, such as choosing between appetitive snack foods (Krajbich et al. 2010). This suggests that such tasks—and, perhaps, goal-directed valuation more generally—might be accomplished by sequentially accumulating random samples of the decision variables, in this case perhaps drawn internally from a world model. In the case of model-based reinforcement learning in an MDP, this could involve averaging value over random state transition trajectories rather than conducting a more systematic search.

Caching and Partial Evaluation

Finally, in search over a large state space, the model-based/model-free distinction may be a false, or at least a fuzzy, dichotomy. Although maintaining a world model allows an agent, in principle, to recompute the action values at every decision, such computation is laborious and one may prefer to simply store ("cache") and reuse the results of previous searches. In one version of this idea (the "model-based critic," which has some neural support; Daw et al. 2011), values derived from model search could drive prediction errors (e.g., dopaminergic responses) so as to update stored values or policies using precisely the same temporal-difference learning machinery otherwise used for model-free updates. Then, until relearned from experience or recomputed by a further search, such cached representations will retain their inflexible, model-free character: insensitive to devaluation.

Related algorithms from reinforcement learning, such as prioritized sweeping or Dyna, similarly store values and update them with sporadic model-based searches, even mixing model-based and model-free updates (Sutton 1990; Moore and Atkeson 1993). Neural phenomena, such as the replay of neural representations of previously experienced routes between trials or during sleep, may serve a similar purpose (Johnson and Redish 2005).

Moreover, the recursive nature of Equations 12.4 and 12.5 demonstrates another way that search and model-free values can interact. In particular, it is possible at any state in a search to substitute learned model-free estimates of $Q(s, a)$ rather than expanding the tree further. Again, this will entail devaluation insensitivity for outcomes in the part of the tree not explored.

All of these examples suggest different sorts of interactions between model-based and model-free mechanisms. Thus, although previous work has tried to explain the balance between goal-directed and habitual behaviors (i.e., under what circumstances animals exhibit devaluation sensitivity), by considering which of two separate controllers is dominant, the correct question may be, instead: What triggers update or recomputation of stored values using search, and what determines how far that search goes?

Conclusion

Model-based reinforcement learning extends successful model-free reinforcement learning accounts of the phasic dopaminergic response and its role in action choice to include action planning by searching a learned cognitive map or model. Although this proposal is still in its early days—in particular, the neural mechanisms underpinning such search are as yet relatively unknown—the proposal offers a quantitative set of hypothetical mechanisms which may guide further experimentation, and leverages existing knowledge of the neural substrates for model-free reinforcement learning. Moreover, compared to conceptualizations of search for action planning in other areas of artificial intelligence or cognitive science, model-based reinforcement learning inherits a number of unique and potentially important characteristics from its successful model-free cousin: for instance, mechanisms aimed at optimizing aggregate reward rather than attaining a single goal, and a fundamental focus on coping with stochasticity and uncertainty.

Acknowledgments

I am supported by a Scholar Award from the McKnight Foundation, a NARSAD Young Investigator Award, Human Frontiers Science Program Grant RGP0036/2009-C, and NIMH grant 1R01MH087882-01, part of the CRCNS program. I wish to thank my collaborators on related work, particularly Aaron Bornstein, Dylan Simon, Sara Constantino, Yael Niv, and Peter Dayan, for helpful conversations and ideas, as well as the participants of the Ernst Strüngmann Forum, especially Trevor Robbins and James Marshall, for extensive and very helpful feedback on this manuscript.

13

Cognitive Control, Cognitive Search, and Motivational Salience

A Systems Neuroscience Approach

K. Richard Ridderinkhof and Helga A. Harsay

Abstract

An essential facet of adaptive and versatile behavior is the ability to prioritize actions in response to dynamically changing circumstances, in particular when circumstances require the coordination of a planned course of action vis-à-vis instantaneous urges and extraneously triggered reactions. This chapter focuses on one aspect of cognitive search: the exploration of internal and external milieu for motivationally salient events (stimuli that are novel, ambiguous, infrequent, deviant, or unexpected, or register as a risk for undesirable outcomes or a risk for the exhaustion of resources) which may require appropriate adaptive action. A neurocognitive framework is described for understanding how cognitive control and cognitive search are modulated by motivationally salient events. This framework emphasizes the integration of a salience network in the brain with other large-scale neural networks, neurotransmitter systems, and homeostatic (autonomic nervous system) functioning.

The anterior insula cortex and anterior cingulate cortex are core nodes of a salience network that monitors for motivationally salient stimuli. This framework helps to amalgamate findings from disparate literatures into a common conjecture and highlights the role of motivational salience in modulating cognitive search and cognitive control. The salience network transforms salience signals into an orienting response which serves to recruit the necessary physiological arousal and to engage task-relevant networks (involving attentional, working-memory, and adaptive action selection processes) while disengaging task-negative networks. Using representative examples as instructive points in case, it is argued that this integrative systems-neuroscience framework provides a parsimonious account of salience processing, and may provide novel insights into the neural basis of individual differences among healthy as well as pathological populations.

Introduction

To begin our discussion on the modulation of cognitive control and cognitive search through motivationally salient events, let us discuss what we mean by these terms.

Cognitive control refers descriptively to the capacity to orchestrate, coordinate, and direct basic attentional and cognitive processes and their temporal structure, in accordance with internal goals and or external demands, so as to optimize behavioral outcomes. Such control serves to prioritize our actions, in particular when circumstances require the coordination of a planned course of action vis-à-vis instantaneous urges and extraneously triggered reactions. We often find ourselves confronted with a variety of alluring and potentiating opportunities for action in a particular situation. Our responsiveness to such action affordances is shaped, constrained, and guided by our current concerns, intentions, and prior experience, such that we are not immediately captivated by the one action affordance that presents the most potent solicitation.

Cognitive search has been conjectured to be a central concept in a variety of human and animal behavior (Hills 2006). Cognitive search may range from relatively open to relatively closed search. *Open search* refers to the exploration of the internal and external milieu for motivationally salient events (i.e., stimuli that are novel, ambiguous, infrequent, deviant, or unexpected, or register as a risk for undesirable outcomes or a risk for the exhaustion of resources) that may require appropriate adaptive action. *Closed search* refers to the exploration of the internal and external milieu for specific targets (e.g., an item in long-term memory or an object in a visual scene). Here, we are concerned with the open type of cognitive search. *Motivational salience* is used here as a descriptive term for an emerging construct that unifies how the brain organizes its response to signals that call for adaptive action. Salient events may indicate opportunities (e.g., for obtaining desirable outcomes), but will more often indicate challenges (e.g., a risk for undesired outcomes).

Some situations require immediate, *online* cognitive control. Proficient traffic navigation, for example, requires one to arrest conversation with a passenger when approaching a complex roundabout or to overrule the habit of driving on the right side of the road when navigating traffic in England. Such online control, exerted to suppress and overcome incorrect, inappropriate, or undesirable actions in favor of intention-driven action selection, should be distinguished from the *anticipatory* processes that regulate them (Ridderinkhof et al. 2011). Anticipatory regulation refers to those modulatory processes that either strengthen online control proactively or preempt the need for such online action control. If a traffic accident (e.g., resulting from an experienced tendency to drive on the right side of an English road) was barely avoided, anticipatory action regulation might lead one to tighten online action control to preempt further error.

Orthogonal to this proactive/preemptive dimension, anticipatory regulation may be prospective or reactive in nature. Prospective regulation refers to tightening control in anticipation of demanding situations: one may slow down when anticipating busy traffic or make use of explicit cues or instructions to guide adjustments of processing priorities. In other instances, anticipatory regulation will be more *reactive* in nature; that is, adjustments of online control will be contingent upon alerting salient events. Motivationally salient events require that appropriate adaptive actions are generated immediately, such as when a child unexpectedly crosses the street ahead of an approaching car driver.

Current Aims

In an attempt to advance our understanding of how cognitive control and cognitive search are modulated by motivationally salient events, we aim to describe a neurocognitive framework for appreciating the cognitive and neural bases of salience processing. This framework emphasizes the integration of a salience network in the brain with other large-scale neural networks, neurotransmitter systems, and homeostatic (autonomic nervous system) functioning.

Using errors, error awareness, and lapses of task engagement as points in case, we will argue that this integrative systems neuroscience approach will help us frame salience-driven processes of cognitive search in a unified fashion. We suggest that this framework provides a parsimonious account of salience processing and may provide novel insights into the neural basis of individual differences among healthy as well as pathological populations.

A Systems Neuroscience Approach

Consensus is now emerging that to appreciate the neural underpinnings of salience processing, we need to focus on structural and functional connectivity profiles rather than zoom in on the isolated operations of individual brain regions. Thus, we adopt a systems neuroscience perspective that considers complex and multifaceted functions to arise from the dynamic interactions of distributed brain areas, operating in large-scale networks (Ridderinkhof et al. 2011; Bressler and Menon 2010; Harsay, submitted). This principled perspective may aptly guide our exploration of how coherent structural and functional networks can promote as well as constrain the emergence of salience signaling.

Brain networks can be defined based on structural connectivity or functional interdependence. Neuronal ensembles can be characterized as network nodes if their large-scale structural connectivity patterns are sufficiently distinct from those of other neuronal ensembles. The architecture of structural networks provides the hard-wiring from which functional interactions can emerge in the form of dynamic interactions within and between networks. In humans, structural and functional connectivity profiles are studied using a variety of methods. Using electrophysiological recording techniques, time/frequency analyses of inter-electrode phase coherence reveal the extent of synchrony in neural oscillations between populations (or even very small ensembles) of neurons, with synchronous firing patterns indicating functional connectivity. Using functional magnetic resonance imaging (fMRI), psychophysiological interaction analyses reveal functional coupling between task-related activations recorded from different brain regions. Using resting-state fMRI, analyses of interregional physiological coupling reveal functional connectivity profiles while test subjects are at rest. Using diffusion tensor imaging (DTI), probabilistic fiber-tracking analyses reveal structural connectivity profiles as associated with specific cognitive functions.

Together, these techniques have helped characterize a number of large-scale brain networks. Such networks may be configured dynamically and transiently, in response to current task demands, whereas other networks may be more fundamental and constant, so as to deal consistently and generically with common or recurrent demands.

Generic Networks

Perhaps the most prominent among these generic networks is the default mode network (DMN), a tonically coupled network that will typically display decreased activation during a cognitive task while showing increased activation during task disengagement. The DMN comprises, among other areas, the posterior cingulate, regions in the parietal and medial temporal lobes, and anterior portions of ventromedial prefrontal cortex (Amodio and Frith 2006). DMN is a functional network believed to participate in an organized, baseline "idling" default mode state of brain function. This default mode state comprises a free flow of thought and self-referential processing that is typically suspended during specific goal-directed behaviors (Greicius et al. 2003; Amodio and Frith 2006; Raichle et al. 2001). Interestingly, activation of the DMN is often observed to be suppressed during cognitively demanding tasks, and behavioral performance accuracy increases as a function of this DMN deactivation (Kelly et al. 2008; Weissman et al. 2006). Almost complementary to the DMN is a frontoparietal network, sometimes referred to as the central executive network. The frontoparietal network, with areas in dorsolateral prefrontal cortex and posterior parietal cortex as its key elements, is critical for top-down guidance of goal-directed behavior and is almost ubiquitously reported to be activated during the performance of cognitively demanding tasks (Dosenbach et al. 2007; Menon and Uddin 2010).

Interestingly, the engagement and disengagement of the frontoparietal network and DMN are often reported to be complementary, as if balanced adaptively in response to cognitive demands (Greicius et al. 2003; Sridharan et al. 2008). Yet, their precise interrelationships, their degree of overlap, their interactions, and the functional significance of their anticorrelation is currently subject to theoretical debate and experimental scrutiny.

The Salience Network

A third network comprises the dorsal anterior cingulate cortex (ACC) and the frontal operculum/anterior insula cortex (AIC). This cingulo-opercular network was initially thought to be task-specific, involved in the initiation and maintenance of task set, in task monitoring and error feedback, and in subsequent performance adjustments (Dosenbach et al. 2007). When a similar AIC-ACC network was subsequently identified in task-free states, it was termed the salience network (Menon and Uddin 2010), thought to be involved in orientation to homeostatically relevant (salient) intrapersonal and extrapersonal events.

Von Economo Neurons

Very large brains, such as those of most large (semi-)aquatic mammals—various whales and dolphins, walrus, manatee—as well as a few large land-mammals—African and Asian elephants, and hominoids (humans and great apes, but not other primates)—contain a class of bipolar layer V neurons called *von Economo neurons* (VENs) that are specialized in the high-speed relay of signals across large axons (Von Economo 1926). One feature common to species whose brains contain VENs, in addition to the relative size of their brains, is the apparent richness of their social networks and interactions. Among hominoids, the absolute and relative number of VENs appears to increase as a function of phylogenetic development, and therefore as a function of the complexity of their brains and social behavior rather than merely brain size. Among the great apes, the orangutan has the smallest brain and the smallest social networks and, indeed, the smallest (absolute as well as relative) number of VENs. Interestingly, this phylogenetic evolution appears to be paralleled by ontological development in humans, with VENs not emerging until just before birth, gradually increasing in abundance across infancy, and reaching adult levels that remain relatively stable from early childhood onward (Allman et al. 2010).

In post-mortem stereological analyses, VENs are found in ventral parts of the AIC and rostral parts of ACC (or their homologs), but not much in other parts of the brain, potentially endowing the salience network with the capacity to modulate the activity of other networks rapidly. That the AIC and ACC might act in concert is supported by findings of reciprocal projections in monkeys as well as by recent work confirming the existence of white-matter pathways between AIC and ACC in humans. Resting-state fMRI studies also indicate functional connectivity between the AIC and ACC.

Coactivation of the Anterior Cingulate Cortex and Anterior Insula Cortex

Not surprisingly, the AIC and ACC are often found to be coactivated in functional neuroimaging studies, in particular in response to the degree of subjective salience across domains (Craig 2009; Sridharan et al. 2008). For instance, in the virtual ball-throwing game *CyberBall*, subjects experience social isolation and pain when they are suddenly excluded from the game; this sudden social exclusion triggers immediate activation of the ACC and AIC. Coactivation of these core components of the salience network has been associated with orienting to and facilitating the processing of personally and motivationally salient information, in the broad spectrum of emotional, social, cognitive, sensorimotor, homeostatic, and sympathetic efferent and interoceptive autonomic domains. Within the salience network, AIC appears more specialized in receiving multimodal sensory input, whereas the ACC is connected more to action selection and action execution systems in cortical and subcortical brain regions, allowing the salience network to influence not only attention (to facilitate the further processing of salient signals) but also adaptive action in response to such signals.

Salience Network Function

Identifying motivationally salient stimuli has been proposed as the core function of the salience network; once a stimulus activates the salience network, it will have preferential access to the brain's attentional and working memory resources (Menon and Uddin 2010). That is, once sensory areas detect a salient stimulus, this signal is transmitted to the salience network which in turn generates a control signal to engage brain areas mediating attentional, working memory, and action selection processes while disengaging the DMN. Critically, these switching mechanisms help focus attention on stimuli that signal deviant events or undesirable outcomes, as a result of which they take on added significance or saliency.

Orienting to salient events or states that are associated with motivational significance could take various guises. One may orient attention to extraneous stimuli that call for action updating to secure valued outcomes and avoid undesired outcomes (i.e., stimuli that are novel, infrequent, deviant, unexpected, threatening, or which serve as instructed targets or distractors); one may become receptive to induced emotions or affective states that call for approach or avoidance; or one may seek to monitor one's internal and external milieu for signals that register as a risk for undesirable outcomes (e.g., slips of action, performance errors, response capture, action conflict, negative feedback, punishment, lack of expected reward). In general, the salience network appears to be central to monitoring for specifically those motivationally important changes that require autonomic regulation (Critchley 2009).

The AIC and ACC have direct anatomical connections to the autonomic nervous system, mostly via brainstem nuclei that provide feedback on bodily states and changes in autonomic arousal (Craig 2002). In particular, these cortical areas have robust connectivity to the locus coeruleus/norepinephrine (LC/NE) system involved in boosting and maintaining phasic and tonic arousal (Aston-Jones and Cohen 2005a). The LC is the main NE-generating nucleus in the brainstem, and the LC/NE system is central to regulating the sympathetic discharge and the inhibition of parasympathetic tone in arousal responses. Indeed, salient events are consistently associated with increased pupil-dilation response and skin conductance and with decelerated heart rate, the more so for more unexpected events (Critchley 2005). Taken together, these patterns lend weight to the notion that AIC and ACC are jointly involved in the adaptive regulation of physiological (bodily and neural) arousal states in accordance with current concerns and environmental demands.

Tipping the Balance

These observations provide a starting point for investigating how the salience network might modulate the operation of other core networks. Its functional and structural architecture, at the juxtaposition of cognitive, affective, and homeostatic systems, render the salience network highly suitable for dynamically interfacing other brain networks involved in orienting to salient events or states, on the one hand, and the ignition, guidance, and marshalling of adaptive action, on the other. The salience network orients to salient events or states that are associated with motivational significance and facilitates further processing of these events by recruiting physiological arousal and tipping the balance between brain networks, such that activation and functional connectivity in task-related networks is enhanced in favor of task-unrelated networks. The AIC plays a critical and causal role in engaging and disengaging the DMN and the cingulo-opercular network (Sridharan et al. 2008). This new understanding of the AIC as a critical node for initiating network switching provides key insights into various phenomena related to inter- and intra-individual differences in salience processing, as discussed below. Future efforts aimed at capturing these functions in computational models might help to provide an even more solid footing for this conceptualization in terms of a salience network.

Points in Case

Errors as Salience Signals

Empirical (Notebaert et al. 2009) and theoretical work (Ullsperger et al. 2010) has emphasized notable parallels between the processing of errors and of other rare, deviant, or novel stimuli (or otherwise potentially significant or motivationally relevant events). Erroneous outcomes and other performance problems can be considered as salient events that trigger a reflex-like orienting response in the salience network, which is accompanied by a cascade of central and autonomic nervous system reactions associated with increased autonomic arousal as needed to recruit the mental and physical resources required for adaptive action.

Meta-analyses have shown that the AIC and ACC are consistently reported to be activated during errors and other instances when performance monitoring becomes necessary. Consistent with these observations, indices of autonomic arousal co-vary with conflicts, errors, and feedback. For example, error commission results in robust heart-rate deceleration and enhanced pupil-dilation responsivity, and these changes (which represent the recruitment of arousal so as to prepare the organism for adaptive action) tend to correlate with activity in the AIC and ACC.

In a refined meta-analysis of 55 fMRI studies, Ullsperger et al. (2010) focused on the patterns of coactivation of AIC and ACC across conditions that call for adjustments. Both pre-response conflict (which arises when a stimulus elicits competing response tendencies) and decision uncertainty (referring to situations when information about the correct response is underdetermined) indicate an increased risk of error, but the error might still be countermanded if the conflict is resolved or the uncertainty is reduced in time. These conditions primarily activate the dorsal part of AIC. By contrast, action slips and negative feedback cannot be repaired, but do call for remedial actions, compensating the failure and/or subsequent adjustments improving future performance. These conditions predominantly activate the ventral part of AIC.

The dorsal and ventral AIC tend to coactivate with the dorsal and pregenual ACC, respectively (Seeley 2010). Thus, the different subregions of the salience network appear to play partially different roles processing the salience of errors. The dorsal AIC appears to be involved in signaling increased risk (and hence the anticipation of imminent errors); the ventral AIC appears to register prediction error. Consistent with differential connectivity profiles, the dorsal AIC appears important in prospective control (recruiting the necessary effort to preempt potential risks and failures), whereas the ventral subdivision appears more important for salience processing (monitoring for the need to undertake remedial action and homeostatic regulation) (Lamm and Singer 2010; Ullsperger et al. 2010).

Fluctuations in Task Engagement

Fluctuations in activity of the LC/NE system have been found to index variability in performance efficiency and to co-vary with lapses of task engagement. The phasic LC/NE response has been hypothesized to serve task engagement by providing an orienting signal that triggers the interruption of ongoing processing in favor of the processing of and acting upon the salient event that triggered the response (Aston-Jones and Cohen 2005a). Baseline pupil diameter (before a stimulus) and evoked pupil diameter (after a stimulus) serve as indices for tonic and phasic modes of LC/NE function (Gilzenrat et al. 2010). Following an inverted U-function, the middle firing range of LC, associated with adequate effortful processing, is accompanied by constrictions in baseline pupil diameter and increased stimulus-evoked pupil dilations; task disengagement occurs when the LC firing rate (and associated pupil dilation) is below the phasic middle range. Thus, preparatory autonomic arousal before the stimulus, as indexed by pupil diameter before the participant's response, should account for at least some of the variance in performance fluctuations. Preparatory pupil dilation may thus provide overt indications of task disengagement, presaging performance lapses and failures to balance DMN and task-related networks (Ullsperger et al. 2010).

Indeed, tendencies toward improved performance appear to be foreshadowed in the activation of the salience and task-related control networks, whereas increased activation in the DMN often presage performance lapses (Eichele et al. 2008; Weissman et al. 2006). The AIC might be involved in these preludes to performance fluctuations in terms of preparatory engagement (e.g., through the allocation of cognitive and physical resources) of salience processing and deliberate adaptive control networks while simultaneously disengaging the DMN (Sridharan et al. 2008).

Error Awareness versus Error Blindness

Salience signals sometimes go unnoticed. They might need an appropriate potential in order for them to alert and engage the salience network and tip the balance between other large-scale networks. For example, for errors to elicit an orienting reaction in the salience network, error awareness might be crucial. Performance errors are almost routinely registered in the ACC, even if the individual does not consciously recognize the error as such. However, subsequent post-error slowing and changes in autonomic activity are observed only when subjects were aware of their error (Overbeek et al. 2005; Wessel et al. 2011). Neuroimaging studies confirmed that the AIC and ACC are modulated by error awareness and error blindness (Hester et al. 2005; Klein et al. 2007).

In a recent fMRI experiment, we found that baseline pupil diameter did indeed predict subsequent activity in areas associated with error awareness (Harsay et al., submitted). Specifically, pupil dilation (prior to and after aware errors) co-varied with activation increases in the salience network (ACC and AIC), in task-related areas in the oculomotor network, and with a concurrent deactivation in the DMN. Moreover, pupil dilation before the aware error predicted increased functional connectivity of AIC with oculomotor areas; simultaneously, it also decreased connectivity with areas of the DMN during error awareness. This suggests coordinated activity of AIC with distant brain regions presumably in an effort to amplify the neural salience-signal of the detected error and to preset task-relevant oculomotor structures.

The AIC and its relation to the autonomic response appear to be crucial for error awareness. Errors may elicit an orienting response (Notebaert et al. 2009), which serves to increase LC/NE-based arousal and to recruit large-scale brain networks sufficient to cause conscious experience (Dehaene et al. 2006). In other words, instead of actually becoming aware of the error itself, we may first become aware of the orienting response generated by the salience network (Ullsperger et al. 2010).

Individual Differences in the Normal and Pathological Range

The conjecture of cognitive search in relation to a salience network that can tip the balance between other networks may provide parsimonious insights into the potential for individual differences in cognitive function, both within the normal population as well as among clinical groups. Any impairment of the salience network´s operations or connections might compromise the potential of salient signals to alert and engage the salience network. Here we briefly evaluate the cognitive deficits and neuropsychiatric sequelae that might ensue when the integrity of the salience network is compromised. As an extreme but representative example, we focus on what has come to be known as the behavioral variant of frontotemporal dementia (bvFTD).

Frontotemporal dementia generically refers to a clinical syndrome caused by degeneration of the frontal and temporal lobes from the sixth decade of life onward. Already in the early stages, bvFTD is characterized by atrophy of specific subregions of AIC and ACC within the salience network as well as various subcortical targets; during later stages, degeneration extends throughout the salience network and into neighboring frontal and temporal areas involved in cognitive and affective control (Seeley et al. 2008). Interestingly, and conspicuously, VENs are among the neurons most vulnerable to bvFTD-related atrophy.

During the early stages of bvFTD, patients experience difficulties in representing the salience of social signals, and in using these representations to guide behavior. During later stages, symptoms become more severe and extend to loss of initiative, loss of control over impulsive or compulsive tendencies, and loss of interpersonal consideration (Seeley 2010). Compared to controls, patients with bvFTD show blunted autonomic and behavioral responses in socially embarrassing situations (such as when being shown one's public karaoke performance), loss of theory of mind, loss of care about the social impact of one's own behavior, and loss of empathy. As an apparent common denominator of these deficits, bvFTD patients show deficiencies in the capacity to process the personal significance of salient signals (especially in social contexts), and in using such signals for appropriate adaptive behavior.

Conclusion

The anterior insula cortex and anterior cingulate cortex are structurally and functionally coupled key nodes in a salience network that operates as an integral hub in mediating interactions between other large-scale brain networks involved in cognitive control and cognitive search. The salience network monitors the internal and external milieu for motivationally salient events, marks such events for further processing, recruits the necessary physiological arousal, and tips the balance between other networks so as to generate appropriate behavioral responses. This systems neuroscience framework provides an integrative and parsimonious synthesis of a variety of findings and may provide novel insights into the neural basis of individual differences in salience processing among healthy as well as pathological populations.

14

Convergent and Divergent Operations in Cognitive Search

Bernhard Hommel

Abstract

Human goal-directed action emerges from the interaction between stimulus-driven sensorimotor online systems and slower-working control systems that relate highly processed perceptual information to the construction of goal-related action plans. This distribution of labor requires the acquisition of enduring action representations; that is, of memory traces which capture the main characteristics of successful actions and their consequences. It is argued here that these traces provide the building blocks for off-line prospective action planning, which renders the search through stored action representations an essential part of action control. Hence, action planning requires cognitive search (through possible options) and might have led to the evolution of cognitive search routines that humans have learned to employ for other purposes as well, such as searching for perceptual events and through memory. Thus, what is commonly considered to represent different types of search operations may all have evolved from action planning and share the same characteristics. Evidence is discussed which suggests that all types of cognitive search—be it in searching for perceptual events, for suitable actions, or through memory—share the characteristic of following a fixed sequence of cognitive operations: divergent search followed by convergent search.

Introduction

The phylogenetic development of humans and many other species is characterized by a transition from reactivity to proactivity. In contrast to the dominant experimental paradigm in behavioral and neuroscientific research—where the presentation of experimenter-controlled stimuli marks the starting point of theoretical and empirical analysis—humans rarely await environmental triggers to get going but are instead driven by internal needs, goals, and passions. Proactive behavior guided by internal anticipations and predictions requires executive functions that operate off-line rather than in real time. Indeed, beginning to plan an action only after its execution conditions have been encountered often makes little sense, which is why, for instance, goalkeepers prepare themselves for jumping, catching, and pushing the ball long before they see it coming.

Planning an action in the absence of the object as well as the situational cues to which it relates requires the means to represent and simulate them in advance (i.e., off-line). This calls for cognitive abilities that go beyond what our basic sensorimotor online systems have to offer (i.e., the systems that translate stimulus input into motor output more or less in real time and that we share to some degree with almost all living organisms). In humans and perhaps in other primates, this reliance of planning ahead on longer-term internal representation has promoted the development of a dual-system architecture. In humans, for example, manual actions emerge from the interaction between a stimulus-driven sensorimotor online system (mediated by the dorsal pathway; e.g., Milner and Goodale 1995) and a slower-working (ventral) control system that relates highly processed perceptual information to the construction of goal-related action plans (Glover 2004; Hommel et al. 2001a, b). The emergence of off-line systems did not lead to the replacement of online systems; having both systems provides the opportunity to restrict off-line action planning to the specification of the goal-relevant features of an action but to leave the filling-in of the less important motoric details to the sensorimotor online system (Turvey 1977).

This distribution of labor requires the acquisition of enduring action representations; that is, of memory traces that capture the main characteristics of successful actions and their consequences. I will argue that these traces provide the building blocks for off-line action planning, which renders the search through stored action representations an essential part of action control. In other words, action planning requires cognitive search (through possible options) and might have led to the evolution of cognitive search routines that we now can also employ for other purposes, such as searching for perceptual events and through memory. Thus, what are commonly considered to be different types of search operations may all have evolved from action planning, suggesting that they might share the same characteristics.[1] Indeed, I will argue that all types of cognitive search (be it in searching for perceptual events, for suitable actions, or through memory) share the characteristic of following a fixed sequence of cognitive operations.

---

[1] From the perspective of a cognitive system, there is no logical difference between searching for a visual target; searching through (i.e., retrieving) one's memory of one's last birthday present; searching for (i.e., selecting) an action alternative suitable to produce a particular song by means of a keyboard; searching for a particular metaphor; or searching for the possible uses of a pen. In all these cases, the searcher consults an internal representation of past and/ or present events and matches their content against some sort of search template, which represents the target or intended outcome, until some reasonable match is obtained. In that sense, there is no logical reason to believe that the cognitive operations underlying visual search, memory search, action selection, or the production of options in verbal planning, creativity, or problem-solving tasks differ in principle, and I know of no empirical evidence that enforces this assumption.

Searching for Suitable Actions

Evolution does not care so much about the deep insights and interesting memories an organism may or may not have, but selects instead for appropriate actions. So how do we identify and choose appropriate actions, and how do we tailor them flexibly to the current situational requirements? In view of the dominant stimulus-response paradigm in the experimental analysis of action control and other cognitive processes, it is not surprising that many theoretical approaches to action selection attribute the greatest responsibility in the selection process to the stimulus. Preparing for an action is viewed as the activation of task-relevant stimulus-response rules or associations, which then make sure that processing a task-relevant stimulus leads to the spreading of activation to the associated response code so that this code is likely to win the internal competition for controlling the output (e.g., Anderson 1993; Cohen et al. 1990; Kornblum et al. 1990). Obviously, this approach presupposes either extensive experience of the agent with the task at hand or some sort of instruction describing which rules are acceptable in a given situation—much like in the standard experimental setup. How people choose actions under less constrained conditions and how they can ever act in the absence of stimuli remains unclear (Hommel et al. 2001b).

Carrying out an action presupposes the existence of a goal,[2] the intention to create a particular outcome. This requires some sort of anticipation regarding the action's outcome, some expectation that the action will produce particular effects, and some motivation to produce them. The question of how these anticipations are created and how they guide the eventual selection of one concrete action has been addressed by two different approaches: the *ideomotor approach*, which focuses on the perceptual aspects of action outcomes, and the *motivational approach*, which emphasizes their affective implications.

The ideomotor approach to goal-directed action (James 1890; for an overview, see Shin et al. 2010) assumes that agents automatically register the perceptual consequences of their movements and integrate the motor patterns underlying the movements with the representations of the consequences they produce (see Figure 14.1, left panel). Hence, moving in one's environment is assumed to lead to the acquisition of bidirectional associations between movement patterns and codes of their perceptual outcomes. Given this bidirectionality, agents can then use the associations in either direction and thus intentionally reactivate a particular motor pattern by anticipating ("thinking of") its

---

[2] In this chapter, I make the assumption that all sorts of cognitive search, including perceptual search and action selection, are under the control of goals. How, according to which principles, and by what kind of mechanism goals are searched for and identified will not be discussed. However, it may well be that what I consider a goal is no more than the next level of what is actually a multilayered search-driven decision-making hierarchy. Accordingly, goals might be selected according to the same principles, and by means of the same mechanisms, that are involved in selecting a visual target or a manual action.

B. Hommel

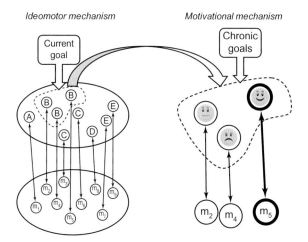

Figure 14.1 Distribution of labor between (A) the preselection of actions (from motor patterns, $m_1 - m_9$) associated with goal-related action effects (B in this example) and (B) the weighting of the preselected actions according to the state they are expected to produce. Chronic goals bias this process toward alternatives which satisfy them; in this example, m_5 is the most likely candidate for execution.

sensory consequences. The ideomotor approach has received ample empirical support. Novel action-produced perceptual effects are indeed spontaneously acquired and integrated with the corresponding action in adults, children, and infants, so that effect-related stimuli become effective primes of that action (for an overview, see Hommel 2009). Brain-imaging studies suggest that the hippocampus provides the bidirectional link between action plans stored in and/or generated by the supplementary motor area and the perceptual representations of action effects in the respective sensory cortices (Elsner et al. 2002; Melcher et al. 2008).

According to the ideomotor approach, translating an intended goal into actual action requires the cognitive representation of the desired sensory consequences or, more precisely, of the sensory implications of the desired effect. Once this representation has been formed or activated, the first step of action selection can be considered a kind of feature match: the desired outcome's sensory consequences (i.e., the description of the action goal) can be matched against the sensory consequences of all the actions in the agent's repertoire (see Figure 14.1, left panel). The result of this matching operation is the activation of all candidate actions that would be suited to create the intended effect in principle, or at least an effect that is perceptually similar.

Identifying action opportunities is commonly not part of experimental analyses, where the options are almost always specified by the task and/or arbitrarily defined by the experimenter. Accordingly, it is not surprising that this aspect of action selection is not very well understood while much more is known about selection of actions from prespecified response sets. Apart from the above mentioned stimulus-centered accounts, which assume some sort of translation of stimulus information into response activation, research on this topic has emphasized two (related) motivational criteria that underlie action selection: reward and efficiency. Generations of learning theorists have pointed out that carrying out some actions provides more reward than carrying out others, and that this is likely to affect the probability with which an action is selected. Recent neuroscientific findings have provided strong support for the idea that action selection is systematically biased by the anticipation of reward or punishment (Schultz 2006) and/or the related affective states (Damasio 1996). Another line of research that has focused on the impact of efficiency on action selection showed that agents prefer action variants that imply less cognitive effort (e.g., Kool et al. 2010) and metabolic cost (e.g., Chapman et al. 2010). If one considers that both reward and efficiency correspond to something like chronic goals and that they are likely to be correlated with specific affective states, these findings seem to fit with the assumption that the anticipation of reward and/or positive affect biases decision making toward the associated action (see Figure 14.1, right panel).

Ideomotor and motivational approaches capture important aspects of the internal search for the action that is best suited to reach an intended goal. Interestingly, the purposes that ideomotor and motivational processes seem to serve are complementary (de Wit and Dickinson 2009): defining which actions would be suited to reach a particular goal (the purpose of ideomotor mechanisms) does not itself provide sufficient criteria for making the eventual selection, whereas comparing candidate goals with respect to the reward they may provide or the effort they require (the purpose of motivational mechanisms) presupposes some rather limited set of action alternatives that are all suitable in principle. This suggests that ideomotor and motivational mechanisms operate in a sequence, as indicated in Figure 14.1, with motivational mechanisms selecting from the set provided by ideomotor mechanisms.

In the present context, it is important to note that this suggested sequence of operations implies a succession of two rather different search modes. Ideomotor mechanisms start with one representation, the description of the goal, and try to diverge and activate as many perceptually related representations as possible. In contrast, motivational mechanisms start with a limited number of representations and then try to converge onto one optimal solution. In the following sections, I will discuss evidence which suggests that

1. convergent and divergent search operations can be found and distinguished in various types of cognitive search, including the search for perceptual targets and the search through memory for problem solutions;

2. all these types of search are likely to consist of a fixed sequence of divergent search operations followed by convergent search;

3. convergent and divergent search are likely to require different configurations of cognitive control.

To substantiate these claims, I will proceed by discussing evidence for convergent and divergent search operations in the context of searching for to-be-perceived objects (e.g., as in visual search), and in the context of searching through memorized objects and events (e.g., as with problem solving). I will conclude by suggesting a rudimentary control architecture that may underlie convergent and divergent search and present some evidence supporting this suggestion.

Searching for Perceived Targets

People tend to spend a great deal of their time searching for objects and other people—just think of parents looking for their kids, or scientists looking for a particular paper that they could swear was on their desk a few minutes ago. Searching for external events has been mostly studied in the visual modality, and there is consensus that at least two different types of visual search exist: feature search (e.g., looking for a red target among green distracters) and conjunction search (e.g., looking for a green X—i.e., the conjunction of the color green and the shape X—among red Xs and green Os) (Wolfe 1994; Wolfe, this volume). These two types of search differ in ease and efficiency: searching for a feature goes fast and is not much affected by the number of distractors, whereas searching for a feature conjunction is slow and highly sensitive to the number of distractors. These different characteristics have motivated the assumption that feature search can proceed in parallel and in a more or less bottom-up fashion, whereas conjunction search requires serial operations that are controlled top-down.

Perceptual search processes are commonly studied and theoretically addressed under complete neglect of action-related processes. The underlying idea is that the control of perceptual search is primarily input control whereas action-related processes deal with output control: two types of control that most researchers consider independent and unrelated (Johnston et al. 1995). Recent observations, however, tend to undermine this implicit conviction. As summarized elsewhere (Hommel 2010), a number of findings suggest that the efficiency of searching for a particular feature depends on the action carried out to signal the presence of the target or of actions that are being planned in the context of the search operation. For instance, searching for shape-defined targets is more efficient after preparing a grasping action, whereas searching for location- or intensity-defined targets is more efficient after preparing a pointing action (Fagioli et al. 2007; Wykowska et al. 2009). Hence, visual search is modulated by, and thus cannot be independent of, action planning.

The reason why action planning and search are related may have to do with the distribution of labor between the off-line perception-action system and the online sensorimotor system discussed above (Hommel 2010). While this distribution makes action planning and execution more flexible, it also raises a number of serious control problems. For instance, how does the sensorimotor system know which information is relevant for steering the motor activity selected by the perception-action system? As Wykowska et al. (2009) and Hommel (2010) have suggested, this problem might be solved by the perception-action system through increasing the gain of feature information coming from action-relevant feature dimensions (see Figure 14.2). For example, when preparing for a grasp, the perception-action system might increase the weight given to feature values coming from feature maps coding for shape and orientation (in addition to some weighting of location codes to end up at the right place), whereas preparing for a pointing action might lead to comparatively stronger weighting of feature values coded on location maps. Interestingly, the stronger weighting of stimulus attributes coded on feature maps that provide task-related information has been assumed to be part of the mechanism underlying the attentional control of visual search processes (e.g., Found and Müller 1996; Wolfe et al. 2003). If the functionality attributed to this mechanism is what action control provides, it makes sense to assume that what we call visual

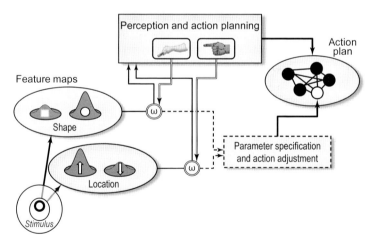

Figure 14.2   A process model of action-induced attention (after from Hommel 2010). Feature maps provide information both for off-line perception and action planning and for online specification of current action parameters. Perception provides contextual information, and action planning prepares an action plan with some parameters specified in advance (forward modeling; see black nodes) and others left for online specification (white nodes). To make certain that online specification uses appropriate information, the perception-action system modulates the output gain ω from the feature maps, so that information from goal-relevant feature maps has more impact on sensorimotor processing.

attention is a phylogenetic derivative of action control (Hommel 2010), which again would render observations of interactions between action control and attention less surprising than it might seem.

If visual attention is really an evolutionary by-product of improving action control mechanisms, one would expect perceptual search processes to show the same characteristics as action control. Thus, if the search for the right action proceeds through a sequence of divergent and convergent search operations, one would expect the same sequence for perceptual search. That seems to be far-fetched at first sight, especially if we consider the classical paradigms employed to study feature and conjunction search. Take, for instance, a display in a typical feature-search task: In what sense would searching for a red circle surrounded by twenty green circles require any sequence of divergent and convergent processes?

Single-cell recordings in monkeys provide considerable evidence for such a sequence (Lamme and Roelfsema 2000). Facing a number of stimuli is assumed to trigger a nonselective (i.e., not yet attentionally modulated) spread of neural activation throughout the visual cortex all the way up to frontal areas—the so-called "fast feedforward sweep." It is so fast that after about 100 ms, even the highest levels of visual coding (i.e., brain systems coding for complex stimulus characteristics and stimulus identities) have responded to a presented stimulus. Neuroscientific methods allowed for following the spread of stimulus-induced activation throughout the entire brain and revealed that the speed of spreading is mainly determined by the brain's hierarchical structural and functional architecture—with each layer adding about 10 ms (Lamme and Roelfsema 2000; Tovee 1994). Neurally speaking, the fast feedforward sweep can be considered decidedly divergent, as it activates as many stimulus-related representations as possible, presumably including various alternative interpretations of a given stimulus (Marcel 1983): it also activates both representations of currently relevant, attended stimuli and stimulus features as well as representations of irrelevant stimuli and features to the same extent. Even so, this nonselective spread of information might well be sufficient for performing a number of tasks, such as the detection of the presence of a particular feature (Treisman and Gelade 1980).

The visual fast feedforward sweep is reliably followed by a second phase of neural activation with entirely different characteristics. This so-called "recurrent" processing wave works its way back to early visual areas and differentiates relevant and irrelevant (attended and unattended) information by selectively enhancing that part of the sweep-induced activation that relates to the relevant stimulus (features) (e.g., Chelazzi et al. 1993; Lamme and Spekreijse 1999). This recurrent wave is apparently necessary for the emergence of conscious representations (Lamme 2003) as well as for the segregation and integration of stimulus features (Lamme 2003; Lamme and Roelfsema 2000). This implies that the fast feedforward sweep may often be sufficient to detect particular features but that searching for feature conjunctions requires recurrent processing. If we consider that the latter serves to integrate stimulus features, this scenario fits perfectly with the feature integration theory (FIT) suggested by Treisman and Gelade (1980). As FIT implies, searching for a feature may be mastered by monitoring the activation level of dedicated feature maps. If the monitored level increases during the feedforward sweep, the participant does not need to await the recurrent processing wave to give a response. This can explain why the search for simple features is often fast and insensitive to the number of distractors (for additional views, see Wolfe, this volume). When searching for conjunctions of features, however, detecting the presence of a particular feature is insufficient. Rather, the features making up the conjunction would need to be integrated, which, according to FIT, is a serial process; thus, search time increases with the number of visible objects being considered. If we consider that the recurrent processing wave is selective and converging onto one given object, conjunction search may indeed require a whole sequence of convergence operations (i.e., a sequence of recurrent waves targeting alternative objects).

As can be seen, conjunction search can be characterized as a sequence of divergent processing (the fast feedforward sweep) followed by a convergent processing (the recurrent wave). But what about feature search? It is interesting to note that this kind of search does not really capture the ecological essence of everyday search performance. People are commonly looking for objects (or people) that in some cases may have features with a particular pop-out quality but are not selectively defined by them. Hence, we rarely search for single features. If we have to serially process a visual scene to locate a conjunctively defined target, we do not scan the scene randomly but are instead guided by features that are part of the conjunction (Wolfe 1994). This suggests that the main function of the divergent feedforward sweep is to determine the feature database which the following convergent operations can use to home in on possible targets. We can thus conclude that at least the bulk of everyday visual search can be aptly characterized as a sequence comprising a divergent, stimulus-driven spread of activation—an operation that seems to serve the purpose of identifying as many candidate targets as possible—followed by a convergent, goal-driven selection of one specific event representation. Exactly the same sequence is seen in the case of searching for appropriate actions.

Searching for Solutions

Even though the ultimate purpose of selecting to-be-perceived targets and to-be-produced actions relates to external, environmental states of affairs, the search operations involved are without exception targeting internal representations. As we have seen, some characteristics seem to be shared by both search operations aiming at representations of currently perceived events, as in visual search, and search operations aiming at representations of future events, as in action planning. Given that the representations themselves are likely to differ in various ways, this commonality in search is remarkable and suggests that the characteristics we can identify are not restricted to direct interactions with our environment.

Indeed, divergent and convergent operations can also be found in problem solving and similar entirely internal search processes. They are particularly obvious in the domain of creative thinking. Even though the importance of human creativity cannot be overestimated, the processes underlying it are understudied and poorly understood (Sternberg et al. 2002). In part, this is due to strong traditions in this field that either focus on creativity as a personal trait— hence, as a characteristic that a given person does or does not have—or emphasize the products, rather than the functional characteristics, of the creative process (see Brown 1989; Runco 2007). Only more recently have researchers begun to agree that truly creative acts do not reflect the operation of just one process, brain area, or intellectual faculty but rather the interplay of multiple cognitive processes and neural networks (e.g., Dietrich 2004; Eysenck 1993; Heilman 2005). Still, there is no agreement as to what these processes and networks might be and how they are to be identified.

Guilford (1967) was one of the first to distinguish between two basic types of thinking that might underlie creative acts: (a) divergent thinking serves the purpose of producing as many possible solutions for a given problem as possible and (b) convergent thinking serves to find the one best solution to problems that require the satisfaction of multiple constraints. Two classical tasks provide good examples: The *alternate uses task* (Guilford 1967) requires participants to name as many appropriate uses of a simple object, such as a pen, as possible, which calls for a literal "brainstorm" through memory. In contrast, the *remote associations task* (Mednick 1962) presents participants with three concepts (e.g., time, hair, and stretch) per trial, who are then asked to identify the one concept that is best related to all three (long).

Unfortunately, the distinction between divergent and convergent thinking is seldom heeded in creativity studies. Instead of studying both types of process together, they often employ only divergent tasks (for overviews and discussion, see Baas et al. 2008; Davis 2009) or convergent tasks (e.g., Isen et al. 1987) or ad-hoc developed and difficult-to-categorize tasks to study "the creativity" (for an overview, see Plucker and Makel 2010). This seems particularly problematic as divergent and convergent thinking not only differ with respect to their computational goals but also seem to rely on different functional and neural mechanisms (cf. Dietrich 2004). A first hint is provided by the observation that individual convergent-thinking performance is not correlated with divergent-thinking performance (Akbari Chermahini and Hommel 2010) and that performing convergent- and divergent-thinking tasks induce opposite mood states (Akbari Chermahini and Hommel 2012). Moreover, there is evidence that divergent-thinking performance relates to the individual dopamine level of participants in the form of an inverted U-shape, with medium levels allowing for the best performance, whereas convergent-thinking performance shows a linear, negative relationship with dopamine levels (Akbari Chermahini and Hommel 2010).

Even though many researchers have focused on one type of creative thinking or the other, entire creative acts (e.g., the invention of a new tool or the conception of a new painting) are likely to require both: a first phase of brainstorming that identifies as many options as possible and a subsequent phase of zooming in on one option and thinking it through. Indeed, Wallas (1926)—as various authors since—suggested that creative acts run through four stages:

1. Preparation, where the problem is investigated
2. Incubation, where the problem is thought about unconsciously
3. Illumination, where ideas come together to form a possible solution
4. Verification, the stage in which the chosen option is evaluated and confirmed

Even if more processes are likely to contribute to a creative act, it makes sense to characterize the first two stages as emphasizing divergent processes and the final two stages as emphasizing convergent processes.

Control States Underlying Convergent and Divergent Search

Summarizing the discussion so far, there is increasing evidence that convergent and divergent search operations can be observed in a broad range of cognitive activities, including the search for perceptual events, the search through problem solutions, and the search through representations of possible actions. Two types of operations seem to come as a fixed sequence, with divergent search followed by convergent search—a sequence that may sometimes be cycled through repeatedly, such as when the sought-for target, action alternative, or memory is not found and/or when goals are changing. Moreover, there are reasons to assume that the two types of search operations are controlled by different cognitive control states. Let us now consider how these states may be characterized.

Figure 14.3 sketches the basic idea underlying many biological models of decision making (for a review, see Bogacz 2007). Most models assume that the representations of multiple alternatives, such as A and B in the figure, compete against each other. As alternative decisions are commonly mutually exclusive, collecting more evidence for (or increasing the tendency toward) one alternative increases the activation of the corresponding representation (e.g., A), which leads to the suppression of other alternatives (such as B). If the evidence is clear-cut, decision making might proceed automatically: at some point, sufficient evidence is collected for one of the alternatives and/or the competing alternatives have received sufficient suppression so that the winner can be determined. However, biological systems are noisy and evidence is not always as

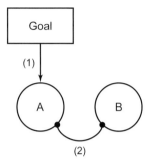

Figure 14.3   Possible mechanisms involved in decision making. The goal-relevant alternative A is supported by the goal representation (1) but competes with choice alternative B through mutual inhibition (2). Thus, in addition to the competition, bias is provided by the goal.

clear-cut as one might wish, so many researchers have assumed contributions from top-down processes that bias decision making toward goal-consistent solutions (e.g., Duncan et al. 1997).

This scenario suggests that different control states might be created by modulating the strength of the top-down bias (control route 1) and/or local competition (control route 2; see Colzato et al. 2008). Strengthening top-down bias and/or increasing local competition would establish a relatively "convergent" control mode that goes for singular targets and "exclusive" decision making. In contrast, relaxing top-down control and/or decreasing local competition would establish a relatively "divergent," integrative control mode that is able to tolerate the selection of multiple targets. Such focused and relaxed control modes may underlie convergent and divergent processing in perceptual search, creative thinking, and action selection, and thus represent general control states of the human cognitive system.

Interestingly, similar pairs of states have been claimed to exist in other cognitive domains as well. For instance, both functional (Dreisbach and Goschke 2004) and neuroscientific (Cools 2008; Cools and D'Esposito 2009) considerations suggest that executive control seeks a balance between two extreme control states: one mode guarantees the stability of goal representations in the face of obstacles and resistance, whereas the other mode allows for giving up and trading the present goal for a more reasonable or promising alternative. Cools and d'Esposito (2009; see also Cools, this volume) suggest that the stability part of this delicate balance might be mediated by the prefrontal dopaminergic pathway, whereas the flexibility part is mediated by the striatal dopaminergic pathway. It is interesting to note that the prefrontal mechanisms that Cools and d'Esposito consider relevant for maintaining stability have also been assumed to provide the top-down bias in competitive decision making (Desimone and Duncan 1995); this might suggest that there is a tight relationship between the control modes responsible for stability and for convergent thinking. Indeed, the individual efficiency of both top-down control (Duncan et al. 1996) and convergent thinking (Akbari Chermahini and Hommel 2010) has been reported to correlate with intelligence. Conversely, a behavioral genetics study revealed that individuals with the DRD2 TAQ IA polymorphism, which results in a 30–40% reduction in dopamine D2 receptor density (the receptor type found primarily in the striatal dopaminergic pathway), show significantly better performance in divergent thinking (Reuter et al. 2006). This fits with the fact that antipsychotic D2-antagonistic drugs reduce the so-called "positive symptoms" of schizophrenia, which have been described as a kind of "widening of the associative horizon" (Eysenck 1993). It thus seems that the functional dialectic between convergent and divergent operations is mirrored to at least some degree in the relationship between stability and flexibility, and this seems to imply some overlap of the underlying neural substrate. Nevertheless, until now the logic of the stability-flexibility concept has only been applied to action goals, whereas the convergent-divergent concept can potentially be applied to any type of decision making—be it between to-be-attended targets, memory traces, representations of alternative actions, or goals. However, given that the search for a target, memory item, or action needs to be goal-directed, decisions between goals need to precede, and selected goals need to outlive, more specific decisions, which requires at least some sort of temporal hierarchy of decision making (cf. Hommel 2009).

A similar, possibly related pair of control states has been referred to as exploitation and exploration modes (Cohen et al. 2007; Daw et al. 2006; see also Daw, this volume, and Hills and Dukas, this volume). The concepts of exploitation and exploration are almost identical to what others have referred to as stability and flexibility, but exploitation-exploration approaches have focused more on the strategies driving control toward one or the other pole of this dimension and the information and neural signals informing such strategies. Moreover, although dopamine has been assumed to control the balance between stability and flexibility (Cools and D'Esposito 2009), the control of balance between exploitation and exploration has also been attributed to norepinephrine (Aston-Jones and Cohen 2005b) as well as to dopamine (Hills 2006; Hills and Dukas, this volume). Expectations and uncertainty are assumed to be important parameters, with moderate degrees of certainty and expected uncertainty promoting exploitation, and perfect certainty (producing boredom) and unexpected uncertainty (undermining confidence in one's assumptions) promoting exploration (Cohen et al. 2007). Future research is needed to test the interesting hypothesis that the same information that promotes exploitation also induces a convergent operation style, while information that promotes exploration induces a divergent operation style.

If we assume that comparable convergent and divergent search modes exist in perceptual search, memory search, and action selection, and that in all these cases the search modes are controlled by the same cognitive control states, one would expect specific interactions between all sorts of tasks that are likely to require the establishment of such control states. In particular, one would expect that interleaving or quickly switching between any two tasks would yield better performance if they call for the same (focused or relaxed) control state than if they imply different states. Two recent studies suggest that this is indeed the case.

Hills et al. (2008) demonstrated that participants, who in a visual foraging task searched through clumpier distributions in space, spent more time on constructing possible words from a set of letters in a Scrabble-like task. One possible interpretation is that a clumpier environment is more likely to propagate a convergent control style than a more diffuse distribution of possible targets, and that a convergent style would lead to more endurance when working on a Scrabble problem. Along similar lines, Hommel et al. (submitted) had participants switch between blocks of convergent- and divergent-thinking tasks and other tasks that are commonly taken to tap into cognitive control processes. Tasks suspected to require rather strong top-down control—like Navon's (1977) global-local task, the Stroop task, and the Simon task—yielded better performance when mixed with a convergent-thinking rather than a divergent-thinking task. This fits with the prediction that types of tasks which rely on a rather focused control mode benefit more when mixed with each other than with a task that calls for a relaxed mode, such as the divergent-thinking task. Hommel et al. (submitted) also employed the attentional blink task, which has been suspected to benefit from lesser top-down control (Olivers and Nieuwenhuis 2006; Shapiro et al. 2006). As predicted, this task yielded better performance when mixed with a divergent-thinking task.

Conclusion

The evolutionary emergence of a cognitive off-line system that allows for both the anticipation and generation of external events has made perceivers/agents more or less independent of current situational circumstances and rendered them proactive rather than reactive. Proactive processes require choices, however, and choices imply the search for a suitable or, ideally, even the best option. Accordingly, humans have developed search strategies that serve two different goals. Divergent search operations identify useful and feasible options without necessarily comparing them, whereas convergent search operations try to pick the best (i.e., most rewarding and/or least demanding) option from this restricted set. There is evidence that these two types of operations can be found in perceptual and memory search, as well as in action selection—hence, in all sorts of searching through cognitive representations. Moreover, there is evidence that these two operations differ with respect to the neural underpinnings and that they are controlled by dissociable control states.

The observed similarities across various sorts of search processes suggest a common phylogenetic source, and I have speculated that the emergence of the ability to plan actions prospectively (i.e., off-line, in the absence of response-triggering external cues) was the driving force. If planning involves decision making between alternative stored action representations, it can be considered a process of cognitive search, and it is possible that it represented the prototype for the development of other types of cognitive search (Hommel 2010). What I did not discuss was how the ability to plan ahead evolved. An interesting possibility is discussed in Hills and Dukas (this volume), who suggest that cognitive search—the internal checking of a number of representations for a match against some goal-relevant representation—might represent the internalization of the ability to search the environment overtly (Hills 2006; Hills et al. 2008). In other words, cognitive search through object and event representations might in some sense simulate overt, active search for external objects and events. This view is consistent with my suggestion that action control is the prime mover in the evolution of cognitive search (and other attentional operations; Hommel 2010), and it may help in extending the present discussion to the analysis of cognitive skills and processes in general.

Moreover, the perspective of Hills and Dukas (this volume) points to a possible origin of the divergent-convergent sequence in cognitive search operations that I have considered. Overt search, as in food foraging behavior, logically and empirically alternates between (overt) exploration (looking around for possible food) and exploitation (collecting and/or eating the food). The cognitive control of overt exploration behavior is likely to require a more divergent decision-making style, as discussed above, whereas the control of overt exploitation calls for a convergent style. This implies a systematic sequence of action-control styles over time, commonly beginning with the divergent control style, followed up by convergent control. If so, seeing the same sequence of control operations in various versions of cognitive search seems to be a logical consequence of the internalization of overt search behavior into a cognitive skill.

First column (top to bottom): Peter M. Todd, Eddy J. Davelaar, Bernhard Hommel, Sean M. Polyn, Eddy J. Davelaar in discussion, Sean M. Polyn, Peter M. Todd
Second column: Thorsten Pachur, Jeremy M. Wolfe, Jeroen G. W. Raaijmakers, Jeremy M. Wolfe, Michael R. Dougherty, Nathaniel D. Daw, Michael D. Lee
Third column: K. Richard Ridderinkhof, Jeroen G. W. Raaijmakers, Michael R. Dougherty, Nathaniel D. Daw, Michael D. Lee, Thorsten Pachur, K. Richard Ridderinkhof

15

Unpacking Cognitive Search

Mechanisms and Processes

Thorsten Pachur, Jeroen G. W. Raaijmakers,
Eddy J. Davelaar, Nathaniel D. Daw, Michael R. Dougherty,
Bernhard Hommel, Michael D. Lee, Sean M. Polyn,
K. Richard Ridderinkhof, Peter M. Todd, and Jeremy M. Wolfe

Abstract

This chapter discusses commonalities and differences in the cognitive mechanisms underlying different search tasks, such as spatial search, visual search, memory retrieval, action search, problem solving, and decision making. Three key issues relevant across all types of search are distinguished: (a) the initiation of search, (b) the maintenance and adaptive modification of the search process, and (c) the termination of search. As to search initiation, research is summarized concerning the effect of the number of cues on difficulty for executing search, and which factors structure the cue hierarchy. Discussion follows on how knowledge about metacognitive processes in memory might be used for better understanding the processes in maintenance of search, and heuristic principles for stopping search, possibly shared across different search tasks, are identified. Finally, consideration is given to how search processes might change as a function of experience and aging.

Introduction

In *The Disappearance of Lady Frances Carfax* (Doyle 1917), Sherlock Holmes is commissioned to track down a wealthy noblewomen who mysteriously vanished while traveling through Europe. To find Carfax, the detective and his ally, Dr. Watson, meticulously reconstruct the Lady's itinerary and visit the places where she had been seen prior to her disappearance. The investigation starts in Lausanne, where Watson is informed that Carfax has moved to Baden-Baden; there, he is sent to her long-term maid in Montpellier, who tells Watson that Carfax laid her off after making the acquaintance of a certain Dr. Shlessinger.

This information takes Holmes and Watson back to London, where they search for further clues as to the Lady's whereabouts. Although few of us engage in detective work regularly, Holmes' investigation resembles, in many respects, our more mundane search activities. In particular, it seems fair to say that most of our cognitive activities involve search of some kind, whether for a name to go with a face, a word to describe how we are feeling, an object hidden somewhere in the scene before us, or a solution to a problem encountered on the job.

But how do we search? As a starting point, consider how animals go about searching for resources in space (Bell 1991). In general, animals attempt to find as much resource in as short a time as possible. If there are cues to locations of resources that can be sensed from afar (e.g., seeing prey, chemically sensing conspecifics already at a resource), then these should govern the search; this is similar to visual search being guided to areas of interest detected in peripheral vision. Otherwise, in cases of uncertain resource location, organisms should tend to search in a way that brings them to new locations without going over recently visited locations again (akin to sampling without replacement). A random search (e.g., Brownian motion) does not accomplish this well (as evident, e.g., in the protest among iPod users against Apple's original random shuffle algorithm, which brought up recently played songs too frequently). Therefore, animals often use search strategies that move across the environment on a roughly straight course, or use a more systematic "space-filling" path (e.g., spiraling outward from a starting point).

Spatial foraging is but one example of a task that involves search. Search is also a key factor in memory retrieval, visual search, action search, problem solving, and decision making. In this chapter we discuss both the commonalities and differences between these different types of search. To structure our discussion, we distinguish three basic issues in search: (a) how search is initiated, (b) how search is maintained and adaptively modified, and (c) when and how search is terminated. In addition, we discuss individual differences in search that may arise due to developmental changes, due to prior experience in these or similar tasks, or due to preexisting (possibly genetic) differences in information processing.

How Is Search Initiated?

Cue Selection

The first step to get the search process going is to establish a set of features (or cues) that define the object of the search. To illustrate, consider a visual search task where you set out to look for a turquoise ring in the bedroom: What are the prerequisites for initiating the search? Search for the ring will not proceed randomly; rather, attention will be guided to items that share basic features with the target. These basic features (e.g., size, shape, color of the desired ring) serve as a template for comparing items encountered as search proceeds, and the goal is to find an adequate match between this abstract representation of the target item and the visual image encountered during search. Interestingly, guiding features are not the same as perceptual features. Guidance seems to be based on a coarse and categorical representation of a set of basic features. To illustrate: although the ring may clearly be a particular shade of "turquoise," your ability to use color for guidance is limited to directing your attention to items that are broadly, categorically "blue" (Daoutis et al. 2006). Moreover, as rings occur in some places (e.g., on dressers) and not in others (e.g., mid-air), search will be guided by scene-based properties, or context features (Biederman 1972).

Similar principles hold for search in memory, where it is assumed that a template representation consisting of a set of "retrieval cues" is used to constrain the output of the memory system during search. As in visual search, the retrieval cues contain information that distinguishes the to-be-retrieved item from all of the other traces that may reside in the memory system. Examples of these constraining retrieval cues are semantic characteristics (e.g., animals) or the temporal circumstances of the item's occurrence (e.g., recall the items that were on list A). There is also evidence that people can use multiple cues to constrain simultaneously what is being retrieved during memory search (e.g., recall all the animals that were on list A; Polyn et al. 2011).

In some search tasks, the set of features guiding search may arise directly from the task. In visual search tasks, for instance, the description of the target (e.g., turquoise ring) readily provides the features that will lead to the target (e.g., round object, has a hole). In other search tasks, however, the set of features has to be actively generated by the participant (below we discuss factors that can affect the construction of the feature set, such as the predicted effectiveness of the cues). In memory search, the set of target features might also be defined by the specific recall strategy used by the participant (e.g., search for items in alphabetical order). Whereas there is considerable research on memory and visual search, we still know relatively little about cue selection in nonvisual search, such as auditory (e.g., speaker identification) or tactile search. As discussed below, given that several principles in search are shared across different search types, it is likely that aspects of feature or cue selection described above also generalize to these types of search.

How Do Multiple Cues Affect Search?

Often, a target is defined by a set of multiple features, such as when one searches for an item that is both a ring *and* blue. How does the complexity of the target affect the difficulty of search? Interestingly, the answer could vary across different types of search. For instance, visual search based on conjunctive rules (e.g., find the red X) seems to be more difficult than when based on a single cue (e.g., find the X). Similarly, it is assumed that search prior to probability judgments is more difficult for judgments of conditional probability (e.g., the probability of breast cancer given a positive mammogram), which are based on multiple cues, than search with only one cue (because cues are processed sequentially; e.g., Dougherty et al. 1999). Memory models such as search of associative memory or SAM (Raaijmakers and Shiffrin 1981), by contrast, do not necessarily assume that combining multiple cues complicates search.

Which Factors Guide the Selection of Cues?

The selection of retrieval cues used in standard memory-retrieval paradigms is relatively well understood, at least compared to cue-selection processes in real-world tasks (e.g., medical diagnosis). For example, in laboratory tasks, each item (or in some cases an entire list) is generally associated with a single and unique cue (e.g., in paired-associates learning; Calkins 1894). In contrast, in many real-world retrieval tasks, cues are shared across items or "lists" and are thus only probabilistically related to the target item. To illustrate, in medicine a retrieval cue such as "high white-blood cell count" is associated with several different pathologies, ranging from bacterial infection to disorders of bone marrow (e.g., leukemia). These pathologies are often organized hierarchically, such that there are many specific examples of the general class of bacterial infection and many specific examples of the general class of bone-marrow disorders. Within each class of pathologies, individual examples (which could be called "hypotheses") might be associated with specific symptoms ("data"). Given a representation that can be expressed in terms of hypotheses and data, we can now ask the question: What is the probability of the data (a symptom) given a particular hypothesis (a disease)? The answer is the diagnosticity or validity of that symptom cue. Though not a deterministic cue, the presence of a high white-blood cell count may still be a diagnostic piece of information. In the context of memory retrieval tasks, one can imagine that the diagnosticity (or validity) of a particular memory retrieval cue can be exploited to help guide the retrieval of potential hypotheses from long-term memory (Thomas et al. 2008; Dougherty et al. 2010). For example, in a simplified environment, imagine that the diagnosticity of a particular cue (symptom) for discriminating between two mutually exclusive and exhaustive categories of diseases is 2:1. This would imply that twice as many hypotheses from disease category 1 are related to the observed symptom compared to disease category 2. Such cue diagnosticity provides valuable information that can and should be used in determining how to search through memory in diagnosis tasks; namely, search using the most diagnostic cues available. Put more generally, the statistical properties of a cue likely inform basic memory search processes. Unfortunately, there is little work on how statistical properties of the retrieval cues affect cue selection in memory search (see, however, Anderson 1991).

The idea that search for cues is guided by their usefulness is, by contrast, a common one in other realms of judgment and decision making. For instance, the take-the-best heuristic (Gigerenzer and Goldstein 1996) assumes that cues are inspected in sequential order according to their validity (defined as the probability that the cue leads to a correct response given that it discriminates between two options). The large literature on multiple-cue probability learning has examined the processes by which people acquire knowledge about the validity of cues (e.g., Klayman 1988; for other approaches, see Dieckmann and Todd 2012). Alternatively, people may use cues in an order, based on how likely they are to lead to any decision (i.e., their "discrimination rate"; cf. Rakow et al. 2005), or a combination of validity and discrimination rate (i.e., their "success"; Martignon and Hoffrage 1999), on intuitive causal beliefs about the cues' importance (Chapman and Chapman 1969).

Search Initiation in Action Selection

While both visual search and memory search usually have a clearly specified target, other types of search are more open-ended and, as a consequence, may be guided in a rather different fashion. For instance, consider exploring which out of many possible actions will yield desired outcomes (or will avoid undesirable outcomes). Animals and humans are often confronted with a variety of opportunities for action in a particular situation. Some of these options might be more alluring or potentiating than others; some might be more risky or more effort-consuming.

Action selection in these circumstances implicates search in at least two senses: external (i.e., traversing the environment and exploring the results of actions so as to learn action-outcome relationships, reward contingencies, or cognitive maps) and internal (i.e., the use of these learned representations to evaluate candidate courses of action to guide subsequent action selection toward those most likely to maximize reward). (Here reward may be determined by a cost-benefit analysis of potential outcomes vis-à-vis current motivational states.) The search for those actions that have maximal (subjective) expected utility (another way of talking about reward) is well captured by reinforcement learning models, which describe how regularities among action-outcome contingencies are extracted from experience. Broadly, this type of action search will be initiated, constrained, guided, and terminated by an agent's current concerns, intentions, and prior experience, as well as by its present motivational state (e.g., fatigue, satiation). In these respects, search based on reinforcement learning may differ from visual and memory search, in which initiation, guidance, and termination are generally influenced more explicitly by instructions and cues.

Although it is traditionally assumed that search occurs over actions, computing their values by averaging over the possible reward outcomes to which they might lead, a recent alternative proposes that agents might first choose between outcomes, then search over action plans for how best to obtain the desired outcome (Padoa-Schioppa and Assad 2006; Krajbich et al. 2010). The initial *goal choice* in this case may occur in a similar fashion as initiation of memory or visual search (e.g., based on feature templates).

Construction of the Search Space

In addition to coming up with a set of cues that define *what* to look for, some types of search also require the definition of the search space; that is, *where* it is possible to look. In visual search, it has been hypothesized that individuals need to construct the search space by "parsing" the scene into *proto-objects*, regions that will be selected by attention (Rensink 2000a). Moreover, in searches that are extended in time, there may be an initial plan for a search path, which is refined during search as a function of what is found (in the next section, we elaborate on such search maintenance processes). For instance, when asked, in a verbal fluency task, to retrieve all movies seen over the last six months, one might first search among the films seen in a particular movie theater and then move on to search among films of a particular genre, rather than probing memory for movies in general. In memory search, the refinement of search can thus consist of switching between different sets of retrieval cues.

A similar construction of a search space is relevant in problem solving and in multi-attribute choice, where a set of possible options needs to be generated from which a final choice can be made (Marewski et al. 2010; Tversky 1972). Sometimes, such a consideration set might be generated more or less automatically—and efficiently. In a study that examined action selection in sports, Johnson and Raab (2003) found that options which are quickly generated tend to be of higher quality than options generated more slowly (see also Dougherty et al. 1997; Gettys and Fisher 1979).

The construction of the search space can have a considerable effect on the efficiency of search. For instance, in a verbal fluency task, search becomes more difficult the larger the category from which objects are recalled (though the effect can depend on the retrieval strategy; Indow and Togano 1970; see also Murdock and Okada 1970).

Open Questions

While some of the principles guiding search initiation seem to be similar across different types of search, there are also some differences. What is currently unclear, however, is the extent to which the observed differences between various types of search may be due to the experimental paradigms used to study the different types of search. Natural environments may provide a much richer context than the rather artificial settings used in the laboratory. Consequently, navigation through search spaces in the real world may be much easier, due to the constraints imposed. Furthermore, the selection of cues and the construction of the search space are likely to arise from a dynamic interplay of divergent (i.e., global) and convergent (i.e., local) search strategies, possibly applied sequentially; methods must be developed to investigate such dynamic processes, to which we turn to next.

How Is Search Maintained and Dynamically Modified?

After initiation, how is search maintained? The answer might depend strongly on whether a search targeted just one single thing (e.g., a nest or partner) or whether search is ongoing (e.g., for food). Whereas in the first case search is (often) stopped after the target has been found, in the latter case, search may continue after finding a target, seeking other targets.

Global versus Local Search Strategies

In many situations, search may be characterized as switching between exploration (or divergent search) and exploitation (or convergent search). The respective contributions of exploration and exploitation are influenced by the structure of the environment, in particular by whether the desired resource occurs in patches or not. If resources are patchy (i.e., distributed in clumps with relatively empty regions between them), then finding one resource indicates that others may be nearby. Here, the organism can benefit from switching from exploration between patches to exploitation of the discovered patch. Because the resources within a patch are themselves often not immediately detectable, and thus also require search (e.g., a berry bush is a patch in which berries must be sought by looking underneath leaves), this switching can also be thought of as going from global to local search. Local within-patch search can be implemented by taking smaller steps or making smaller movements to stay within the patch, turning more to stay in the same vicinity, and turning back if the edge of the patch is detected (Bell 1991).

A popular way to study the dynamic interplay between exploration and exploitation is with so-called *bandit problems*, in which there are M choices you can make for a sequence of N trials (e.g., Gittins 1979; Kaelbling et al. 1996). Each choice has some fixed, but unknown, rate of providing a binary reward. The goal is to maximize the total number of rewards obtained, and the search problem is then to explore the M choices sufficiently to determine which one(s) to exploit on further trials (for experimental studies, see Daw et al. 2006; Lee et al. 2011).

When to Leave the Patch?

When resources are distributed in patches and one is currently being exploited, another problem arises: as the resources in the patch are increasingly being depleted, the benefit of staying in the patch decreases, and at some point the organism must decide to leave that patch and return to exploring for other patches. The general principle guiding animals in this situation is captured in optimal foraging theory by the *marginal value theorem* (Charnov 1976). Accordingly, the highest rate of return of resources can be achieved if the patch is left as soon as the rate of finding things in that patch falls below the expected mean rate of finding things across the environment as a whole when the optimal strategy is followed.

Although a useful benchmark, the marginal value theorem makes strong and often unrealistic assumptions about the organism's knowledge and computational capacities with respect to determining instantaneous and expected rates of return. Consequently, a variety of heuristics for patch-leaving decisions have been proposed that are based on simple, easy-to-compute cues: how much time one has already spent in the patch, how many items one has found in the patch, how long it has been since the previous item was found in the patch, and how long it took to get to this patch in the first place. The effectiveness of specific patch-leaving heuristics depends in part on how resources are distributed across patches. For instance, if resources are aggregated such that there are some very good patches along with many middling ones, then it is appropriate to leave the patch after some giving-up-time has passed since the previous item was found. Humans seem to use such a rule in some spatial and memory search tasks (Wilke et al. 2009; Hutchinson et al. 2008; see also Payne et al. 2007).

Another way to conceptualize the dynamic transition between global and local search is area-restricted search, in which an organism performs more high-angle turns when resources are encountered and so stays in a local area, gradually returning to low-angle turns when resources are not encountered for some time. Area-restricted search can yield more continuous transitions back and forth between local and global search over time, and may be more appropriate where patch boundaries are fuzzy (for an overview, see Hills 2006). In addition to factors such as the current and expected rate of return and the time spent in a patch, it has also been shown that animals sometimes take into account the variability of the patches they seek. For instance, when they must reach a threshold amount of food to survive the night, they might prefer a patch with greater variability but lower overall mean return rate over a less variable but higher mean one if the former, but not the latter, has a chance of providing enough food for survival (as described in risk-sensitive foraging theory; for an overview, see McNamara and Houston 1992).

How Is Search Monitored?

Memory Search

Managing the search process effectively requires keeping track of the contents of the current as well as past search space. This monitoring probably relies heavily on what are termed metacognitive processes; that is, processes which keep track of how aspects of cognition are proceeding (Koriat et al. 2000; Metcalfe and Shimamura 1994; Nelson 1996). Although we still know relatively little about the exact nature of the metacognitive processes involved in search, it is possible that they are similar to those used in other domains, such as (a) monitoring with respect to the contents of memory and (b) monitoring with respect to the acquisition or learnability of study material. Several paradigms have been developed to investigate these processes (Nelson 1996; Nelson et al. 2004). Monitoring of the contents of memory is often studied by asking people to assess their confidence in the accuracy of a retrieved piece of information, or by asking them to assess the likelihood that they will be able to retrieve a particular piece of information in the future, given that it cannot be retrieved at the present time (*feeling-of-knowing judgments*). The monitoring of the acquisition of information is studied by asking people to assess how well learned a piece of material is (*judgments-of-learning*). People's assessments in these tasks are often rather accurate and have been shown to predict future recallability. A second method to study monitoring of information acquisition is by asking people to assess how easily they will be able to learn a newly experienced piece of information (*ease-of-learning*); for instance, when estimating how much study time to allocate to studying for a test based on the difficulty of the material. Ease-of-learning judgments may play out in cognitive search by influencing how long one spends in an exploration mode, assuming that one goal of exploration is to discover or learn environmental or statistical contingencies (see also Metcalfe and Jacobs 2010; for a review of different types of metacognitive judgments, see Nelson 1996).

Although some work has examined how metacognitive monitoring limits or informs search behavior in single-item recall tasks (e.g., Dougherty et al. 2005; Nelson et al. 1986), there is no work on more complex search tasks. For instance, in verbal fluency tasks (e.g., name all animals you can think of) it is necessary to monitor how much of a semantic space has already been exploited, or to estimate the size of the remaining unused portion of the "information patch." Another important gap in the understanding of metacognitive monitoring of memory is how it might relate to error monitoring and detection, as carried out by functions localized to the prefrontal cortex. Shimamura (2008) proposed a neurocognitive model of metacognition that postulates a fundamental role of cognitive control for regulating and monitoring metacognitive representations.

Decision Making and Problem Solving

Metacognitive monitoring processes in other search tasks are even less well studied. For example, in decision-making tasks, which are often assumed to be based on sequential search of cues (e.g., Payne et al. 1993; Gigerenzer et al. 1999), how does one monitor which cues have been previously accessed in the course of a decision? Does a physician use a similar process to monitor symptoms that have already been checked or evaluated while generating a diagnosis? Finally, monitoring processes might also be important for searching and navigating the solution space in problem-solving tasks, where one has to monitor one's current location in the solution space and which locations have already been visited (cf. hill climbing; Newell and Simon 1972).

Open Questions

Although the categorical distinction between exploration and exploitation describes some search processes quite well, in other cases it may be more appropriate to use a continuous approach. In addition, it is still relatively unclear what mediates the switch between exploration and exploitation. One possibility is that switching is based on a form of conflict signaling, indicating that there is a mismatch between the encountered stimuli and the target (see Hommel, this volume). Specifically, mild conflict might lead to increased top-down control (exploitation), whereas stronger conflict might lead to stress and a change in the search strategy (exploration).

Another issue concerns the metaphors and analogies we use to conceptualize search. We often liken internal search in memory to external search in a spatially laid out environment. Might this spatial metaphor critically constrain the way we think about and understand search? Clearly, there are alternative conceptualizations, such as distributed, symbolic, or temporal representations, which might highlight different aspects of the search process rather than portray search in spatial terms (see Schooler et al., this volume). For instance, the importance of navigation costs may be less important if search occurs within a distributed representation.

How Are Search Processes Controlled?

As mentioned above, effective search often requires maintenance and control processes (e.g., to switch dynamically between exploration and exploitation). What are the proximate psychological capacities that are tapped by these control processes? A general assumption in influential models of cognitive control (inspired by the cybernetic approach; Wiener 1948) is that information is sampled and matched against a goal representation until a reasonable fit is achieved (e.g., Botvinick et al. 2001; Miller et al. 1960). Top-down control over cognitive search might be achieved in a similar manner. In a visual search task, for example, this would suggest that a representation of the target stored in working memory is matched against stimuli encountered during search until the target is identified. In tasks requiring action search, it has been proposed that conflict—that is, when there is a mismatch between the target and the stimuli encountered—leads to an increase of top-down control (e.g., Botvinick et al. 2001). Control, however, can sometimes also be governed by local priming (i.e., arising from the stimuli) rather than managed in a top-down fashion.

For instance, in memory search, the search for the next item to be considered will be influenced by both top-down constraints (the target representation) and the similarity between the current and the previous items (and the priming the previous item generates).

Given that controlling the search process requires continuous updating of the information currently in the focus of attention, processes in working memory are likely to play a key role. Within cognitive psychology, the construct of working memory has been defined as the ability to maintain focus of attention on goal-relevant information in the face of distraction (Kane et al. 2001). Factor analysis and experimental work have revealed that working memory capacity (as measured by operation-related tasks) is correlated with performance in a number of laboratory and nonlaboratory tasks, including response inhibition tasks (anti-saccade, Stroop), auditory tasks (dichotic listening tasks), resistance to proactive interference (Brown-Peterson task), measures of general fluid abilities, note taking, and planning (Engle 2002).

Increasing evidence indicates that key characteristics of cognitive control during search are indeed correlated with working memory capacity. For instance, Hills et al. (2010b) have proposed that a higher working memory capacity is associated with a lower frequency of switching between patches. Currently it is unclear how exactly working memory capacity affects the switching behavior. For instance, working memory could affect the signal-to-noise ratio in information processing (i.e., the ability to discriminate between targets and distractors), which might help focusing on the current task. Alternatively, a higher working memory capacity could lead to better conflict resolution (Bäckman et al. 2010; Li et al. 2001), for instance, by facilitating the identification of the actual signal within the noise or by suppressing task-irrelevant information. Moreover, it is likely that not all subcomponents of working memory affect control processes equally during search (Friedman et al. 2008; Miyake et al. 2000). Thus, further investigation is needed to distinguish more precisely the relevant components.

In light of the current evidence for the influence of cognitive control on switching behavior, it might be useful to distinguish between switching which results from a strategic decision and switching that occurs due to unsystematic factors (i.e., distraction). On one hand, higher working memory is assumed to help individuals stay focused on searching within a patch (while a patch still yields successful outcomes), thus decreasing the switching rate, as shown by Hills and Pachur (2012) and Hills et al. (2011). On the other hand, to the extent that strategic patch switching (e.g., when disengaging from a patch and switching to exploration once the current patch has been depleted) involves task-switching costs, higher cognitive control might be associated with an increased switching rate. For instance, Mayr (2001) found that older adults (who are likely to have a reduced working memory capacity) display higher switching costs than younger adults in a task-switching paradigm. Given the potentially multiple roles of working memory in exploitation and exploration, future research should delineate more clearly the factors that moderate the relationship between working memory and search.

Modes of Control versus Levels of Control

There is agreement that agents can change their strategy in search-related tasks, but how can we describe this change between strategies? One approach is to group the strategies in terms of binary dimensions (e.g., exploitation vs. exploration), so that changes between them can be seen as moving agents toward one or the other pole of each dimension. For instance, starting to search within a patch (spatial foraging) or a visual group (visual search) or item category (memory search) can be described as moving out of exploration toward exploitation. Alternatively, changing between strategies can be viewed as up- or down-movements in a goal hierarchy (Miller et al. 1960). Accordingly, the same strategic choice can be considered as moving down one level in a hierarchy of possible representations of search targets, from a more general level, which includes all available patches, groups, or categories as possible target locations, to a more specific level that restricts the search space to one patch, group, or category. The advantage of viewing the dynamics in search maintenance in terms of different levels of control is that it allows further levels that are more concrete (lower) or abstract (higher) to be added without giving up the general theoretical scheme.

How Is Search Stopped?

Earlier, in our discussion of the maintenance of search, we addressed the issue of how to decide when to modify the current search behavior (e.g., leaving a patch to move on to the next one). Similar principles apply to decide when to terminate the search process altogether. Although the decision to stop search is relevant for most search tasks, relatively little is known about the extent to which similar principles govern people's stopping behavior across these tasks. In any case, for search to be effective, stopping rules need to be sensitive to the characteristics of the task. In some tasks, for instance, it might be crucial to find at least one object (e.g., in food search or mate choice), whereas in others one can be more selective and stop search if a threshold is not met (e.g., in consumer product search or information foraging), irrespective of whether anything has been found at all.

Several empirical tasks have been developed to investigate the effectiveness of people's stopping rules in sequential choice. A prominent approach uses *optimal stopping problems*, for which optimal points to end search can, in principle, be determined. In one type of optimal stopping problem, known as the *secretary* or *dowry problem* (Ferguson 1989; Gilbert and Mosteller 1966), there is a sequence of N numbers distributed in some unknown way and independently sampled. The searcher's goal is to choose the maximum number in the sequence, under the constraint that only the current number can be chosen at the time it is presented and that one cannot return to a previous number. In this version of the task, the searcher only learns the rank of the current number relative to all those previously seen. In other versions, the numbers themselves are seen, N may be unknown, the distribution may be known, and the utility function may differ (e.g., with continuous payoff rather than just success or failure; Bearden 2006; Smith et al. 2007). Investigations of people's performance in the secretary problem have been conducted, for instance, by Dudey and Todd (2001) and Lee (2006). Finally, in *deferred decision tasks*, searchers have to decide whether to continue information search (e.g., conduct another test) or to stop search and make a diagnosis about a situation (e.g., which of two diseases a patient has). Models of stopping rules to describe people's search behavior in such a task have been tested, for instance, by Busemeyer and Rapoport (1988; see also Browne et al. 2007).

Is There Evidence for Similar Stopping Rules across Different Types of Search?

As mentioned above, in many situations the determination of optimal stopping rules will exceed the cognitive capacities of an organism. In such situations, decisions to stop will need to be based on heuristic principles which can, under some circumstances, approximate the optimal solutions. Given that the need to decide when to stop search is relevant across many different tasks, we must ask whether similar heuristics for stopping search may be used across various domains. Although only very few studies have directly compared stopping behavior in different search tasks, the existing evidence hints at some commonalities. Comparing patch-leaving rules—akin to stopping rules at the patch level—in spatial and memory search, an interval-based rule (specifically, time since the last encountered item) accounted in both tasks for the data best (Hutchinson et al. 2008; Wilke et al. 2009). Similarly, findings suggest that people's decision to terminate retrieval from memory is a function of the number of retrieval failures, which is usually highly correlated with the temporal interval since the last retrieval (Harbison et al. 2008).

Process Tests of Stopping Rules in Decision Making

How can people's stopping behavior be studied and measured? Whereas search in memory is usually not directly observable, decision-making paradigms have been developed that enable tracking of external information search (for an overview, see Schulte-Mecklenbeck et al. 2011). In multi-attribute decision making, where people have to search for attributes to evaluate the alternatives, process tracing methodologies such as Mouselab (Payne et al. 1993) or eye-tracking have been used to test how people stop search. For instance, according to the take-the-best heuristic (Gigerenzer and Goldstein 1996), alternatives are compared by sequentially inspecting their attributes (in the order of their validity or importance for this decision) and stopping that search and inspection as soon as the alternatives differ on an attribute. Thus, to infer which of two cities has more inhabitants, take-the-best starts by comparing the cities on the highest validity attribute (e.g., whether it is a state capital): if both cities have the same value on that attribute (e.g., if neither is a state capital) then the second most valid attribute is inspected (e.g., whether the city has an international airport). If this attribute discriminates (e.g., if only one of the two cities has an international airport), search is stopped and no further attribute is inspected. Using the Mouselab experimental tool, several studies have shown that people's stopping behavior indeed follows such a simple rule when information costs are high (Bröder 2003), there is time pressure (Rieskamp and Hoffrage 2008), cognitive resources are limited (Mata et al. 2007), or the number of alternatives is high (Ford et al. 1989). More recently, Khader et al. (2011) developed a neuroimaging paradigm that allows tracking the neural correlates of information search in memory-based decision making. The authors obtained evidence that people using take-the-best show reduced retrieval activity in the brain areas representing attribute knowledge when the heuristic stops search early as compared to when the heuristic searches more extensively. Pachur and Scheibehenne (2012) used a sequential sampling paradigm to show that when pricing a lottery, people stopped information search about the lotteries differently depending on whether they were asked for a maximum buying price or a minimum selling price.

Open Questions

Most search situations that are investigated in empirical studies are relatively artificial. It is not clear whether tasks studied in the laboratory make search more or less difficult compared to more natural search situations. On one hand, experimental search contexts usually do not offer as much information to help navigate the search process as more natural search environments. On the other, search environments outside the laboratory are also more complex, for instance because the target object is less well defined (e.g., find an appropriate partner to start a family), or because the search process is more difficult to control. Consequently, researchers need to study search and stopping rules also in real-world domains.

Individual Differences in Cognitive Search

The efficiency of an individual's adaptive control, in general, and of searching for objects, memory traces, and problem solutions, in particular, is known to vary with intelligence, operation span, and age. For instance, the development of people's performance in visual search tasks across the life span shows an inverted U-shaped trajectory (Hommel et al. 2004). Older adults have particular problems with excluding irrelevant distractors; they seem to recheck more often when a target is absent. Interestingly, the opposite tendency is observed in decision making: older adults seem to search for less information than younger adults when making a decision (Mata and Nunes 2010). Nevertheless, older adults still show a general ability to adapt their information search to the structure of the environment. When a more extended search affords better decisions, older adults acquire more information than when extended search pays only little (Mata et al. 2007). This suggests that elderly people actively employ context-specific search control strategies, presumably to compensate for (real or assumed) effects of age-related cognitive decline.

Although investigations of search behavior in decision making have found evidence for the use of a considerable variety of strategies, variation in strategy use seems to be due primarily to external factors, such as time pressure and the statistical structure of the task, with individual differences playing only a minor role (Bröder 2011). There are, however, some exceptions. In addition to the age differences described above, search strategies in decision making have been shown to differ reliably as a function of expertise. For instance, Garcia-Retamero and Dhami (2009) found that crime experts (burglars, police officers) tend to follow a strategy with simple search and stopping rules (take-the-best) to judge the security of a property, whereas novices (students) tended to follow a strategy involving more extensive search (see also Shanteau 1992).

To the extent that search is associated with a person's willingness to take risks, there is some evidence for gender differences in search. For instance, in a task where extended search increased gains but also the risk of a large loss, young male participants were more willing to take risks and to search longer than female participants (Slovic 1966). In addition, individual differences in motivation or persistence may lead people to stay engaged versus disengage from search (Dougherty and Harbison 2007).

Associations between control processes and working memory (as measured by operation-span performance) suggest that individual differences in search might also be related to individual differences in working memory. The influence of working memory on search seems to be due, in particular, to operational capabilities (i.e., manipulating material stored in working memory) rather than to storage capacity (i.e., the number of items that can be stored). Standard measures of working memory, such as the operation-span task, reading span, listening span, and symmetry span, rely on a process-versus-maintenance distinction: participants are asked to maintain a growing list of to-be-remembered items simultaneously while engaging in a processing task. In the operation-span task, for example, participants are presented with a list of letters serially (one at a time), with a simple mathematics problem interleaved between each successive letter presentation. Performance on the operation-span task is given by the number of letters correctly retrieved across multiple sequences of to-be-remembered items. Individuals high in operation span show advantages in rejecting irrelevant information in memory and search-like tasks (e.g., Vogel et al. 2005) and in the attentional blink (Colzato et al. 2007). This might be due to the fact that both operation span and age have an impact on a person's ability to distinguish between signal (i.e., targets) and noise (i.e., distractors). Indeed, older adults seem to spend more time sampling sensory evidence to achieve a reliable signal-to-noise ratio than young adults (e.g., by engaging in more rechecking operations to make sure that the signal actually belongs to the searched object; Hommel et al. 2004). However, it is currently unclear which search behavior fosters a high signal-to-noise ratio. On one hand, having a reliable signal-to-noise ratio might reduce cognitive conflict (because relevant items and distractors can be better distinguished) and therefore foster exploitation. On the other, a higher signal-to-noise ratio will also increase the sensitivity to detect conflict signals, which should foster exploration. Overall, individual differences in the adaptivity of switching between exploration and exploitation can be due to both perceptual abilities to detect (external or internal) signals to switch and the ability to perform the switch (cf. Mayr 2001).

Engle and colleagues have found that an individual's working memory span predicts aspects of their performance on longer-term memory search tasks, such as free recall. Unsworth and Engle (2007) suggest that these differences are related to the difficulty of individuals with low working memory span to use cues effectively to constrain memory search (resulting in more intrusions from prior lists and fewer correct retrievals). Recent work suggests that more strategic aspects of search show reliable individual differences: people who tend to organize recalled items with a temporal strategy reliably recall more items than individuals whose recalls are temporally disorganized (Sederberg et al. 2010).

There is also some evidence for individual differences in visual search resulting from cultural influences. Specifically, Nisbett and colleagues (e.g., Nisbett and Miyamoto 2005) found that Asians, who show a more collectivist orientation, are more sensitive to context information, and thus seem to have a more divergent search behavior, than individually oriented Westerners. Similar attentional biases have also been found as a function of religious orientation (Colzato et al. 2010b), suggesting that cultural practices might shape the way individuals configure their cognitive system for search operations.

Future Directions

In our discussion of the cognitive mechanisms underlying search, we distinguished three different aspects of search: the initiation of search, the maintenance of search, and the termination of search. We discussed commonalities and differences between different types of cognitive search tasks (e.g., visual, memory, spatial, action search), potential proximate mechanisms, as well as individual differences in search. Although several experimental paradigms have been developed to investigate the cognitive processes during the different stages in search, little is known about how these processes are implemented and biologically mediated. There is evidence that some search behavior is linked to dopamine (e.g., for an overview, see Hills 2006; Hills, this volume), yet to what degree does this link hold across different domains (such as search in memory, visual search, spatial search, and search for actions)? Moreover, the mechanisms underlying an individual's adaptive use of different search strategies (e.g., to compensate for age-related decline) are not well understood, nor are the mechanisms that drive cultural influences on the control of cognitive search.

An important application of research on cognitive search may lie in developing methods to train individuals to change their search behavior (e.g., brain training), for instance, to be more flexible in switching (exploration or innovation) or more persistent in concentrating (exploitation or focus). Important questions here include how long the training effects last (long-term or short-term), and whether they transfer from one domain to another (for evidence, see, e.g., Karbach and Kray 2009; Hills et al. 2010b).

Sherlock Holmes' adventures offer some inspiration for hoping that people can be trained to adopt different search methods in some instances. Holmes often attempted to instruct Watson about his investigative methods in searching for clues and solutions to puzzling mysteries. Even though this was not always a success, in *The Disappearance of Lady Frances Carfax*, Holmes and Watson's search ends successfully as they manage to find the Lady, at the mercy of Shlessinger, just in time before he could bury her alive.

Search Environments,
Representation, and Encoding

16

Foundations of Search

A Perspective from Computer Science

James A. R. Marshall and Frank Neumann

Abstract

Since Alan Turing, computer scientists have been interested in understanding natural intelligence by reproducing it in machine form. The field of artificial intelligence is characterized, to a large extent, by search algorithms. As search is a computational process, this too has been well studied as part of theoretical computer science, leading to famous results on the computational hardness of problems. This chapter provides an overview of why most search problems are known to be hard and why general search strategies are impossible. It then discusses various heuristic approaches to computational search. The fundamental message intended is that any intelligent system of sufficient complexity, using search to guide its behavior, should be expected to find solutions that are good enough, rather than the best. In other words, it is argued that natural and artificial brains should *satisfice* rather than *optimize*.

Introduction

Almost since the first digital computers were created, computer scientists have speculated on their potential capacity for intelligent behavior (Turing 1950). Such thinking prompted the creation of the modern discipline of "artificial intelligence" (AI), which seeks to reproduce animal or human-level intelligence. Classic problem domains for AI include formal games such as chess (Shannon 1950). Other forms of richer interaction are even more interesting, the most stringent of which is probably Turing's famous "imitation game" (typically referred to now as the "Turing test") or variants thereof, in which a computer attempts to fool a human interrogator that it is itself human, by maintaining a conversation on any topic (Turing 1950). AI techniques are also applied to solve computationally hard constraint satisfaction and optimization problems, such as the well-known traveling salesman problem, in which a salesman must find the shortest circular route visiting all cities on his itinerary exactly once. In all these areas of AI, computational search plays a key role.

The earliest AI approaches to chess used search methods to choose promising moves (Shannon 1950), and contemporary chess computers have managed to beat human grandmasters by deploying massive computational power alongside dictionaries of expert-provided openings and gambits. Similarly, computational search can be used in developing a conversational program to play Turing's imitation game. Finally, AI approaches to traveling salesman problems and their like use computational search to find a good quality solution.

Thus, search appears to be a mainstay of AI. In fact, it could be claimed that all intelligence is search (natural as well as artificial). This is likely to be an overstatement; a human chess expert can only evaluate a fraction of the moves considered by a computer, yet can still reliably beat their artificial opponent; similarly it is not obvious that we perform a search process analogous to the computer's when we talk to each other, yet our conversational ability is much greater. Still, it seems likely that search processes are involved in many important aspects of behavior and intelligence, both human and animal. By search process, we mean an internal search process over different representations of a problem within a brain. In this chapter, we explore what is known about computational search and its limitations, and speculate about how the study of natural intelligence might benefit from this information.

The Problem with Computational Search

Given their pervasiveness and general importance, much research effort in theoretical computer science has been invested in analyzing search problems and algorithms. A *search problem* is defined as considering a set of alternative *solutions X*, where the quality of each solution x in X can be evaluated using an *objective function f(x)*. The search problem is then usually to find the solution x with the "best" value *f(x)* (typically by minimizing or maximizing *f*). In this case, the search problem is one of *optimization* according to the objective function; however, the search could also be to *satisfice* by finding a solution whose objective value satisfies some minimum requirement. The definition just given is very general; there are almost no constraints on what the solutions in X and the objective function can represent. A *search algorithm* is then an automatic procedure for attempting to find the required solution to a given problem (i.e., for *solving* the problem), whether that requirement is to find the best available solution or simply one of sufficient quality. As we will discuss, some very powerful results have been derived showing that finding a good algorithm for search problems of the kind just described can present considerable difficulties.

Most Interesting Search Problems Are Hard

Before considering if search problems are hard, it is necessary to define what is meant by "hard." In theoretical computer science, this is done in terms of the efficiency of algorithms to solve problems. Briefly, an *efficient algorithm* is one that runs in *polynomial time*; in our search terms, this means that the time to find the best solution in a set having size n is no longer than a polynomial function of n, such as log n, n, n^2, etc. This upper bound is denoted with "big-oh" notation, such as $O(n^2)$, and one says that such an algorithm is in $O(n^2)$. In contrast, an *inefficient algorithm* is one that runs in exponential time; in other words, the upper bound is an exponential function of the size of the problem set n, such as 2^n, n^n, etc. As before, this upper bound is notated as $O(n^n)$, and we say that an algorithm is in $O(n^n)$, for example. This approach to studying algorithms neglects a lot of detail and focuses instead on what is really important: how the running time of the algorithm increases with the size of the solution set to which it is applied. The approach also ignores the detail of the computational device on which the algorithm is running, since all discrete computers of a certain complexity are able to do the same kinds of computation (Church 1936; Turing 1936).

Now consider the following apparently simple problem. The problem is from Boolean logic, where all formulae are written in terms of *variables*, which can be TRUE or FALSE, logical AND (TRUE if *both* arguments are TRUE, denoted ∧), logical OR (TRUE if *either* argument is TRUE, denoted ∨), and logical NOT (TRUE if the argument is FALSE, and FALSE if the argument is TRUE, denoted ¬). The problem is then to find a *satisfying assignment* of truth values to variables, such that a formula of the following kind evaluates to TRUE:

$$(A \lor C \lor \neg D) \land (B \lor \neg B \lor C). \tag{16.1}$$

The formula above is *satisfiable* if values of the variables can be found such that the first clause (in brackets) *and* the second clause are both true. Each clause is true if *any* of its *literals* (variables or their negation) are true. Since this is a satisfiability problem (i.e., is the formula satisfiable or not?), and since each clause has three literals, it is referred to as 3-SAT.

The above may seem rather technical and arcane, but 3-SAT has some fascinating and very useful properties. First, there is no known algorithm that can solve 3-SAT in less than exponential time, so as the number of clauses in the formula grows, the search time grows exponentially. This effectively means that in the worst case, the search for a solution might need to include every member of the solution set, which is clearly bad. However 2-SAT, in which the number of literals per clause is 2 instead of 3, can be solved with a polynomial-time algorithm; this transition in hardness is also seen in other kinds of problems. The particularly interesting thing about 3-SAT, however, is that it is representative of the difficulty of all interesting search problems. 3-SAT can be converted by a polynomial-time algorithm to all other problems for which no efficient algorithm is known, such as the traveling salesman problem mentioned earlier. This equivalence may not be immediately apparent, since 3-SAT is a yes/no problem, whereas the traveling salesman problem is one of optimization. A traveling salesman problem can, however, be turned into a decision problem by phrasing it as such: Is there a tour of length no more than k in this graph? Actually, the perceptive reader will see that this formulation is closer to a description of a satisficing problem than an optimization problem; the link to optimization further requires that k be reduced progressively until the answer to the preceding question is "no," at which point the optimal solution is that most recently found in determining the answer to the question for a larger value of k. Thus, finding an efficient algorithm for 3-SAT, or any of these other equivalent problems, would result in an efficient algorithm for *all* such problems. Computer scientists refer to these problems as belonging to the *complexity class* NP-Complete (NP-C). For a problem to be a member of NP-C, it means that no efficient algorithm for it is known to exist, so the only algorithms known for them run in exponential time. In contrast, those problems for which efficient algorithms *are* known belong to the complexity class P (for polynomial time). It is not known whether efficient algorithms for problems in NP-C do not exist, or whether they simply have not yet been discovered. However, given the decades of research into such problems, the consensus among computer scientists is that efficient algorithms for them really do not exist. This could be significant for brains, if they use computational search procedures for certain problems of that nature.

Efficient yet General Search Algorithms Are Impossible

The computational hardness of most interesting search problems, described in the last section, has led computer scientists to consider a number of heuristic approaches to finding solutions that are of good quality. Some of this research has been biologically inspired, although much mathematically grounded heuristics work has also been done. Some heuristics researchers, primarily in evolution-inspired algorithms, began to make claims that their heuristics were generally applicable to all problems, or even superior to alternative heuristics. In response to this, the *no-free-lunch* theorems for search were developed (Wolpert and Macready 1997). These results appear to prove that, across all possible search problems, and for any objective function, all search algorithms have equivalent performance. Given the strength of their results, these theorems require very stringent and unrealistic assumptions about the nature of the set of problems and the behavior of the algorithms. Critics countered that since these assumptions do not correspond to real-world search problems and algorithms, the no-free-lunch theorems do not offer useful results, and indeed some algorithms *can* be generally superior. A more recent extension of the no-free-lunch framework relaxes these assumptions and concludes that in fact there is a generally superior search algorithm which maximizes the expected quality of the solutions it finds in any finite amount of time, but it is blind enumeration of the set of possible solutions (Marshall and Hinton 2010). Less formally, the intuitive message is that when playing a game where the aim is to draw numbered balls out of a bag to find as high a value as possible in a given number of attempts, the best strategy is not to put balls you have already seen back in the bag before drawing again! Of course, such results do not mean that a particular search algorithm cannot be designed to perform well on a particular set of related problems. However, in conjunction with the computational hardness of most interesting problems, no-free-lunch theorems do seem to rule out general, efficient search algorithms, that are able to find the optimal solution to any problem in less time than it takes to enumerate all the solutions to that problem.

Why Things Might Not Be So Bad

Our discussion thus far has shown how most interesting search problems are computationally hard and that there is no generally superior search heuristic other than blind enumeration of all possible solutions. While algorithms can still be designed on a problem-by-problem basis to find good quality solutions, these results suggest that finding general search principles in the brain might be futile, and that search processes in the brain might only be applied to comparatively simple problems. In practice, however, computational search might be easier than it first appears.

Average Case versus Worst Case

The first way in which computational search might not be so difficult is that problems which are hard in the *worst case* might be easy *on average*. In describing the class of NP-C problems above, we defined it in terms of problems whose best-known algorithms run in exponential time. However, for exponential-time algorithms, such as those in $O(2^n)$, remember that the 2^n is an *upper bound* on the running time, so the running time can actually be lower on a particular instance of a problem. This upper bound is derived in terms of *worst-case* difficulty of a problem. However, the *average-case* difficulty of a problem is much more relevant, for brains as well as for computer scientists. Returning to the 3-SAT problem, it is easy to see that many instances of the problem can quickly be discovered to be satisfiable or unsatisfiable, such as the formula:

$$(A \vee A \vee \neg A) \wedge (A \vee A \vee \neg A), \tag{16.2}$$

where *any* value of A makes the formula true, or

$$\left(A \vee A \vee A\right) \wedge \left(\neg A \vee \neg A \vee \neg A\right), \tag{16.3}$$

where *no* value of A makes the formula true. In fact, it is interesting to know that for 3-SAT, there is a *phase transition* in the difficulty of problem instances. Below a critical threshold of the ratio of number of clauses to number of variables, almost all instances are satisfiable; above that threshold, almost all instances are unsatisfiable (Kirkpatrick and Selman 1994). The computationally difficult instances of 3-SAT are clustered around this critical threshold. Since 3-SAT is a representative computationally hard problem, this could represent a general characteristic of other hard search problems. Although a brain could be tackling a search problem that is, in theory, computationally infeasible, in practice, for most of the instances of that problem, it either readily encounters an optimal solution or it will be quickly established that such a solution does not exist. What matters for the brain is the kinds of problems that it has encountered over evolutionary time; since these problems are unlikely to all be hard instances, effective shortcuts in the search process might evolve.

Performance of Simple Heuristics

Another way in which shortcuts might be taken by brains doing computational search is in the use of heuristics. Although earlier we pointed out that the only general search heuristic is blind enumeration, for limited classes of problems certain very simple classes of heuristic can be shown to have better-than-average performance. One particularly simple local-search heuristic is *gradient descent*. In this framework, some local structure over the set of solutions is induced by defining a neighborhood operator, such as assignments to variables that differ in only one truth-value in the 3-SAT example discussed earlier. Local search then iterates a simple procedure: evaluate the quality of the current solution (in the 3-SAT example, this could be number of true clauses), evaluate the qualities of all neighboring solutions, then move to the neighbor giving the best improvement. If no improvement is possible, the search procedure terminates and the solution arrived at is chosen as the best found during the search. It is hard to imagine a more simple-minded search procedure, yet it has been shown that, for a variety of NP-C problems (e.g., the traveling salesman problem), choosing a neighborhood function having certain properties results in some interesting performance guarantees for the search process (Grover 1992). In particular, it can be shown that the local search process always converges on a solution whose quality is better than the average quality of the solution set, and that it will do so efficiently, in time proportional to the size of the solution set. Thus, even if faced with a hard search problem, in which the solution is neither easily found nor easily shown not to exist, a brain could efficiently arrive at a better-than-average solution, by following a very simple heuristic.

Learning and Evolvability

Thus far we have considered the optimization of a given target function; here we turn to another relevant topic related to search: *learning*. Humans learn all the time and develop new skills. Essentially, the brain is solving a lot of classification problems. Considering such classification problems, one tries to learn a function that gives a good classification for a given set of examples. In the simplest case, consider a function f that takes elements from a given set X and classifies them as either positive or negative. The field of machine learning (Mitchell 1997) is an integral part of computer science, whose goal is to design algorithms that make use of empirical data to do classification. Based on given observed examples (training data) and their classification, a learning algorithm has to generalize this classification to unknown examples coming from the same domain.

Again, theoretical computer scientists are interested in which classes of functions can be learned in polynomial time and which classes require exponential time to be learned. The field of computational learning theory (Kearns and Vazirani 1994) studies learning from a theoretical point of view and classifies which functions can be learned efficiently. *Efficient* always means in polynomial time with respect to the given input size n and the inverse of a tolerance error ε. The goal is to determine which classes of functions can be learned in polynomial time and which ones require more computational effort.

Recently, these techniques have been used to gain new insight into evolutionary learning by considering which classes of functions are learnable through an evolutionary algorithm. This is done under the term *evolvability*. Below, we introduce the most popular models in computational learning and relate them to the notion of evolvability. Later we will introduce a kind of evolutionary algorithm that is used for learning unknown functions in practice.

PAC Learning

The most popular model of learning in computational learning theory is the *probably approximately correct* (PAC) learning model developed by Valiant (2009). This model introduces complexity theory concepts, of the kind described in earlier sections, to machine learning and thus allows one to determine which classes of functions are learnable in an efficient way.

To make the task precise, the goal is to learn an unknown function, $f: X \rightarrow Y$, mapping elements from some input space X to their corresponding *class values* in Y. The function f comes from a known concept class C which contains functions of similar structure.

In the PAC learning model, the algorithm is given random examples of X according to an unknown distribution D and their corresponding class values. The goal is to compute a hypothesis h which approximates f in the following sense: Whenever a new example x from X is drawn according to the distribution D, h makes with probability $1 - \delta$ (where δ is positive but close to zero) an error of at most ε; that is, $|h(x) - f(x)| < \varepsilon$ holds with probability at least $1 - \delta$. A concept class C is *learnable* if an algorithm exists to solve the given task for every function in C in polynomial time. Note that there is no restriction on how an algorithm learns the given class of functions.

Often $Y = \{+1, -1\}$ holds; that is, the function can only take on these two class values. The reader may think of examples that are classified either as positive or negative, such as "there is a predator in the grass" or "there is not a predator in the grass" to give a biologically relevant example.

The basic PAC learning model is also referred to as distribution-independent learning as it works for any fixed distribution D. In the distribution-specific PAC learning model, the algorithm is required to learn the function f with respect to a distribution D that is known in advance. A more restricted model of PAC learning is *statistical query* (SQ) learning (Kearns 1998). SQ learning is motivated by random noise in the learning process. SQ learning is a natural restriction of PAC learning, where the algorithms are only allowed to use statistical properties of the data set rather than the individual examples.

Evolvability

Using these formal models of learning, theoretical insights can be gained on how an evolutionary process is able to learn. Recently, the learnability of evolutionary algorithms has been studied under the term evolvability. These studies provide insights into the process of evolution from the perspective of theoretical computer science. Feldman and Valiant (2008) motivate their studies with the following example: Consider the human genome of roughly 20,000 genes. For each gene, the condition under which the protein corresponding to it is expressed, in terms of all the other proteins, is encoded in its regulatory region. This means that each protein is controlled by a function f of the other 20,000 proteins. The question is: How expressive can this function be, such that it is able to perform the complex tasks of biology as well as be efficiently learnable by evolution?

Considering how difficult it is for an evolutionary process to discover a particular learning or classification algorithm and the representations used, evolution *is* relevant here. Since individual learning can also be thought of as an evolutionary process, such results can also be relevant for understanding the discovery of search and learning methods *within* individuals.

As in the PAC learning model, classes of functions are considered and examined as to whether they are evolvable (i.e., learnable by an evolutionary algorithm). Thus, similar to PAC learning—given a target function f from a concept class C of ideal functions, a class of *representations* R, and a probability distribution D over the input space—the task is to compute a representation r from R which with high probability outputs the same function value as f when choosing an input element according to D.

Evolvability (Feldman and Valiant 2008) considers mechanisms that can evaluate many argument functions. New functions are explored by mutation. Here it is crucial that only a small amount of the whole function set can be explored in each iteration of the evolution process, and that the evolution process only takes a limited number of generations. Furthermore, it is assumed that the performance of a function can be measured. This is crucial for evolution since better functions should have a higher chance of being transferred to the next generation. Selection of which functions to transfer to the next generation is based on this performance measure.

Valiant shows that his model of evolvability is a constrained form of PAC learning (Valiant 2009). The main difference between evolvability and PAC learning is that the general PAC learning framework allows the update of a hypothesis in an arbitrary way, depending on the examples that have been considered so far. In evolution, the update only depends on the aggregated knowledge that has been obtained during the process. This knowledge is given by the set of functions of the current generation. In contrast to the general PAC learning framework, one cannot look at a particular example presented in the past.

Valiant showed that parity functions which are learnable in the PAC framework are not evolvable (Valiant 2009). Furthermore, Feldman has given a new characterization of SQ learning and shown that if a function is SQ learnable, then it is also evolvable (Feldman 2008). This shows that a broad class of functions is learnable by evolutionary algorithms that run in polynomial time.

Having examined learning and its relation to evolvability from a theoretical point of view, we now introduce a class of evolutionary algorithms used to learn functions for classification and learning.

Genetic Programming

After having stated some theoretical results on learning, we want to examine how computer scientists make use of mechanisms in nature to come up with computer algorithms. Many scientists are acquainted with evolutionary algorithms, such as genetic algorithms. Genetic programming, developed by Koza (1991), is a type of evolutionary algorithm designed to learn certain types of functions; one evolves functions to solve the given task. Individuals are therefore functions, usually represented as trees describing mathematical expressions. Similar to the other evolutionary approaches, a set of individuals constitutes a population. A parent population creates an offspring population using *crossover* and *mutation*. The *fitness* of a function is measured in terms of its performance with respect to some test cases, possibly with penalties for unduly complicated functions to avoid overfitting. Based on their fitness, individuals from the combined populations of parents and children are selected to build the new parent population. The process is iterated until some stopping criterion is satisfied. In the case of crossover, two trees are combined to construct a new tree, which represents a new function. Mutation usually changes the tree slightly such that a similar tree is obtained. A crucial difference to Valiant's notion of evolvability is that genetic programming uses less powerful operators for constructing new solutions to the given problem. Valiant only uses mutation, but allows a much more powerful mutation operator. Here, a new function can be constructed by any algorithm; the only restriction is that it must run in polynomial time. Thus, a basic question is: How powerful are operators actually for evolution, and which setting is realistic to explain the evolutionary learning process?

Genetic programming has had success in the fields of symbolic regression, financial trading, medicine, biology, and bioinformatics. A particularly relevant application of genetic programming is that of Trimmer (2010, chapter 5) in an attempt to learn the well-known Rescorla-Wagner rule (Rescorla and Wagner 1972), which describes classical conditioning:

$$V \leftarrow V + \alpha\beta(\lambda - V). \tag{16.4}$$

This rule specifies an update mechanism for learning the value of a stimulus (V) based on experienced rewards (λ) and learning rate parameters (α and β). The work of Trimmer is interesting in that it takes a *fitness landscape* approach and considers the relative performance of Rescorla-Wagner, as well as other rules which could plausibly be discovered by the evolutionary process, to examine how hard learning that particular rule might be.

As discussed above, there are many applications of genetic programming but the theoretical foundations of this type of algorithm are still in their infancy. This is due to the complex stochastic processes of such algorithms, which are hard to analyze. Different approaches have been applied to understand the behavior of genetic programming in a theoretical way, such as Markov chain analyses, convergence, and computational complexity analyses (see Poli et al. 2010). The goal of these approaches is to understand the learning process and determine which structural properties make the learning task hard or easy.

Don't Optimize, Satisfice

The predominant approach in theoretical studies of behavior is to consider the optimal solution to a particular problem as a benchmark against which observed behavior is assessed (Parker and Maynard Smith 1990). This approach is possible because typically the problem under consideration is sufficiently simple so that an optimal solution can be derived. Classic examples relevant to behavioral ecology include bandit problems, secretary problems, and statistical decision problems. As soon as sufficiently complex search problems are considered, however, the optimality approach becomes impossible, because optimal solutions to these kinds of problems are unknown and may not even exist. In this new field, therefore, the problem is no longer one of *optimization* but of *satisficing*; that is, finding solutions that are *good enough*. Herbert

A. Simon (1996) referred to this as procedural rationality, as opposed to substantive rationality. Animals have been argued to satisfice, even when optimal solutions are possible (Gigerenzer et al. 1999); yet in computational search, satisficing is typically not a shortcut to the best known solution, it *is* the best known solution. It might appear that satisficing is no more computationally feasible than optimization, given its link with NP-C problems, such as 3-SAT (outlined above). The important point is, provided that the search criteria are set appropriately for the search problem, that the average case complexity of satisficing is much lower that optimization. If search criteria are set too high for the distribution of solution values in some class of search problems, satisficing will be akin to optimization; however, if the criteria are set low enough, but not so low as to accept anything, a useful satisfactory solution will usually be found with a relatively small amount of searching.

In conclusion, we hope that our discussion has explained why optimal search is so uniformly impossible in computational search problems. We suggest that the results on heuristic search from the computational science community offer a rich store of ideas for those interested in behavior and cognition.

Acknowledgments

We are grateful to Nathaniel D. Daw and Thomas T. Hills for helpful comments on an earlier draft and to the Ernst Strüngmann Forum for the invitation to participate in this extended discussion.

17

Problem Solving and Search in Networks

David Lazer and Ethan S. Bernstein

Abstract

This chapter examines the role that networks play in facilitating or inhibiting search for solutions to problems at both the individual and collective levels. At the individual level, search in networks enables individuals to transport themselves to a very different location in the solution space than they could likely reach through isolated experimental or cognitive search. Research on networks suggests that (a) ties to diverse others provide a wider menu of choices and insights for individuals, and (b) strong ties will be relatively more useful for complex information, and weak ties for simple information. At the collective level, these conclusions become less clear. The key question is how the collective operates to coordinate within the group versus beyond it so as to balance experimentation and convergence toward a solution. Collective coordination of search and collective evaluation of potential solutions may significantly influence the optimal network structure for collective problem-solving search.

Introduction

Millions of problems go to work each day in search of solutions. The process of search, or "investigation of a question" (as defined in the Oxford English Dictionary), is in part defined by networks. While only a decade ago "problem solving" evoked images of Rodin's *Thinker*, we now think of Obama's Blackberry, IBM's smarter planet campaign, and project managers being able to "Google" all the brains of their organizations (Douglas 2009). Although these are modern images, our capacity to solve complex problems based in part on the solutions of others is certainly a distinctive feature of human intelligence. When confronted with a problem, the search for a solution may happen in isolation, but it may also involve help from other human or nonhuman sources accessible through a network of ties; that is, "networked search." In networked search, the network of sources from which help may be received defines problem solvers' access to potential pieces of a solution, whereas strategies to create and search networks define problem solvers' approach to traverse the path to connect those pieces. The construction of problem solving as a networked search, in turn, poses a series of critical questions across multiple levels of analysis, including: Where do people go to find answers? What are the collective, emergent consequences of those behaviors?

Other chapters in this volume highlight the role of asocial search; for example, how individuals search for visual patterns (Wolfe, this volume) or search memory for a relevant fact or word (Davelaar and Raaijmakers, this volume). The search of our networks is analytically distinct but part of the broader picture of search; indeed, as we discuss below, networked search and isolated search can often substitute for each other. Asking one's spouse if they remember where you put the keys may be a substitute for wracking one's memory for where you may have thrown them earlier. Conceptualizing human search as being, in part, a networked process also offers distinct practical implications: with improved understanding of how collaborative networks operate comes the opportunity, and challenge, to design networks for improved efficiency of networked, social search by individuals, groups, organizations, institutions, and communities.

Here we focus on networked search as a core process of problem solving. We begin by providing a typology for understanding existing search research, categorized by types of search behavior. We then turn to our principal task of investigating similarities and paradoxes in networked search theory across two levels of analysis: individual and collective. In the process of connecting what has been very disparate literature, our hope is not only to solidify the theory of search in networks but also to distill some important themes and opportunities for future research.

The Role of Networks in Problem Solving

Let us begin by envisioning "solutions" to a problem as a basket of activities, where, generally speaking, the permutations of possible activities are limitless. Searching through the space of possible solutions presents an extraordinary challenge, especially if one assumes (as we do) that synergies among activities are endemic—where, for example, activities A and B may be harmful singly but beneficial together. Given a very large solution space, with high levels of synergy among activities, incremental search (e.g., hill climbing without first determining the highest peak) will be a recipe for being stuck in a local optimum.

A Typology of Search

Search, at its broadest interpretation, may be classified based on the strategy used to navigate through a problem space. Figure 17.1 offers a typology of

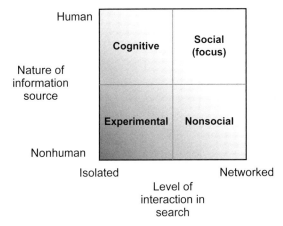

Figure 17.1 Typology of search across two dimensions. X-axis represents the level of interaction in search (isolated or networked); Y-axis indicates nature of the information source (human or nonhuman).

search useful for focusing our discussion across two common dimensions: whether search is isolated or networked (X-axis) and whether the information source searched is human or nonhuman (Y-axis). Individually, these dimensions are common in relevant literatures; however, the combination is novel and results in four distinct (although combinable) categories of search: cognitive, experimental, social sources, or nonsocial sources.

Isolated search may be *cognitive* when the information source is human (the individual searcher's mind) and the "hardware" is a brain, deriving solutions through mental models of how the world works that remain relatively consistent over time. Alternatively, isolated search may be *experimental*, involving interpreting feedback from attempted activities, adjusting hypotheses, and attempting an activity again, as foraging behavior may be characterized (e.g., McNamara and Fawcett, this volume). When search is networked rather than isolated, external sources of information may be consulted from either other humans (*social*) or nonhuman sources (*nonsocial*, e.g., files). One might imagine an individual searching for a Starbucks in a city. If this person had previously been to that city, the location of a Starbucks might be recalled so that an isolated human search based on memory of that location could be conducted (cognitive search). The person could simply begin walking, assuming that there is a high density of Starbucks and that one would likely be found within a few blocks by circling around the focal location (experimental search). Alternatively, the individual could ask someone walking by for directions (social search) or simply consult a smartphone (nonsocial search).

Using this typology, our first proposition would be to assert that most individuals, when search is isolated, will not make large changes in their solutions to problems they confront, in part because in a complex world, it is difficult or impossible to anticipate the impact of radical change. As in the model of *exploratory information foraging* presented by Fu (this volume), search may begin without sufficiently precise criteria to judge the relevance of uncovered radical information to form a solution. If the objective of search were to thwart a terrorist attack, it may be hard to determine if increased activity in a suspected cell of a suspicious group is a relevant clue or a false lead. The social component (networked, human), however, offers the capacity for major change, with less risk, through observation of the activities of others. Relevance (or lack thereof) of radical new information to an optimal solution may be inferred from the choices of other human investigators proximate to you; that is, using others as prototypes allows searchers to make larger changes, based on radical new information, with lower risk.

Our focus here is thus on social search, where friendship, trust, belief, and expertise are all dyadic variables that have been examined as drivers of search in networks. Substantial research highlights positional factors that are likely to be related to successful search. For example, Burt (2004) has argued that a position of brokerage (i.e., knowing people who do not know each other) provides advantage by (a) providing ongoing flows of diverse information, (b) facilitating access to nonredundant information in extant cases, and (c) enhancing individual cognitive capacity (see also Burt 1992).

Levels of Analysis

Social search may be executed by individuals or collectives. Following the vast majority of prior treatments of search, we begin our discussion with the individual level, where the impetus of social search emanates from a single individual. We then turn to the collective level, which becomes analytically relevant when outcomes are not simply the sum of individual efforts, but rather the result of some interaction among individual efforts (e.g., the purposeful coordination of a group or where there are informational spillovers from one individual to the next).

Taking our cues from prior literature, our discussion of the collective will begin by assuming the same theory of networked search operates at both the individual and collective levels, with the primary difference being the expansion of the locus of search impetus from a single individual to a collection of individuals. In effect, collective search simply shifts the boundary between "inside" and "outside." At the individual level, inside is an individual brain, and outside is everything else. At the collective level, the boundary expands what is inside to include multiple individuals (e.g., a group), with a shared set of networks on the outside. As we progress, we identify what we believe may be at least one key theoretical tension between the individual and collective levels.

Locus of Problem Solving: Individuals

Individual networked search, by definition, locates the impetus for problem solving squarely in the hands of one central individual (ego), who may draw on various baskets of activities, situated in diverse networks, to find solutions. Despite the substantial attention devoted to team-based problem solving over the past decade, the locus of most theory on network-related search is still the individual. Here we explore two tensions in the individual networked search literature that lie at the heart of current research: creating versus conforming connections (related to number and strength of ties) and tacit versus explicit knowledge (content that flows across the ties).

Individual Creating versus Conforming

In the quest for theories of performance in networked search, perhaps the most frequently studied tension is that between creation and conformity, exploration and exploitation, innovation and copying (March 1991). Search networks, for example, provide not only information but also exert control, for example, through conformity pressures.

The visibility of one's behavior to others creates the opportunity for pressure on the individual to conform to others' solutions, whether optimal or not. Agent-based simulation models have demonstrated that the more efficient the network is at disseminating information, the better the performance of the system is on the short run but that it is worse over the long term (Lazer and Friedman 2007): connectedness encourages fast conformity at the expense of optimality. In this model of parallel problem solving, a system is made up of a set of agents, each of whom is independently searching for answers (Lazer and Friedman 2007). The performance of each agent is independent, in the sense that the performance of agent A has no direct bearing on any other agent, making this a set of individuals rather than a collective. Performance is, however, interdependent in the sense that there is a network connecting agents which allows them to observe the behaviors and performances of other agents (but not otherwise communicate). The essential conclusion from these simulations, as well as similar experimental studies (e.g., Mason et al. 2008), is that for *complex* problems, networks that were inefficient at disseminating information enabled a more thorough search of the problem space by agents, and thus better long-run performance by the system. For performance, the conformity imposed by connectedness was more troublesome than the creativity enabled by access was productive.

Such findings are consistent with an array of research that highlights the dangers of processes of rapid consolidation of individual theories and experimentation (Janis 1972; Page 2007), including McNamara and Fawcett's research on premature stopping behavior in this volume. We would expect these dangers to be particularly salient in the case of network closure (Uzzi 1997), where one's contacts can see each other. Conversely, we hypothesize that an "opaque" network, which provides more "spatial separation" (increased communication costs) between nodes (Duncan 1976; Raisch and Birkinshaw 2008), will therefore encourage experimentation, reduce copying, and lengthen exploration while limiting premature stopping.

We also note that for a particular problem, there may be multiple useful paths to finding a solution, and a critical and understudied question involves which direction of search an individual takes. Binz-Scharf, Lazer, and Mergel (unpublished), for example, study how individuals in a DNA forensics laboratory search for answers to problems they encounter. In this study, a wide range of sources are utilized, ranging from nonhuman sources (manuals, journals) to institutional support (a help desk for software) to social resources (friends). Further, people often use a distinctive sequence in their search: some, for example, will thoroughly search nonhuman sources first, because no reputational consequences are at stake for getting an answer from a journal or Google, whereas asking for help from a person could entail loss of face. Given the path dependencies of many answers, study of the behaviors that drive directions for search is an area of promise for future work.

Knowledge Transfer for Simple versus Complex Problems

The literature on knowledge transfer distinguishes between tacit and explicit knowledge. Explicit knowledge is knowledge that is easy to codify (Nonaka 1994; Gavetti and Levinthal 2000; Edmondson et al. 2003), such as directions to a restaurant (at least in most geographies). Tacit knowledge is knowledge that is difficult to codify, because of its complexity or contingent nature (e.g., an answer that begins with "it depends" likely tends toward the tacit end of the scale).

Because it is easy to codify, explicit knowledge is more likely accessible through nonhuman sources of information, such as a reference manual or materials that could be found, for example, through Google. Alternatively, one could consult with an individual or set of individuals about possible answers, where weak ties will likely suffice in providing an answer. Even if an answer is not provided, a reliable path to the optimal answer—a well-tested routine that has proven to be a fruitful path to find an answer (Nelson and Winter 1982)—may be provided such that the individual has a stable roadmap to the solution, like a treasure map, and need only to execute it to succeed.

For tacit knowledge, nonsocial sources of information become less useful because (by definition) tacit knowledge cannot easily be formally represented. Less trivially, strong ties are particularly important to transfer tacit knowledge (Hansen 1999). The reason for this is that transferring tacit knowledge smoothly is likely costly, requiring that both actors have background understanding of each other and speak a similar (and similarly situated) language (Bechky 2003). These requirements are presumably more likely given strong ties, and thus transfer of tacit knowledge is eased when embedded in a broader set of exchanges between two individuals.

Individual Social Search: Summary

Even our very limited treatment here is sufficient to distill one key issue in individual networked search; namely, that the complexity of the problem space may dictate the characteristics of an optimal network. We return to this point in more detail below (see section on Discussion and Implications).

Locus of Problem Solving: Collective

The collective level is relevant if collective-level consequences result from how individuals are connected together. This might be the case where there is a functional interdependence among the activities of different individuals (e.g., the value produced by activity one by person A depends on whether person B engages in activity two). It would also be the case where there is informational interdependence among actors: person A learns something and transmits it to person B.

There are many constructions of the collective in the social sciences. The literature on groups focuses on small sets of people (typically less than a dozen), with well-defined boundaries, usually structured around some homogeneous, shared purpose. The literature on organizations generally focuses on formal bureaucratic structures, often structured around heterogeneous purposes, on a scale of hundreds or thousands. The literature on communities, broadly construed, can span collectives from thousands to billions. Given the nested nature of these constructs, our focus here is largely on problem solving in the most fundamental form of collective: groups.

Following Alderfer (1977), we define a group as an intact social system, complete with boundaries, interdependence for some shared purpose, and differentiated members—that which Hackman (2012) refers to as *purposive groups*, real groups that exist to accomplish something. This definition incorporates two key identifiers which distinguish a group from other collections of individuals (Hackman 2012):

1. Members can be distinguished from non-members, by both members and non-members.
2. Members depend on each other to achieve a collective purpose, accepting specialized roles in the process.

Although other definitions of groups may differ, because of our focus on search as a form of problem solving, we follow Hackman (2012:430) in excluding "casual gatherings…, reference groups, identity groups, and statistical aggregations of the attributes, estimates, or preferences of people who do not actually interact with one another." We would argue that this definition holds even in an age where groups may never meet face-to-face or may only stay together for a limited time, such as distributed teams in large organizations (Hackman and Wageman 2005; O'Leary and Cummings 2007; Hackman 2012).

From Individual to Group

The key conceptual question about networked search by groups is how one aggregates from the individual to collective. We begin with the proposition that the theory of networked search operating at the individual level remains consistent when analyzing the collective level—only the boundary between inside and outside shifts outward to include multiple individuals on the inside. In other words, with collective problem solving, the search for the best basket of activities to form a solution is distributed among a set of individuals; there is a defined division of labor and rewards for reaching a solution that is distributed across members of the group (although not necessarily equally). The key questions then become:

- How are these networked search tasks coordinated inside the group to yield performance?
- Does the relationship between external network structure and search performance change as a result of the actor being a collective rather than an individual?

Coordination of Search Tasks

Many, perhaps even most, important complex problems are not solvable in an efficient manner by an individual because the scale of the effort may be too great, or the scope of the skills required too broad. It is for precisely this reason that, when individuals are the locus of search, they often supplement their own cognitive and experimental search with networked search to access solutions and capabilities held by others. Such an individual-centric model for collective search by humans faces, however, a key limitation: failure to account for *coordinated* search through a problem space.

For example, if we take the basic parallel problem-solving paradigm (a set of agents, all of whom are working on the same problem, with independent payoffs), but allow agents to communicate about *how* to search through the problem space, as a group would be expected to do, collective search behavior might change dramatically, especially if rewards for finding a solution were shared by the group. It is possible that a group might decide to diversify behaviors so as to make collective search more thorough or to focus search on what are seen as promising areas of the problem space. Thus, within the parallel problem-solving framework, the question is: How does the network affect how groups search through a problem space? One might also ask: How does the network affect how groups *decide* to search through a problem space? We are not familiar with research directly on this point; partially relevant is the work on the performance implications of transactive memory (Wegner 1987; Liang et al. 1995; Austin 2003; Brandon and Hollingshead 2004) and team familiarity (Huckman et al. 2009), which focuses on how people learn to work with specific others as well as work on self-organization in groups (Trist et al. 1963; Barker 1993; Arrow and Burns 2003; Arrow and Crosson 2003).

The general set of questions around division of labor and coordination of individual efforts in a collective transcends issues around collective problem solving. Many problems require some division of labor, splitting the problem into subproblems, each of which is in turn solved by individuals (or smaller groups). Some activities may require efforts by multiple people or multiple individuals with special and mutually exclusive skills. There is a vast literature in organizational theory on process and coordination (e.g., Mintzberg 1979; Schein 1985, 1987; Hackman 2012). Relatively little of this literature addresses problem solving per se; most focuses on the execution of well-defined, if sometimes complex, tasks (e.g., how to create an effective assembly process). A full mapping of how this literature might apply to problem-solving search is beyond the scope of this chapter. Key questions that we would highlight, however, include:

- *How does performance of individuals map to the performance of the whole?* Steiner (1976) offers a particularly useful typology: Some search tasks are additive, essentially the sum of the contributions of every member of the group. Others are disjunctive (only the best performer matters) or conjunctive (only the worst performer matters).
- *What is the structure of interdependence among individuals?* Some search tasks require synchronous, coordinated action among different agents; others require asynchronous action. Creating a Wikipedia page with a compendium of facts about some notable individual, for example, requires little coordination; contributors can simply assess what is missing at a given point in time and fill gaps. Investigation of a crime, however, requires coordinated action among the involved investigators.

Both well-functioning groups and networks facilitate coordination, and thus a simple hypothesis would be that higher levels of interdependence among agents require denser networks between those agents. There are, however, many mechanisms to facilitate coordination beyond networks in human systems. Standardization, for example, is one major mechanism for coordinating behavior without communicating. The need to communicate at a given moment to allow for synchronized action is eliminated by our ability to track time accurately and the convergence of particular conventions around time keeping. The question regarding the role of networks thus becomes one of the (sometimes large) residual: Given the other mechanisms for coordination, which network structures, both inside and outside of the collective, support group performance in solving a problem?

Relationship between Network Structure and Search Performance for Collectives

Just as was the case for individuals, a blanket assertion that more and stronger ties would be better is clearly not the right answer for the collective.

Inside

With regard to the network inside the group, consider the classic Asch experiment (1956), in which individuals conformed to the (false) group norm; the choices of subjects were visible to the other members of the group. One difference between individual and collective networked search lies on the inside of the collective: collectives do not always have access to all of the knowledge within the collective the way that individuals ordinarily do. Put differently, collectives "forget" a lot more than individuals do. This finding comes from the particularly substantial thread of related research focused on the issue of information aggregation within groups, especially on *hidden profile* tasks (Stasser and Titus 1985, 2003). In a hidden profile task, information is distributed among group members—some of which is redundant, some of which is (privately) held by single individuals—and the group is searching for a "right" answer that requires individuals to combine their privately held information. The robust, and paradoxical, finding of this research is that despite incentives to maximize group performance, individuals will tend to focus their discussion on commonly held information and not discuss (or reveal) information that is privately held, even though that information is necessary for group success. This has led to substantial research on the conditions that will lead individuals to reveal the information that they alone have (Sunstein 2006).

The hidden profile paradigm is based on group discussion; however, an older vein of research, which came out of the Small Group Network Laboratory at MIT in the 1950s (Bavelas 1950; Guetzkow and Simon 1955; see also Leavitt 1951), examined information aggregation in the context of distributed information in networks. In this research, information would be distributed in a group, where members each had a signal about the state of the world. Successful answering of the problem by the group required pooling all of these signals together and disseminating the right answer to the entire group. Individuals were connected to a subset of the entire group and could pass a signal on to one of their contacts. The key question was: What network structure facilitated group success? The robust answer was that centralized networks worked best for simple problems whereas decentralized networks functioned best for complex problems that required more individual effort.

Neither of the above research paradigms, however, incorporated the idea of individual experimentation (i.e., individuals might proactively seek information that the group does not have) through coordinated search via external networks. Therefore, we turn our attention to the other side of the collective boundary.

Outside

Just as with individuals, groups that are well connected to external networks run a risk of suffering reduced performance. Through a field experiment in a manufacturing context, Bernstein (2012) has demonstrated that a modest increase in group-level privacy (reduced observability through stronger group boundaries) can improve sustainably and significantly assembly-line performance by as much as 10–15% on a simple assembly task, by supporting productive deviance, localized experimentation, distraction avoidance, and continuous improvement.

In the context of problem solving, experimentation necessarily requires nonconformity; visibility through the network (whether internal or external to the collective) may therefore stymie new behaviors. Given that perhaps the dominant small group unit is, even today, the family (i.e., a group made up of people with shared genetics), we speculate as to whether certain individual behaviors that might be viewed as dysfunctional (e.g., stubbornness) might actually be beneficial at the group level because they maintain diversity within the group, yielding greater group success, and thus improved propagation of genes.

While the importance of maintaining access to diverse perspectives was also relevant at the individual level, the question of how network structure influences performance at the collective level is complicated by the fact that the collective has both an internal and external component to its network. We believe this complication calls for more research to build a more nuanced theory of networked search by collectives, a recommendation we explore in the next section.

Discussion and Implications

Two focal points have been identified for thinking about search in networks and problem solving: the individual and the collective. At the individual level, network research highlights the value of having diverse information sources as well as strong ties for complex information and weak ties for simple. At the collective level, we argue that problem complexity requires an external network structure that slows the consolidation processes in the system (see Figure 17.2), given the internal tendencies of groups.

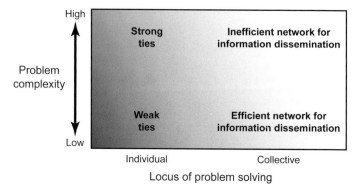

Figure 17.2 Preconditions for successful search in external networks.

There is a potential tension between what is optimal at these two levels. As Lazer and Friedman (2006) describe, when groups confront complex problems, there is a potential "tragedy of the network": individuals have an interest in not engaging in costly experimentation, but in positioning themselves to receive information from others quickly, whereas the group has an interest in individual experimentation and putting the brakes on information spread.

Research into that tension is made more interesting, and more urgent, in light of modern information and communication technologies, which offer the potential for vastly more efficient communication outside of collectives. Bernstein's (2012) finding of substantial value to group-level privacy, even in contexts like simple assembly manufacturing where complete transparency and observability is the standard, suggests the possibility of rather perverse consequences to rewiring the network of communication to make it more efficient. Indeed, given that most of human existence has been under conditions of much more limited global communication, this raises the question of whether there is a fundamental misalignment between individual psychology (which is to work on problems together) and collective outcomes in an age where the technical limits to working together and learning from one another have been radically reduced.

The more nuanced question regarding modern information and communication technologies is how the mechanisms for global coordination interplay with those of local coordination. Nonhuman foraging, with some exceptions, typically allows for just local coordination, because the means to communicate nonlocally is lacking. Thus, a key analytic question must focus on the global logic of purely local search behaviors. If one is looking at swarming, for example, key questions become: How do agents distribute themselves over a landscape, based on local spacing decisions? How does the swarm allocate enough agents to resource retrieval when a resource is found? Nonlocal communication is, however, eminently possible for humans. There are mechanisms to apprise a whole population of certain facts and shortcuts that rapidly diffuse relevant information.

While we only raise the questions here, a useful avenue for further research would be on the interplay of these different levels of mechanisms to coordinate search, particularly in this contrast between the operation of theory at the individual and collective levels. One potential flaw in a hive/swarm metaphor for human behavior is that information is constantly flowing into groups, in part because most individuals belong to many distinct groups. There is a natural osmosis of information among groups, where groups actively manage ties to the external environment as necessary to help in problem solving. These observations point to the need for study of search in networks with many methodologies, as individual and collective research tend to be executed in different contexts with different methods. Classic experimental work offers great promise, for example, for studying how people choose to balance experimentation and exploration with manipulated network structures. However, it is equally clear that problem solving in organizations, families, and societies comes with contexts that interplay and structure the directions that people can search. This highlights the need for field research that uses replicable methods systematically across settings to evaluate which patterns of search are robust, and which patterns interplay with particular contextual factors.

In concluding, we would like to step beyond future research possibilities to offer one hypothesis we find particularly intriguing. A common theme throughout this chapter has been the importance of complexity in influencing how increasing connectedness will impact performance. The literature suggests, as presented in Figure 17.2 at the individual level, that more complexity requires more connectedness. This seems consistent with common perceptions of the world today: the world's problems have become more complex, but our ability to address these problems has improved with modern technologies, which in turn permit substantially better connectedness for networked search. The anomaly, however, is in the increased prevalence of teams. As networked search has become more efficient, current theory would suggest that groups would become less important, not more—that the network has become so powerful that individuals could harness it for problem solving without the need for well-performing teams, which are not easy or costless to build. Why, then, in the age of Google, Facebook, e-mail, texting, instant messaging, and costless phone calls is there apparently an increased reliance on teams as a key unit of production (Arrow and McGrath 1995; Edmondson and Nembhard 2009; Hackman 2002, 2012)?

One possibility is that it is precisely *because* networked search has become so much more powerful that teams have become more prevalent. By giving the group some power to balance inside and outside activities, collective search solves many of the counterproductive aspects of increasingly powerful networks in networked search. The construction of boundaries may buffer individuals from outside control, allowing a more deliberative, exploratory space within the group. If that were the case, in a world where ever-escalating connectivity enables exploitation of what is collectively known, teams would be increasingly important as instruments of exploration.

18

From Plato to the World Wide Web

Information Foraging on the Internet

Wai-Tat Fu

Abstract

Generally speaking, two conditions make cognitive search possible: (a) symbolic structures must be present in the environment and (b) these structures must be detectable by a searcher, whose behavior changes based on the structures detected. In this chapter, information search on the Internet is used to illustrate how a theoretical framework of these two conditions can assist our understanding of cognitive search. Discussion begins with information foraging theory (IFT), which predicts how general symbolic structures may exist in an information environment and how the searcher may use these structures to search for information. A computational model called SNIF-ACT (developed based on IFT) is then presented and provides a good match to online information search for specific target information. Because a further component important to cognitive search is the ability to detect and learn useful structures in the environment, discussion follows on how IFT can be extended to explain search behavior that involves incremental learning of the search environment. Illustration is provided on how different forms of semantic structures may exist in the World Wide Web, and how human searchers can learn from these structures to improve their search. Finally, the SNIF-ACT model is extended to characterize directed and exploratory information foraging behavior in information environments.

Introduction

The ability to search for useful resources has long been taken as a prime indicator of intelligence. The first decade or so of research on artificial intelligence (AI) focused almost exclusively on the study of search processes (Nilsson 1971), and AI was almost synonymous for search. The problem of search, however, has a much longer history than AI research. In the *Meno*, for example,

Plato (in his account of Socrates) posed the problem of search (inquiry) as a basic conundrum for understanding human intelligence (Plato 380 BCE):

> *Meno*: And how will you inquire, Socrates, into that which you know not? What will you put forth as the subject of inquiry? And if you find what you want, how will you ever know that that is what you did not know?

In the *Meno*, Plato reasoned that whenever we are in a state where there is a lack of knowledge (or information), we are compelled to search (inquire) for the information, even though we may not know exactly what it is that we seek; thus we face the problem of evaluating whether the information we find is that which we lack. The problem posed by Plato is fundamental: *How do we know how to search for something that we do not know?* Plato's solution is that we possess preexisting knowledge that allows this search. Although the origin of this preexisting knowledge is debatable (Plato argued in favor of a previous existence), for our purpose, let it suffice to assume that an agent has the ability to detect symbolic structures and to behave differentially to the detected structures. Indeed, perhaps one major characteristic of cognitive search is the *intelligence* exhibited by this particular ability to detect structures in the environment, in the general sense that an intelligent search is one that allows the searcher to decide *how* to find *relevant* information. This may sound trivial for humans (or at least many believe that humans always know what they are searching for), yet answering the question "how can an agent search intelligently" proves to be very challenging. In fact, in areas such as AI and cognitive science, *search is considered to be a central process that makes intelligence possible*, and thus has been a primary emphasis of AI research for decades (see Newell and Simon 1976).

The focus of this chapter is on a specific kind of search: information search. My goal is to demonstrate how the nature of cognitive search is manifested through the systematic investigation of the complex activities involved when people search for information. Although the Internet was not invented when Plato contemplated the question of search, I will demonstrate how the major questions that he raised are still relevant and can be used to guide understanding and theoretical development of information search on the Internet. In particular, I emphasize two important aspects of information search: (a) the structure of the Internet's information environment and (b) the means by which humans detect this structure and use it to guide their search for information.

Information Search

Searching for information has increasingly become an indispensable part of our daily activities: from checking the weather to planning a trip; from finding recipes to conducting a literature review for scientific research. While these activities may seem mundane, many scientific questions lurk behind them and are relevant (or even equivalent) to those in research on different kinds of cognitive activities, such as problem solving (finding a solution to an algebra problem), decision making (finding an apartment), or foraging (finding high- or low-calorie food).

One important aspect of search is that the searcher often needs to extract information incrementally from the task environment to find the desired resource. Consider an extreme case in which resources are randomly distributed in the task environment and the searcher is unable to detect any structures or patterns in the environment. In this situation, the searcher can be said to have no more intelligence than a random (without knowledge) searcher. In most cases, however, the environment has some structure or patterns that are detectible by the searcher, so that the searcher can use this structure to acquire knowledge about the environment and improve search. Knowledge about the environment allows the searcher to behave differentially based on the detected structure and to search selectively on one path instead of others so that a resource can be reached in as few steps as possible.

An important question in the study of cognitive search is how *intelligence* is manifested through the search process. Following Newell and Simon (1976), I argue that intelligence in information search can only be found when two conditions are met:

1. Detectable structures must be present in the information environment.
2. The searcher must be able to detect these structures and use them to control search activities.

The first condition is usually determined by the nature of the environment or the task, whereas the second involves the characteristics of the searcher. It is important to note that the amount of search is not a direct measure of the amount of intelligence being exhibited. To the contrary, I argue that the study of cognitive search is concerned with the question about how an agent is able to behave differentially as it acquires information from the environment, such that a large amount of search *would* be required if the agent *did not behave* in such a way. Before I elaborate on this point, by demonstrating a specific model of information foraging that captures the efficient nonrandom search behavior of people on the Internet, I will first highlight the evidence for structure in the Internet that facilitates search. Then I will demonstrate how an intelligent searcher can navigate these environments both to find specific information and to learn about the underlying information structure in an exploratory fashion.

Structure of the Internet's Information Environment

In a world in which the Internet has become pervasive, information search is almost synonymous with search on the World Wide Web, which is dominated by the use of search engines. Those who have experience with Internet search engines find that they work reasonably well in most cases. The major reason why search engines perform well (and appear intelligent) can, indeed, be attributed to their ability to exploit the inherent structure of the Web's environment. Take the algorithm *PageRank*, used by the popular search engine *Google*, as an example. PageRank works by analyzing the link structure of Web pages to assign each page a *PageRank score* (Brin and Page 1998). The exact method to derive the PageRank score (and how it is combined with other methods) is beyond the scope of this chapter; however, the general idea is to derive the score of a page based on its links to other pages, such that each link represents a "vote" to the page. Pages that have higher PageRank scores have more weight in their votes. Thus, a page with a high PageRank score is linked to many pages that also have high PageRank scores. PageRank scores can then be used to rank the list of pages returned from a search engine; the assumption is that the page with the highest score will most likely lead the searcher to find the target information.

The primary reason why link structures in the WWW can be exploited to facilitate search is that Web pages tend to occur in "patches"; that is, there tends to be a few "hubs" that connect to many pages, and many pages that are only loosely connected to other pages. The formation of these hubs is often the result of two related processes:

1. There is a general tendency for people to link new pages to "authoritative" or "high-quality" pages; once a page becomes a hub, it attracts even more pages to link to it, creating a rich-gets-richer effect.
2. When a new page is created and linked to other pages, the linked pages tend to have related topics to the new page.

Because of these tendencies, the information environment becomes "patchy": pages that contain related topics tend to be within short distances of one another and a common "hub" (measured by the number of clicks required to move between two pages). This characteristic is commonly found in the growth of a *scale-free network* (Barabási 2009). A scale-free network has the characteristic that the size of the network (i.e., number of Web pages) may increase without significantly increasing the average distance between any two nodes (i.e., the number of clicks between two random Web pages). A common example of a scale-free network is the air transportation system: The existence of "hub" airports allows new airports to be introduced without significantly increasing the average number of transfers between any two random airports. As long as the new airports are connected to nearby hubs, one can reach any airport through the hubs.

In general, exploiting link structures (and identifying hub pages) in the WWW allows the searcher to navigate more quickly to the target information. This method works well as long as the information for which they are searching is connected to one another through hub pages. Search engines that exploit link structures work well *on average* for two interrelated reasons: (a) "rich patches" (hub pages) exist in the information environment and (b) most people are interested in information in one of the rich patches. However, when searching for information outside of a rich patch (e.g., when searching for information related to topics that are not yet sufficiently well connected to form hub pages), the likelihood that search engines can find the information decreases dramatically (e.g., searching for "cognitive search" on the Web will be unlikely to lead to information as rich as the chapters in this volume).

In summary, search engines generally support the exploitation of popular, well-connected information patches (reflected by the link structures constructed by Web page designers), but they do not generally support exploration for new information that is not already connected to rich information patches.

Targeted Search in the Internet Information Environment

Information foraging theory is an important theory of human information search (Fu and Pirolli 2007; Pirolli 2007; Pirolli and Card 1999). It predicts how humans interpret information cues and use these to decide how to navigate in an information environment to find specific information targets (e.g., evaluating and selecting hyperlinks when navigating in the WWW; Fu and Pirolli 2007). IFT assumes that people adapt their information-seeking behavior to maximize their rate of gaining useful information to meet their task goals (similar to optimal foraging theories developed in behavioral ecology; Stephens and Krebs 1986), and selectively to proceed along information paths based on their utility (McFadden 1974) by following cues encountered in the information environment. The theory further assumes that adaptive information systems evolve toward states that maximize gains of valuable information per unit cost. Thus IFT provides a principled method to understand how humans detect and adapt to the information structures in an environment and differentially follow an information path based on the interpretation of the detected structures.

The crucial element in IFT is the measure of *information scent*, which is defined based on a Bayesian estimate of the relevance of a distal source of information (whether the target information can be found) conditional on the proximal cues (e.g., a text snippet, such as the title of a page or the link text on a search page). Search by following an information scent is adaptive because search strategies are sensitive to the inherent predictive structures in the environment. In other words, similar to foraging behavior by animals, the decisions on *where* to search for information (food) and *when* to stop searching (patch-leaving policy) are assumed to be adapted to the statistical structures of the information environment. The detection and utilization of the structures are characterized as an adaptive response to the demands and constraints imposed by the information environments.

To a certain extent, this adaptive principle integrates the two conditions for exhibiting intelligence in the above-mentioned search. First, IFT assumes that information structures exist and that these structures emanate from two sources. The first source is the semantic structures embedded in text, and these are inherent language structures from which we derive meaning (Kintsch 1998). When a searcher sees a text snippet of a hyperlink (e.g., the link text or short description of a link that is returned from search engines), he/she can infer the relevance of the information on the page by estimating the semantic similarities between the text snippet and the information goal. The second source is the link structures between Web pages. As discussed earlier, patches which contain similar information contents (in terms of topical or semantic relevance assumption) tend to be closer to each other (in terms of number of links between them). The second condition of IFT is that people detect these structures by interpreting information cues (e.g., text snippets) and, by inferring their relevance to their information goal through a process that is inherent in human semantic memory (Anderson et al. 2004), they reach a decision on an information path through a stochastic choice process (McFadden 1974). Therefore, when a searcher selects a link that has high semantic overlap between the link text and the information goal, the searcher is getting closer to the information patch that contains the target information (i.e., assuming that a hill-climbing strategy works well).

To illustrate how IFT captures the essence of intelligence exhibited by information search, let us consider one instance of IFT: a computational model called *SNIF-ACT* (Fu and Pirolli 2007), which was developed as an extension of ACT-R (Anderson et al. 2004). The model was fit to detailed moment-by-moment Web surfing behavior of individuals studying in a controlled laboratory setting. The basic structure of the SNIF-ACT model is identical to that of a cognitive model called the *Bayesian satisficing model* (BSM) (Fu 2007; Fu and Gray 2006), which was developed to explain individual learning and choice behavior in repeated sequential decision situations. BSM is composed of a Bayesian learning mechanism and a local decision rule. SNIF-ACT applies the BSM to Web information search and assumes that, when users evaluate links on a Web page, they will incrementally update their perceived relevance of the Web page according to a Bayesian learning process. A local decision rule then decides when to stop evaluating links. Evaluation of additional links continues until the perceived relevance of the new links is lower than the cost of evaluating them. At that point, the best link encountered thus far will be selected.

To illustrate the behavior of the model, consider a case where the model is facing a single Web page with multiple links. Three actions are possible, each represented by a separate production rule (hereafter referred to as a "production"; see Anderson et al. 2004): Attend-to-Link, Click-Link, and Backup-a-Page. Similar to BSM, these productions compete against each other according to the random utility theory (McFadden 1974). That is, at any point in time, the model will attend to the next link on the page, click on a link on a page, or decide to leave the current page and return to the previous page. The utilities of the three productions are derived from the link likelihood equation and can be calculated as:

$$\text{Attend-to-Link: } U(n+1) = \frac{U(n) + IS(Link)}{1 + N(n)} \tag{18.1}$$

$$\text{Click-Link: } U(n+1) = \frac{U(n) + IS(BestLink)}{1 + k + N(n)} \tag{18.2}$$

$$\text{Backup-a-page: } U(n+1) = MIS(\text{Previous Pages}) \\ - MIS(\text{Links 1 to } n) - GoBackCost \tag{18.3}$$

$U(n)$ represents the utility of the production at cycle n. $IS(Link)$ represents the information scent of the currently attended link, calculated by the method called *pointwise mutual information* (Manning and Schutze 1999), which calculates the semantic similarity of two sets of words by some function of their base frequencies and collocation frequencies in large corpus of text. $N(n)$ represents the number of links already attended on the Web page after cycle n (one link is attended per cycle). $IS(BestLink)$ is the link with the highest information scent on the Web page; k is a scaling parameter; $MIS(page)$ is the mean information scent of the links on the Web page; and $GoBackCost$ is the cost of going back to the previous page. The values of k and $GoBackCost$ are estimated to fit the data.

Figure 18.1 illustrates how the probabilities of selecting the three productions change (Figure 18.1b) as the model sequentially processes links on a single page (Figure 18.1a). Initially the probability of choosing Attend-to-Link is high. This is based on the assumption that when a Web page is first processed, there is a bias in learning the utility of links on the page before a decision is made. However, as more links are evaluated, the utilities of the productions decrease (i.e., the denominator gets larger as $N(n)$ increases). Because the utility of Attend-to-Link decreases faster than that of Click-Link—since $IS(Best)$ = 10, but $IS(link)$ decreases from 10 to 2—the probability of choosing Attend-to-Link decreases but that of Click-Link increases. The implicit assumption of the model is that since evaluation of links takes time, the more links that are evaluated, the more likely it is that the best link evaluated so far will be selected; otherwise, time cost may outweigh the benefits of finding a better link.

As shown in Figure 18.1, after four links on the hypothetical Web page have been evaluated, the probability of choosing Click-Link is larger than that of Attend-to-Link. At this point, if Click-Link is selected, the model will choose the best (in this case the first) link and move on to process the links on the next page. Since the selection process uses a stochastic choice rule (i.e., a softmax rule; see Fu and Pirolli 2007), Attend-to-Link may, however, still be selected. If this is the case, as more links are evaluated—that is, as $N(n)$ increases—the probability of choosing Attend-to-Link and Click-Link decreases. If not, the

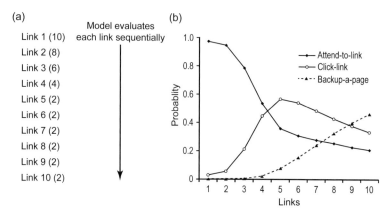

Figure 18.1 (a) A hypothetical Web page in which the information scent values (number in parenthesis) of links on the page decreases linearly from 10 to 2. (b) The probabilities of choosing each of the competing productions change as the model processes each additional link on the page; the mean information scent of the previous page was assumed to be 10.

probability of choosing Backup-a-Page is initially low because of the high GoBackCost. The utility for Backup-a-Page is calculated based on a moving average of the information scent encountered in previous pages. However, since the mean information scent of the links evaluated on the present page, MIS(links 1 to n), decreases relative to the information scent of links evaluated on previous pages, MIS(Previous Pages), the probability of choosing Backup-a-Page increases. This happens because the mean information scent of the current page is "perceived" to be dropping relative to the mean information scent of the previous page. In fact, after eight links are evaluated, the probability of choosing Backup-a-Page becomes higher than Attend-to-Link and Click-Link, and the probability of choosing Backup-a-Page keeps on increasing as more links are evaluated (i.e., as the mean information scent of the current page decreases). This demonstrates how competition between the productions can serve as a local decision rule that decides when to stop exploration.

Figure 18.2 shows the results of matching the SNIF-ACT model to the link selection data from a group of 74 users who conducted a search using the Yahoo! Web site (Fu and Pirolli 2007) across a range of information search tasks (e.g., "find the 2002 holiday schedule"). During the experiments, all pages visited were saved and all Web links on the pages selected by both the model and human subjects were extracted; the total frequencies of visits for each of these links are plotted in Figure 18.2. We see that the model provided good fits to the data ($R^2 = 0.91$), suggesting that the dynamic selection mechanism in the Bayesian satisficing model describes the human link selection process well.

In summary, the SNIF-ACT model demonstrates how IFT can be applied to search for specific information on the Internet. It thus creates a link with a wide range of other search domains found in this volume. Furthermore, the model

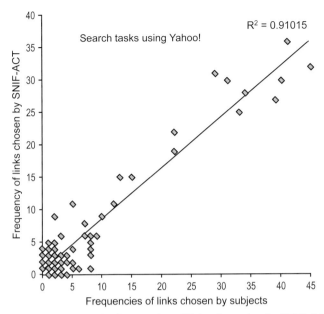

Figure 18.2 Scatterplot for the frequencies of links chosen by the SNIF-ACT model and human subjects when searching using the Yahoo! Web interface.

is very useful in predicting what links will be selected by users when they are engaged in different information search tasks. For example, the SNIF-ACT model can provide direct quantitative predictions on how likely users will find information produced by different designs of Web pages (e.g., what link text should be used, their layouts, etc.).

Exploratory Search in the Internet Information Environment

As discussed earlier, Web search engines are designed to exploit link structures to facilitate search of popular information. In many cases, people do indeed use the Web to retrieve simple facts, such as to search for the address of a restaurant, information about a person, or deadlines for filing taxes. When a person is engaged in a more open-ended or "ill-defined" search task, search engines may help, but they do not allow people to explore related information that is less popular and which may be found on pages far away from hub pages. In other words, while the "patchy" nature of Web pages allows search engines to find relevant information quickly in a patch (pages closely linked to certain hub pages), search engines are not designed specifically to facilitate search for information domains that are not patchy (i.e., information that does not overlap much in terms of topical relevance and thus may not share sufficient links to form a patch).

Going back to the questions posed in the *Meno*, while we may not know exactly what will be found, our ability to detect whether something is relevant often improves during the search process as we gather more information about the task and the environment. For example, when pursuing interest in the topic of "anti-aging," a person might find that it is related to many disjoint sets of topics: cosmetics, genetic engineering, nutrition, etc. When co-occurrences of these topics are repeatedly encountered during search, the searcher may be able to learn that these topics are related and relevant to the broader information goal. Typically, this does not reflect the design and intent of search engines; the ability to learn the association of topics may depend on whether the searcher can detect the structures (the co-occurrences of these topics returned from search engines) during the search. As more people use the Web to perform this kind of *exploratory information foraging*, new tools are being developed to augment search engines. However, before we discuss these new tools, I will briefly discuss the characteristics of exploratory information foraging.

In general, exploratory information foraging refers to the situation in which the information searcher has only a rough idea of the object of the search, and judgment of relevance depends greatly on the external information encountered during the search process. Furthermore, there is often no clear criterion for deciding when to stop searching. This is in sharp contrast to specific or targeted information foraging (Fu and Pirolli 2007; Pirolli and Card 1999), where the forager has a clear criterion for judging whether the target information is found. This criterion is mostly driven internally and is seldom changed or is dependent on the external information encountered during the search process. The challenge is: How do we extend the IFT so that it has the capability of learning incrementally to detect structures in the environment during the search process? Incremental changes to internal knowledge structures during search is perhaps one way that humans overcome the challenge posed in the *Meno*: how to search for "that which you know not."

Intuitively, the capability to learn from the environment seems a natural way of raising intelligence in cognitive search. For example, empirical research shows that one important difference between novice and expert chess players is that expert chess players have more stored information, which allows the expert players to recognize a large number of specific features and patterns of features on a chessboard, and information that uses this recognition to select actions based on the features recognized (e.g., Chase and Simon 1973a). While sophisticated chess programs often require search over tens of thousands of moves, chess masters seldom need to search more than a hundred of these potential moves. What makes this possible is apparently their ability to recognize patterns in the environment that are more *meaningful* than others. In other words, experiences accumulated from previous searches allow a person to derive a rich set of *semantic information* about the task environment that makes search more intelligent. Research on this in AI and cognitive science, which allows artificial systems to develop semantic information to exhibit human-level intelligence, is still extremely limited.

Semantic Structures in the Information Environment

As discussed above, when retrieving popular information, search engines that exploit link structures tend to be effective in guiding users to the information. However, when searching for information not linked to "hub pages" (i.e., pages in which most people are interested), link structures do not help. For example, a recent study (Kang et al. 2010) found that when searching for information that was less popular, following the links between Web pages often led to a restricted set of information, presumably because less popular information tended to be distributed across patches in the information environment that were not directly connected by hyperlinks. In contrast, people who had more knowledge about the domain (e.g., experts) were able to utilize their knowledge to explore more efficiently for relevant information by coming up with better search terms; this allowed for better identification of relevant information patches, which subsequently allowed them to select better links and pages as they navigated in the information environment.

From observations, it appears that people can acquire knowledge during search. For example, during a Web search, a searcher may recognize certain Web sites to be more authoritative, or remember how to navigate from one page to another through a sequence of hyperlinks. Whereas traditional search engines fail to capitalize on this form of search knowledge, *social information Web sites* have been developed to allow searchers to share their knowledge with other users to facilitate exploration of information on the Web. In a recent study (Fu and Dong 2012), we examined how people learn from the social information Web site Del.icio.us—a social tagging Web site that allows people to assign short text descriptions to Web pages and share them on the site. The popularity of social tagging arises from its benefits for supporting information search and exploration. When these user-generated sets of tagged documents are aggregated, a bottom-up semantic structure, often referred to as *folksonomy*, is formed. Many argue that folksonomies provide platforms for users in a distributed information space to share knowledge among users, as social tags can reveal relationships among structures in the resources that others can follow. We have shown that as users interpret tags created collaboratively by others, these tags not only help a user explore for more relevant information, they also help the learning of the conceptual structures of other tags (Fu and Dong 2012; further details discussed in the next section).

Here I analyze this new form of social information ecology and show how emergent structures in such an ecology may guide the use of these semantic structures during exploratory information foraging (Fu and Dong 2010). To highlight the characteristics of these semantic structures, this form will be compared to link structures extracted using a method similar to the PageRank algorithm (see earlier discussion). We conducted a simulation study on an existing system called Bibsonomy (Bibsonomy.org)—a public social tagging Web site that allows multiple users to post articles, Web pages, and other media to share with other users. The goal of this study was to show how different structures may help people perform exploratory information foraging.

We compared the empirical probability distribution functions of the predictive probabilities of topics and tags in each set of resources (see Figure 18.3). We defined experts broadly as people who have more domain-specific concepts which allow them to differentiate between relevant information or to make better inferences in their topic of expertise. Experts are thus generally more proficient in selecting tags that better describe topics in a resource. Quality of resources was defined as those that are most referred to by others, such as Web pages that have many links pointing to them (i.e., in-links). The definition of quality is therefore similar to that used by the PageRank algorithm, which assumes that each in-link is a "vote" by another page; the more votes a page receives, the higher its quality. By comparing how well expertise and quality can distinguish between resources, the goal is to test the extent to which experts

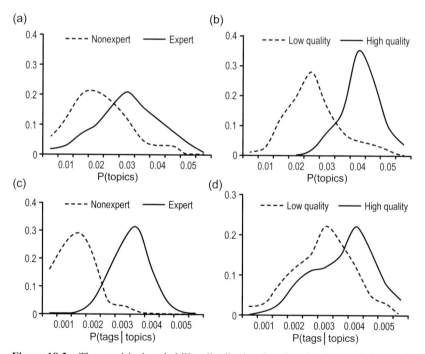

Figure 18.3   The empirical probability distribution function for the predictive probabilities of topics and tags in each of the four sets of resources. P(topics) represent the probability that a given topic to be found will be contained in the documents; P(tag|topics) indicate the probability that a tag is predictive of the topic.

(who index resources based on contents) and quality (which rank resources based on link structures) can help people explore for information.

The topic distributions between experts and nonexperts (Figure 18.3a) were less distinguishable than those between low- and high-quality resources (Figure 18.3b); however, the reverse was true for tag distributions (Figure 18.3c, d). This suggests that the quality of resources is generally better at predicting "hot" topics—that is, higher P(topics)— and that expert-generated tags tended to be more predictive of "cold" topics than resource quality. For example, resources tagged by a focused group of domain experts could contain cold topics associated with high-quality tags, but these resources were less likely picked up by quality (i.e., ranking of resources based on link structures). These results are consistent with the notion that content-based semantic structures are more useful for exploration of less popular topics, whereas link structures are more useful for finding popular information. For example, when presenting information cues (e.g., a recommended list of Web links as a person is exploring for information on the Web), a system can utilize either semantic structures (based on topical relevance of contents) or link structures (based on number of in-links and out-links) to select pages which may be relevant. In general, results show that following cues derived from semantic structures can more likely lead a person to explore patches that are less explored by others than those derived from link structures.

Detecting and Learning Semantic Structures during Search

Having demonstrated the different characteristics between semantic and link structures in social information Web sites for exploratory information foraging, let us turn to an experiment that directly tests how people utilize and learn from the semantic structures. In this experiment, we developed a set of exploratory information foraging tasks and observed the search behavior of people over a period of eight weeks (Fu and Dong 2012). In all tasks, participants started with a rough description of the topic and gradually acquired knowledge about the topic through iterative search-and-comprehend cycles. Participants were told to imagine that they had to write a paper and give a talk on the given topic to a diverse audience and that all kinds of questions related to the topic might be posed. Two general topics were chosen: (a) find out relevant facts about the independence of Kosovo (IK task) and (b) find out relevant facts about anti-aging (AA task). These two tasks were chosen because the IK task referred to a specific event; thus information related to it tended to be more specific, and there many Web sites contained multiple pieces of well-organized information relevant to the topic. By contrast, the AA task was more ambiguous and related to many disjoint areas, such as cosmetics, nutrition, or genetic engineering. Thus, Web sites relevant to the IK task contained more overlapping concepts (which can be found on the same pages) than those relevant to the AA task (which must be found on different pages).

Each of the eight participants performed one of the tasks for eight sessions over a period of eight weeks, with each session approximately one week apart. Participants were told to think aloud during the task in each session. Participants were instructed to provide a verbal summary of every Web page they read before they created any tags for the page. They could then bookmark the Web page and create tags for the page. After they finished reading a document, they could either search for new documents by initiating a new query or select an existing tag to browse documents tagged by others. This exploratory search-and-tag cycle continued until a session ended. All tags used and created during each session were extracted to keep track of changes in the shared external representations, and all verbal description on the Web pages were extracted to keep track of changes in the internal representations during the exploratory search process. These tags and verbal descriptions were then input as contents of the document. At the end of each session, participants were given printouts of all Web pages that they had read and bookmarked, and were asked to "put together the Web pages that go together on the basis of their information content into as many different groups" as the participants saw fit. These categories were then used to judge how much they had learned during the search.

To keep track of how people learn new knowledge during search, we extended the SNIF-ACT model to predict how the searcher incrementally learns to incorporate semantic structures extracted from the information system to improve their search. The idea is to assume that each searcher has a set of mental concepts R and a set of semantic nodes S. The information goal is to predict whether node S_j (some useful information) can be found by following a link with tags T. That is, the user is trying to estimate this probability, $P(S_j|R,T_k)$, when deciding which links can be broken down into two components:

$$\underset{\substack{\text{Predict internal rep} \\ \text{from external rep}}}{\downarrow} \qquad \underset{\substack{\text{Predict information} \\ \text{from a given mental} \\ \text{(internal) category}}}{} \qquad (18.4)$$

$$P(S_j|R,T) = \sum_m P(R_m|T)P(S_j|R_m) \nearrow$$

In other words, to predict whether node S_j can be found in a particular document, one must first estimate $P(R_m|T)$: the probability that the document with tags T belongs to a particular concept R_m. The second estimate $P(S_j|Rm)$ involves the probability that Sj can be found in mental concepts R_m. This estimate depends on the "richness" of the mental concepts: the richer the set of mental concepts, the better the model will be able to predict whether the information can be found in the concept R_m. As the model incrementally learns to enrich the mental categories (for details, see Fu and Dong 2012), its ability to predict which links should be selected improves.

In addition, the model learns new concepts as it encounters new tags (and contents). Based on the rational model of categorization, a new concept R_0

is formed when $P(R_0|T)$ is larger than $P(R_m|T)$ for all m when a new tag is encountered. $P(R_0|T)$ and $P(R_m|T)$ can be calculated based on Bayes's theorem, and prior probabilities $P(R_m)$ and $P(R_0)$ can be estimated using standard methods which reduce a multi-class to a binary categorization problem. One such method is to define the prior probabilities based on a *coupling probability*—the probability (which is independent of items seen thus far) that any two items belong to the same category in the environment. The higher the coupling probability, the higher the likelihood that two items can be found in the same category (e.g., when two related items can be found on the same Web page), and the higher the likelihood that they will be in one of the existing categories. (It can be shown that when the number of viewed items increases, there is a higher tendency to put an new item into the largest category—a property that is consistent with the effect of base rate in categorization; see Fu and Dong 2012.) On the other hand, when the coupling probability is low, the likelihood that a new category will be formed will be higher, as the prior probability that any two items are from the same category is lower.

We tested the model against the data to understand how well this integration of learning and search is able to capture exploratory information foraging behavior. We used the verbal protocol data to perform model tracing to predict how well the model predicted search behavior. Figure 18.4 shows the proportion of new tags assigned to each page that participants bookmarked and the corresponding proportions of tags that were assigned by the model to the pages that it bookmarked.

Interestingly, even though participants assigned fewer tags in the AA task, the *proportions* of new tag assignment over the total number of tag assignments were higher in the AA task than in the IK task. This is consistent with the lower rate of return of relevant information in the AA task. This lower rate could be caused by the fact that existing tags were less informative for the AA task. Indeed, concepts extracted from the documents by the participants in the AA task were more often different from existing tags in the IK task, which suggests that the existing tags did not serve as good cues to information contained in the documents. The general trends and differences between the two tasks were closely matched by the model (average $R^2 = 0.83$, min = 0.62, max = 0.98). We also matched the categories of bookmarks selected by the participants as well as by the model and found good correlations between these categories (mean $R^2 = 0.83$). The current set of results demonstrates the good match of the model in keeping track of how the incremental extraction of semantic structures helped search performance. It clearly shows how the participants incrementally developed semantic structures to improve their exploration of information. Results, therefore, demonstrate how internal conceptual structures are influenced by external information structure, and how their interaction influences the success of exploratory information foraging.

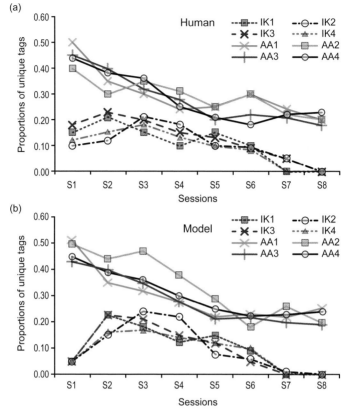

Figure 18.4 Mean proportions of unique tag assignment for the high-overlap (IK) and low-overlap (AA) tasks by participants (a) and the model (b) over eight sessions. IK1 represents participant 1 in the IK task and AA1 represents participant 1 in the AA task, etc.

General Discussion

Technology has greatly changed since Plato's *Meno*. Information search has become much more efficient through the help of the Internet and powerful Web search engines. These technological advances, however, merely *help* us carry out search much faster; they do not possess the same level of intelligence as humans or animals searching in their environments. Indeed, the vast amount of empirical research shows that cognitive search has distinct intelligence that is not yet completely understood.

In this chapter, empirical results and computational models were used to illustrate how structures exist in information environments, and how humans can detect and use these structures to guide their search. Results show that while exploiting link structures can facilitate simple fact retrieval, semantic structures are more important for people to learn and explore as their information goals evolve. Analysis on the probability distribution of topics on the Web shows that, when resources are ranked based on link structures, the probability distribution of topics tends to be more distinct in "hot" topics than in "cold" topics; however, the reverse is true when resources are ranked by semantic structures derived from the contents. Empirical studies on how people perform exploratory information foraging show that people not only assimilate new information into their existing conceptual structures, they also develop new conceptual structures as they explore for information on the Web. Results further demonstrate the coupling of internal conceptual structures and external information structures during exploratory information foraging.

I have argued that for both fact retrieval and exploratory information foraging, two conditions are necessary for cognitive search: structures must exist and searchers must be able to detect and utilize them. In addition, different levels of intelligence can be observed as an organism searches in response to the structures detected in the environment. In the domains of AI and cognitive science, it is customary to believe that the critical test for understanding any behavior is to develop a machine (or program) that *exhibits the same level of intelligence as the behavior*. A major challenge is to capture the intelligence behind cognitive search to the extent that a machine can be developed to search (and learn) as humans or animals do in their natural environments. This is particularly true when search is initiated for an unknown object; for example, when a searcher is engaged in exploratory information foraging and information goals evolve as new information is found during the search process.

19

Optimal Strategies and Heuristics for Ecological Search Problems

John M. McNamara and Tim W. Fawcett

Abstract

All animals, including humans, search for a variety of different things in their natural environment, from food to mates to a suitable place to live. Most types of search can be represented as stopping problems of varying complexity, in which the animal has to decide when to stop searching and accept the current option. All forms of search take time, and in solving a stopping problem the animal has to trade off this time cost against the expected benefits of continuing to search.

This chapter discusses two main approaches to predicting search behavior: the optimality approach and the heuristics approach. The optimality approach identifies the best possible solution to a search problem and thereby sets an upper bound to what natural selection can achieve. The heuristics approach considers simple decision algorithms, or "rules of thumb," which animals may use to implement efficient search behavior. Although few studies have tried to integrate these functional and mechanistic perspectives, they are likely to provide complementary insights. Often, the form of an optimal strategy suggests which kinds of heuristics might be expected to evolve.

Stopping problems may be simple, repeated, or embedded in other stopping problems. For example, if searchers assess the value of each encountered option by examining a series of cues, the assessment process can be considered as another stopping problem. When the searcher is uncertain about the environment it is in, its previous experiences during search can strongly influence the optimal behavior. Where a limited number of items can be accepted, as in mate search, a key constraint is whether the searcher can return to previously encountered items. Some search problems are complicated by the fact that the encountered items are themselves searching. The chapter concludes with a discussion of some open questions for future research.

Introduction

Our aim in this chapter is to give an overview of how animals solve some common search problems in their natural environment. Animals may search for items in many different contexts, but here we concentrate mostly on foraging and mate search, which have been extensively studied. We discuss two main approaches to analyzing these problems. The first is *optimality theory* (Parker and Maynard Smith 1990), which seeks to identify strategies of search that maximize fitness, where fitness can be thought of loosely as expected lifetime reproductive success. This approach sheds light on the selective forces shaping the evolution of search behavior. The second approach we consider focuses on so-called *heuristics* or rules of thumb (Gigerenzer and Todd 1999; Hutchinson and Gigerenzer 2005), simple problem-solving algorithms that enable animals to reach a good, though not necessarily optimal, solution. In our view, these two approaches are complementary. Optimality theory is needed to identify the best possible solution to a problem, and hence set an upper bound on the performance of a simple rule. The form of the optimal strategy may also suggest simple heuristics, although sometimes simple rules that do well are very different in form to the optimal solution. At various points in our analysis, we explore the connections between the two perspectives. We highlight general principles of adaptive search with a view to generating insights for those interested in search problems outside biology.

Types of Search Problems

Broadly speaking, we can group search problems in the following two categories:

1. *Finding a unique object.* There are situations in which the searcher is looking for a certain specific object, and no other object will do. Examples include the spring journey of a migrating bird, which must get to a specific location if it is to breed successfully; the recall of someone's name from memory; and search for a specific person or piece of information on the Internet. The classic secretary problem (Freeman 1983), in which the criterion is to maximize the probability of getting the best secretary and there is no reward unless this particular individual is chosen, is also a search problem of this type.
2. *Maximization of expected net reward.* In many other search problems, the sought object(s) is (are) not unique; different objects have different values and the objective of the search is to maximize the expected net value of the item(s) chosen minus any search costs. Examples of such search problems include a female searching for a mate; an animal foraging on a food patch where the fitness of the animal is maximized by maximizing the mean total amount of food found minus search costs; partner choice by client fish attempting to find a good cleaner fish that will remove parasites; job search; and most consumer choice situations, including Internet search for products.

The distinction between these two categories is not absolute; in fact, the first type of scenario could be regarded as an extreme case of the second type of scenario in which all but one of the available objects have zero value. Whether real search problems fit this situation exactly is debatable, even for the examples mentioned. For instance, when searching for the name "Philip," "Phil" may well be a close enough approximation. However, by and large it is useful to distinguish between these two categories. Behavioral ecologists are usually concerned with the second case; that is maximization of expected net reward. Consider, for example, mate search: We expect natural selection to produce search strategies that maximize the expected number of surviving offspring. Males differ in the quality of their genes and in the amount of parental care they will provide. Thus mating with some males is more valuable than mating with others. Often the later a female breeds, the fewer offspring will survive. Thus a female is not always after the best male, but must find a compromise between male quality and breeding early. Such trade-offs are a key feature of many search problems in behavioral ecology. Our focus here is mainly on problems of this type.

Types of Search Cost

Search costs can arise from various sources (e.g., Pomiankowski 1987). The fundamental cost in most search problems is a time cost. Typically, time spent searching is costly because the searcher loses the opportunity to do other things. Mate choice by a female illustrates two other time costs: there may be a seasonal decline in fecundity and/or there may be fewer and lower-quality males available over time if males are no longer available once chosen by other competing females. This kind of competitive effect is not unique to mate choice; in foraging problems, food may be depleted by other foragers. Other costs of search arise when the search process is deleterious to the searcher. For example, search may be energetically expensive, particularly if options are widely spaced. Search may also incur a predation risk. When there is the risk of death during search, the value of the object(s) sought and the cost of losing one's life must be combined into a common currency. The animal's reproductive value provides an appropriate currency (Houston and McNamara 1999); for an application of this currency to the problem of when to leave a patch of food, see Brown (1988) and Houston and McNamara (1999).

Here we concentrate on time costs, which are clearly relevant to a wide range of search problems outside biology. For simplicity, we assume a constant cost per unit time (γ).

Simple, Repeated, and Embedded Stopping Problems

The simplest decision a searcher has to make is when to stop searching; we refer to this as a stopping problem. In many situations, the stopping problem is repeated several times, or it may even be embedded within other stopping problems. Below we consider the essential features of simple, repeated, and embedded stopping problems in turn. We finish by highlighting some open questions for future research.

Simple Stopping Problems

Stopping in Food Search

Consider a foraging animal which is searching a patch that contains food items. The number of items on the patch is not known in advance. However, the animal has some prior information specifying the possible number of items and the probabilities of each possibility. This prior information can come from past experience and its evolutionary history (McNamara and Houston 1980; McNamara et al. 2006). The animal may also not know how difficult it is to find each item. Assume that the search path on the patch is given (e.g., random movement). As the animal searches, it encounters a series of food items. Over time, the duration between successive encounters tends to be longer as the patch depletes. At every instant the animal must decide whether to continue its search or to leave the patch and seek better sources of food elsewhere. This decision can be based on the number of items found so far and the time at which these items were encountered.

If the cost per unit time while searching is γ, then it might be reasonable to assume the animal's fitness is maximized by maximizing

$$W = E\{\text{Net energy gain on the patch}\}$$
$$-\gamma \times E\{\text{Time on the patch}\},$$

(19.1)

where E denotes the expected or mean value. When energy is gained as a smooth flow that decreases over time, as with a hummingbird feeding on flower nectar, it is optimal to leave the patch (flower) when the rate of net energy gain falls to γ. At that point, the hummingbird should then move on to probe another flower. Note that in this particular example, the flower may be one of a cluster of flowers making up an inflorescence, which could be considered a patch at a higher level. Zooming out still further, the inflorescence is part of a larger patch comprising all the inflorescences on that plant. At each of these levels, the hummingbird may be selected to optimize its patch-leaving decision. Later we will consider this kind of "embedded" search problem in more detail.

When food is found as discrete items, the optimal strategy is not so simple. In this case finding items gives information about the type of patch the animal is on and hence the likelihood of more items in the future. In abstract terms we may characterize the experience of the forager on the patch by a vector $\mathbf{x}$, which specifies quantities such as the number of items found and the time taken to find each of them. We can define the potential function W as the function of $\mathbf{x}$ defined by

$$W(\mathbf{x}) = \max \begin{bmatrix} E\{\text{Net further energy gain on the patch}|\mathbf{x}\} \\ -\gamma \times E\{\text{Further time on patch}|\mathbf{x}\} \end{bmatrix}. \quad (19.2)$$

The optimal strategy of the animal is to leave the patch when the potential drops to zero (McNamara 1982). The potential declines smoothly between finding food items and jumps when an item is found. However, a jump may be up or down, depending on the prior probability distribution of prey items on the patch. If the number of items has low variance, then finding an item means there are fewer left, and the potential jumps downward after encountering an item. An extreme case is when there is at most one item per patch; in this case, a forager should always leave the patch after encountering an item. In contrast, if the distribution of the number of items has high variance so that some patches contain many items and some contain few, then finding an item indicates likelihood that there are a lot more items present, and the potential jumps upward. In this latter case of clumped prey, it pays to be "optimistic" in the sense that even when the (mean) rate of energy intake falls to γ, it is not optimal to leave; instead the animal should persevere a little longer (McNamara 1982; Hutchinson et al. 2008).

Heuristics for Food Search

The previous discussion classifies optimal behavior. However, behavioral ecologists do not expect the action of natural selection to produce search rules that are exactly optimal, but rather to produce rules that perform well in an animal's natural environment. Rules based on a variable that behaves like the potential could provide a simple heuristic, and such rules have been proposed to account for the behavior of parasitoids searching for patchily distributed hosts (Waage 1979). Various other simple rules have also been proposed in the context of patch exploitation. One simple rule is to leave after a fixed number of items have been found. Another is to leave after a fixed time. More generally, let n denote the total number of items found so far and t denote the total search time so far. Then any subset S of the two-dimensional space of vectors of the form (n, t) defines a rule of the form: continue searching until $(n, t) \in S$, and then leave. The optimal rule is only of this form under very restrictive and unrealistic assumptions; for example, when all items are equally easy to find. Nevertheless it can be a useful conceptualization. A simple rule that is not of this form is to leave when no item has been found for a fixed amount of time (giving-up-time rule; McNair 1982; Waage 1979). For information on the performance of these simple rules, see Hutchinson et al. (2008) and references therein.

Stopping in Mate Search

Mate search is also a stopping problem, but it differs from the foraging situations considered earlier in that, in a given reproductive attempt, the searcher can choose just one of the available options. Consider a female selecting a mate from a sequence of males that vary in quality, in terms of the genetic or resource-based benefits they can provide. In this one-off choice situation, she need only consider the value of the current male she is inspecting and compare this with the fitness consequences of continuing to search. This gives a simple optimal stopping rule: she should accept a male if his value exceeds the expected future net payoff from rejecting him and continuing her search (Real 1990; Collins et al. 2006).

Fixed versus Adjustable Thresholds

When males vary in quality and the quality distribution is known to the female, it is relatively straightforward to determine the optimal stopping rule. Theory predicts an acceptance threshold, with the female stopping her search and mating with the current male when his quality exceeds this threshold. The threshold may be fixed at a constant value or, if time is limited, it may decline as the female nears the end of the search period to reduce the risk of ending up unpaired (Real 1990).

What makes the problem more difficult is that in the real world, the distribution of male qualities is typically variable and uncertain. Under these conditions, the female might estimate the general quality of available males from the males she has seen so far and compare the current male with this estimate (Dombrovsky and Perrin 1994; Mazalov et al. 1996; Collins et al. 2006). Thus, rather than using a fixed acceptance threshold, her threshold may be adjusted in the light of her earlier experiences during search.

Return to Previously Encountered Options

When modeling mate search, a key issue is whether females can return to males they encountered earlier in the search process. This possibility is a feature of fixed-sample search rules such as "best-of-*n*," according to which a female assesses a fixed number (*n*) of males and then mates with the best of them. If the distribution of male qualities is fixed and time is not limiting (so that the critical acceptance threshold is constant), it never pays to revisit previously encountered options; if a male was not good enough in the past, it follows that he will not be good enough now either (Collins et al. 2006). Formal models of mate search have confirmed that the best-of-*n* rule can never outperform a fixed threshold under these conditions (Real 1990; Luttbeg 2002), even when search costs are negligible (Wiegmann et al. 2010).

This is puzzling, because in real systems it is frequently observed that females make repeated visits to several different males before deciding with whom to mate (reviewed by Luttbeg 1996). This has been interpreted by some as empirical support for the best-of-n rule. There are three important points to make here:

1.   Observed patterns of search behavior may shed little light on the underlying decision rules. There are countless other conceivable rules besides best-of-n that entail return to previously sampled males, and some of these might be superior to a fixed threshold.

2.   The assumptions of standard models may misrepresent key features of real mate-search problems, leading to erroneous predictions. For example, a common assumption is that females can assess male quality without error; however, Luttbeg (2002) showed that biased estimates of mean quality may favor a fixed-sample rule (e.g., best-of-n) over a sequential search rule (e.g., fixed threshold). More generally, a trade-off between the speed and accuracy of assessment (Trimmer et al. 2008; Chittka et al. 2009) may mean that, after an initial screening, it pays for females to return to a subset of males for a more in-depth assessment. In addition, if females learn about the distribution of male qualities and adjust their acceptance criteria accordingly, a male who was previously rejected may be worth returning to at a later point in time.

3.   Claiming that one search rule is superior to another is problematic, because this depends greatly on the scenario in which they are compared. Fixed thresholds may do well when the distribution of male qualities is static, but the best-of-n rule is better at adjusting to any changes. If locally available males are of higher quality than expected, a female using a fixed threshold may pair up too hastily, whereas if they are of lower quality than expected, she may wait too long. The best-of-n rule, in contrast, automatically adjusts its choice criteria in response to the quality of males sampled.

Heuristics for Mate Search

It would seem highly implausible that a female consciously computes her expected net future payoff from rejecting a given male, even though selection should produce behavior that makes it appear as though she is taking this into account. Instead, her search behavior is likely to be implemented through simple heuristics (Gigerenzer and Todd 1999; Hutchinson and Gigerenzer 2005) which lead her close to the optimal solution. Comparing a fixed number of males before selecting the best, as in the best-of-n rule, and selecting the first male whose quality exceeds a given level, as in the fixed-threshold rule, are both examples of search heuristics. The question is: Which heuristic is selection likely to favor? For simple scenarios it is easy to find the value of n that maximizes the success of a best-of-*n* rule, or the threshold value that maximizes the success of a fixed-threshold rule, but comparing across different classes of rules is less straightforward.

Historically, much of the work on heuristics has focused on simple, well-defined problems in which there is a known solution, and the interest is in how quickly and accurately different heuristics locate that solution. As we will see below, mate-search problems may have several layers of complexity, and instead of trying to find the single best option the female typically tries to maximize her expected number of offspring. Heuristics are appropriate for these kinds of situations as well, but to determine their success we need to consider their evolutionary properties: how they impact on reproductive success, and whether they prevail when pitted against alternative rules.

Variability among Options

Variability has important implications for search strategies. Consider a patch-leaving problem where the patches contain an average of five items of unit value, and it takes five time units to search the patch exhaustively at unit cost per time spent. If all patches contain five items (i.e., no variability between patches) then it may be difficult for the forager to make a positive net gain. In contrast, if half of the patches contain ten items while the other half are empty, then by being flexible and leaving the patch if no items are found in the first time unit, the animal can get a high mean payoff.

In mate search, one possible decision the female can make is to mate with the first male she encounters and not bother searching for alternatives. Although this is likely to be a poor strategy under most conditions, it is in fact the optimal stopping rule when there is insufficient variability in male quality; there is no point in continuing to search if this is unlikely to yield a significantly better mate. In general, the greater the variability in male quality (for a given mean quality), the more choosy females should be and therefore the more willing they should be to search. Where this variability is unknown, the female may have to search simply to discover whether it is worth searching at all.

The variability among options has a critical influence on how searchers resolve the trade-off between speed and choosiness in their decision making. If variability is low, it does not matter too much what the searcher chooses and thus speed should be prioritized. If variability is high, it is important to be choosy.

Game-Theoretical Aspects

So far we have assumed that the behavior of other individuals has no influence on the searcher's strategy. This can be a useful simplification for exposing some of the selective forces involved, but in many circumstances a fuller understanding of search behavior needs to take a game-theoretical perspective and consider what the searcher's conspecifics are doing.

Competitive Search

When a forager is exploiting a limited resource, its gains will deplete faster if there are others foraging on the same patch. This might be expected to shorten the optimal time spent on the patch, but precisely how it affects the leaving decision depends on whether competitors will also be present on other patches. If individuals distribute themselves across patches according to an ideal free distribution (Fretwell and Lucas 1969), such that richer patches are more heavily exploited, this will tend to equalize net intake rate between the patches (Bernstein et al. 1988). In some cases the presence of competitors may benefit a searcher, if the searcher is able to gain social information from its competitors' searching behavior and exploit some of the food that they find (Barnard and Sibly 1981).

Mate search is also pressured by competition with same-sex rivals, but the impact of this depends strongly on the mating system (Emlen and Oring 1977). In highly polygynous systems with no male care and little effect of sperm depletion, female search behavior will be largely unaffected by whether a given male has previously been chosen by other females. At the other extreme, in strictly monogamous species with biparental care and an extended pair bond, the options available to a searching female are rapidly depleted by rivals that choose more quickly. This problem is compounded if the sex ratio is skewed toward females, increasing the risk that she fails to pair up at all. In such cases, speed may be prioritized over accuracy in decision making. For the solution of this game between competing searchers in a simple setting, see Collins and McNamara (1993). As in search for food, the presence of competitors could potentially have beneficial effects if females capitalize on the social information provided by their rivals, via mate-choice copying (Galef and White 2000). This has the potential of reducing search costs but the benefits depend critically on the mating system; in a strictly monogamous species, there is little point choosing the same male as another female (Brown and Fawcett 2005).

Two-Sided Search

In mate search, there is an additional game-theoretical element to the problem if males are also choosy. In that case, the options being searched for are themselves also searching, which complicates matters considerably. Mutual choice entails an added risk in that the female's preferred mate might not be willing to accept her; however, it may also prolong the availability of other males who refuse to pair with the first females they encounter.

Mutual mate search was first formally analyzed by McNamara and Collins (1990), who framed it in terms of the analogous two-sided problem of job search. Their model assumed that searchers have perfect information, but uncertainty is likely to be a prominent feature of real-world mutual-choice systems. Attractiveness in such systems depends not only on an individual's own quality, but on the quality distributions of potential mates and same-sex rivals, which may be impossible to observe directly. Under these conditions, the interest shown by potential mates may be used as a cue to a searcher's mating prospects as well as to adjust his/her acceptance threshold adaptively (Fawcett and Bleay 2009). A possible heuristic suggested to implement this flexible search strategy is adjust-relative, which lowers its acceptance threshold after being rejected by potential mates of lower quality and raises it after being courted by potential mates of higher quality (Todd and Miller 1999). The evolutionary properties of this rule have not been addressed, but evidence from speed dating in humans is at least consistent with the use of adjust-relative or something similar (Beckage et al. 2009).

Repeated Stopping Problems

Foraging animals often visit a series of food patches, exploiting food found in each. A forager is then faced with the repeated stopping problem of when to leave each patch and move on to another. When food patches are not well defined, a foraging animal faces a similar problem: when to search locally (area-restricted search; see Stephens et al., this volume) and when to stop searching intensively and take a longer "flight" to a new location. There is now a large literature discussing the characteristics of the resulting search paths, and in particular when these paths can be described as a Lévy process. For an application of these ideas to human memory retrieval, see Rhodes and Turvey (2007). The fundamental biological phenomenon is, however, not the search path but the underlying strategy that gives rise to this path. A search strategy is a rule that determines the decisions an animal takes during search, where the decision taken at any time can depend on what the animal has encountered. The search path only gives indirect evidence of the underlying search strategy; just looking at search paths is a poor substitute for determining the strategy.

When a foraging animal visits a series of food patches, exploiting food found on each, it is often reasonable to assume that the fitness of the animal is maximized by maximizing its mean net rate of energy gain. Let γ^* be the maximum possible mean rate. While on one patch an animal has an opportunity cost of γ^* per unit time, as this is the rate of gain it can obtain in the environment as a whole. Thus its search on each patch can be regarded as a stopping problem with this cost per unit time. Note the circularity implicit in this characterization; to experience rate γ^*, the animal must forage optimally, but to forage optimally it must know γ^* (Houston and McNamara 1999).

An animal that experiences a series of food patches for the first time may have to learn about this environment. An animal such as a hummingbird, which experiences a smooth decreasing flow of reward from a flower, can learn to forage optimally by simply updating its estimate of γ^* after visiting each flower and then leaving the next flower when its reward rate falls to this estimate

(McNamara and Houston 1985). However, when food items are found as discrete items, an animal faces a difficult estimation problem since environments may vary in the distribution of numbers of items per patch and the distribution of difficulty in finding items. Under these circumstances it seems unlikely that the animal can effectively learn all this information. Instead we might expect it to learn some information about how its experience on a patch affects future prospects on that patch (the joint distribution of capture times; McNamara and Houston 1987), and employ a simple rule which integrates past experience in a way that effectively exploits gross features of the environment.

Much of this rationale could also apply to mate search, if males are distributed in patches. Leks are the most obvious case of this (Höglund and Alatalo 1995), although as Hutchinson and Halupka (2004) argue, there may be many non-lekking systems in which males have a patchy distribution. While females examine the males within a given patch, their search costs will be low compared to search costs when moving between different patches. This predicts an acceptance threshold that declines gradually while sampling the males in a patch, but drops sharply to a lower threshold for the last male when the female has to decide whether to mate now or move on to the next patch.

Embedded Stopping Problems

In the previous sections we ignored the details of how the searcher assesses the various items it encounters. Bringing this into focus, we find a second stopping problem embedded within the first: How much time and effort should the searcher expend on assessing the current item before deciding to accept it and/or resuming search for the next item? Embedded stopping problems are found in most of the standard examples of search in biology, from prey choice to mate choice to habitat choice. In each case, the benefit of careful inspection—an accurate assessment—is counterbalanced by the cost of possibly missing out on more profitable options elsewhere.

Consider a female inspecting a sequence of males, in a one-sided choice problem (i.e., males will happily mate with any female). While inspecting a given male she has to decide constantly between (a) accepting him, (b) continuing to assess him by gathering further information, and (c) rejecting him and moving on to inspect the next male. Her decision making can be modeled as a procedure based on the sequential probability ratio test (McNamara et al. 2009). That is, she will continue to assess the male until either she is confident that he is good enough to mate with, or confident that he is bad enough to be discarded. The costs and benefits in this situation depend on both the expected quality of the males yet to be encountered and the female's future strategy, which means that to find the optimal strategy one cannot just consider single males in isolation. The same principle applies to other embedded stopping problems. Importantly, modeling these types of decisions as a sequential probability ratio test might have some mechanistic grounding, in that the predictions appear to fit patterns of decision making in the basal ganglia (Bogacz 2007), a group of nuclei in the vertebrate brain that are associated with learning.

Heuristics for Assessment

Several of the best-studied heuristics address discrimination between a set of options, specifying an explicit procedure for examining the characteristics, or cues, of each option (Gigerenzer and Todd 1999; Hutchinson and Gigerenzer 2005; Todd and Gigerenzer 2007). Tallying, for example, examines all cues and picks the option that is favored by the greatest number of cues; it is, in other words, a majority rule. Take-the-best, in contrast, uses a lexicographic criterion: it first compares all the options on the basis of the most reliable cue, then if no difference is found it considers the second-best cue; then if still no difference is found it moves on to the third-best cue, and so on, until it encounters a cue that enables discrimination (whereupon it chooses the option that scores highest for that cue). Take-the-best performs impressively well on a range of simple discrimination tasks (Hutchinson and Gigerenzer 2005), but whether animals (including humans) have evolved to use something similar to this heuristic in their everyday tasks is a different matter. In principle, animals might be able to judge the reliability of cues by learning from past experiences, or because they have adapted to these cues during their evolutionary history. Navigation by birds and bees might be similar in some respects to take-the-best, in that there appears to be a hierarchical ranking of the cues used by the animal to find its destination. Celestial and landmark cues tend to dominate magnetic cues, which are used only when visual cues are unavailable, for example because of a cloudy sky (Able 1993; Frier et al. 1996; Muheim et al. 2006).

An interesting feature of take-the-best is that it compares all available options for one cue before moving on to the next cue. That is, it embeds the assessment of options within the inspection of each cue, rather than embedding the inspection of cues within the assessment of each option as in the mate-choice model of McNamara et al. (2009). This has important implications for search behavior. If options are encountered sequentially, as is assumed to be the case in most biological scenarios, the former assessment strategy implies that the searcher will return to previously visited options, whereas the latter implies that it will not. The order of cue assessment during mate choice has been carefully studied in only a handful of cases (e.g., Christy et al. 2002), for which evidence suggests that females assess a series of cues in one male before discarding him and moving on to the next male. Again, we are left with the puzzle of why females sometimes return to males they assessed earlier. Are they just forgetful?

In some situations, the particular way in which options are assessed—for example, whether the searcher gathers all the information it needs in one visit or spreads its assessment over several repeated visits—can affect the final decision. Hills and Hertwig (2010) analyzed a set of experiments in which human subjects could freely sample the payoffs from two options before choosing one of them. Some people switched frequently between the two options while sampling, whereas others sampled each option for a more extended bout and switched only rarely. These two strategies were associated with different final choices: frequent switchers preferred the option that was better in the majority of its short sampling bouts, whereas rare switchers preferred the option that gave the higher average payoff over the long term. Thus, sampling behavior and choice behavior may be closely connected.

Search Costs versus Assessment Costs

To make predictions about the type of strategy searchers should use in embedded stopping problems, it is important to distinguish between search costs (i.e., the time or effort spent in locating an option) and assessment costs (i.e., the time or effort invested in inspecting that option) (Sullivan 1994; Fawcett and Johnstone 2003). Search costs will be high if males are spread out in the environment (e.g., strictly territorial) as opposed to clustered together (e.g., on a lek), but they may be mitigated if the assessment of males can be made from a distance (e.g., if they signal their quality vocally rather than visually). On the other hand, if males signal their quality via conspicuous morphological cues, this may enable much more rapid assessment than if they do so via dynamic, behavioral traits, which are potentially time consuming to assess (Sullivan 1994). Thus the spatial distribution and the manner in which males signal their quality will affect the relative magnitude of search and assessment costs. If the search costs greatly outweigh the assessment costs, it will not be worth the effort of returning to reassess a previously encountered male, whereas if the reverse is true then females may visit the same males repeatedly. This will determine whether females examine a sequence of cues within each male, as in the model by McNamara et al. (2009), or compare a set of males within each cue, as in the take-the-best heuristic.

Collective Search

All the situations described above address a single individual concerned with its own interests, often in competition with others. In insect societies, however, individuals often perform actions that are in the best interests of the colony (Wilson 1974). There are two obvious search problems that colony members face: search for resources that can be consumed by the colony and search for a new nest site for the colony as a whole. Search for a new nest site is particularly demanding because colony members must coordinate their search strategies to choose a good nest site and must ensure that the whole colony then emigrates to this site rather than being split between sites. This coordinated activity is achieved by decentralized control; individuals interact locally with others (e.g., Marshall et al. 2006, 2009). For example, in the ant *Temnothorax albipennis*, some colony members initially search, returning to recruit other ants to their chosen site by a process known as tandem running. Once a quorum of individuals is present at a new site, behavior changes so that all individuals at the old site are transported rapidly to this new site (Pratt et al. 2002). Thus in this problem, search is conducted by individual agents but the stopping decision is made at the colony level.

Open Questions

In problems such as search for patchily distributed food, it might be reasonable to assume that an animal is born with "prior information" on the likely statistical properties of its environment. From a theoretical point of view we might ask: To what extent can we expect evolution to produce animals that are Bayesians? From an empirical point of view we might ask: Do priors really differ between organisms whose ancestors inhabited different environments? To what extent is an animal's prior information on patch type molded by previous experience, as opposed to its evolutionary history?

Why do searchers sometimes return to previously encountered options? Does this reflect a cognitive constraint (e.g., limited memory)? Does it reflect high assessment costs, for which in-depth assessment only pays after some options have been eliminated by preliminary screening? Or does it reflect changing choice criteria, such that a rejected option may become acceptable at a later point in time?

Which search heuristics should we expect from an evolutionary point of view? Psychologists have compared the performance of selected heuristics in several well-defined tasks, but this does not tell us which ones are likely to be favored in the course of evolution. Is there a systematic way that we can investigate the evolutionary properties of these search heuristics, or are they simply too numerous and too diverse to compare?

Nearly all models of search in behavioral ecology assume that options are encountered sequentially. Is this a realistic assumption? Does it reflect a cognitive constraint that individuals can only pay attention to one option at a time? How would our predictions of search behavior change if simultaneous assessment is possible?

To what extent can we infer underlying decision rules from observing the behavior of a searching animal? Experimental manipulation of the search problem might enable us to discard certain candidate rules, but is this kind of approach likely to be sufficient? Should we be concentrating instead on studying the neurobiological basis of decision making?

How are search rules affected when individuals can use the social information provided by other searchers? How does this interact with competitive effects (i.e., depletion of resources)?

Acknowledgments

TWF acknowledges support from a European Research Council grant on "The evolution of mechanisms that control behavior" (grant number 250209 to Alasdair Houston). We thank Thomas Hills, James Marshall, Lael Schooler, and an anonymous reviewer for comments.

20

Search Environments, Representation, and Encoding

Lael J. Schooler, Curt Burgess, Robert L. Goldstone,
Wai-Tat Fu, Sergey Gavrilets, David Lazer,
James A. R. Marshall, Frank Neumann, and Jan M. Wiener

Abstract

This chapter explores the benefits of restructuring search spaces and internal representations so as to make search more efficient. It begins by providing a formal definition of search, and proposes a method for shifting search between low- and high-dimensionality problem spaces. Consideration is given to how learning shapes the representations that help people search efficiently as well as on constraints that people face. Some constraints are considered biases necessary to make sense out of the world; others (e.g., working memory) are taken as both "limiters" to be overcome and "permitters" that make learning in a finite amount of time possible at all. Further constraints on search are tied to the physical structure of the world. The chapter concludes with a discussion of social search, where communication can promote exploration and exploitation in an environment that often consists of other agents searching for similar solutions.

Introduction

In 1975, Allen Newell and Herbert Simon received the Turing award for their contributions to computer science and psychology. In large part, they were being honored for their work in artificial intelligence. In their acceptance address, Newell and Simon (1976, 1987) described how they approached problems in artificial intelligence by studying the natural intelligence of people. These studies of humans and machines led them to conclude that the key to intelligence was the ability to manipulate symbols. They believed that all intelligent behavior, whether human or machine, arises from composing symbols into entities called symbol structures that can be manipulated by prescribed sets of operators. Some operators can construct new structures, whereas others modify or destroy existing ones. The combination of symbol structures and the corresponding operators define what Newell and Simon called a symbol system. These symbol systems were at the heart of their *physical symbol system hypothesis*: "A physical symbol system has the necessary and sufficient means for general intelligent action" (Newell and Simon 1987:293).

Their claim with the physical symbol system hypothesis (or symbol system hypothesis; Newell 1980) was that symbol systems not only support intelligent behavior, they are essential for the display of intelligent behavior. They viewed the symbol system hypothesis as the guiding principle that should organize research on human and artificial intelligence. For Newell and Simon, symbol systems were as fundamental to the study of intelligence as the theory of plate tectonics is to geology or germ theory is to the study of disease. This is a radical view, but one that was proposed as a hypothesis to be tested. They were, after all, empiricists at heart. The hypothesis that intelligent behavior rests on symbol structures flowing one into the next, transformed by operators, led them to see problem solving as search through a space of symbol structures that represent possible solutions to particular problems. Thus, intelligent behavior was a form of search in a problem space of symbol structures.

Their belief in the fundamental importance of search led to their second guiding principle, the *heuristic search hypothesis*: "A physical symbol system exercises its intelligence in problem solving by search; that is, by generating and progressively modifying symbol structures until it produces a solution structure" (Newell and Simon 1987:230). Their *general problem solver* (GPS) algorithm worked by transforming one solution into the next until a dead end (requiring back-tracking) or goal was reached. Just as a rat might search for food in a field by moving from patch to patch, GPS moved in an abstract solution space from symbol set to symbol set. They argued that problem solving must depend on "heuristic (i.e., knowledge-controlled) search" (Newell 1980), because intelligent behavior can be observed even when problem spaces are so vast that they cannot be exhaustively searched. The importance of basic notions of symbol systems and heuristic search in our report is a testament to the lasting legacy of Newell and Simon's formalization of search processes.

We start by providing a formal definition of search. Inspired by results showing that high-dimensionality spaces imply that good solutions should be well connected to each other, we propose a method for shifting search between low- and high-dimensionality problem spaces. Turning from formal methods to people, we consider the ways in which learning shapes the representations that help people search efficiently. Thereafter we discuss constraints that people face: some are considered biases necessary to make sense out of the world; others (e.g., working memory) are taken as both "limiters" to be overcome and "permitters" that make learning in a finite amount of time possible at all. Further constraints on search are tied to the physical structure of the world. Finally, we turn to social search, which complements heuristic search by supplementing internal cognitive constraints on search within an individual with the constraints provided by an environment that often consists of other agents searching for similar solutions.

A Formal Definition of Search

To aid concrete discussion of iterative search algorithms, we define search problems in a formal way that is consistent with Newell and Simon's notion of symbol systems. A search problem is given by a triplet (S, f, W), where S is the considered search space, $f: S \rightarrow R$ is a function assigning objective values to the elements of S (representing all possible solutions), and W is a set of constraints.

To illustrate this, let us consider the well-known traveling salesman problem (TSP). Input is given by a set of n cities $\{1, ..., n\}$, and between each pair of cities, i and j, there is a distance, $d_{i,j}$. A tour in the TSP problem visits each city exactly once and returns to the origin. We focus on two variants:

1. Satisficing version: Is there a tour of cost at most k?
2. Optimization version: Find a tour of minimal cost.

To fit the TSP problem into our search framework, the search space S is given by all permutations of the n cities (i.e., ordered tours through all the cities, as opposed to the locations of the individual cities themselves in physical space). The cost of a permutation π is then computed by starting at the first city in the permutation, $\pi(1)$, moving to the second city in the permutation, $\pi(2)$, then to the third, $\pi(3)$, and so on. The cost of this permutation is given by the sum of the distances traveled to construct the tour:

$$\text{cost}(\pi) = d_{\pi(1),\pi(2)} + d_{\pi(2),\pi(3)} + \dots + d_{\pi(n-1),\pi(n)} + d_{\pi(n),\pi(1)}. \quad (20.1)$$

Let us now consider optimization problems tackled by iterative search algorithms. The task is to find an element x^* in S which minimizes the function value:

$$x^* = \arg\min_{x \in S} f(x). \quad (20.2)$$

In the TSP example, we would search through the space S for a tour that has minimal cost. To apply iterative search algorithms to optimization problems, three steps are necessary:

1. Choose a representation of the elements in the search space S.
2. Define a fitness function (might be different from f) that assigns fitness values to points in the search space S.
3. Define operators that construct, from a set of solutions, a new set of solutions. The combination of the search representation in step (1) and the operators gives a structure to the search space in terms of how local neighbors in the search space are related to each other.

This framework fits many successful algorithms for optimization, such as local search and simulated annealing. Furthermore, many successful bio-inspired algorithms (e.g., evolutionary algorithms, ant colony optimization, and particle swarm optimization) fit into this framework. They differ from each other in the representation chosen and the operators used to produce new solutions. As we have seen, possible solutions for the TSP problem can be represented by permutations of the *n* cities. Furthermore, the fitness assignment can be straightforward by taking the length of the tour that is encoded by the permutation. Given a permutation of the input elements, we next have to think about what operators could be used to construct a new solution.

A well-known operator for solving the TSP problem is the state-of-the-art 2-OPT operator. It takes the current tour, chooses two edges of the tour (i.e., connections between cities), and removes them, yielding three disconnected part-tours. The parts are then reconnected in a different order (by two new edges) such that a new tour is obtained. Using a local search procedure, one would start with an initial solution and try all possible 2-OPT operations until a better permutation has been found. If no improvement is possible, the algorithm stops. Note that 2-OPT defines a neighborhood for each point (tour) in the search space in terms of all the possible new arrangements of three parts of that tour. The size and the structure of such neighborhoods are crucial for the success of these algorithms.

Once a neighborhood in a local search algorithm is defined, we can address the problem of becoming trapped in local optima. By choosing a large neighborhood, local optima become less likely. In the extreme case, one might think of defining the neighborhood of a solution as the set of all other solutions in the entire search space, which by definition would include the globally optimal solution. However, it is obvious that this would lead to neighborhoods that are usually not searchable in an efficient way, as the number of elements in them would be exponential with respect to the given problem size.

Considering how to choose good representations and operators, and hence neighborhoods, in our setting can be done by examining the fitness landscape, defined by the search space S, the function f to be optimized, and the chosen neighborhood $N: S \rightarrow 2^S$. We can think of the fitness landscape as a graph whose elements of S are nodes that have certain values, and with an arc from x to y if y is an element of the neighborhood of x, that is, $y \in N(x)$. Fitness landscapes are often visualized by plotting the surface of fitness values over the search space. Solutions that are neighbors are close to each other, that is, they can be easily reached using the operators from (3) above. Because the fitness function f often produces similar values for nearby solutions, one can observe local and global optima in the fitness landscape.

High-Dimensionality Fitness Spaces

Finding the global optimum requires a search algorithm to avoid being trapped in any one of possibly very many local maxima. Recent work done within the context of fitness landscapes defined on genotype spaces suggests that landscapes with extremely high dimensionality have certain features that may simplify searching the space of solutions. To illustrate this work, consider the following model. Assume that the search space consists of genotypes each comprising a very large number L of diallelic loci (i.e., positions at which they can have one of two different alleles). Each genotype has L one-step neighbors (single mutants). Let us assign fitnesses randomly and independently to each genotype so that they are equal either to 1 (a viable genotype) or 0 (inviable genotype), with probabilities P and $1 - P$, respectively. In general, viable genotypes will tend to form connected networks—that is, they will be connected by steps of a single mutation. For small values of P, there are two qualitatively different regimes: (a) subcritical, in which all connected components of the genotype network are relatively small (which takes place when $P < P_c$, where P_c is the percolation threshold), and (b) supercritical, in which the majority of viable genotypes are connected in a single giant component, which takes place when $P > P_c$ (Gavrilets and Gravner 1997). A very important, though counterintuitive, feature of this model is that the percolation threshold is approximately the reciprocal of the dimensionality of the genotype space: $P_c \approx 1/L$, and thus P_c is very small if L is large (see Gavrilets 2004; Gavrilets and Gravner 1997). Therefore, increasing the dimensionality of the genotype space, L, while keeping constant the probability of being viable, P, makes the formation of the giant component unavoidable. (Similar findings hold when the model is generalized to use continued fitness values; see Gavrilets and Gravner 1997).

In the literature, the connected networks discussed in the previous paragraph are often referred to as neutral networks, where the word "neutral" means that there is no difference in fitness between the genotypes in the network. In certain applications, small differences in fitness are allowed and the resulting networks are called "nearly neutral." The earlier work on neutral and nearly neutral networks in multidimensional fitness landscapes concentrated exclusively on genotype spaces in which each individual was characterized by a discrete set of genes. However, many features of biological organisms that are actually observable and/or measurable are described by continuously varying variables such as size, weight, color, or concentration. A question of particular biological interest is whether (nearly) neutral networks are as prominent in a continuous phenotype space as they are in the discrete genotype space. Recent results provide an affirmative answer to this question. Specifically, Gravner et al. (2007) have shown that in a simple model of random fitness assignment, viable phenotypes are likely to form a large connected cluster even if their overall frequency is very low, provided the dimensionality of the phenotype space L (i.e., the number of phenotypic characters) is sufficiently large. In fact, the percolation threshold, P_c, for the probability of being viable scales with L as $1/2^L$ and thus decreases much faster than $1/L$, which is characteristic of the analogous discrete genotype space model.

Earlier work on nearly neutral networks was also limited to consideration of the direct relationship between genotype and fitness. Any phenotypic properties that usually mediate this relationship in real biological organisms were neglected. Gravner et al. (2007) studied a novel model in which phenotype is introduced explicitly. In their model, the relationships—both between genotype and phenotype as well as between phenotype and fitness—are of the many-to-one type, so that neutrality is present at both the phenotype and the fitness levels. Moreover, their model results in a correlated fitness landscape in which similar genotypes are more likely to have similar fitnesses. Gravner et al. (2007) showed that phenotypic neutrality and correlation between fitnesses can reduce the percolation threshold, making the formation of percolating networks easier.

Overall, the results of Gravner and colleagues reinforce the previous conclusion (Gavrilets 1997, 2004; Gavrilets and Gravner 1997; Reidys and Stadler 2001, 2002; Reidys et al. 1997) that extensive networks of genotypes with approximately similar fitnesses are a general feature of multidimensional fitness landscapes (both uncorrelated and correlated, as well as in both genotype and phenotype spaces). An important question is whether such concepts could inform internal search over cognitive representations. If so, they would suggest that moving to higher-dimensional search spaces could facilitate internal search by allowing the system to escape from local search optima.

High- and Low-Dimensionality Search

As discussed by Marshall and Neumann (this volume), choosing an appropriate neighborhood representation can make hard computational search problems much easier. Intuitively, one may think that reducing the dimensionality of a search space would make search easier. In machine classification problems, however, appropriately increasing the dimension of the search space (using "kernel methods") can turn a hard nonlinear classification problem into an easy linear one (e.g., Shawe-Taylor and Cristianini 2004), and neural models have been proposed which suggest that brains might also do this (e.g., Huerta et al. 2004). For internal cognitive search, could dynamic adjustment of the dimensionality of the internal space improve search performance? For low-dimensional search landscapes, a well-defined "fitness gradient" at any point in the space exists, but following it can lead a searcher to become trapped in local optima. However, higher-dimensional fitness landscapes have highly connected components (as described in the previous section) with much smaller fitness gradients, allowing neutral diffusion through the entire search space without having to suffer large losses in fitness. The proposal then is that internal search might first search in a low-dimensional internal space, climbing fitness gradients, until a local optimum is reached and no further improvement can be found. This could then be followed by an increase in the dimensionality of the internal space and an episode of neutral diffusion through the space. This would, in turn, be followed by a return to the low-dimensional representation of internal space and a further episode of hill climbing, which may climb a gradient to a new and better local optimum than the one found prior to the preceding episode of neutral diffusion. Several iterations of this process could be used in an attempt to find successive improvements in the quality of local optima discovered.

An approximation of this process can be seen in high-dimensional semantic memory models such as HAL and LSA (Burgess and Lund 2000; Landauer and Dumais 1997). These models capitalize on lexical co-occurrence and acquire word meaning by bootstrapping conceptual representations via the inductive encoding of statistical regularities in language. In the case of HAL, words are represented by vectors, typically with 200–140,000 vector elements, where each element corresponds to another word in the input stream that occurred near the word being represented. The meaning is thus a representation of the contexts in which the word occurred, and input samples can be very large (one billion words has been one of the larger language samples). The vectors are formed by encoding weighted lexical co-occurrence values as a window (typically 5–10 words) moves along the text calculating the vector values for each target word and the words in the window before and after it. Although these models are usually used statically (i.e., the vector values for words are extracted after the model passes through the entire text), they could be used dynamically, in line with the changing dimensionality approach suggested above. Such a model would start small (with about five encoded words and hence five vector dimensions) and add dimensions (and encoded words) as it encounters each unique word. The resulting model would have very sparse dimensionality in that most of the space defined by the dimensions would be unoccupied. Once the model has experienced a large amount of text, dimensionality can be reduced again by retaining the most contextually diverse columns. Regardless of the final number of dimensions, both models can usually undergo a dimensionality reduction to around 200–300 dimensions without losing resolution in their cognitive predictability (e.g., predicting word relatedness, semantic priming, typicality effects, and grammatical and semantic categorization). Both HAL and LSA have been shown to account for various phenomena in the concept acquisition process (Landauer and Dumais 1997; Li et al. 2000) and demonstrate the plausibility of dynamically increasing and decreasing dimensionality of the space, as needed, to represent the language input.

Representations Learned by Humans and Machines

As the foregoing analysis of fitness landscapes attests, a central factor for a search process is how the search space is represented. Relatedly, in the domain of cognitive science there is a history of research showing that representations change as people gain experience during search. Prominent examples are when people learn how to solve a complex problem or acquire a complex skill, such as when one learns how to navigate in a city or learns how to play chess. Studies on expert-novice differences in chess consistently show that one important element that defines chess expertise is whether the person can effectively represent the states of a chessboard to promote inferring the best move. For example, expert chess players are often found to have exceptional memory of chess positions and are able to recall them accurately even after a short (< 5 s) encoding time. Exceptional memory, however, is only found when the chess positions are meaningful (Chase and Simon 1973b). When chess pieces are randomly located on the chessboard, recall accuracy decreases dramatically. This is often taken as evidence that experts have more efficient internal representations of the chess positions that allow them to interpret quickly the functional state of the game. In other words, extensive experience with the search space (possible moves in a chess game) allows experts to reduce the dimensionality of the search space, making their search more efficient than for novices.

Chess playing is also studied extensively in the domain of machine learning. In fact, developing algorithms that can beat human chess players is often considered a major benchmark test for success in the field of artificial intelligence. One common approach is to compute the optimal depth of win (minimum number of moves to win) for a given state, and use this as a fitness function in the search algorithm, based on which the computer selects the "best" move. Finding the best move often requires extensive search in a very large space of possible moves, and it must be done over and over, because the search space changes after each move by the opponent. Nevertheless, rapid advances in machine learning techniques and computational power have led to machines that can beat even the most skilled human chess players. On the other hand, the way a computer plays chess is very different from the way in which a human plays. Specifically, it is believed that the search process is much more efficient for humans than computers in the sense that humans consider vastly fewer moves. The reduction of the search space through experience is often considered the primary reason why cognitive (human) search is more efficient than machine search.

The human ability to develop better representations that facilitate search becomes even clearer in cases where the size of the search space is larger than it is for chess. For example, while machines can beat a human chess player, no machine algorithm has yet been developed to beat expert players of the game of Go—an ancient board game for two players that is noted for being rich in strategy despite its relatively simple rules. Because Go utilizes a much simpler set of rules than chess, the search space becomes much less constrained, thus making it difficult for a machine to search. On the other hand, expert Go players, like expert chess players, can learn more effective representations of the search space by perceptually recognizing "loosely defined" functional states through experience, which practically reduces the dimensions of the search space they use.

As discussed by Fu (this volume), the way that representations and search processes interact is often considered a fundamental aspect of intelligence. The discussion above leads to the perhaps paradoxical conclusion that the amount of search is not necessarily a measure of the amount of intelligence being exhibited by the agent (human, animal, or machine). What makes search intelligent is not that a large number of search steps are required for reaching the target, but that a large amount of search would be required if a requisite level of knowledge were not applied by the cognitive system (Newell and Simon 1976, 1987). While it seems that there is still no deep theoretical explanation for the distinction in performance between human experts and machines, there are three general conclusions that can be based on the observations. First, some part of the human superiority in tasks with a large perceptual component, as in chess or even the traveling salesman problem (MacGregor et al. 2000), can be attributed to the special-purpose, built-in, parallel processing structure of the human perceptual-spatial system. Second, many of the tasks in which humans excel seem to involve a large amount of semantic information. For example, master-level chess players are estimated to have knowledge of approximately 50,000 relevant chess patterns. This suggests that experts can substitute recognition for search (at least partially) because these patterns contain an enormous amount of information that helps the experts to reduce the search space significantly. Finally, there may be a distinction between local and nonlocal use of search knowledge (see Hills and Dukas, this volume). Many chess algorithms tend to use information gathered during the course of search (we refer to this kind of information broadly as "search knowledge") only locally to help make decisions at the specific (or neighboring) node where the information was gathered. Hence, the same facts have to be rediscovered repeatedly at multiple locations in the search space. Humans, however, are good at taking search knowledge "out of context" and generalizing it to apply to a wider range of areas. Thus, if a weakness in a chess position can be traced back to a series of moves that led to it, then the same weakness can be expected in other positions if the same (or similar) series of moves is executed. Indeed, much progress has been made in machine learning in this kind of nonlocal use of knowledge to improve search. Just how (e.g., mechanistically) humans are able to do so is still relatively unknown. However, the importance of choosing the appropriate representations seems to be a key factor that influences search performance.

In summary, we argue that dimension reduction of the search space by experience is one critical characteristic of cognitive search that distinguishes it from formal methods of search developed by machine learning researchers. This type of representational change seems to be the main reason why cognitive search can be more efficient than machine search. More research is needed to uncover how this kind of dimension reduction in the representation of search space is accomplished and what neurocognitive mechanisms are involved.

Built-In and Learned Constraints

The importance of constraints for search is strongly supported by both theoretical and empirical arguments. Classic work on heuristics has shown that efficient search depends on the searcher being able to apply operators that usually bring the searcher closer to its goal. An unbiased or unconstrained searcher will typically be unable to find goals in reasonable amounts of time.

Consider the vast space of possible language grammars. Gold and Chomsky formally showed that there are too many possible grammars to learn a language in a finite amount of time, let alone the two years required by most children, if there were no constraints on what those grammars might look like (Gold and The RAND Corporation 1967; Chomsky 1965). In a related analysis, Wolpert (1996) showed that there is no such thing as a truly general and efficient learning device. Developmental psychologists have argued that children need to have built-in constraints, biases, or implicit assumptions that fit well with their environment (Gelman 1990; Spelke and Kinzler 2007).

One exciting alternative to built-in constraints is that experience with a richly and diversely structured world can allow agents to devise some of the constraints that they will then use to make searching their world for adaptive behaviors more efficient. While some constraints are surely provided by evolution, others can be acquired during an organism's lifetime and are no less powerful for being learned. In fact, acquired constraints have the advantage of being tailored to an individual's own circumstances. For example, early language experience establishes general hypotheses about how stress patterns inform word boundaries (Jusczyk et al. 1999). Children are flexible enough to acquire either the constraints imposed by a stress-timed language (e.g., English) or a syllable-timed language (e.g., Italian), but once the systematicities within a language are imprinted, children are constrained to segment speech streams into words according to these acquired biases. When exposed to new objects, people create new descriptions for the objects' parts and then are constrained to use these descriptions to represent still later objects (Schyns and Rodet 1997). As a final example, Madole and Cohen (1995) describe how 14-month-old children learn part-function correlations that violate real-world events. These correlations cannot be learned by 18-month-old children, which suggest that children younger than this acquire constraints on the types of correlations that they will learn. In all of these cases, constraints are acquired that subsequently influence how people will search for regularities in their environment.

A search system must have strong constraints on the possibilities it will pursue if it wants to find solutions in a practical amount of time, but a considerable amount of flexibility is still needed when a system faces different environments and tasks. This dilemma can be resolved by again making constraints themselves learnable. Kemp et al. (2010a, b) present a quantitative, formal approach to learning constraints. Their hierarchical Bayesian framework describes a method for learning constraints at multiple levels. For example, upon seeing several normal dogs, their system would develop expectancies of various strengths that a new dog will have four legs, that mammals have four legs, and that animals have four legs. Upon seeing a set of both dogs and swans, their system would expect dogs to have four legs, swans to have two legs, and, more generally, all animals of a particular species to have a characteristic number of legs. This latter hypothesis will in turn help the system to quickly find the hypothesis "all beetles have six legs" upon seeing only a single beetle exemplar. Representations at higher levels capture knowledge that supports learning at the next level down. In this manner, constraints can be learned at a higher level that facilitate search for valid inferences at a lower level.

Bayesian approaches are not the only models that can search for constraints for further search. Some neural network models provide working examples of systems that learn new constraint structures because of the inputs provided to them. Bernd Fritzke's (1994) *growing neural gas model* provides a compelling example of this. When inputs are presented, edges are grown between nodes that are close to the input, and new nodes are created if no node is sufficiently close to the input. The result is a graph-based "skeleton" that can aptly accommodate new knowledge because the skeleton was formed exactly in order to accommodate the knowledge. This skeleton-creating approach appears also in "Rethinking Innateness" (Elman et al. 1996), where one of the primary ideas is that the existence of modularity does not implicate innateness. Modules can be learned through the process of systems self-organizing to have increasingly rich and differentiated structure. Computational modeling suggests that the eventual specialization of a neural module often belies its rather general origins (Jacobs et al. 1991). Very general neural differences, such as whether a set of neurons has a little or a lot of overlap in their receptive fields, can lead to large-scale functional differences, such as specializing spontaneously to handle either categorical or continuous judgment tasks or snowballing into "what" versus "where" visual systems (Jacobs and Jordan 1992). Without belaboring the details of these models, there are a sufficient number of examples of constraint-creating mechanisms to believe that systems can achieve both efficient and flexible search routines by learning how to constrain themselves.

Working Memory Constraints

Beyond imprecise or incomplete knowledge about the search space, biological systems face constraints, such as limited working memory capacities, that make the actual calculation (and memorization) of the optimal solution to many kinds of problems impossible. To help overcome these constraints, humans employ a variety of easy-to-compute strategies and heuristics. Moreover, it appears reasonable to assume that humans create internal representations of the problem space (e.g., the environment) that facilitate the search process. Memory representations of large-scale environments are often described as being hierarchically structured with multiple layers of abstraction (e.g., Stevens and Coupe 1978). A possible function of this organization is that it reduces memory and computation costs when searching for paths between (multiple) locations. For example, by using different levels of detail simultaneously (i.e., by using high resolution only for the current surrounding while using coarser representations for distant locations), search costs and working memory load are reduced.

Planning a novel route through a familiar environment can be conceptualized as searching for a path through state- or search-space from a given start location to a destination. From a computational perspective, such planning tasks become challenging if the environment is large such that many path alternatives are possible and/or if multiple target locations have to be considered (e.g., when solving the TSP). Wiener et al. (2008) recently studied human performance in solving TSPs under conditions that required working memory as opposed to conditions that did not tax memory. When working memory was required, participants performed better if the optimal solution to the TSP required visiting all targets in one region before entering another region. This is best described by a planning (search) algorithm that utilizes an abstraction of the actual problem space to compute an initially coarse solution that is subsequently refined (see also Pizlo et al. 2006). Again, this algorithm operates on a reduced search space that represents an abstraction of the actual search space, thus reducing working memory load and the computational complexity of the problem. We note, however, that search algorithms which operate on abstractions of the actual search space are obviously vulnerable to suboptimal or distorted solutions (e.g., direction judgments; Stevens and Coupe 1978) and may require replanning during actual navigation (Wiener and Mallot 2003). Such additional costs appear to result from the trade-off between the quality of the solution and the constraints inherent to the system.

Working memory can be construed not just as a limitation to be overcome, but also in some cases as a constraint that may serve important functions (Hertwig and Todd 2003). Consistent with this view, Kareev and colleagues have suggested that short-term memory limitations can actually benefit correlation detection (Kareev et al. 1997). They show that smaller sample sizes of environment observations amplify correlations, because both the median and the mode of the sampling distribution of the Pearson correlation exceed the population correlation. As the size of these observed samples is presumably bounded by short-term memory capacity, people with lower short-term memory capacity would be expected to consider smaller samples than those with higher capacity. The result is that the lower-capacity individuals should be more likely to perceive correlations that have been amplified by their more limited short-term memory. Kareev found empirical support for this hypothesis, although some questions have been raised about both the theoretical analysis and the interpretation of the empirical results. For example, small samples lead to high false alarm rates (Juslin and Olsson 2005), and the advantage can only hold if one assumes a decision threshold (Anderson et al. 2005) and relatively large correlations (Kareev 2005). Gaissmaier et al. (2006) suggest that the apparent empirical advantage in detecting correlations for those with lower memory capacity may be confounded with an increased likelihood of those with higher capacity to explore.

As another example of possible advantages of memory constraints, Elman (1991) developed a neural network simulation of a task that a young child faces when learning aspects of a language—essentially, searching for a grammar that accounts for the language inputs being heard. For example, the network had to predict number agreement between subject and verb in a sentence, or whether a verb was transitive or intransitive. The network could not learn the full underlying complex grammar when trained from the outset with "adult" language. However, the network succeeded when its limited "short-term memory" (realized as windows on the input sentences) was allowed to grow gradually. Starting with smaller windows helped the network find the statistical regularities across the input sentences. Whether a limited working memory also helps people learn a hierarchical organization of spatial memory (as opposed to semantic or syntactic memory) is an open question.

Constraints on Physical and Cognitive Search Space Topology

Two of the major goals of this Forum were to explore the relationship between search in different domains, especially external "spatial" search and internal "cognitive" search, and to investigate how search strategies scale from low- to high-dimensional environments. In considering the relationship between external search in the environment and internal search over representations of solutions to problems, one might implicitly assume that the primary difference is that external search is low dimensional (typically two or three) and internal search is high dimensional. We propose, however, that this is not the primary distinction between internal and external search. Rather, as we have reviewed, the important difference is that representation of the space for internal search can vary, both in topology and in dimensionality. It is more difficult to change representations in external space. For example, it is relatively difficult for people and ants to build bridges that reduce distances in external space, while in contrast we argue that distances between points in a cognitive search space can be more easily altered by changes to the representation (e.g., by increasing or decreasing the dimensionality of the search space).

In abstract terms, the topology of a search space is defined by the neighborhood function that specifies how points in the search space relate to each other. In external space this has a natural interpretation: on the surface of the Earth, the neighbors of a particular point in space have an intuitive definition, which similarly holds for the three-dimensional spaces inhabited by animals able to fly or swim. Animals searching in these environments must move through spatially neighboring points before they can get to other more distant points; they cannot teleport. Thus, if an animal wishes to search for something (e.g., food or mates at a distant point), it must move through other points to get there and might take the opportunity to search at intermediate points as well along the way. In transferring the concept of external search to internal search, however, one should realize that the spatial structure or topology of an environment is outside the animal's control, while for internal search, the representation of the space, and hence the topology and dimensionality of the space itself, can be changed. This could, in turn, affect the difficulty of a search process in that internal space; hence, a useful representation for an internal search problem might itself be searched for, or selected, by the animal or by evolutionary processes in the "space of possible representations" (Newell and Simon 1976, 1987).

Animals do have some ability to change the dimensionality of their environment. Consider, for example, an ant colony reducing a two-dimensional surface to a network of one-dimensional pheromone trails and manipulating the nature of that network to facilitate navigation (e.g., Jackson et al. 2004), or a terrestrial animal that increases the dimensionality of its environment by acquiring the ability to fly. Animals may also directly adapt the dimensionality of their search to achieve some objective; for example, switching between trail following and more exploratory behavior in the case of ants (Edelstein-Keshet et al. 1995) or changing between local terrestrial search and long-distance flights between areas in the case of a bird or other flying animal (Amano and Katayama 2009). Nonetheless, an animal's ability to manipulate the external space in which it searches is limited by dimensionality and the basic laws of physics. In contrast, internal search spaces should be subject to much less restriction, both in terms of dimensionality and topology.

Social Search

Newell and Simon focused on the intelligence of individuals, but groups also need to act intelligently to search for solutions. A key distinction is between group search and individual search with a social component (for an extended discussion, see Lazer and Bernstein, this volume). Group search involves group-level payoff, whereas individual search involves individual-level payoff. In both cases, one can still examine the collective implications of individual behavior, but the presence of a group payoff potentially reduces the conflict of interest among individuals. Individual success is some function of collective and individual components, and the relative magnitude of these components. At one end of the spectrum, individual success is purely a function of group success (social insects may be closer to this end). In other group systems, individual success might be empirically separable from group success, or there might be no group component to individual success whatsoever. Thus, for example, there might be individual benefits to putting less effort into foraging, even though the group (and individual) also gains benefits from finding resources. The general conundrum is that exploration is individually costly but offers benefits to the collective (more on this below), so the potential risk for the group is underinvestment in exploration. How then to achieve group search? From a behavioral ecology perspective, the conditions needed for group selection to emerge at the genetic level (e.g., very low levels of genetic mixing) are quite narrow and unlikely to have characterized humans or human predecessors. Instead, culture might be a potential avenue for group selection because of the speed of cultural relative to genetic change.

Communication in Social Search

The individual-group dimension is actually part of the general question of what the structure of payoff interdependence among actors is. While the dominant idea of foraging is that there is an exhaustible resource, creating a potential conflict of interest among actors, there are many examples of other types of interdependence. Most notably, there is an array of scenarios where agents benefit from the presence of other individuals. For example, one explanation for the existence of cities is the ease with which individuals can communicate information (Glaeser et al. 1992).

Another important dimension is how advertent and inadvertent communication helps coordinate search. Communication, most critically, facilitates exploitation across agents. Agent A discovers resource X, communicates that to Agent B, which exploits resource X. Communication may thus facilitate efficient exploitation of resources, but may also create the social dilemma of over-rewarding exploiting agents compared to exploring agents. If agents explore and what is found remains private until the agent shares the information, then reciprocity may be needed to resolve the collective dilemma. If agents explore and what is found is clearly visible to all, and it is not possible to exclude other agents from consuming the good, then an under-investment in exploration will occur. In particular cases, variation in visibility (e.g., some solutions may not be visible or possible to copy, while others are) may occur, which would create a bias toward search for nonvisible resources.

Communication may also be important in efficient exploration. Organized search may be more efficient than uncoordinated search. For example, a group search for missing keys can be more efficient if the searchers look in mutually exclusive sets of rooms—but if Agents A and B have no way of communicating which rooms they have inspected, there is a risk that they both search the same room. In addition, copying behavior may allow for more efficient collective search by focusing search on promising areas of the solution space (i.e., effective exploration sometimes requires effective exploitation).

Often, a contrast is drawn between the emergent patterns of self-organized groups and groups that are driven top-down by a leader, rule system, or hierarchical structure (Resnick 1994). What this rhetorical antithesis misses is that self-organized groups do elect leaders, form rule systems, and institute hierarchies (akin to changing the search space representation as described earlier). Most groups that follow rules are typically self-organized, and the rule systems themselves are self-organized. The rules are the tangible products of courts, parliaments, congresses, and governments at city, regional, national, and global levels. For example, in the absence of an existing governmental structure to regulate lobster harvesting effectively, the harvesters themselves created a structure (Acheson 2003). Rules and norms (their less explicit cousin) are complex systems in their own right, no less so than beehives or traffic jams. They do not exist on their own, but rather depend upon supporting structures for their continuation. They require legal and governmental systems to be created, changed, and eliminated (Ostrom et al. 2003).They require monitoring systems (e.g., police) to insure adherence and sanctioning systems (e.g., jails) to punish discovered rule violations. Originally unorganized groups will propose, vote upon, and live under rule, monitoring, and sanction systems that they construct themselves (Janssen et al. 2008; Samuelson and Messick 1995). In this manner, groups that face scarce resources are often importantly not simple decentralized systems, but rather decentralized systems that spontaneously create rule systems that are themselves decentralized.

Humans are not alone in adaptively creating organization structures that help them achieve their goals. Some ant species tune their level of egalitarianism to the level of informational uncertainty of individuals within the colony (Sueur et al. 2011). When individuals have little uncertainty about the relative advantages of different resources in their environment, they adopt more despotic decision regimes in which group choices are controlled by relatively few individuals (for a related point, see Pierce and White 1999). When informational uncertainty is low, or when decisions must be made quickly, there are benefits for social search processes that concentrate effective voting power in relatively few individuals. As informational uncertainty increases, so does the importance of pooling information across many individuals. In related work, bee swarms searching for new nesting sites have been aptly modeled as a population of agents that accumulate evidence for alternative choices (Marshall et al. 2009; Seeley et al. 2012). Assuming that the colony has adapted to achieve at least a certain level of accuracy at discovering the best available nest site, this accumulation process involving many individuals minimizes search time. Similarly for human groups, when the complexity of a problem space is low, centralized networks in which a single individual communicates with others are effective in a manner that no longer is found as problem complexity increases (Leavitt 1962); but distributed networks become important as the ruggedness of a problem space increases (Lazer and Friedman 2007).

Conclusion

As Newell and Simon famously eschewed disciplinary boundaries, one can only imagine how pleased they would be to see how search informs and connects the cognitive, biological, and social sciences today. In this chapter, we have described the benefits of restructuring search spaces and internal representations so as to make searches more efficient. Whereas Newell and Simon focused on the application of heuristics to fixed and well-defined search spaces, biological and social systems often engage in higher-level searching for more effective representations to make their lower-level searches more effective. This can be achieved by either increasing or decreasing the dimensionality of internal representations, or by restructuring the representations altogether.

As clever as they were, Newell and Simon could not be expected to predict perfectly the developments in science 35 years later. For example, Newell and Simon (1976, 1987) thought that mimicking the way people play chess was the most promising way forward for chess programs. At the time of their Turing award, such programs had only just begun "to compete with serious amateurs." They believed the route computers would take to beat the best human players would be to buttress heuristic search with knowledge. In the end, although heuristics certainly played a role in the computer victory over people, Hitech and its successor Deep Blue depended more on the "massive" search of game trees than Newell and Simon had imagined; a triumph of Moore's law regarding exponentially increasing computer processing power. In their words: "It's fun to be wrong" (Newell and Simon 1987:316). Although they admittedly missed the mark with respect to the extent that human-inspired heuristics would solve the problems of artificial intelligence, their take on the key role of heuristic search for human intelligence does appear to have been largely substantiated. As we have reviewed here, human intelligence depends on constraining search in a variety of ways. It's also fun to be right.

Acknowledgments

We thank Iain Couzin and John M. C. Hutchinson for helpful comments.

Bibliography

Able, K. P. 1993. Orientation cues used by migratory birds: A review of cue-conflict experiments. *Trends Ecol. Evol.* **8(10)**:367–371. [19]

Acheson, J. M. 2003. Capturing the Commons: Devising Institutions to Manage the Maine Lobster Industry. Lebanon: Univ. Press of New England. [20]

Adams, C. D. 1981. Variations in the sensitivity of instrumental responding to reinforcer devaluation. *Q. J. Exp. Psychol.* **34B**:77–98. [7]

Adams, C. D., and A. Dickinson. 1981. Instrumental responding following reinforcer devaluation. *Q. J. Exp. Psychol.* **33B**:109–121. [7]

Addolorato, G., L. Leggio, L. Abenavoli, and G. Gasbarrini. 2005. Neurobiochemical and clinical aspects of craving in alcohol addiction: A review. *Addict. Behav.* **30(6)**:1209–1224. [6]

Adler, F. R., and D. M. Gordon. 1992. Information collection and spread by networks of patrolling ants. *Am. Nat.* **140**:373–400. [3]

Adler, F. R., and M. Kotar. 1999. Departure time versus departure rate: How to forage optimally when you are stupid. *Evol. Ecol. Res.* **1**:411–421. [2]

Agster, K. L., N. J. Fortin, and R. Eichenbaum. 2002. The hippocampus and disambiguation of overlapping sequences. *J. Neurosci.* **22(13)**:5760–5768. [6]

Ahmed, S. H. 2010. Validation crisis in animal models of drug addiction: Beyond non-disordered drug use toward drug addiction. *Neurosci. Biobehav. Rev.* **35(2)**:172–184. [6]

Ainge, J. A., M. Tamosiunaite, F. Wörgötter, and P. A. Dudchenko. 2011. Hippocampal place cells encode intended destination, and not a discriminative stimulus, in a conditional T-maze task. *Hippocampus* doi:10.1002/hipo.20919. [6]

Ainge, J. A., M. A. van der Meer, R. F. Langston, and E. R. Wood. 2007. Exploring the role of context-dependent hippocampal activity in spatial alternation behavior. *Hippocampus* **17(10)**:988–1002. [6]

Akbari Chermahini, S., and B. Hommel. 2010. The (b)link between creativity and dopamine: Spontaneous eye blink rates predict and dissociate divergent and convergent thinking. *Cognition* **115**:458–465. [14]

———. 2012. Creative mood swings: Divergent and convergent thinking affect mood in opposite ways. *Psychol. Res.*, in press. [14]

Alcock, J. 1987. Leks and hilltopping in insects. *J. Nat. Hist.* **21**:319–328. [4]

Alderfer, C. P. 1977. Group and intergroup relations. In: Improving Life at Work, ed. J. R. Hackman and J. L. Suttle, pp. 227–296. Santa Monica: Goodyear. [17]

Alexander, G. E., and M. D. Crutcher. 1990. Functional architecture of basal ganglia circuits: Neural substrates of parallel processing. *Trends Neurosci.* **13**:266–271. [7]

Alexander, G. E., M. D. Crutcher, and M. R. DeLong. 1990. Basal ganglia-thalamo-cortical circuits: Parallel substrates for motor, oculomotor, prefrontal and limbic functions. *Prog. Brain Res.* **85**:119–146. [9]

Alexander, G. E., M. DeLong, and P. Stuck. 1986. Parallel organisation of functionally segregated circuits linking basal ganglia and cortex. *Ann. Rev. Neurosci.* **9**:357–381. [9]

Alexander, W., and J. W. Brown. 2010. Computational models of performance monitoring and cognitive control. *Top. Cogn. Sci.* **2**:658–677. [5]

———. 2011. Medial prefrontal cortex as an action-outcome predictor. *Nat. Neurosci.* **14(10)**:1338–1344. [5]

Allman, J. M., N. A. Tetreault, A. Y. Hakeem, et al. 2010. The Von Economo neurons in frontoinsular and anterior cingulate cortex in great apes and humans. *Brain Struct. Funct.* **214(5–6)**:495–517. [13]

Alpern, S., and S. Gal. 2003. The Theory of Search Games and Rendezvous. Boston: Kluwer. [4]

Alt, W., and G. Hoffmann, eds. 1990. Biological Motion. Lecture Notes in Biomathematics. Heidelberg: Springer-Verlag. [3]

Altman, J., B. J. Everitt, T. W. Robbins, et al. 1996. The biological, social and clinical bases of drug addiction: Commentary and debate. *Psychopharmacol.* **125(4)**:285–345. [6, 9]

Altmann, E. M. 2003. Task switching and the pied homunculus: Where are we being led? *Trends Cogn. Sci.* **7(8)**:340–341. [5]

Altmann, E. M., and W. D. Gray. 2002. Forgetting to remember: The functional relationship of decay and interference. *Psychol. Sci.* **13(1)**:27–33. [5]

Alvarez, P., and L. R. Squire. 1994. Memory consolidation and the medial temporal lobe: A simple network model. *PNAS* **91**:7041–7045. [6]

Amador, N., M. Schlag-Rey, and J. Schlag. 2000. Reward-predicting and reward-detecting neuronal activity in the primate supplementary eye field. *J. Neurophysiol.* **84(4)**:2166–2170. [5]

Amano, T., and N. Katayama. 2009. Hierarchical movement decisions in predators: Effects of foraging experience at more than one spatial and temporal scale. *Ecology* **90**:3536–3545. [4, 20]

Amiez, C., J. P. Joseph, and E. Procyk. 2005. Anterior cingulate error-related activity is modulated by predicted reward. *Eur. J. Neurosci.* **21(12)**:3447–3452. [5]

Amodio, D. M., and C. D. Frith. 2006. Meeting of minds: The medial frontal cortex and social cognition. *Nat. Rev. Neurosci.* **7(4)**:268–277. [13]

Anderson, A. K., K. Christoff, I. Stappen, et al. 2003. Dissociated neural representations of intensity and valence in human olfaction. *Nat. Neurosci.* **6**:196–202. [7]

Anderson, J. R. 1974. Retrieval of prepositional information from long-term memory. *Cogn. Psychol.* **6**:451–474. [11]

———. 1983. The Architecture of Cognition. Cambridge, MA: Harvard Univ. Press. [11]

———. 1991. Is human cognition adaptive? *Behav. Brain Sci.* **14**:471–484. [15]

———. 1993. Rules of the Mind. Hillsdale, NJ: Lawrence Erlbaum. [14]

Anderson, J. R., D. Bothell, M. D. Byrne, et al. 2004. An integrated theory of the mind. *Psychol. Rev.* **111**:1036–1060. [18]

Anderson, J. R., D. Bothell, C. Lebiere, and M. Matessa. 1998. An integrated theory of list memory. *J. Mem. Lang.* **38**:341–380. [11]

Anderson, J. R., and R. Milson. 1989. Human memory: An adaptive perspective. *Psychol. Rev.* **96**:703–719. [11]

Anderson, J. R., and L. J. Schooler. 1991. Reflections of the environment in memory. *Psychol. Sci.* **2**:396–408. [11]

Anderson, R. B., M. E. Doherty, N. D. Berg, and J. C. Friedrich. 2005. Sample size and the detection of correlation—a signal detection account: Comment on Kareev (2000) and Juslin and Olsson (2005). *Psychol. Rev.* **112**:268–279. [20]

Andersson, M. 1981. An optimal predator search. *Theor. Pop. Biol.* **19**:58–86. [3]

Andrade, E. B., and D. Ariely. 2009. The enduring impact of transient emotions on decision making. *Org. Behav. Hum. Decis. Proc.* **109(1)**:1–8. [6]

Arbilly, M., U. Motro, M. W. Feldman, and A. Lotem. 2010. Co-evolution of learning complexity and social foraging strategies. *J. Theor. Biol.* **267**:573–581. [4]

Archer, J., and L. Birke. 1983. Exploration in Animals and Humans. Cambridge: Van Nostrand Reinhold. [9]

Arnsten, A. F. T. 1998. Catecholamine modulation of prefrontal cortical cognitive function. *Trends Cogn. Sci.* **2(11)**:436–446. [9]

———. 2009. Stress signalling pathways that impair prefrontal cortex structure and function. *Nat. Rev.* **10**:410–422. [8, 9]

Aron, A. R. 2010. From reactive to proactive and selective control: Developing a richer model for stopping inappropriate responses. *Biol. Psych.* **69(12)**:e55–68. [9]

Aron, A. R., T. E. Behrens, S. Smith, M. J. Frank, and R. A. Poldrack. 2007. Triangulating a cognitive control network using diffusion-weighted magnetic resonance imaging (MRI) and functional MRI. *J. Neurosci.* **27(14)**:3743–3752. [9]

Arrow, H., and K. L. Burns. 2003. Self-organizing culture: How norms emerge in small groups. In: The Psychological Foundations of Culture, ed. M. Schaller and C. Crandall, pp. 171–199. Mahwah, NJ: Lawrence Erlbaum. [17]

Arrow, H., and S. Crosson. 2003. Musical chairs: Membership dynamics in self-organized group formation. *Small Group Res.* **5**:523–556. [17]

Arrow, H., and J. E. McGrath. 1995. Membership dynamics in groups at work: A theoretical framework. In: Research in Organizational Behavior, ed. B. M. Staw and L. L. Cummings, pp. 373–411. Greenwich, CT: JAI. [17]

Asch, S. E. 1956. Studies of independence and conformity: A minority of one against a unanimous majority. *Psychol. Monogr.* **70(9)**:1–70. [17]

Aston-Jones, G., and J. D. Cohen. 2005a. Adaptive gain and the role of the locus coeruleus-norepinephrine system in optimal performance. *J. Comp. Neurol.* **493(1)**:99–110. [13]

———. 2005b. An integrative theory of locus coeruleus-norepinephrine function: Adaptive gain and optimal performance. *Ann. Rev. Neurosci.* **28**:403–450. [8, 9, 14]

Atallah, E. H., D. Lopeq-Paniagua, J. W. Rudy, and R. C. O'Reilly. 2007. Separate neural substrates for skill learning and performance in the ventral and dorsal striatum. *Nat. Neurosci.* **10(1)**:126–131. [6]

Atance, C. M., and D. K. O'Neill. 2001. Episodic future thinking. *Trends Cogn. Sci.* **5(12)**:533–539. [9]

Atkinson, R. C., J. E. Homlgren, and J. F. Juola. 1969. Processing time as influenced by the number of elements in a visual display. *Perc. Psychophys.* **6(6A)**:321–326. [10]

Atkinson, R. C., and R. M. Shiffrin. 1968. Human memory: A proposed system and its control processes. In: The Psychology of Learning and Motivation: Advances in Research and Theory, ed. K. W. Spence and J. T. Spence, pp. 89–195. New York: Academic Press. [11]

Aubert, A. E., D. Ramaekers, F. Beckers, et al. 1999. The analysis of heart rate variability in unrestrained rats: Validation of method and results. *Comput. Methods Programs Biomed.* **60(3)**:197–213. [9]

Austin, J. R. 2003. Transactive memory in organizational groups: The effects of content, consensus, specialization, and accuracy on group performance. *J. Appl. Psychol.* **88(5)**:866–878. [17]

Austin, K. B., L. H. White, and M. L. Shapiro. 1993. Short- and long-term effects of experience on hippocampal place fields. *Abstr. Soc. Neurosci.* **19**:797. [9]

Averbeck, B. B., J. W. Sohn, and D. Lee. 2006. Activity in prefrontal cortex during dynamic selection of action sequences. *Nat. Neurosci.* **9(2)**:276–282. [9]

Awh, E., E. K. Vogel, and S. H. Oh. 2006. Interactions between attention and working memory. *Neuroscience* **139(1)**:201–208. [5]

Baas, M., C. K. W. De Dreu, and B. A. Nijstad. 2008. A meta-analysis of 25 years of mood-creativity research: Hedonic tone, activation, or regulatory focus? *Psychol. Bull.* **134**:779–806. [14]

Bäckman, L., U. Lindenberger, S.-C. Li, and L. Nyberg. 2010. Linking cognitive aging to alterations in dopamine neurotransmitter functioning: Recent data and future avenues. *Neurosci. Biobehav. Rev.* **34**:670–677. [15]

Backwell, P. R. Y., and N. I. Passmore. 1996. Time constraints and multiple choice criteria in the sampling behaviour and mate choice of the fiddler crab, *Uca annulipes. Behav. Ecol. Sociobiol.* **38**:407–416. [4]

Baddeley, A. D. 1986. Working Memory. Oxford: Clarendon Press. [8]

Badre, D., and A. D. Wagner. 2002. Semantic retrieval, mnemonic control, and prefrontal cortex. *Behav. Cogn. Neurosci. Rev.* **1(3)**:206–218. [9]

Bainton, R. J., L. T. Tsai, C. M. Singh, et al. 2000. Dopamine modulates acute responses to cocaine, nicotine and ethanol in *Drosophila. Curr. Biol.* **10**:187–194. [2]

Baker, S. C., R. D. Rogers, A. M. Owen, et al. 1996. Neural systems engaged by planning: A PET study of the Tower of London task. *Neuropsychologia* **34(6)**:515–526. [9]

Baldo, J. V., S. Schwartz, D. Wilkins, and N. F. Dronkers. 2006. Role of frontal versus temporal cortex in verbal fluency as revealed by voxel-based lesion symptom mapping. *J. Intl. Neuropsychol. Soc.* **12(6)**:896–900. [9]

Balleine, B. W. 2001. Incentive processes in instrumental conditioning. In: Handbook of Contemporary Learning Theories, ed. R. M. S. Klein, pp. 307–366. Hillsdale, NJ: LEA. [6, 7]

Balleine, B. W., N. D. Daw, and J. P. O'Doherty. 2008. Multiple forms of value learning and the function of dopamine. In: Neuroeconomics: Decision Making and the Brain, ed. P. W. Glimcher et al. New York: Academic Press. [12]

Balleine, B. W., M. R. Delgado, and O. Hikosaka. 2007. The role of the dorsal striatum in reward and decision-making. *J. Neurosci.* **27**:8161–8165. [7]

Balleine, B. W., and A. Dickinson. 1998a. Goal-directed instrumental action: Contingency and incentive learning and their cortical substrates. *Neuropharmacol.* **37(4–5)**:407–419. [6, 7]

———. 1998b. The role of incentive learning in instrumental outcome revaluation by specific satiety. *Anim. Learn. Behav.* **26**:46–59. [7]

Balleine, B. W., and S. Killcross. 2006. Parallel incentive processing: An integrated view of amygdala function. *Trends Neurosci.* **29(5)**:272–279. [7]

Balleine, B. W., A. S. Killcross, and A. Dickinson. 2003. The effect of lesions of the basolateral amygdala on instrumental conditioning. *J. Neurosci.* **23(2)**:666–675. [7]

Balleine, B. W., and S. B. Ostlund. 2007. Still at the choice-point: Action selection and initiation in instrumental conditioning. *Ann. NY Acad. Sci.* **1104**:147–171. [9]

Barabási, A.-L. 2009. Scale-free networks: A decade and beyond. *Science* **325**:412–413. [18]

Bar-Gad, I., G. Morris, and H. Bergman. 2003. Information processing, dimensionality reduction and reinforcement learning in the basal ganglia. *Prog. Neurobiol.* **71(6)**:439–473. [9]

Barker, J. R. 1993. Tightening the iron cage. Concertive control in self-managing teams. *Adm. Sci. Q.* **38**:408–437. [17]

Barnard, C. J. 1984. When cheats may prosper. In: Producers and Scroungers: Strategies of Exploitation and Parasitism, ed. C. J. Barnard, pp. 6–33. New York: Chapman and Hall. [3]

Barnard, C. J., and R. M. Sibly. 1981. Producers and scroungers: A general model and its application to captive flocks of house sparrows. *Anim. Behav.* **29(2)**:543–550. [3, 4, 19]

Barnea, A., and F. Nottebohm. 1995. Patterns of food storing by black-capped chickadees suggest a mnemonic hypothesis. *Anim. Behav.* **49**:1161–1176. [4]

Barnes, T. D., Y. Kubota, D. Hu, D. Z. Jin, and A. M. Graybiel. 2005. Activity of striatal neurons reflects dynamic encoding and recoding of procedural memories. *Nature* **437(7062)**:1158–1161. [6, 7]

Barnes, T. D., J. B. Mao, D. Hu, et al. 2011. Advance-cueing produces enhanced action-boundary patterns of spike activity in the sensorimotor striatum. *J. Neurophysiol.* **105**:1861–1878. [6]

Barron, A. B., E. Søvik, and J. L. Cornish. 2010. The roles of dopamine and related compounds in reward-seeking behavior across animal phyla. *Front. Behav. Neurosci.* **4**:1–9. [2]

Barta, Z., R. Flynn, and L.-A. Giraldeau. 1997. Geometry for a selfish foraging group: A genetic algorithm approach. *Proc. R. Soc. B* **264**:1233–1238. [3]

Bartumeus, F. 2005. Animal search strategies: A quantitative random-walk analysis. *Ecology* **86**:3078–3087. [3]

———. 2007. Lévy processes in animal movement: An evolutionary hypothesis. *Fractals* **15**:151–162. [3]

———. 2009. Behavioral intermittence, Lévy patterns, and randomness in animal movement. *Oikos* **118**:488–494. [3]

Bartumeus, F., J. Catalan, U. L. Fulco, M. L. Lyra, and G. M. Viswanathan. 2002. Optimizing the encounter rate in biological interactions: Lévy verses Brownian strategies. *Phys. Rev. Lett.* **88**:097901. [3]

Bartumeus, F., L. Giuggioli, M. Louzao, et al. 2010. Fishery discards impacts on seabird movement patterns at regional scales. *Curr. Biol.* **20**:1–8. [3]

Battaglia, F. P., G. R. Sutherland, and B. L. McNaughton. 2004. Local sensory cues and place cell directionality: Additional evidence of prospective coding in the hippocampus. *J. Neurosci.* **24(19)**:4541–4550. [6, 9]

Bauer, B., P. Jolicoeur, and W. B. Cowan. 1996. Distractor heterogeneity versus linear separability in colour visual search. *Perception* **25(1)**:1281–1294. [10]

Baum, E. B., and W. D. Smith. 1997. A Bayesian approach to relevance in game playing. *Artif. Intell.* **97(1–2)**:195–242. [12]

Bavelas, A. 1950. Communication patterns in task oriented groups. *J. Acoust. Soc. Am.* **57**:271–282. [17]

Baxter, M. G., A. Parker, C. C. Lindner, A. D. Izquierdo, and E. A. Murray. 2000. Control of response selection by reinforcer value requires interaction of amygdala and orbital prefrontal cortex. *J. Neurosci.* **20(11)**:4311–4319. [9]

Bazazi, S., J. Buhl, J. J. Hale, et al. 2008. Collective motion and cannibalism in locust marching bands. *Curr. Biol.* **18(10)**:735–739. [3]

Bazazi, S., C. C. Ioannou, S. J. Simpson, et al. 2010. The social context of cannibalism in Mormon cricket collective movement. *PLoS ONE* **5**:e1511. [3]

Bazazi, S., P. Romanczuk, S. Thomas, et al. 2011. Nutritional state and collective motion: From individuals to mass migration. *Proc. R. Soc. B* **278(1704)**:356–363. [3]

Bean, D., G. J. Mason, and M. Bateson. 1999. Contrafreeloading in starlings: Testing the information hypothesis. *Behaviour* **136**:1267–1282. [4]

Bearden, J. N. 2006. A new secretary problem with rank-based selection and cardinal payoffs. *J. Math. Psychol.* **50**:58–59. [15]

Bechky, B. A. 2003. Sharing meaning across occupational communities: The transformation of understanding on a production floor. *Organ. Sci.* **14(3)**:312–330. [17]

Beck, A. T., A. J. Rush, A. F. Shaw, and G. Emery. 1979. Cognitive Therapy of Depression. New York: Guildford. [9]

Beckage, N., P. M. Todd, L. Penke, and J. Asendorpf. 2009. Testing sequential patterns in human mate choice using speed-dating. In: Proc. of the 31st Ann. Conf. of the Cognitive Science Society, ed. N. Taatgen and H. van Rijn, pp. 2365–2370. Amsterdam: Cognitive Science Society. [19]

Behrens, T. E., M. W. Woolrich, M. E. Walton, and M. F. Rushworth. 2007. Learning the value of information in an uncertain world. *Nat. Neurosci.* **10(9)**:1214–1221. [5, 9]

Bell, W. J. 1990. Searching behavior patterns in insects. *Ann. Rev. Entomol.* **35**:447–467. [2]

———. 1991. Searching Behaviour: The Behavioural Ecology of Finding Resources. New York: Chapman and Hall. [3, 15]

Benhamou, S. 1992. Efficiency of area-concentrated searching behavior in a continuous patchy environment. *J. Theor. Biol.* **159**:67–81. [2, 4]

———. 2007. How many animals really do the Lévy walk? *Ecology* **88**:1962–1969. [3]

Berendse, H. W., Y. Galis-de Graaf, and H. J. Groenewegen. 1992. Topographical organization and relationship with ventral striatal compartments of prefrontal corticostriatal projections in the rat. *J. Comp. Neurol.* **316**:314–347. [9]

Berke, J. D., and H. Eichenbaum. 2009. Striatal versus hippocampal representations during win-stay maze performance. *J. Neurophysiol.* **101(3)**:1575–1587. [6]

Bernoulli, D. 1738/1954. Exposition of a new theory on the measurement of risk. *Econometrica* **22**:23–36. [12]

Bernstein, C., A. Kacelnik, and J. R. Krebs. 1988. Individual decisions and the distribution of predators in a patchy environment. *J. Anim. Ecol.* **57**:1007–1026. [19]

Bernstein, E. 2012. The transparency paradox: A role for privacy in organizational learning and operational control. Boston: Harvard Business School working paper. [17]

Berridge, K. C. 1996. Food reward: Brain substrates of wanting and liking. *Neurosci. Biobehav. Rev.* **20(1)**:1–25. [6]

———. 2007. The debate over dopamine's role in reward: The case for incentive salience. *Psychopharmacol.* **191(3)**:391–431. [6]

Bichot, N. P., and J. D. Schall. 2002. Priming in macaque frontal cortex during popout visual search: Feature-based facilitation and location-based inhibition of return. *J. Neurosci.* **22(11)**:4675–4685. [10]

Bickel, W. K., and L. A. Marsch. 2001. Toward a behavioral economic understanding of drug dependence: Delay discounting processes. *Addiction* **96**:73–86. [6]

Biebach, H., J. R. Krebs, and H. Falk. 1994. Time-place learning, food availability and the exploitation of patches in garden warblers, *Sylvia borin. Anim. Behav.* **48**:273–284. [4]

Biederman, I. 1972. Perceiving real-world scenes. *Science* **177**:77–80. [15]

Birn, R. M., J. B. Diamond, M. A. Smith, and P. A. Bandettini. 2006. Separating respiratory-variation-related fluctuations from neuronal-activity-related fluctuations in fMRI. *NeuroImage* **31(4)**:1536–1548. [9]

Birrell, J. M., and V. J. Brown. 2000. Medial frontal cortex mediates perceptual attentional set shifting in the rat. *J. Neurosci.* **20(11)**:4320–4324. [9]

Blair, R. J. 2008. The amygdala and ventromedial prefrontal cortex: Functional contributions and dysfunction in psychopathy. *Phil. Trans. R. Soc. Lond. B* **363(1503)**:2557–2565. [9]

Blair, R. J., and D. G. Mitchell. 2009. Psychopathy, attention and emotion. *Psychol. Med.* **39(4)**:543–555. [9]

Bogacz, R. 2007. Optimal decision-making theories: Linking neurobiology with behavior. *Trends Cogn. Sci.* **11**:118–125. [14, 19]

Bond, A. B. 1980. Optimal foraging in a uniform habitat: The search mechanism of the green lacewing. *Anim. Behav.* **28**:10–19. [4]

———. 1981. Giving-up as a Poisson process: The departure decision of the green lacewing. *Anim. Behav.* **29**:629–630. [10]

Bonnevie, T., M. Fyhn, T. Hafting, et al. 2010. Hippocampal contribution to maintenance of entorhinal grid fields. *Abstr. Soc. Neurosci.* **36**:101.04. [6]

Botvinick, M. M., T. S. Braver, D. M. Barch, C. S. Carter, and J. C. Cohen. 2001. Conflict monitoring and cognitive control. *Psychol. Rev.* **108**:624–652. [5, 15]

Botvinick, M. M., Y. Niv, and A. C. Barto. 2009. Hierarchically organized behavior and its neural foundations: A reinforcement learning perspective. *Cognition* **113(3)**:262–280. [12]

Bousfield, W. A. 1953. The occurrence of clustering in the recall of randomly arranged associates. *J. Gen. Psychol.* **49**:229–240. [2, 4]

Bousfield, W. A., and H. W. Sedgewick. 1944. An analysis of sequences of restricted associative responses. *J. Gen. Psychol.* **30**:149–165. [11]

Bousfield, W. A., H. W. Sedgewick, and B. H. Cohen. 1954. Certain temporal characteristics of the recall of verbal associates. *Am. J. Psychol.* **67**:111–118. [11]

Bouton, M. E. 2004. Context and behavioral processes in extinction. *Learn. Mem.* **11(5)**:485–494. [9]

Bovet, P., and S. Benhamou. 1988. Spatial analysis of animals' movements using a correlated random walk model. *J. Theor. Biol.* **131**:419–433. [3]

Bower, M. R., D. R. Euston, and B. L. McNaughton. 2005. Sequential-context-dependent hippocampal activity is not necessary to learn sequences with repeated elements. *J. Neurosci.* **25(6)**:1313–1323. [6]

Brandon, D. P., and A. B. Hollingshead. 2004. Transactive memory systems in organizations: Matching tasks, expertise, and people. *Organ. Sci.* **15(6)**:633–644. [17]

Brandon, M. P., C. Libby, M. Connerney, A. Bogaard, and M. E. Hasselmo. 2010. Grid cell spiking depends on intact activity in the medial septum. *Abstr. Soc. Neurosci.* **36**:101.19. [6]

Bray, S., A. Rangel, S. Shimojo, B. W. Balleine, and J. P. O'Doherty. 2008. The neural mechanisms underlying the influence of Pavlovian cues on human decision making. *J. Neurosci.* **28**:5861–5866. [7]

Bressler, S. L., and V. Menon. 2010. Large-scale brain networks in cognition: Emerging methods and principles. *Trends Cogn. Sci.* **14(6)**:277–290. [13]

Briggs, J. S., and S. B. Vander Wall. 2004. Substrate type affects caching and pilferage of pine seeds by chipmunks. *Behav. Ecol.* **15**:666–672. [4]

Brin, S., and L. Page. 1998. The anatomy of a large-scale hypertextual Web search engine. *Comp. Netw. ISDN Syst.* **30**:107–117. [18]

Brockmann, D., L. Hufnagel, and T. Geisel. 2006. The scaling laws of human travel. *Nature* **439**:462–465. [3]

Bröder, A. 2003. Decision making with the "adaptive toolbox": Influence of environmental structure, intelligence, and working memory load. *J. Exp. Psychol. Learn. Mem. Cogn.* **29**:611–625. [15]

———. 2011. The quest for take-the-best. In: Heuristics: The Foundations of Adaptive Behavior, ed. G. Gigerenzer et al. New York: Oxford Univ. Press. [15]

Bröder, A., and B. R. Newell. 2008. Challenging some common beliefs: Empirical work within the adaptive toolbox metaphor. *Judgm. Decis. Mak.* **3**:205–214. [4]

Bröder, A., and S. Schiffer. 2003. Take the best versus simultaneous feature matching: Probabilistic inferences form memory and effects of representation format. *J. Exp. Psychol. Gen.* **132**:277–293. [4]

Bromberg-Martin, E. S., M. Matsumoto, and O. Hikosaka. 2010a. Dopamine in motivational control: Rewarding, aversive, and alerting. *Neuron* **68(5)**:815–834. [9]

Bromberg-Martin, E. S., M. Matsumoto, S. Hong, and O. Hikosaka. 2010b. A pallidus-habenula-dopamine pathway signals inferred stimulus values. *J. Neurophysiol.* **104(2)**:1068–1076. [12]

Bromberg-Martin, E. S., M. Matsumoto, H. Nakahara, and O. Hikosaka. 2010c. Multiple timescales of memory in lateral habenula and dopamine neurons. *Neuron* **67(3)**:499–510. [9]

Brown, E. N., L. M. Frank, D. Tang, M. C. Quirk, and M. A. Wilson. 1998. A statistical paradigm for neural spike train decoding applied to position prediction from ensemble firing patterns of rat hippocampal place cells. *J. Neurosci.* **18(18)**:7411–7425. [6]

Brown, G. D. A., I. Neath, and N. Chater. 2007a. A temporal ratio model of memory. *Psychol. Rev.* **114**:539–576. [11]

Brown, G. D. A., T. Preece, and C. Hulme. 2000. Oscillator-based memory for serial order. *Psychol. Rev.* **107**:127–181. [11]

Brown, G. R., and T. W. Fawcett. 2005. Sexual selection: Copycat mating in birds. *Curr. Biol.* **15**:R626–R628. [19]

Brown, J. S. 1988. Patch use as an indicator of habitat preference, predation risk and competition. *Behav. Ecol. Sociobiol.* **22**:37–47. [19]

Brown, J. W., and T. S. Braver. 2005. Learned predictions of error likelihood in the anterior cingulate cortex. *Science* **307(5712)**:1118–1121. [5]

———. 2007. Risk prediction and aversion by anterior cingulate cortex. *Cogn. Affect. Behav. Neurosci.* **7(4)**:266–277. [5]

Brown, J. W., J. R. Reynolds, and T. S. Braver. 2007b. A computational model of fractionated conflict-control mechanisms in task switching. *Cogn. Psychol.* **55**:37–85. [5]

Brown, R. T. 1989. Creativity: What are we to measure? In: Handbook of Creativity, ed. J. A. Glover et al., pp. 3–32. New York: Plenum. [14]

Brown, S. D., and A. Heathcote. 2008. The simplest complete model of choice response time: Linear ballistic accumulation. *Cogn. Psychol.* **57(3)**:153–178. [10]

Brown, V. J., and E. M. Bowman. 2002. Rodent models of prefrontal cortical function. *Trends Neurosci.* **25**:340–343. [7]

Browne, G. J., and M. G. Pitts. 2004. Stopping rule use during information search in design problems. *Org. Behav. Hum. Decis. Proc.* **95**:208–224. [11]

Browne, G. J., M. G. Pitts, and J. C. Wetherbe. 2007. Cognitive stopping rules for terminating information search in online tasks. *MIS Quarterly* **31**:89–104. [15]

Brunel, N., and X. J. Wang. 2001. Effects of neuromodulation in a cortical network model of object working memory dominated by recurrent inhibition. *J. Comput. Neurosci.* **11(1)**:63–85. [5]

Buchel, C., R. J. Dolan, J. L. Armony, and K. J. Friston. 1999. Amygdala-hippocampal involvement in human aversive trace conditioning revealed through event-related functional magnetic resonance imaging. *J. Neurosci.* **19(24)**:10,869–10,876. [9]

Buchel, C., J. Morris, R. J. Dolan, and K. J. Friston. 1998. Brain systems mediating aversive conditioning: An event-related fMRI study. *Neuron* **20(5)**:947–957. [9]

Buckner, R. L., and D. C. Carroll. 2007. Self-projection and the brain. *Trends Cogn. Sci.* **11(2)**:49–57. [6, 9]

Bundesen, C. 1990. A theory of visual attention. *Psychol. Rev.* **97**:523–547. [10]

———. 1996. Formal models of visual attention: A tutorial review. In: Converging Operations in the Study of Visual Selective Attention, ed. A. Kramer et al., pp. 1–44. Washington, D.C.: American Psychological Association. [10]

Burgess, C., and K. Lund. 2000. The dynamics of meaning in memory. In: Cognitive Dynamics: Conceptual Change in Humans and Machines, ed. E. Dietrich and A. B. Markman, pp. 117– 156. Hillsdale, NJ: Lawrence Erlbaum. [20]

Burgess, N., and G. J. Hitch. 1999. Memory for serial order: A network model of the phonological loop and its timing. *Psychol. Rev.* **106**:551–581. [11]

Burgess, N., J. O'Keefe, and M. Recce. 1993. Toward a mechanism for navigation by the rat hippocampus. In: Proc. of the 2nd Ann. Computation and Neural Systems Meeting CNS*93. Dordrecht: Kluwer. [6]

Burgess, N., M. Recce, and J. O'Keefe. 1994. A model of hippocampal function. *Neural Netw.* **7(6/7)**:1065–1081. [6]

Burgess, P. W., E. Veitch, A. de Lacy Costello, and T. Shallice. 2000. The cognitive and neuroanatomical correlates of multitasking. *Neuropsychologia* **38**:848–863. [9]

Burt, R. S. 1992. Structural Holes: The Social Structure of Competition. Cambridge, MA: Harvard Univ. Press. [17]

———. 2004. Structural holes and good ideas. *Am. J. Soc.* **110(2)**:349–399. [17]

Busemeyer, J. R., and A. Rapoport. 1988. Psychological models of deferred decision making. *J. Math. Psychol.* **32**:91–143. [15]

Bush, G., B. A. Vogt, J. Holmes, et al. 2002. Dorsal anterior cingulate cortex: A role in reward-based decision making. *PNAS* **99(1)**:507–512. [5, 9]

Buzsáki, G. 1989. Two-stage model of memory trace formation: A role for "noisy" brain states. *Neuroscience* **31(3)**:551–570. [6]

Cabeza, R., F. Dolcos, R. Graham, and L. Nyberg. 2002. Similarities and differences in the neural correlates of episodic memory retrieval and working memory. *NeuroImage* **16(2)**:317–330. [5]

Cabeza, R., and L. Nyberg. 2000. Imaging cognition II: An empirical review of 275 PEt and fMRI studies. *J. Cogn. Neurosci.* **12(1)**:1–47. [9]

Calkins, M. W. 1894. Association. *Psychol. Rev.* **1**:479–483. [15]

Cancho, R. F., and R. V. Solé. 2001. The small world of human language. *Proc. R. Soc. B* **268**:2261–2265. [2]

Candolin, U. 2003. The use of multiple cues in mate choice. *Biol. Rev.* **78**:575–595. [4]

Cantin, L., M. Lenoir, E. Augier, et al. 2010. Cocaine is low on the value ladder of rats: Possible evidence for resilience to addiction. *PLoS ONE* **5(7)**:e11592. [6]

Cantin, L., M. Lenoir, S. Dubreucq, et al. 2009. Choice reveals that rats are majoritarily resilient to cocaine addiction. *Nature Precedings* http://hdl.handle.net/10101/npre.2009.3738.1. (accessed 11 January 2012). [6]

Cantwell, J., ed. 2004. Globalization and the Location of Firms. Cheltenham: Edward Elgar. [20]

Carelli, R. M., and S. A. Deadwyler. 1994. A comparison of nucleus accumbens neuronal firing patterns during cocaine self-administration and water reinforcement in rats. *J. Neurosci.* **14(12)**:7735–7746. [6]

Caron, M. G., and R. M. Wightman. 2009. "To learn, you must pay attention": Molecular insights into teachers' wisdom. *PNAS* **106(18)**:7267–7268. [2]

Carrasco, M., and B. McElree. 2001. Covert attention accelerates the rate of visual information processing. *PNAS* **98(9)**:5363–5367. [10]

Carroll, M. E. 1993. The economic context of drug and non-drug reinforcers affects acquisition and maintenance of drug-reinforced behavior and withdrawal effects. *Drug Alcohol Depend.* **33(2)**:201–210. [6]

Carter, C. S., T. S. Braver, D. M. Barch, et al. 1998. Anterior cingulate cortex, error detection, and the online monitoring of performance. *Science* **280(5364)**:747–749. [9]

Carter, C. S., A. W. MacDonald, III, L. L. Ross, and V. A. Stenger. 2001. Anterior cingulate cortex activity and impaired self-monitoring of performance in patients with schizophrenia: An event-related fMRI study. *Am. J. Psychiatry* **158(9)**:1423–1428. [9]

Cattaneo, L., and G. Rizzolatti. 2009. The mirror neuron system. *Arch. Neurol.* **66(5)**: 557–560. [9]

Chafee, M. V., and P. S. Goldman-Rakic. 2000. Inactivation of parietal and prefrontal cortex reveals interdependence of neural activity during memory-guided saccades. *J. Neurophysiol.* **83(3)**:1550–1566. [5, 9]

Chamberlain, S. R., U. Muller, A. D. Blackwell, et al. 2006. Neurochemical modulation of response inhibition and probabilistic learning in humans. *Science* **311(5762)**:861–863. [8, 9]

Chance, M. R. A., and A. P. Mead. 1955. Competition between feeding and investigation in the rat. *Behavior* **8**:174–181. [9]

Changizi, M. A., and W. G. Hall. 2001. Thirst modulates a perception. *Perception* **30(12)**:1489–1497. [9]

Changizi, M. A., Q. Zhang, and S. Shimojo. 2006. Bare skin, blood and the evolution of primate colour vision. *Biol. Lett.* **2(2)**:217–221. [10]

Chao, A., M.-C. Ma, and M. C. K. Yang. 1993. Stopping rules and estimation for recapture debugging with unequal failure rates. *Biometrika* **80**:193–201. [11]

Chao, L. L., and A. Martin. 1999. Cortical regions associated with perceiving, naming, and knowing about colors. *J. Cogn. Neurosci.* **11(1)**:25–35. [9]

———. 2000. Representation of manipulable man-made objects in the dorsal stream. *NeuroImage* **12(4)**:478–484. [9]

Chapman, K. M., D. J. Weiss, and D. A. Rosenbaum. 2010. Evolutionary roots of motor planning: The end-state comfort effect in lemurs (*Lemur catta*, *Eulemur mongoz*, *Eulemur coronatus*, *Eulemur collaris*, *Hapalemur griseus*, and *Varecia rubra*). *J. Comp. Psychol.* **124**:229–232. [14]

Chapman, L. J., and J. P. Chapman. 1969. Illusory correlation as an obstacle to the use of valid psychodiagnostic signs. *J. Abnorm. Psychol.* **74**:271–280. [15]

Charnov, E. L. 1976. Optimal foraging, the marginal value theorem. *Theor. Pop. Biol.* **9**:129–136. [2–4, 15]

Chase, W. G., and H. A. Simon. 1973a. The mind's eye in chess. In: Visual Information Processing, ed. W. G. Chase, pp. 215–281. New York: Academic Press. [18]

———. 1973b. Perception in chess. *Cogn. Psychol.* **4**:55–81. [20]

Chelazzi, L., E. K. Miller, J. Duncan, and R. Desimone. 1993. A neural basis for visual search in inferior temporal cortex. *Nature* **363(6427)**:345–347. [14]

Cheng, K., and D. F. Sherry. 1992. Landmark-based spatial memory in birds (*Parus atricapillus* and *Columba livia*): The use of edges and distances to represent spatial positions. *J. Comp. Psychol.* **106**:331–341. [4]

Cheng, S., and L. M. Frank. 2008. New experiences enhance coordinated neural activity in the hippocampus. *Neuron* **57(2)**:303–313. [9]

Chittka, L., P. Skorupski, and N. E. Raine. 2009. Speed–accuracy tradeoffs in animal decision making. *Trends Ecol. Evol.* **24**:400–407. [19]

Chomsky, N. 1965. Aspects of the Theory of Syntax. Cambridge, MA: MIT Press. [20]

Christy, J. H., P. R. Y. Backwell, S. Goshima, and T. Kreuter. 2002. Sexual selection for structure building by courting male fiddler crabs: An experimental study of behavioral mechanisms. *Behav. Ecol.* **13**:366–374. [19]

Chun, M. M., and J. M. Wolfe. 1996. Just say no: How are visual searches terminated when there is no target present? *Cogn. Psychol.* **30**:39–78. [10]

Church, A. 1936. An unsolvable problem of elementary number theory. *Am. J. Math.* **58**:345–363. [16]

Churchland, A. K., R. Kiani, and M. N. Shadlen. 2008. Decision-making with multiple alternatives. *Nat. Neurosci.* **11(6)**:693–702. [9]

Clark, C. W., and R. Dukas. 2003. The behavioral ecology of a cognitive constraint: Limited attention. *Behav. Ecol.* **14(2)**:151–156. [5]

Clark, R. E., and L. R. Squire. 1998. Classical conditioning and brain systems: The role of awareness. *Science* **280(5360)**:77–81. [9]

Clark, R. E., S. M. Zola, and L. R. Squire. 2000. Impaired recognition memory in rats after damage to the hippocampus. *J. Neurosci.* **20(23)**:8853–8860. [9]

Clatworthy, P. L., S. J. Lewis, L. Brichard, et al. 2009. Dopamine release in dissociable striatal subregions predicts the different effects of oral methylphenidate on reversal learning and spatial working memory. *J. Neurosci.* **29(15)**:4690–4696. [8, 9]

Cohen, J. D., K. Dunbar, and J. L. McClelland. 1990. On the control of automatic processes: A parallel distributed processing account of the Stroop effect. *Psychol. Rev.* **97**:332–361. [14]

Cohen, J. D., S. M. McClure, and A. J. Yu. 2007. Should I stay or should I go? Exploration versus exploitation. *Phil. Trans. R. Soc. Lond. B* **362**:933–942. [14]

Cohen, N. J., and H. Eichenbaum. 1993. Memory, Amnesia, and the Hippocampal System. Cambridge, MA: MIT Press. [6, 9]

Collins, E. J., and J. M. McNamara. 1993. The job-search problem with competition: An evolutionarily stable dynamic strategy. *Adv. Appl. Probab.* **25**:314–333. [4, 19]

Collins, E. J., J. M. McNamara, and D. M. Ramsey. 2006. Learning rules for optimal selection in a varying environment: Mate choice revisited. *Behav. Ecol.* **17**:799–809. [19]

Collins, P., L. S. Wilkinson, B. J. Everitt, T. W. Robbins, and A. C. Roberts. 2000. The effect of dopamine depletion from the caudate nucleus of the common marmoset (*Callithrix jacchus*) on tests of prefrontal cognitive function. *Behav. Neurosci.* **114(1)**:3–17. [8]

Colwill, R. M., and R. A. Rescorla. 1985. Postconditioning devaluation of a reinforcer affects instrumental responding. *J. Exp. Psychol. Anim. Behav. Proc.* **11**:120–132. [7]

———. 1986. Associative structures in instrumental learning. *Psychol. Learn. Motiv.* **20**:55–104. [7]

———. 1988. Associations between the discriminative stimulus and the reinforcer in instrumental learning. *J. Exp. Psychol. Anim. Behav. Proc.* **14(2)**:155–164. [7]

Colzato, L. S., M. T. Bajo, W. van den Wildenberg, et al. 2008. How does bilingualism improve executive control? A comparison of active and reactive inhibition mechanisms. *J. Exp. Psychol. Learn. Mem. Cogn.* **34**:302–312. [14]

Colzato, L. S., J. Pratt, and B. Hommel. 2010a. Dopaminergic control of attentional flexibility: Inhibition of return is associated with the dopamine transporter gene (DAT1). *Front. Hum. Neurosci.* **4**:53. [2]

Colzato, L. S., M. M. A. Spapè, M. M. Pannebakker, and B. Hommel. 2007. Working memory and the attentional blink: Blink size is predicted by individual differences in operation span. *Psychon. Bull. Rev.* **14**:1051–1057. [15]

Colzato, L. S., I. van Beest, W. P. M. van den Wildenberg, et al. 2010b. God: Do I have your attention? *Cognition* **117**:87–94. [15]

Coolen, I., L.-A. Giraldeau, and M. Lavoie. 2001. Head position as an indicator of producer and scrounger tactics in a ground feeding bird. *Anim. Behav.* **61**:895–903. [3]

Cools, R. 2006. Dopaminergic modulation of cognitive function-implications for L-DOPA treatment in Parkinson's disease. *Neurosci. Biobehav. Rev.* **30(1)**:1–23. [8, 9]

———. 2008. Role of dopamine in the motivational and cognitive control of behavior. *Neuroscientist* **14(4)**:381–395. [14]

Cools, R., R. A. Barker, B. J. Sahakian, and T. W. Robbins. 2001. Enhanced or impaired cognitive function in Parkinson's disease as a function of dopaminergic medication and task demands. *Cereb. Cortex* **11**:1136–1143. [9]

Cools, R., and M. D'Esposito. 2009. Dopaminergic modulation of flexible cognitive control in humans. In: Dopamine Handbook, ed. A. Björklund et al. Oxford: Oxford Univ. Press. [2, 14]

———. 2011. Inverted-U-shaped dopamine actions on human working memory and cognitive control. *Biol. Psychol.* **69(12)**:e113–125. [8, 9]

Cools, R., M. F. Frank, S. E. Gibbs, et al. 2009. Striatal dopamine synthesis capacity predicts dopaminergic drug effects on flexible outcome learning. *J. Neurosci.* **29(5)**:1538–1543. [8]

Cools, R., S. J. G. Lewis, L. Clark, R. A. Barker, and T. W. Robbins. 2007a. L-DOPA disrupts activity in the nucleus accumbens during reversal learning in Parkinson's disease. *Neuropsychopharmacol.* **32**:180–189. [8]

Cools, R., A. Miyakawa, M. Sheridan, and M. D'Esposito. 2010a. Enhanced frontal function in Parkinson's disease. *Brain* **133(Pt 1)**:225–233. [8]

Cools, R., K. Nakamura, and N. D. Daw. 2011. Serotonin and dopamine: Unifying affective, activational, and decision functions. *Neuropsychopharmacol.* **36(1)**:98–113. [8]

Cools, R., and T. W. Robbins. 2004. Chemistry of the adaptive mind. *Phil. Trans. A* **362(1825)**:2871–2888. [2, 9]

Cools, R., R. Rogers, R. A. Barker, and T. W. Robbins. 2010b. Top-down attentional control in Parkinson's disease: Salient considerations. *J. Cogn. Neurosci.* **22(5)**:848–859. [8]

Cools, R., M. Sheridan, E. Jacobs, and M. D'Esposito. 2007b. Impulsive personality predicts dopamine-dependent changes in frontostriatal activity during component processes of working memory. *J. Neurosci.* **27(20)**:5506–5514. [8]

Corbit, L. H., and B. W. Balleine. 2000. The role of the hippocampus in instrumental conditioning. *J. Neurosci.* **20(11)**:4233–4239. [9]

———. 2003. The role of prelimbic cortex in instrumental conditioning. *Behav. Brain Res.* **146(1–2)**:145–157. [7]

———. 2005. Double dissociation of basolateral and central amygdala lesions on the general and outcome-specific forms of pavlovian-instrumental transfer. *J. Neurosci.* **25(4)**:962–970. [7]

Corbit, L. H., and P. H. Janak. 2007. Inactivation of the lateral but not medial dorsal striatum eliminates the excitatory impact of Pavlovian stimuli on instrumental responding. *J. Neurosci.* **27(51)**:13,977–13,981. [7]

Corbit, L. H., P. H. Janak, and B. W. Balleine. 2007. General and outcome-specific forms of Pavlovian-instrumental transfer: The effect of shifts in motivational state and inactivation of the ventral tegmental area. *Eur. J. Neurosci.* **26(11)**:3141–3149. [7]

Corbit, L. H., J. L. Muir, and B. W. Balleine. 2001. The role of the nucleus accumbens in instrumental conditioning: Evidence of a functional dissociation between accumbens core and shell. *J. Neurosci.* **21(9)**:3251–3260. [7]

Couzin, I. D. 1999. Collective Animal Behaviour. PhD diss., Univ. of Bath. [3]

Craig, A. D. 2002. How do you feel? Interoception: The sense of the physiological condition of the body. *Nat. Rev. Neurosci.* **3(8)**:655–666. [13]

———. 2009. How do you feel—now? The anterior insula and human awareness. *Nat. Rev. Neurosci.* **10(1)**:59–70. [13]

Critchley, H. D. 2005. Neural mechanisms of autonomic, affective, and cognitive integration. *J. Comp. Neurol.* **493(1)**:154–166. [13]

———. 2009. Psychophysiology of neural, cognitive and affective integration: fMRI and autonomic indicants. *Intl. J. Psychophysiol.* **73(2)**:88–94. [13]

Crofts, H. S., J. W. Dalley, J. C. M. Van Denderen, et al. 2001. Differential effects of 6-OHDA lesions of the frontal cortex and caudate nucleus on the ability to acquire an attentional set. *Cereb. Cortex* **11(11)**:1015–1026. [8]

Cross, F. R., and R. R. Jackson. 2010. Olfactory search-image use by a mosquito-eating predator. *Proc. R. Soc. B* **277**:3173–3178. [2, 4]

Crusio, W. E. 2001. Genetic dissection of mouse exploratory behaviour. *Behav. Brain Res.* **125(1–2)**:127–132. [9]

Csicsvari, J., J. O'Neill, K. Allen, and T. J. Senior. 2007. Place-selective firing contributes to the reverse-order reactivation of CA1 pyramidal cells during sharp waves in open-field exploration. *Eur. J. Neurosci.* **26(3)**:704–716. [6]

Curtis, C. E., and M. D'Esposito. 2003. Persistent activity in the prefrontal cortex during working memory. *Trends Cogn. Sci.* **7(9)**:415–423. [8]

Dahlin, E., A. S. Neely, A. Larsson, L. Backman, and L. Nyberg. 2008. Transfer of learning after updating training mediated by the striatum. *Science* **320(5882)**:1510–1512. [8]

Damasio, A. R. 1994. Descartes' Error: Emotion, Reason, and the Human Brain. New York: Putnam. [6, 9]

———. 1996. The somatic marker hypothesis and the possible functions of the prefrontal cortex. *Phil. Trans. R. Soc. Lond. B* **351**:1413–1420. [14]

Daoutis, C. A., M. Pilling, and I. R. L. Davies. 2006. Categorical effects in visual search for colour. *Vis. Cogn.* **14(2)**:217–240. [10, 15]

Daselaar, S. M., Y. Porat, W. Huijbers, and C. M. Pennartz. 2010. Modality-specific and modality-independent components of the human imagery system. *NeuroImage* **52(2)**:677–685. [9]

Davelaar, E. J. 2007. Sequential retrieval and inhibition of parallel (re)activated representations: A neurocomputational comparison of competitive queuing and resampling models. *Adapt. Behav.* **15**:51–71. [11]

Davelaar, E. J., Y. Goshen-Gottstein, A. Ashkenazi, H. J. Haarmann, and M. Usher. 2005. The demise of short-term memory revisited: Empirical and computational investigations of recency effects. *Psychol. Rev.* **112**:3–42. [11]

Davidson, T. J., F. Kloosterman, and M. A. Wilson. 2009. Hippocampal replay of extended experience. *Neuron* **63**:497–507. [6]

Davis, M. A. 2009. Understanding the relationship between mood and creativity: A meta-analysis. *Org. Behav. Hum. Decis. Proc.* **108**:25–38. [14]

Daw, N. D. 2003. Reinforcement Learning Models of the Dopamine System and Their Behavioral Implications. PhD diss., School of Computer Science, Carnegie Mellon Univ. [6]

———. 2011. Trial-by-trial data analysis using computational models. In: Affect, Learning and Decision Making, Attention and Performance XXIII, ed. E. A. Phelps et al. New York: Oxford Univ. Press. [12]

Daw, N. D., and K. Doya. 2006. The computational neurobiology of learning and reward. *Curr. Opin. Neurobiol.* **16(2)**:199–204. [12]

Daw, N. D., S. J. Gershman, B. Seymour, P. Dayan, and R. J. Dolan. 2011. Model-based influences on humans' choices and striatal prediction errors. *Neuron* **69(6)**:1204–1215. [12]

Daw, N. D., Y. Niv, and P. Dayan. 2005. Uncertainty-based competition between prefrontal and dorsolateral striatal systems for behavioral control. *Nat. Neurosci.* **8(12)**:1704–1711. [6, 12]

Daw, N. D., J. P. O'Doherty, P. Dayan, B. Seymour, and R. J. Dolan. 2006. Cortical substrates for exploratory decisions in humans. *Nature* **441(7095)**:876–879. [5, 7–9, 14, 15]

Day, L. B., M. Weisand, R. J. Sutherland, and T. Schallert. 1999. The hippocampus is not necessary for a place response but may be necessary for pliancy. *Behav. Neurosci.* **113(5)**:914–924. [9]

Dayan, P., and N. D. Daw. 2008. Decision theory, reinforcement learning, and the brain. *Cogn. Affect. Behav. Neurosci.* **8**:429–453. [12]

de Araujo, I. E., M. L. Kringelbach, E. T. Rolls, and F. McGlone. 2003. Human cortical responses to water in the mouth, and the effects of thirst. *J. Neurophysiol.* **90**:1865–1876. [7]

de Araujo, I. E., E. T. Rolls, M. I. Velazco, C. Margot, and I. Cayeux. 2005. Cognitive modulation of olfactory processing. *Neuron* **46(4)**:671–679. [7]

de Fockert, J. W., G. Rees, C. D. Frith, and N. Lavie. 2001. The role of working memory in visual selective attention. *Science* **291(5509)**:1803–1806. [5]

De Groot, A. D. 1965. Thought and Choice in Chess. The Hague: Mouton. [4]

Dehaene, S. 1989. Discriminability and dimensionality effects in visual search for featural conjunctions: A functional pop-out. *Perc. Psychophys.* **46(1)**:72–80. [10]

Dehaene, S., J. P. Changeux, L. Naccache, J. Sackur, and C. Sergent. 2006. Conscious, preconscious, and subliminal processing: A testable taxonomy. *Trends Cogn. Sci.* **10(5)**:204–211. [13]

de Kroon, H., and L. Mommer. 2006. Root foraging theory put to the test. *Trends Ecol. Evol.* **21**:113–116. [4]

Dember, W. N., and C. L. Richman. 1989. Spontaneous Alternation Behavior. New York: Springer-Verlag. [6]

Derdikman, D., and M.-B. Moser. 2010. A dual role for hippocampal replay. *Neuron* **65(5)**:582–584. [6]

Desimone, R., and J. Duncan. 1995. Neural mechanisms of selective visual attention. *Ann. Rev. Neurosci.* **18**:193–222. [14]

Detrain, C., J. L. Deneubourg, S. Goss, and Y. Quinet. 1991. Dynamics of collective exploration in the ant *Pheidole pallidula. Psyche* **98**:21–29. [3]

DeVito, L. M., and H. Eichenbaum. 2011. Memory for the order of events in specific sequences: Contributions of the hippocampus and medial prefrontal cortex. *J. Neurosci.* **31(9)**:3169–3175. [6]

DeVries, D. R., R. A. Stein, and P. L. Chesson. 1989. Sunfish foraging among patches: The patch departure decision. *Anim. Behav.* **37**:455–467. [10]

de Wit, S., and A. Dickinson. 2009. Associative theories of goal-directed behaviour: A case for animal-human translational models. *Psychol. Res.* **73**:463–476. [14]

Diba, K., and G. Buzsáki. 2007. Forward and reverse hippocampal place-cell sequences during ripples. *Nat. Neurosci.* **10**:1241–1242. [6]

Dickerson, M., and J. O'Connor. 2006. Gambling as an Addictive Behavior. Cambridge: Cambridge Univ. Press. [6]

Dickinson, A. 1985. Actions and habits: The development of behavioural autonomy. *Phil. Trans. R. Soc. Lond. B* **308(1135)**:67–78. [12]

Dickinson, A., and B. W. Balleine. 1993. Actions and responses: The dual psychology of behaviour. In: Spatial Representation, ed. N. Eilan et al., pp. 277–293. Oxford: Basil Blackwell Ltd. [9]

———. 1995. Motivational control of instrumental action. *Curr. Dir. Psychol. Sci.* **4**:162–167. [7]

———. 2002. The role of learning in the operation of motivational systems. In: Learning, Motivation and Emotion, vol. 3 of Steven's Handbook of Experimental Psychology (3rd edition), ed. C. R. Gallistel, pp. 497–533. New York: Wiley. [7, 12]

Dickinson, A., and C. W. Mulatero. 1989. Reinforcer specificity of the suppression of instrumental performance on a non-contingent schedule. *Behav. Processes* **19**:167–180. [7]

Dickinson, A., S. Squire, Z. Varga, and J. W. Smith. 1998. Omission learning after instrumental pretraining. *Q. J. Exp. Psychol.* **51B**:271–286. [7]

Dieckmann, A., and P. M. Todd. 2012. Simple rules for ordering cues in one-reason decision making. In: Ecological Rationality: Intelligence in the World, ed. P. M. Todd, G. Gigerenzer, and the ABC Research Group, pp. 274–306. New York: Oxford Univ. Press. [15]

Dietrich, A. 2004. The cognitive neuroscience of creativity. *Psychon. Bull. Rev.* **11**:1011–1026. [14]

Diller, D. E., P. A. Nobel, and R. M. Shiffrin. 2001. An ARC-REM model for accuracy and response time in recognition and cued recall. *J. Exp. Psychol. Learn. Mem. Cogn.* **27**:414–435. [11]

Dombrovsky, Y., and N. Perrin. 1994. On adaptive search and optimal stopping in sequential mate choice. *Am. Nat.* **144**:355–361. [19]

Donderi, D. C., and D. Zelnicker. 1969. Parallel processing in visual same-different decisions. *Perc. Psychophys.* **5(4)**:197–200. [10]

Dosenbach, N. U. F., D. A. Fair, F. M. Miezin, et al. 2007. Distinct brain networks for adaptive and stable task control in humans. *PNAS* **104(26)**:11,073–11,078. [13]

Dosenbach, N. U. F., K. M. Visscher, E. D. Palmer, et al. 2006. A core system for the implementation of task sets. *Neuron* **50(5)**:799–812. [9]

Dosher, B. A., S. Han, and Z.-L. Lu. 2010. Information-limited parallel processing in difficult heterogeneous covert visual search. *J. Exp. Psychol. Hum. Perc. Perf.* **36(5)**:1128–1144. [10]

Dougherty, M. R., C. F. Gettys, and E. E. Ogden. 1999. MINERVA-DM: A memory processes model for judgments of likelihood. *Psychol. Rev.* **106**:180–209. [15]

Dougherty, M. R., C. F. Gettys, and R. P. Thomas. 1997. The role of mental simulation in judgments of likelihood. *Org. Behav. Hum. Decis. Proc.* **70(2)**:135–148. [15]

Dougherty, M. R., and J. I. Harbison. 2007. Motivated to retrieve: How often are you willing to go back to the well when the well is dry? *J. Exp. Psychol. Learn. Mem. Cogn.* **33**:1108–1117. [11, 15]

Dougherty, M. R., P. Scheck, T. O. Nelson, and L. Narens. 2005. Using the past to predict the future. *Mem. Cogn.* **33**:1096–1115. [15]

Dougherty, M. R., R. Thomas, and N. Lange. 2010. Toward an integrative theory of hypothesis generation, probability judgment, and hypothesis testing. In: The Psychology of Learning and Motivation: Advances in Research and Theory, ed. B. H. Ross, pp. 299–342. San Diego: Academic Press. [15]

Douglas, P. 2009. What if we could google our own brains? http://www.techradar.com/news/world-of-tech/what-if-we-could-google-our-brains-533445 (accessed 26 Oct. 2011). [17]

Downing, P. E. 2000. Interactions between visual working memory and selective attention. *Psychol. Sci* **11(6)**:467–473. [5]

Doya, K. 1999. What are the computations of the cerebellum, the basal ganglia and the cerebral cortex? *Neural Netw.* **12(7–8)**:961–974. [12]

Doyle, A. C. 1917. His Last Bow. London: John Murray. [15]

Dragoi, G., and G. Buzsáki. 2006. Temporal encoding of place sequences by hippocampal cell assemblies. *Neuron* **50(1)**:145–157. [6]

Drai, D., and I. Golani. 2001. SEE: A tool for the visualization and analysis of rodent exploratory behavior. *Neurosci. Biobehav. Rev.* **25(5)**:409–426. [9]

Dreisbach, G., and T. Goschke. 2004. How positive affect modulates cognitive control: Reduced perseveration at the cost of increased distractibility. *J. Exp. Psychol. Learn. Mem. Cogn.* **30**:343–353. [14]

Dudey, T., and P. M. Todd. 2001. Making good decisions with minimal information: Simultaneous and sequential choice. *J. Bioeconomics* **3**:195–215. [15]

Dukas, R. 2002. Behavioural and ecological consequences of limited attention. *Phil. Trans. R. Soc. Lond. B* **357**:1539–1547. [2, 4]

———. 2009. Evolutionary biology of limited attention. In: Cognitive Biology: Evolutionary and Developmental Perspectives on Mind, Brain, and Behavior, ed. L. Tommasi et al., pp. 147–161. Cambridge, MA: MIT Press. [2]

Dukas, R., and S. Ellner. 1993. Information processing and prey detection. *Ecology* **74**:1337–1346. [2]

Dukas, R., and A. C. Kamil. 2000. The cost of limited attention in blue jays. *Behav. Ecol.* **11**:502–506. [2]

———. 2001. Limited attention: The constraint underlying search image. *Behav. Ecol.* **12**:192–199. [4]

Dukas, R., and L. A. Real. 1993. Effects of recent experience on foraging decisions by bumble bees. *Oecologia* **94**:244–246. [2]

Duncan, J., H. Emslie, P. Williams, R. Johnson, and C. Freer. 1996. Intelligence and the frontal lobe: The organization of goal-directed behavior. *Cogn. Psychol.* **30**:257–303. [14]

Duncan, J., and G. W. Humphreys. 1989. Visual search and stimulus similarity. *Psychol. Rev.* **96**:433–458. [10]

Duncan, J., G. W. Humphreys, and R. Ward. 1997. Competitive brain activity in visual attention. *Curr. Opin. Neurobiol.* **7**:255–261. [14]

Duncan, J., and A. M. Owen. 2000. Common regions of the human frontal lobe recruited by diverse cognitive demands. *Trends Neurosci.* **23**:475–483. [9]

Duncan, R. B. 1976. The ambidextrous organization: Designing dual structures for innovation. In: The Management of Organization Design, ed. R. H. Kilmann et al., pp. 167–188. New York: North Holland. [17]

Durstewitz, D., M. Kelc, and O. Güntürkün. 1999. A neurocomputational theory of the dopaminergic modulation of working memory functions. *J. Neurosci.* **19(7)**:2807–2822. [5]

Durstewitz, D., and J. K. Seamans. 2002. The computational role of dopamine D1 receptors in working memory. *Neural Netw.* **15(4-6)**:561–572. [9]

———. 2008. The dual-state theory of prefrontal cortex dopamine function with relevance to catechol-o-methyltransferase genotypes and schizophrenia. *Biol. Psych.* **64(9)**:739–749. [8]

Durstewitz, D., J. K. Seamans, and T. J. Sejnowski. 2000. Dopamine-mediated stabilization of delay-period activity in a network model of prefrontal cortex. *J. Neurophysiol.* **83(3)**:1733–1750. [5, 9]

Durstewitz, D., N. M. Vittoz, S. B. Floresco, and J. K. Seamans. 2010. Abrupt transitions between prefrontal neural ensemble states accompany behavioral transitions during rule learning. *Neuron* **66(3)**:438–448. [9]

Dusenbery, D. B. 2001. Performance of basic strategies for following gradients in two dimensions. *J. Theor. Biol.* **208**:345–360. [4]

Dussutour, A., S. C. Nicolis, G. Shephard, M. Beekman, and D. J. T. Sumpter. 2009. The role of multiple pheromones in food recruitment by ants. *J. Exp. Biol.* **212**:2337–2348. [4]

D'Zmura, M. 1991. Color in visual search. *Vision Res.* **31(6)**:951–966. [10]

Eagle, D. M., and C. Baunez. 2010. Is there an inhibitory-response-control system in the rat? Evidence from anatomical and pharmacological studies of behavioral inhibition. *Neurosci. Biobehav. Rev.* **34(1)**:50–72. [9]

Edelstein-Keshet, L., J. Watmough, and G. B. Ermentrout. 1995. Trail following in ants: Individual properties determine population behaviour. *Behav. Ecol. Sociobiol.* **36**:119–133. [20]

Edmondson, A. C., and I. M. Nembhard. 2009. Product development and learning in project teams: The challenges are the benefits. *J. Prod. Innovat. Manag.* **26(2)**:123–138. [17]

Edmondson, A. C., G. Pisano, R. M. J. Bohmer, and A. Winslow. 2003. Learning how and learning what: Effects of tacit and codified knowledge on performance improvement following technology adoption. *Decision Sciences* **34(2)**:197–223. [17]

Egeth, H., J. Jonides, and S. Wall. 1972. Parallel processing of multielement displays. *Cogn. Psychol.* **3**:674–698. [10]

Egeth, H., R. A. Virzi, and H. Garbart. 1984. Searching for conjunctively defined targets. *J. Exp. Psychol. Hum. Perc. Perf.* **10**:32–39. [10]

Egner, T., and J. Hirsch. 2005. Cognitive control mechanisms resolve conflict through cortical amplification of task-relevant information. *Nat. Neurosci.* **8(12)**:1784–1790. [5]

Ego-Stengel, V., and M. A. Wilson. 2010. Disruption of ripple-associated hippocampal activity during rest impairs spatial learning in the rat. *Hippocampus* **20(1)**:110. [6]

Eich, J. E. 1977. State-dependent retrieval of information in human episodic memory. In: Alcohol and Human Memory, ed. I. M. Birnbaum and E. S. Parker. Hillsdale, NJ: Lawrence Erlbaum. [11]

———. 1980. The cue-dependent nature of state-dependent retrieval. *Mem. Cogn.* **8**:157–173. [11]

Eichele, T., S. Debener, V. D. Calhoun, et al. 2008. Prediction of human errors by maladaptive changes in event-related brain networks. *PNAS* **105(16)**:6173–6178. [13]

Eichenbaum, H. 2000. Hippocampus: Mapping or memory? *Curr. Biol.* **10(21)**:R785–787. [6]

Eichenbaum, H., T. Otto, and N. J. Cohen. 1992. The hippocampus: What does it do? *Behav. Neural Biol.* **57**:2–36. [6]

Eichenbaum, H., C. Stewart, and R. G. Morris. 1990. Hippocampal representation in place learning. *J. Neurosci.* **10(11)**:3531–3542. [9]

Eichenbaum, H., A. P. Yonelinas, and C. Ranganath. 2007. The medial temporal lobe and recognition memory. *Ann. Rev. Neurosci.* **30**:123–152. [6]

Eilam, D., and I. Golani. 1989. Home base behavior of rats (*Rattus norvegicus*) exploring a novel environment. *Behav. Brain Res.* **34(3)**:199–211. [9]

Eisenbach, M., and J. W. Lengeler. 2004. Chemotaxis. London: Imperial College Press. [2]

Elliott, R., J. L. Newman, O. A. Longe, and J. F. Deakin. 2003. Differential response patterns in the striatum and orbitofrontal cortex to financial reward in humans: A parametric functional magnetic resonance imaging study. *J. Neurosci.* **23**:303–307. [7]

Elman, J. L. 1991. Incremental learning, or the importance of starting small. In: Proc. of the 13th Ann. Conf. of the Cognitive Science Society, pp. 443–448. Hillsdale, NJ: Lawrence Erlbaum. [20]

Elman, J. L., E. A. Bates, M. H. Johnson, et al. 1996. Rethinking Innateness: A Connectionist Perspective on Development. Cambridge, MA: MIT Press. [20]

Elsner, B., B. Hommel, C. Mentschel, et al. 2002. Linking actions and their perceivable consequences in the human brain. *NeuroImage* **17**:364–372. [14]

Emery, N. J., and N. S. Clayton. 2004. The mentality of crows: Convergent evolution of intelligence in corvids and apes. *Science* **306**:1903–1907. [4]

Emlen, S. T., and L. W. Oring. 1977. Ecology, sexual selection, and the evolution of mating systems. *Science* **197**:215–223. [19]

Engle, R. W. 2002. Working memory capacity as executive attention. *Curr. Dir. Psychol. Sci.* **11**:19–23. [15]

Eslinger, P. J., and L. M. Grattan. 1993. Frontal lobe and frontal-striatal substrates for different forms of human flexibility. *Neuropsychologia* **31(1)**:17–28. [9]

Estes, W. K. 1955. Statistical theory of spontaneous recovery and regression. *Psychol. Rev.* **62**:145–154. [11]

Euston, D. R., M. Tatsuno, and B. L. McNaughton. 2007. Fast-forward playback of recent memory sequences in prefrontal cortex during sleep. *Science* **318(5853)**:1147–1150. [6]

Everitt, B. J., and T. W. Robbins. 2005. Neural systems of reinforcement for drug addiction: From actions to habits to compulsion. *Nat. Neurosci.* **8**:1481–1489. [6]

Eysenck, H. J. 1993. Creativity and personality: Suggestions for a theory. *Psychol. Inq.* **4(3)**:147–178. [14]

Fagioli, S., B. Hommel, and R. I. Schubotz. 2007. Intentional control of attention: Action planning primes action-related stimulus dimensions. *Psychol. Res.* **71**:22–29. [14]

Falkenstein, M., J. Hohnsbein, J. Hoormann, and L. Blanke. 1991. Effects of crossmodal divided attention on late ERP components. II. Error processing in choice reaction tasks. *Electroenc. Clin. Neurophysiol.* **78(6)**:447–455. [9]

Farooqi, I. S., E. Bullmore, J. Keogh, et al. 2007. Leptin regulates striatal regions and human eating behavior. *Science* **317(5843)**:1355. [9]

Farrell, S., and S. Lewandowsky. 2008. Empirical and theoretical limits on lag-recency in free recall. *Psychon. Bull. Rev.* **15**:1236–1250. [11]

Fasolo, B., G. H. McClelland, and K. A. Lange. 2005. The effect of site design and interattribute correlations on interactive web-based decisions. In: Online Consumer Psychology: Understanding and Influencing Behavior in the Virtual World, ed. C. P. Haugtvedt et al., pp. 325–344. Mahwah, NJ: Lawrence Erlbaum. [4]

Fauchald, P., and T. Tveraa. 2006. Hierarchical patch dynamics and animal movement pattern. *Oecologia* **149**:383–395. [4]

Fawcett, T. W., and C. Bleay. 2009. Pevious experiences shape adaptive mate preferences. *Behav. Ecol.* **20**:68–78. [19]

Fawcett, T. W., and R. A. Johnstone. 2003. Optimal assessment of multiple cues. *Proc. R. Soc. B* **270**:1637–1643. [19]

Feldman, V. 2008. Evolvability from learning algorithms. In: Proc. of the 40th Ann. ACM Symposium on Theory of Computing, pp. 619–628. Victoria, British Columbia: ACM. [16]

Feldman, V., and L. G. Valiant. 2008. The learning power of evolution. In: Proc. of the 21st Ann. Conf. on Learning Theory, pp. 513–551. Helsinki: COLT. [16]

Fenton, A. A., and R. U. Muller. 1998. Place cell discharge is extremely variable during individual passes of the rat through the firing field. *PNAS* **95(6)**:3182–3187. [9]

Ferbinteanu, J., and M. L. Shapiro. 2003. Prospective and retrospective memory coding in the hippocampus. *Neuron* **40(6)**:1227–1239. [6]

Ferguson, T. S. 1989. Who solved the secretary problem? *Stat. Sci.* **4**:282–296. [15]

Fific, M., R. M. Nosofsky, and J. T. Townsend. 2008. Information-processing architectures in multidimensional classification: A validation test of the systems factorial technology. *J. Exp. Psychol. Hum. Perc. Perf.* **34**:356–375. [11]

Fink, J. S., and G. P. Smith. 1980. Mesolimbicocortical dopamine terminal fields are necessary for normal locomotor and investigator exploration in rats. *Brain Res.* **199**:359–384. [2]

Fiorillo, C. D., P. N. Tobler, and W. Schultz. 2003. Discrete coding of reward probability and uncertainty by dopamine neurons. *Science* **299(5614)**:1898–1902. [9]

Fiser, J., P. Berkes, G. Orbán, and M. Lengyel. 2010. Statistically optimal perception and learning: From behavior to neural representations. *Trends Cogn. Sci.* **14(3)**:119–130. [12]

Fleck, M. S., and S. R. Mitroff. 2007. Rare targets are rarely missed in correctable search. *Psychol. Sci.* **18(11)**:943–947. [10]

Fletcher, P. C., and C. D. Frith. 2009. Perceiving is believing: A Bayesian approach to explaining the positive symptoms of schizophrenia. *Nat. Rev. Neurosci.* **10(1)**:48–58. [9]

Floresco, S. B., O. Magyar, S. Ghods-Sharifi, C. Vexelman, and M. T. Tse. 2006. Multiple dopamine receptor subtypes in the medial prefrontal cortex of the rat regulate set-shifting. *Neuropsychopharmacol.* **31(2)**:297–309. [8]

Floresco, S. B., and A. G. Phillips. 1999. Dopamine and hippocampal input to the nucleus accumbens play an essential role in the search for food in an unpredictable environment. *Psychobiology* **27**:277–286. [2]

Flynn, R., and L.-A. Giraldeau. 2001. Producer-scrounger games in a spatially explicit world: Tactic use influences flock geometry of spice finches. *Ethology* **107**:249–257. [3]

Ford, J. K., N. Schmitt, S. L. Schlechtman, B. M. Hults, and M. L. Doherty. 1989. Process tracing methods: Contributions, problems, and neglected research questions. *Org. Behav. Hum. Decis. Proc.* **43**:75–117. [15]

Foreman, J. G. 1977. Differential search game with mobile hider. *SIAM J. Contr. Optim.* **15**:841–856. [4]

Forman, E. H., and N. D. Singpurwalla. 1977. An empirical stopping rule for debugging and testing computer software. *J. Am. Stat. Assoc.* **72**:750–757. [11]

Fortin, N. J., K. L. Agster, and H. B. Eichenbaum. 2002. Critical role of the hippocampus in memory for sequences of events. *Nat. Neurosci.* **5(5)**:458–462. [6, 9]

Foster, D. J., R. G. M. Morris, and P. Dayan. 2000. A model of hippocampally dependent navigation using the temporal difference learning rule. *Hippocampus* **10**:1–6. [6]

Foster, D. J., and M. A. Wilson. 2006. Reverse replay of behavioural sequences in hippocampal place cells during the awake state. *Nature* **440(7084)**:680–683. [6]

Found, A., and H. J. Müller. 1996. Searching for unknown feature targets on more than one dimension: Investigating a "dimension weighting" account. *Perc. Psychophys.* **58**:88–101. [14]

Fourcassie, V., and J. F. A. Traniello. 1995. Ant search behaviour analysis with a video frame grabber. *Insectes Sociaux* **42**:249–254. [3]

Fraenkel, G. S., and D. L. Gunn. 1961. The Orientation of Animals: Kineses, Taxes and Compass Reactions. New York: Dover. [4]

Frank, M. J. 2005. Dynamic dopamine modulation in the basal ganglia: A neurocomputational account of cognitive deficits in medicated and nonmedicated Parkinsonism. *J. Cogn. Neurosci.* **17(1)**:51–72. [8]

Frank, M. J., B. B. Doll, J. Oas-Terpstra, and F. Moreno. 2009. Prefrontal and striatal dopaminergic genes predict individual differences in exploration and exploitation. *Nat. Neurosci.* **12(8)**:1062–1068. [8]

Freeman, P. R. 1983. The secretary problem and its extensions: A review. *Int. Stat. Rev.* **51**:189–206. [4, 11, 19]

Fretwell, S. D., and H. J. Lucas, Jr. 1969. On territorial behavior and other factors influencing habitat distribution in birds. I. Theoretical development. *Acta Biotheor.* **19**:16–36. [19]

Friedman, N. P., A. Miyake, S. E. Young, et al. 2008. Individual differences in executive functions are almost entirely genetic in origin. *J. Exp. Psychol. Gen.* **137**:201–225. [15]

Frier, H. J., E. Edwards, C. Smith, S. Neale, and T. S. Collett. 1996. Magnetic compass cues and visual pattern learning in honeybees. *J. Exp. Biol.* **199**:1353–1361. [19]

Friston, K. J., C. D. Frith, P. F. Liddle, and R. S. Frackowiak. 1991. Investigating a network model of word generation with positron emission tomography. *Proc. Biol. Sci.* **244(1310)**:101–106. [9]

Frith, C. D., K. Friston, P. F. Liddle, and R. S. Frackowiak. 1991a. Willed action and the prefrontal cortex in man: A study with PET. *Proc. Biol. Sci.* **244(1311)**:241–246. [9]

———. 1991b. A PET study of word finding. *Neuropsychologia* **29(12)**:1137–1148. [9]

Fritz, J. B., M. Elhilali, S. V. David, and S. A. Shamma. 2007. Auditory attention: Focusing the searchlight on sound. *Curr. Opin. Neurobiol.* **17**:437–455. [2, 4]

Fritzke, B. 1994. Growing cell structures: A self-organizing network for unsupervised and supervised learning. *Neural Netw.* **7(9)**:1441–1460. [20]

Fu, W.-T. 2007. Adaptive tradeoffs between exploration and exploitation: A rational-ecological approach. In: Integrated Models of Cognitive Systems, ed. W. Gray. New York: Oxford Univ. Press. [18]

Fu, W.-T., and W. Dong. 2010. Facilitating knowledge exploration in folksonomies: Expertise ranking by link and semantic structures. ICCS 2010. http://appliedcogsci.vp.uiuc.edu/admin/upload/1279203819FuDong.CSE10.pdf. (accessed 11 January 2012). [18]

———. 2012. Collaborative indexing to knowledge exploration: A social learning model. *IEEE Intell. Sys.* **27(1)**:39–46. [18]

Fu, W.-T., and W. Gray. 2006. Suboptimal tradeoffs in information seeking. *Cogn. Psychol.* **52(3)**:195–242. [2, 18]

Fu, W.-T., and P. Pirolli. 2007. SNIF-ACT: A cognitive model of user navigation on the World Wide Web. *Hum. Comput. Interact.* **22(4)**:355–412. [2, 18]

Fuhs, M. C., and D. S. Touretzky. 2007. Context learning in the rodent hippocampus. *Neural Comput.* **19(12)**:3172–3215. [6]

Fuster, J. M. 1989. The Prefrontal Cortex. New York: Raven Press. [8]

Fuster, J. M., and G. Alexander. 1971. Neuron activity related to short-term memory. *Science* **173**:652–654. [8]

Fyhn, M., S. Molden, S. Hollup, M. B. Moser, and E. Moser. 2002. Hippocampal neurons responding to first-time dislocation of a target object. *Neuron* **35(3)**:555–566. [9]

Fyhn, M., S. Molden, M. P. Witter, E. I. Moser, and M.-B. Moser. 2004. Spatial representation in the entorhinal cortex. *Science* **305(5688)**:1258–1264. [6]

Gaissmaier, W., L. J. Schooler, and J. Rieskamp. 2006. Simple predictions fueled by capacity limitations: When are they successful? *J. Exp. Psychol. Learn. Mem. Cogn.* **32(5)**:966–982. [20]

Galef, B. G., Jr., and D. J. White. 2000. Evidence of social effects on mate choice in vertebrates. *Behav. Processes* **51**:167–175. [19]

Gallagher, M., R. McMahan, and G. Schoenbaum. 1999. Orbitofrontal cortex and representation of incentive value in associative learning. *J. Neurosci.* **19**:6610–6614. [6]

Garcia-Retamero, R., and M. K. Dhami. 2009. Take-the-best in expert-novice decision strategies for residential burglary. *Psychon. Bull. Rev.* **16**:163–169. [15]

Garrison, J. S. E., and C. L. Gass. 1999. Response of a traplining hummingbird to changes in nectar availability. *Behav. Ecol.* **10**:714–725. [4]

Gavetti, G., and D. Levinthal. 2000. Looking forward and looking backward: Cognitive and experiential search. *Adm. Sci. Q.* **45(1)**:113–137. [17]

Gavrilets, S. 1997. Evolution and speciation on holey adaptive landscapes. *Trends Ecol. Evol.* **12**:307–312. [20]

———. 2004. Fitness Landscapes and the Origin of Species. Princeton: Princeton Univ. Press. [20]

Gavrilets, S., and J. Gravner. 1997. Percolation on the fitness hypercube and the evolution of reproductive isolation. *J. Theor. Biol.* **184**:51–64. [20]

Gehring, W. J., and D. E. Fencsik. 2001. Functions of the medial frontal cortex in the processing of conflict and errors. *J. Neurosci.* **21(23)**:9430–9437. [9]

Gelman, R. 1990. First principles organize attention to and learning about relevant data: Number and animate-inanimate distinction as examples. *Cogn. Sci.* **14**:79–106. [20]

Gemba, H., K. Sasaki, and V. B. Brooks. 1986. "Error" potentials in limbic cortex (anterior cingulate area 24) of monkeys during motor learning. *Neurosci. Lett.* **70(2)**:223–227. [9]

Gen, M., and R. Cheng. 1997. Genetic Algorithms and Engineering Design. New York: Wiley. [4]

Gendron, R. P., and J. E. R. Staddon. 1983. Searching for cryptic prey: The effects of search rate. *Am. Nat.* **121**:172–186. [2]

German, P. W., and H. L. Fields. 2007. Rat nucleus accumbens neurons persistently encode locations associated with morphine reward. *J. Neurophysiol.* **97(3)**:2094–2106. [6]

Gershman, S. J., D. Blei, and Y. Niv. 2010. Context, learning and extinction. *Psychol. Rev.* **117(1)**:197–209. [6]

Gettys, C. F., and S. D. Fisher. 1979. Hypothesis plausibility and hypothesis generation. *Organ. Behav. Hum. Perform.* **24**:93–110. [15]

Ghose, G. M., and J. H. Maunsell. 2002. Attentional modulation in visual cortex depends on task timing. *Nature* **419(6907)**:616–620. [5]

Gibson, K. W., C. L. Hall, and D. L. Kramer. 2006. Time-concentrated sampling: A simple strategy for information gain at a novel, depleted patch. *Can. J. Zool.* **84**:1513–1521. [4]

Gibson, R. M. 1996. Female choice in sage grouse: The roles of attraction and active comparison. *Behav. Ecol. Sociobiol.* **39**:55–59. [4]

Gigerenzer, G., A. Dieckmann, and W. Gaissmaier. 2012. Efficient cognition through limited search. In: Ecological Rationality: Intelligence in the World, ed. P. M. Todd, G. Gigerenzer, and the ABC Research Group, pp. 241–273. New York: Oxford Univ. Press. [11]

Gigerenzer, G., and D. G. Goldstein. 1996. Reasoning the fast and frugal way: Models of bounded rationality. *Psychol. Rev.* **103**:650–669. [15]

Gigerenzer, G., and P. M. Todd. 1999. Fast and frugal heuristics: The adaptive toolbox. In: Simple Heuristics that Make Us Smart, ed. G. Gigerenzer, P. M. Todd, and the ABC Research Group, pp. 3–34. New York: Oxford Univ. Press. [19]

Gigerenzer, G., P. M. Todd, and ABC Research Group. 1999. Simple Heuristics that Make Us Smart. New York: Oxford Univ. Press. [4, 15, 16]

Gilbert, J. P., and F. Mosteller. 1966. Recognizing the maximum of a sequence. *J. Am. Stat. Assoc.* **61**:35–73. [15]

Gill, P. R., S. J. Y. Mizumori, and D. M. Smith. 2011. Hippocampal episode fields develop with learning. *Hippocampus* **21(21)**:1240–1249. [6]

Gillan, C., M. Papmeyer, S. Morein-Zamir, et al. 2011. Disruption in the balance between goal-directed behavior and habit learning in obsessive compulsive disorder. *Am. J. Psychiatry* **168(7)**:18–26. [9]

Gilzenrat, M. S., S. Nieuwenhuis, M. Jepma, and J. D. Cohen. 2010. Pupil diameter tracks changes in control state predicted by the adaptive gain theory of locus coeruleus function. *Cogn. Affect. Behav. Neurosci.* **10**:252–269. [13]

Giraldeau, L.-A., and T. Caraco. 2000. Social Foraging Theory. Princeton: Princeton Univ. Press. [3, 4]

Giraldeau, L.-A., and F. Dubois. 2008. Social foraging and the study of exploitative behavior. *Adv. Stud. Behav.* **38**:59–104. [3, 4]

Giraldeau, L.-A., and B. Livoreil. 1998. Game theory and social foraging. In: Game Theory and Animal Behavior, ed. L. A. Dugatkin and H. K. Reeve. New York: Oxford Univ. Press. [3]

Gittins, J. C. 1979. Bandit processes and dynamic allocation indices. *J. R. Stat. Soc. Series B* **41**:148–177. [15]

Glaeser, E. L., H. Kallal, J. A. Scheinkman, and A. Shleifer. 1992. Growth in cities. *J. Polit. Econ.* **100(6)**:1126–1152. [20]

Gläscher, J., N. D. Daw, P. Dayan, and J. P. O'Doherty. 2010. States versus rewards: Dissociable neural prediction error signals underlying model-based and model-free reinforcement learning. *Neuron* **66(4)**:585–595. [12]

Glimcher, P. W., C. Camerer, and R. A. Poldrack. 2008. Neuroeconomics: Decision Making and the Brain. New York: Academic Press. [6]

Glover, S. 2004. Separate visual representations in the planning and control of action. *Behav. Brain Sci.* **27**:3–24. [14]

Godden, D. R., and A. D. Baddeley. 1975. Context-dependent memory in two natural environments: On land and underwater. *Br. J. Psychol.* **66**:325–331. [11]

Gold, E. M., and The RAND Corporation. 1967. Language identification in the limit. *Information and Control* **10(5)**:447–474. [20]

Gold, J. I., and M. N. Shadlen. 2002. Banburismus and the brain: Decoding the relationship between sensory stimuli, decisions, and reward. *Neuron* **36(2)**:299–308. [12]

Goldman, M. S., S. A. Brown, and B. A. Christiansen. 1987. Expectancy theory: Thinking about drinking. In: Psychological Theories of Drinking and Alcoholism, ed. H. T. Blaine and K. E. Leonard, pp. 181–226. New York: Guilford. [6]

Goldman-Rakic, P. S. 1995. Cellular basis of working memory. *Neuron* **14**:477–485. [8]

Goldsmith, M. 1998. What's in a location? Comparing object-based and space-based models of feature integration in visual search. *J. Exp. Psychol. Gen.* **127(2)**:189–219. [10]

Goldstein, M. H., A. P. King, and M. J. West. 2003. Social interaction shapes babbling: Testing parallels between birdsong and speech. *PNAS* **100**:8030–8035. [4]

Goodwin, D. R., B. Powell, D. Bremer, H. Hoine, and J. Stern. 1969. Alcohol and recall: State dependent effects in man. *Science* **163**:1358–1360. [11]

Gordon, D. M. 1995. The expandable network of ant exploration. *Anim. Behav.* **50**:995–1007. [3]

Goto, Y., S. Otani, and A. A. Grace. 2007. The Yin and Yang of dopamine release: A new perspective. *Neuropharmacol.* **53(5)**:583–587. [9]

Grace, A. A. 2000. The tonic/phasic model of dopamine system regulation and its implications for understanding alcohol and psychostimulant craving. *Addiction* **95(Suppl 2)**:S119–S128. [5]

Grant, D. A., and E. A. Berg. 1948. A behavioral analysis of degree of reinforcement and ease of shifting to new responses in a Weigl type card sorting problem. *J. Exp. Psychol.* **38**:404–411. [5]

Gravner, J., D. Pitman, and S. Gavrilets. 2007. Percolation on fitness landscapes: Effects of correlation, phenotype, and incompatibilities. *J. Theor. Biol.* **248(4)**:627–645. [20]

Graybiel, A. M. 1990. The basal ganglia and the initiation of movement. *Rev. Neurol.* **146(10)**:570–574. [6]

———. 1998. The basal ganglia and chunking of action repertoires. *Neurobiol. Learn. Mem.* **70**:119–136. [6]

Greicius, M. D., B. Krasnow, A. L. Reiss, and V. Menon. 2003. Functional connectivity in the resting brain: A network analysis of the default mode hypothesis. *PNAS* **100(1)**:253–258. [13]

Griffin, A. L., H. Eichenbaum, and M. E. Hasselmo. 2007. Spatial representations of hippocampal CA1 neurons are modulated by behavioral context in a hippocampus-dependent memory task. *J. Neurosci.* **27(9)**:2416–2423. [6]

Groenewegen, H. J., H. W. Berendse, J. G. Wolters, and A. H. M. Lohman. 1990. The anatomical relationship of the prefrontal cortex with the striatopallidal system, the thalamus and the amygdala: Evidence for a parallel organisation. *Prog. Brain Res.* **85**:95–118. [7]

Groenewegen, H. J., E. Vermeulen-van der Zee, A. T. Kortschot, and M. P. Witter. 1987. Organization of the projections from the subiculum to the ventral striatum in the rat: A study using anterograde transport of *Phaseolus vulgaris leucoagglutinin*. *Neuroscience* **23(1)**:103–120. [6, 9]

Gronlund, S. D., and R. M. Shiffrin. 1986. Retrieval strategies in recall of natural categories and categorized lists. *J. Exp. Psychol. Learn. Mem. Cogn.* **12**:550–561. [11]

Grossman, M., and F. J. Chaloupka. 1998. The demand for cocaine by young adults: A rational addiction approach. *J. Health Econ.* **17**:427–474. [6]

Grover, L. K. 1992. Local search and the local structure of NP-complete problems. *Op. Res. Lett.* **12**:235–243. [16]

Grünbaum, D. 1997. Schooling as a strategy for taxis in a noisy environment. In: Animal Groups in Three Dimensions, ed. J. K. Parrish and W. Hamner, pp. 257–282. Cambridge: Cambridge Univ. Press. [3]

Guetzkow, H., and H. A. Simon. 1955. The impact of certain communication nets upon organization and performance in task-oriented groups. *Manag. Sci.* **1(3–4)**:233–250. [17]

Guilford, J. P. 1967. The Nature of Human Intelligence. New York: McGraw-Hill. [14]

Gupta, A. S., M. A. van der Meer, D. S. Touretzky, and A. D. Redish. 2010. Hippocampal replay is not a simple function of experience. *Neuron* **65(5)**:695–705. [6]

Haber, S. N., J. L. Fudge, and N. R. McFarland. 2000. Striatonigral pathways in primates form an ascending spiral from the shell to the dorsolateral striatum. *J. Neurosci.* **20**:2369–2382. [9]

Haber, S. N., K. S. Kim, P. Mailly, and R. Calzavara. 2006. Reward-related cortical inputs define a large striatal region in primates that interface with associative cortical connections, providing a substrate for incentive-based learning. *J. Neurosci.* **26**:8368–8376. [7]

Hackman, J. R. 2002. Leading Teams: Setting the Stage for Great Performances. Boston: Harvard Business School Press. [17]

———. 2012. From causes to conditions in group research. *J. Org. Behav.* **33**:428–444. [17]

Hackman, J. R., and R. Wageman. 2005. When and how team leaders matter. In: Research in Organizational Behavior, ed. B. M. Staw and R. D. Kramer. New York: Elsevier. [17]

Hafting, T., M. Fyhn, S. Molden, M.-B. Moser, and E. I. Moser. 2005. Microstructure of a spatial map in the entorhinal cortex. *Nature* **436**:801–806. [6]

Halikas, J. A. 1997. Craving. In: Substance Abuse: A Comprehensive Textbook, ed. J. H. Lowinson et al., pp. 85–90. Baltimore: Williams and Wilkins. [6]

Haluk, D. M., and S. B. Floresco. 2009. Ventral striatal dopamine modulation of different forms of behavioral flexibility. *Neuropsychopharmacol.* **34(8)**:2041–2052. [8]

Hamblin, S., K. J. Mathot, J. Morand-Ferron, et al. 2010. Predator inadvertent social information use favours reduced clumping of its prey. *Oikos* **119**:286–291. [4]

Hamilton, W. D. 1971. Geometry for the selfish herd. *J. Theor. Biol.* **31**:295–311. [4]

Hammond, L. J. 1980. The effects of contingencies upon appetitive conditioning of free-operant behavior. *J. Exp. Anal. Behav.* **34**:297–304. [7]

Hampton, A. N., P. Bossaerts, and J. P. O'Doherty. 2006. The role of the ventromedial prefrontal cortex in abstract state-based inference during decision making in humans. *J. Neurosci.* **26(32)**:8360–8367. [7, 12]

———. 2008. Neural correlates of mentalizing-related computations during strategic interactions in humans. *PNAS* **105(18)**:6741–6746. [12]

Hansen, M. T. 1999. The search-transfer problem: The role of weak ties in sharing knowledge across organization subunits. *Adm. Sci. Q.* **44(1)**:82–111. [17]

Harbison, J. I., E. J. Davelaar, and M. R. Dougherty. 2008. Stopping rules and memory search termination decisions. In: Proc. of the 30th Ann. Conf. of the Cognitive Science Society, pp. 565–570. Austin: Cognitive Science Society. [15]

Harbison, J. I., M. R. Dougherty, E. J. Davelaar, and B. Fayyad. 2009. On the lawfulness of the decision to terminate memory search. *Cognition* **111**:397–402. [11]

Harley, C. B. 1981. Learning the evolutionarily stable strategy. *J. Theor. Biol.* **89**:611–633. [4]

Haruno, M., and M. Kawato. 2006. Heterarchical reinforcement-learning model for integration of multiple cortico-striatal loops: fMRI examination in stimulus-action-reward association learning. *Neural Netw.* **19(8)**:1242–1254. [9]

Hassabis, D., D. Kumaran, S. D. Vann, and E. A. Maguire. 2007. Patients with hippocampal amnesia cannot imagine new experiences. *PNAS* **104**:1726–1731. [6, 9]

Hasselmo, M. E. 1993. Acetylcholine and learning in a cortical associative memory. *Neural Comput.* **5**:32–44. [6]

Hasselmo, M. E., C. Linster, M. Patil, D. Ma, and M. Cekic. 1997. Noradrenergic suppression of synaptic transmission may influence cortical signal-to-noise ratio. *J. Neurophysiol.* **77(6)**:3326–3339. [5]

Hasselmo, M. E., and M. Sarter. 2011. Modes and models of forebrain cholinergic neuromodulation of cognition. *Neuropsychopharmacol.* **36(1)**:52–73. [8, 9]

Haxby, J. V., M. I. Gobbini, M. L. Furey, et al. 2001. Distributed and overlapping representations of faces and objects in ventral temporal cortex. *Science* **293(5539)**:2425–2430. [9]

Hazy, T. E., M. J. Frank, and R. C. O'Reilly. 2007. Towards an executive without a homunculus: Computational models of the prefrontal cortex/basal ganglia system. *Phil. Trans. R. Soc. Lond. B* **362(1485)**:1601–1613. [8]

Healy, A. F., and M. Kubovy. 1981. Probability matching and the formation of conservative decision rules in a numerical analog of signal detection. *J. Exp. Psychol. Hum. Learn. Mem.* **7(5)**:344–354. [10]

Heilman, K. M. 2005. Creativity and the Brain. New York: Psychology Press. [14]

Heinrich, B. 1995. An experimental investigation of insight in common ravens (*Corvus corax*). *Auk* **112**:994–1003. [4]

Henderson, J., T. A. Hurly, M. Bateson, and S. D. Healy. 2006. Timing in free-living rufous hummingbirds, *Selasphorus rufus*. *Curr. Biol.* **16**:512–515. [4]

Henson, R. N. 1998. Short-term memory for serial order: The start-end model. *Cogn. Psychol.* **36**:73–137. [11]

Hershler, O., and S. Hochstein. 2005. At first sight: A high-level pop out effect for faces. *Vision Res.* **45(13)**:1707–1724. [10]

———. 2006. With a careful look: Still no low-level confound to face pop-out. *Vision Res.* **46(18)**:3028–3035. [10]

Hertwig, R., and P. M. Todd. 2003. More is not always better: The benefits of cognitive limits. In: Reasoning and Decision Making: A Handbook, ed. D. Hardman and L. Macchi, pp. 213–231. Chichester: Wiley. [20]

Hester, R., J. J. Foxe, S. Molholm, M. Shpaner, and H. Garavan. 2005. Neural mechanisms involved in error processing: A comparison of errors made with and without awareness. *NeuroImage* **27(3)**:602–608. [13]

Higgins, S. T., S. M. Alessi, and R. L. Dantona. 2002. Voucher-based incentives: A substance abuse treatment innovation. *Addict. Behav.* **27**:887–910. [6]

Hikosaka, O. 2007. Basal ganglia mechanisms of reward-oriented eye movement. *Ann. NY Acad. Sci.* **1104**:229–249. [7]

Hill, A. J. 1978. First occurrence of hippocampal spatial firing in a new environment. *Exp. Neurol.* **62(2)**:282–297. [9]

Hills, T. T. 2006. Animal foraging and the evolution of goal-directed cognition. *Cogn. Sci.* **30**:3–41. [1, 2, 5, 11, 13–15]

———. 2010. Investigating mathematical search behavior using network analysis. In: Modeling Students' Mathematical Modeling Competencies, ed. R. Lesh et al., pp. 571–581. Boston: Springer-Verlag. [2]

Hills, T. T., and F. Adler. 2002. Time's crooked arrow: Optimal foraging and rate-biased time perception. *Anim. Behav.* **64(4)**:589–597. [4]

Hills, T. T., P. J. Brockie, and A. V. Maricq. 2004. Dopamine and glutamate control area-restricted search behavior in *Caenorhabditis elegans*. *Neuroscience* **24**:1217–1225. [2]

Hills, T. T., and R. Hertwig. 2010. Information search in decisions from experience: Do our patterns of sampling foreshadow our decisions? *Psychol. Sci.* **21**:1787–1792. [2, 4, 19]

Hills, T. T., J. Maouene, B. Riordan, and L. B. Smith. 2010a. The associative structure of language: Contextual diversity in early word learning. *J. Mem. Lang.* **63**:259–273. [2]

Hills, T. T., R. Mata, A. Wilke, and G. R. Samanez-Larkin. 2011. Exploration and exploitation in memory search across the life span. In: Proc. of the 33rd Ann. Conf. of the Cognitive Science Society, ed. L. Carlson et al., pp. 991–996. Austin: Cognitive Science Society. [15]

Hills, T. T., and T. Pachur. 2012. Dynamic search and working memory in social recall. *J. Exp. Psychol. Learn. Mem. Cogn.* **38**:218–228. [2, 15]

Hills, T. T., P. M. Todd, and R. L. Goldstone. 2008. Search in external and internal spaces: Evidence for generalized cognitive search processes. *Psychol. Sci.* **19**:802–808. [2, 14]

———. 2010b. The central executive as a search process: Priming exploration and exploitation across domains. *J. Exp. Psychol. Gen.* **139**:590–609. [2, 15]

Hills, T. T., P. M. Todd, and M. Jones. 2009. Optimal foraging in semantic memory. In: Proc. of the 31st Ann. Conf. of the Cognitive Science Society, ed. N. A. Taatgen and H. van Rijn, pp. 620–625. Austin: Cognitive Science Society. [4, 11]

Hirase, H., A. Czurkó, J. Csicsvari, and G. Buzsáki. 1999. Firing rate and theta-phase coding by hippocampal pyramidal neurons during space clamping. *Eur. J. Neurosci.* **11(12)**:4373–4380. [6]

Hirsh, R., B. Leber, and K. Gillman. 1978. Fornix fibers and motivational states as controllers of behavior: A study stimulated by the contextual retrieval theory. *Behav. Biol.* **22**:463–478. [6]

Hoare, D. J., I. D. Couzin, J.-G. G. Godin, and J. Krause. 2004. Context-dependent group size choice in fish. *Anim. Behav.* **67**:155–164. [3, 4]

Hoffmann, K. L., and B. L. McNaughton. 2002. Coordinated reactivation of distributed memory traces in primate neocortex. *Science* **297(5589)**:2070–2073. [6]

Hogarth, L., A. Dickinson, A. Wright, M. Kouvaraki, and T. Duka. 2007. The role of drug expectancy in the control of human drug seeking. *J. Exp. Psychol. Anim. Behav. Process.* **33(4)**:484–496. [7]

Höglund, J., and R. V. Alatalo. 1995. Leks. Princeton: Princeton Univ. Press. [19]

Holland, P. C. 1979. Differential effects of omission contingencies on various components of Pavlovian appetitive conditioned responding in rats. *J. Exp. Psychol. Anim. Behav. Process.* **5(2)**:178–193. [9]

———. 2004. Relations between Pavlovian-instrumental transfer and reinforcer devaluation. *J. Exp. Psychol. Anim. Behav. Process.* **30(2)**:104–117. [7]

Holland, P. C., and M. E. Bouton. 1999. Hippocampus and context in classical conditioning. *Curr. Opin. Neurobiol.* **9**:195–202. [6]

Holland, P. C., and J. J. Straub. 1979. Differential effects of two ways of devaluing the unconditioned stimulus after Pavlovian appetitive conditioning. *J. Exp. Psychol. Anim. Behav. Process.* **5(1)**:65–78. [9]

Holland, S. M., and T. V. Smulders. 2011. Do humans use episodic memory to solve a what-where-when memory task? *Anim. Cogn.* **14(1)**:95–102. [9]

Hollingworth, A. 2006. Visual memory for natural scenes: Evidence from change detection and visual search. *Vis. Cogn.* **14(4–8)**:781–807. [10]

Holroyd, C. B., and M. G. Coles. 2002. The neural basis of human error processing: Reinforcement learning, dopamine, and the error-related negativity. *Psychol. Rev.* **109(4)**:679–709. [5]

Holroyd, C. B., S. Nieuwenhuis, N. Yeung, et al. 2004. Dorsal anterior cingulate cortex shows fMRI response to internal and external error signals. *Nat. Neurosci.* **7(5)**:497–498. [5]

Holroyd, C. B., N. Yeung, M. G. Coles, and J. D. Cohen. 2005. A mechanism for error detection in speeded response time tasks. *J. Exp. Psychol. Gen.* **134(2)**:163–191. [5]

Hommel, B. 2009. Action control according to TEC (theory of event coding). *Psychol. Res.* **73**:512–526. [14]

———. 2010. Grounding attention in action control: The intentional control of selection. In: Effortless Attention: A New Perspective in the Cognitive Science of Attention and Action, ed. B. J. Bruya, pp. 121–140. Cambridge, MA: MIT Press. [14]

Hommel, B., K. Z. H. Li, and S. Li. 2004. Visual search across the life span. *Dev. Psychol.* **40**:545–558. [15]

Hommel, B., J. Müsseler, G. Aschersleben, and W. Prinz. 2001a. Codes and their vicissitudes. *Behav. Brain Sci.* **24**:910–937. [14]

———. 2001b. The theory of event coding (TEC): A framework for perception and action planning. *Behav. Brain Sci.* **24**:849–878. [14]

Horowitz, T. S., and J. M. Wolfe. 1998. Visual search has no memory. *Nature* **394(6693)**:575–577. [5, 10]

———. 2003. Memory for rejected distractors in visual search? *Vis. Cogn.* **10(3)**:257–298. [10]

Hoshi, E., H. Sawamura, and J. Tanji. 2005. Neurons in the rostral cingulate motor area monitor multiple phases of visuomotor behavior with modest parametric selectivity. *J. Neurophysiol.* **94(1)**:640–656. [9]

Hosokawa, T., K. Kato, M. Inoue, and A. Mikami. 2007. Neurons in the macaque orbitofrontal cortex code relative preference of both rewarding and aversive outcomes. *Neurosci. Res.* **57(3)**:434–445. [9]

Houston, A. I., and J. M. McNamara. 1999. Models of Adaptive Behavior. Cambridge: Cambridge Univ. Press. [19]

Howard, M. W., and M. J. Kahana. 1999. Contextual variability and serial position effects in free recall. *J. Exp. Psychol. Learn. Mem. Cogn.* **25**:923–941. [11]

———. 2002. A distributed representation of temporal context. *J. Math. Psychol.* **46**:269–299. [11]

Huckman, R. S., B. R. Staats, and D. M. Upton. 2009. Team familiarity, role experience, and performance: Evidence from Indian software services. *Manag. Sci.* **55(1)**:85–100. [17]

Huerta, R., T. Nowotny, M. Garcia-Sanchez, H. D. I. Abarbanel, and M. I. Rabinovich. 2004. Learning classification in the olfactory system of insects. *Neural Comput.* **16**:1601–1640. [20]

Huettel, S. A., C. J. Stowe, E. M. Gordon, B. T. Warner, and M. L. Platt. 2006. Neural signatures of economic preferences for risk and ambiguity. *Neuron* **49(5)**:765–775. [9]

Humphreys, M. S., J. Wiles, and J. D. Bain. 1991. Memory retrieval with two cues: Think of intersecting sets. In: Attention and Performance XIV: A Silver Jubilee, ed. D. E. Meyer and S. Kornblum. Hillsdale, NJ: Lawrence Erlbaum. [11]

Hutchings, M. J., and H. de Kroon. 1994. Foraging in plants: The role of morphological plasticity in resource acquisition. *Adv. Ecol. Res.* **25**:159–238. [2]

Hutchinson, J. M. C., C. Fanselow, and P. M. Todd. 2012. Car parking as a game between simple heuristics. In: Ecological Rationality: Intelligence in the World, ed. P. M. Todd, G. Gigerenzer, and ABC Research Group, pp. 454–485. New York: Oxford Univ. Press. [4]

Hutchinson, J. M. C., and G. Gigerenzer. 2005. Simple heuristics and rules of thumb: Where psychologists and behavioral biologists might meet. *Behav. Processes* **69**: 97–124. [4, 19]

Hutchinson, J. M. C., and K. Halupka. 2004. Mate choice when males are in patches: Optimal strategies and good rules of thumb. *J. Theor. Biol.* **231**:129–151. [19]

Hutchinson, J. M. C., and P. M. Waser. 2007. Use, misuse and extensions of "ideal gas" models of animal encounter. *Biol. Rev.* **82**:335–359. [4]

Hutchinson, J. M. C., A. Wilke, and P. M. Todd. 2008. Patch leaving in humans: Can a generalist adapt its rules to dispersal of items across patches? *Anim. Behav.* **75**:1331–1349. [4, 11, 15, 19]

Huxter, J. R., T. J. Senior, K. Allen, and J. Csicsvari. 2008. Theta phase-specific codes for two-dimensional position, trajectory and heading in the hippocampus. *Nat. Neurosci.* **11**:587–594. [6, 9]

Hyman, J. M., E. A. Zilli, A. M. Paley, and M. E. Hasselmo. 2005. Medial prefrontal cortex cells show dynamic modulation with the hippocampal theta rhythm dependent on behavior. *Hippocampus* **15(6)**:739–749. [9]

———. 2010. Working memory performance correlates with prefrontal-hippocampal theta interactions but not with prefrontal neuron firing rates. *Front. Integr. Neurosci.* [6, 9]

Hyman, S. E., and R. C. Malenka. 2001. Addiction and the brain: The neurobiology of compulsion and its persistence. *Nat. Rev. Neurosci.* **2(10)**:695–703. [9]

Indow, T., and K. Togano. 1970. On retrieving sequence from long-term memory. *Psychol. Rev.* **77**:317–331. [11, 15]

Inglis, I. R., S. Langton, B. Forkman, and J. Lazarus. 2001. An information primacy model of exploratory and foraging behaviour. *Anim. Behav.* **62**:543–557. [4]

Isaacs, R. 1965. Differential Games: A Mathematical Theory with Applications to Warfare and Pursuit, Control and Optimization. New York: Wiley. [4]

Isen, A. M., K. A. Daubman, and G. P. Nowicki. 1987. Positive affect facilitates creative problem solving. *J. Pers. Soc. Psychol.* **52**:1122–1131. [14]

Ito, S., V. Stuphorn, J. W. Brown, and J. D. Schall. 2003. Performance monitoring by anterior cingulate cortex during saccade countermanding. *Science* **302**:120–122. [5, 9]

Itskov, V., C. Curto, E. Pastalkova, and G. Buzsáki. 2011. Cell assembly sequences arising from spike threshold adaptation keep track of time in the hippocampus. *J. Neurosci.* **31(8)**:2828–2834. [6]

Itti, L., C. Koch, and E. Niebur. 1998. A model of saliency-based visual attention for rapid scene analysis. *IEEE Trans. Pattern Anal. Mach. Intell.* **20(11)**:1254–1259. [10]

Itti, L., G. Rees, and J. Tsotsos, eds. 2005. Neurobiology of Attention. San Diego: Academic Press Elsevier. [10]

Iversen, S. D., and L. L. Iversen. 2007. Dopamine: 50 years in perspective. *Trends Neurosci.* **30**:188–193. [2]

Iwasa, Y., M. Higashi, and N. Yamamura. 1981. Prey distribution as a factor determining the choice of optimal foraging strategy. *Am. Nat.* **117**:710–723. [4]

Jackson, D. E., M. Holcombe, and F. L. W. Ratnieks. 2004. Trail geometry gives polarity to ant foraging networks. *Nature* **432**:907–909. [20]

Jackson, J. C., J. J. Bos, A. B. Donga, J. V. Lankelma, and C. M. A. Pennartz. 2009. Method of investigating the influence of hippocampal sharp wave-associated ripples on information processing in extrahippocampal structures. *Abstr. Soc. Neurosci.* [6]

Jackson, J. C., A. Johnson, and A. D. Redish. 2006. Hippocampal sharp waves and reactivation during awake states depend on repeated sequential experience. *J. Neurosci.* **26**:12,415–12,426. [6]

Jackson, J. C., and A. D. Redish. 2003. Detecting dynamical changes within a simulated neural ensemble using a measure of representational quality. *Network* **14(4)**:629–645. [9]

———. 2007. Network dynamics of hippocampal cell-assemblies resemble multiple spatial maps within single tasks. *Hippocampus* **17**:1209–1229. [6]

Jacobs, R. A., and M. I. Jordan. 1992. Computational consequences of a bias towards short connections. *J. Cogn. Neurosci.* **4**:323–336. [20]

Jacobs, R. A., M. I. Jordan, and A. G. Barto. 1991. Task decomposition through competition in a modular connectionist architecture: The what and where vision tasks. *Cogn. Sci.* **15**:219–250. [20]

Jacobsen, C. 1936. Studies of cerebral functions in primates. *Comp. Psychol. Monogr.* **13**:1–60. [8]

James, W. 1890. The Principles of Psychology. New York: Dover. [1, 14]

Janis, I. L. 1972. Victims of Groupthink: A Psychological Study of Foreign-Policy Decisions and Fiascoes. Boston: Houghton Mifflin. [17]

Janssen, M. A., R. L. Goldstone, F. Menczer, and E. Ostrom. 2008. Effect of rule choice in dynamic interactive spatial commons. *Intl. J. Commons* **2**:288–312. [20]

Jay, T. M., and M. P. Witter. 1991. Distribution of hippocampal CA1 and subicular efferents in the prefrontal cortex of the rat studied by means of anterograde transport of *Phaseolus vulgaris leucoagglutinin. J. Comp. Neurol.* **313(4)**:574–586. [9]

Jennings, H. S. 1906. Behavior of the Lower Organisms. Bloomington: Indiana Univ. Press. [2]

Jensen, O., and J. E. Lisman. 1996. Hippocampal CA3 region predicts memory sequences: Accounting for the phase precession of place cells. *Learn. Mem.* **3(2–3)**:279–287. [6, 9]

———. 2000. Position reconstruction from an ensemble of hippocampal place cells: Contribution of theta phase encoding. *J. Neurophysiol.* **83(5)**:2602–2609. [6]

Jepma, M., E. T. Te Beek, E. J. Wagenmakers, J. M. van Gerven, and S. Nieuwenhuis. 2010. The role of the noradrenergic system in the exploration-exploitation trade-off: A psychopharmacological study. *Front. Hum. Neurosci.* **4**:170. [8]

Jessup, R. K., J. R. Busemeyer, and J. W. Brown. 2010. Error effects in anterior cingulate cortex reverse when error likelihood is high. *J. Neurosci.* **30(9)**:3467–3472. [5, 9]

Jhou, T. C., H. L. Fields, M. G. Baxter, C. B. Saper, and P. C. Holland. 2009. The rostromedial tegmental nucleus (RMTg), a GABAergic afferent to midbrain dopamine neurons, encodes aversive stimuli and inhibits motor responses. *Neuron* **61(5)**:786–800. [9]

Ji, D., and M. A. Wilson. 2007. Coordinated memory replay in the visual cortex and hippocampus during sleep. *Nat. Neurosci.* **10(1)**:100–107. [6]

Joel, D., and I. Weiner. 2000. The connections of the dopaminergic system with the striatum in rats and primates: An analysis with respect to the functional and compartmental organization of the striatum. *Neuroscience* **96(3)**:451–474. [9]

Jog, M. S., Y. Kubota, C. I. Connolly, V. Hillegaart, and A. M. Graybiel. 1999. Building neural representations of habits. *Science* **286**:1746–1749. [6]

Johnson, A., and D. Crowe. 2009. Revisiting Tolman: Theories and cognitive maps. *Cogn. Crit.* **1(1)**:43–72. [6]

Johnson, A., A. A. Fenton, C. Kentros, and A. D. Redish. 2009. Looking for cognition in the structure in the noise. *Trends Cogn. Sci.* **13(2)**:55–64. [6, 9]

Johnson, A., J. Jackson, and A. D. Redish. 2008. Measuring distributed properties of neural representations beyond the decoding of local variables: Implications for cognition. In: Mechanisms of Information Processing in the Brain: Encoding of Information in Neural Populations and Networks, ed. C. Hölscher and M. H. J. Munk, pp. 95–119. Cambridge: Cambridge Univ. Press. [6]

Johnson, A., and A. D. Redish. 2005. Hippocampal replay contributes to within session learning in a temporal difference reinforcement learning model. *Neural Netw.* **18(9)**:1163–1171. [6, 12]

———. 2007. Neural ensembles in CA3 transiently encode paths forward of the animal at a decision point. *J. Neurosci.* **27(45)**:12,176–12,189. [6, 9]

Johnson, A., M. A. van der Meer, and A. D. Redish. 2007. Integrating hippocampus and striatum in decision-making. *Curr. Opin. Neurobiol.* **17(6)**:692–697. [6]

Johnson, J. G., and M. Raab. 2003. Take the first: Option-generation and resulting choices. *Org. Behav. Hum. Decis. Proc.* **91**:251–229. [15]

Johnston, J. C., R. S. McCann, and R. W. Remington. 1995. Chronometric dissociation of input attention and central attention in human information processing. *Psychol. Sci.* **6**:365–369. [14]

Johnstone, R. A. 1997. The tactics of mutual male choice and competitive search. *Behav. Ecol. Sociobiol.* **40**:51–59. [4]

Jones, B. T., W. Corbin, and F. Fromme. 2001. A review of expectancy theory and alcohol consumption. *Addiction* **96**:57–72. [6]

Jones, M. N., and D. J. K. Mewhort. 2007. Representing word meaning and order information in a composite holographic lexicon. *Psychol. Rev.* **104**:1–37. [4]

Jones, M. W., and M. A. Wilson. 2005. Theta rhythms coordinate hippocampal-prefrontal interactions in a spatial memory task. *PLoS Biol.* **3(12)**:e402. [6, 9]

Jordan, C. Y., and L. D. Harder. 2006. Manipulation of bee behavior by inflorescence architecture and its consequences for plant mating. *Am. Nat.* **167**:496–509. [4]

Jueptner, M., C. D. Frith, D. J. Brooks, R. S. Frackowiak, and R. E. Passingham. 1997. Anatomy of motor learning. II. Subcortical structures and learning by trial and error. *J. Neurophysiol.* **77**:1325–1337. [7]

Jung, M. W., Y. Qin, B. L. McNaughton, and C. A. Barnes. 1998. Firing characteristics of deep layer neurons in prefrontal cortex in rats performing spatial working memory tasks. *Cereb. Cortex* **8(5)**:437–450. [9]

Jusczyk, P. W., D. M. Houston, and M. Newsome. 1999. The beginnings of word segmentation in english-learning infants. *Cogn. Psychol.* **39(3–4)**:159–207. [20]

Juslin, P., and H. Olsson. 2005. Capacity limitations and the detection of correlations: A comment on Kareev (2000). *Psychol. Rev.* **112**:256–267. [20]

Kaelbling, L. P., M. L. Littman, and A. W. Moore. 1996. Reinforcement learning: A survey. *J. Artif. Intell. Res.* **4**:237–285. [5, 15]

Kahana, M. J. 1996. Associative retrieval processes in free recall. *Mem. Cogn.* **24**:103–109. [11]

Kahana, M. J., E. D. Dolan, C. L. Sauder, and A. Wingfield. 2005. Intrusions in episodic recall: Age differences in editing of overt responses. *J. Gerontol. Psych. Sci.* **60**:92–97. [11]

Kahneman, D., P. Slovic, and A. Tversky. 1982. Judgement under Uncertainty: Heuristics and Biases. Cambridge: Cambridge Univ. Press. [6]

Kahneman, D., and A. Tversky. 1979. Prospect theory: An analysis of decision under risk. *Econometrica* **47(2)**:263–292. [6]

———. 2000. Choices, Values, and Frames. Cambridge: Cambridge Univ. Press. [6]

Kalff, C., T. T. Hills, and J. M. Wiener. 2010. Human foraging behavior: A virtual reality investigation on area restricted search in humans. In: Proc. of the 32nd Ann. Conf. of the Cognitive Science Society, ed. R. Catrambone and S. Ohlsson, pp. 1–6. Portland: Cognitive Science Society. [2]

Kane, M. J., M. K. Bleckley, A. R. A. Conway, and R. W. Engle. 2001. A controlled-attention view of WM capacity. *J. Exp. Psychol. Gen.* **130**:169–183. [15]

Kane, M. J., and R. W. Engle. 2002. The role of prefrontal cortex in working-memory capacity, executive attention, and general fluid intelligence: An individual-differences perspective. *Psychon. Bull. Rev.* **9**:637–671. [2]

Kang, R., W.-T. Fu, and T. G. Kannampallil. 2010. Exploiting knowledge-in-the-head and knowledge-in-the-social-web: Effects of domain expertise on exploratory search in individual and social search environments. Proc. of the 28th Intl. Conf. on Human Factors in Computing Systems, pp. 393–402. Atlanta: ACM. [18]

Karbach, J., and J. Kray. 2009. How useful is executive control training? Age differences in near and far transfer of task-switching training. *Dev. Sci.* **12**:978–990. [15]

Kareev, Y. 2005. And yet the small-sample effect does hold: Reply to Juslin and Olsson (2005) and Anderson, Doherty, Berg, and Friedrich (2005). *Psychol. Rev.* **112**:280–285. [20]

Kareev, Y., I. Lieberman, and M. Lev. 1997. Through a narrow window: Sample size and the perception of correlation. *J. Exp. Psychol. Gen.* **126**:278–287. [20]

Kareiva, P. M., and G. Odell. 1987. Swarms of predators exhibit "preytaxis" if individual predators use area-restricted search. *Am. Nat.* **130**:233–270. [2]

Kareiva, P. M., and N. Shigesada. 1983. Analysing insect movement as a correlated random walk. *Oecologia* **56**:234–238. [3]

Katsnelson, E., U. Motro, M. W. Feldman, and A. Lotem. 2011. Individual-learning ability predicts social-foraging strategy in house sparrows. *Proc. R. Soc. B* **278**:582–589. [4]

Kearns, M. J. 1998. Efficient noise-tolerant learning from statistical queries. *J. ACM* **45**:983–1006. [16]

Kearns, M. J., and U. V. Vazirani. 1994. An Introduction to Computational Learning Theory. Cambridge, MA: MIT Press. [16]

Kehagia, A. A., G. K. Murray, and T. W. Robbins. 2010. Learning and cognitive flexibility: Frontostriatal function and monoaminergic modulation. *Curr. Opin. Neurobiol.* **20(2)**:199–204. [8]

Kelemen, E., and A. A. Fenton. 2010. Dynamic grouping of hippocampal neural activity during cognitive control of two spatial frames. *PLoS Biol.* **8(6)**:e1000403. [9]

Kellendonk, C., E. Simpson, H. Polan, et al. 2006. Transient and selective overexpression of dopamine D2 receptors in the striatum causes persistent abnormalities in prefrontal cortex functioning. *Neuron* **49(4)**:603–615. [8]

Kelly, A. M. C., L. Q. Uddin, B. B. Biswal, F. X. Castellanos, and M. P. Milham. 2008. Competition between functional brain networks mediates behavioral variability. *NeuroImage* **39(1)**:527–537. [13]

Kemp, C., N. D. Goodman, and J. B. Tenenbaum. 2010a. Learning to learn causal models. *Cogn. Sci.* **34(7)**:1185–1243. [20]

Kemp, C., J. B. Tenenbaum, S. Niyogi, and T. L. Griffiths. 2010b. A probabilistic model of theory formation. *Cognition* **114(2)**:165–196. [20]

Kennedy, J. S. 1983. Zigzagging and casting as a programmed response to wind-borne odour: A review. *Physiol. Entomol.* **8**:109–120. [4]

Kennerley, S. W., and J. D. Wallis. 2009. Encoding of reward and space during a working memory task in the orbitofrontal cortex and anterior cingulate sulcus. *J. Neurophysiol.* **102(6)**:3352–3364. [9]

Kentros, C., E. Hargreaves, R. D. Hawkins, et al. 1998. Abolition of long-term stability of new hippocampal place cell maps by NMDA receptor blockade. *Science* **280(5372)**:2121–2126. [9]

Kesner, R. P., and J. Rogers. 2004. An analysis of independence and interactions of brain substrates that subserve multiple attributes, memory systems, and underlying processes. *Neurobiol. Learn. Mem.* **82(3)**:199–215. [9]

Khader, P., T. Pachur, S. Meier, et al. 2011. Memory-based decision making with heuristics involves increased activation of decision-relevant memory representations. *J. Cogn. Neurosci.* **23**:3540–3554. [15]

Killcross, S., and E. Coutureau. 2003. Coordination of actions and habits in the medial prefrontal cortex of rats. *Cereb. Cortex* **13(8)**:400–408. [6]

Kim, H., S. Shimojo, and J. P. O'Doherty. 2006. Is avoiding an aversive outcome rewarding? Neural substrates of avoidance learning in the human brain. *PLoS Biol.* **4**:e233. [7]

Kim, J. J., and M. S. Fanselow. 1992. Modality-specific retrograde amnesia of fear. *Science* **256(5057)**:675–677. [9]

Kimball, D. R., T. A. Smith, and M. J. Kahana. 2007. The fSAM model of false recall. *Psychol. Rev.* **114**:954–993. [11]

Kinchla, R. A. 1974. Detecting target elements in multielement arrays: A confusability model. *Perc. Psychophys.* **15(1)**:149–158. [10]

Kintsch, W. 1998. Comprehension: A Paradigm for Cognition. New York: Cambridge Univ. Press. [18]

Kirkpatrick, S., and B. Selman. 1994. Critical behavior in the satisfiability of random Boolean expressions. *Science* **264**:1297–1301. [16]

Klayman, J. 1988. On the how and why (not) of learning from outcomes. In: Human Judgment: The Social Judgment Theory View, ed. B. Brehmer and C. R. B. Joyce. Amsterdam: North Holland. [15]

Klein, R. M. 1988. Inhibitory tagging system facilitates visual search. *Nature* **334**:430–431. [10]

———. 2000. Inhibition of return. *Trends Cogn. Sci.* **4**:138–147. [2, 10]

Klein, R. M., and W. J. MacInnes. 1999. Inhibition of return is a foraging facilitator in visual research. *Psychol. Sci.* **10(4)**:346. [5, 10]

Klein, T. A., T. Endrass, N. Kathmann, et al. 2007. Neural correlates of error awareness. *NeuroImage* **34(4)**:1774–1781. [13]

Knierim, J. J., H. S. Kudrimoti, and B. L. McNaughton. 1998. Interactions between idiothetic cues and external landmarks in the control of place cells and head direction cells. *J. Neurophysiol.* **80**:425–446. [6]

Knudsen, E. I. 2007. Fundamental components of attention. *Neuroscience* **30**:57–78. [2]

Koch, C., and S. Ullman. 1985. Shifts in selective visual attention: Towards the underlying neural circuitry. *Hum. Neurobiol.* **4**:219–227. [10]

Koechlin, E., G. Corrado, P. Pietrini, and J. Grafman. 2000. Dissociating the role of the medial and lateral anterior prefrontal cortex in human planning. *PNAS* **97(13)**:7651–7656. [9]

Koechlin, E., C. Ody, and F. Kouneiher. 2003. The architecture of cognitive control in the human prefrontal cortex. *Science* **302(5648)**:1181–1185. [5, 9]

Koenig, J., A. Linder, and S. Leutgeb. 2010. Grid-like firing of entorhinal cells does not persist during reduced theta activity. *Abstr. Soc. Neurosci.* **36**:203.10. [6]

Koob, G. F., and M. Le Moal. 2006. Neurobiology of Addiction. London: Academic Press. [6]

Kool, W., J. T. McGuire, Z. Rosen, and M. M. Botvinick. 2010. Decision making and the avoidance of cognitive demand. *J. Exp. Psychol. Gen.* **139**:665–682. [14]

Koriat, A., M. Goldsmith, and A. Pansky. 2000. Toward a psychology of memory accuracy. *Ann. Rev. Psychol.* **51**:481–537. [15]

Kornblum, S., T. Hasbroucq, and A. Osman. 1990. Dimensional overlap: Cognitive basis of stimulus-response compatibility—A model and taxonomy. *Psychol. Rev.* **97**:253–270. [14]

Koshland, D. 1980. Bacterial Chemotaxis as a Model Behavioral System. New York: Raven Press. [2]

Kosslyn, S. M., G. Ganis, and W. L. Thompson. 2001. Neural foundations of imagery. *Nat. Rev. Neurosci.* **2(9)**:635–642. [9]

Kouneiher, F., S. Charron, and E. Koechlin. 2009. Motivation and cognitive control in the human prefrontal cortex. *Nat. Neurosci.* **12(7)**:939–945. [5]

Koza, J. R. 1991. Evolving a computer program to generate random numbers using the genetic programming paradigm. In: Proc. of the 4th Intl. Conf. on Genetic Algorithms, ed. R. Belew and L. Booker, pp. 37–44. San Mateo, CA: Morgan Kaufmann Publ. [16]

Krajbich, I., C. Armel, and A. Rangel. 2010. Visual fixations and the computation and comparison of value in simple choice. *Nat. Neurosci.* [12, 15]

Krawitz, A., T. S. Braver, D. M. Barch, and J. W. Brown. 2011. Impaired error-likelihood prediction in medial prefrontal cortex in schizophrenia. *NeuroImage* **54(2)**:1506–1517. [5, 9]

Kringelbach, M. L., J. O'Doherty, E. T. Rolls, and C. Andrews. 2003. Activation of the human orbitofrontal cortex to a liquid food stimulus is correlated with its subjective pleasantness. *Cereb. Cortex* **13**:1064–1071. [7]

Kringelbach, M. L., and A. Stein. 2010. Cortical mechanisms of human eating. *Forum Nutr.* **63**:164–175. [9]

Kristjansson, A., and J. Driver. 2008. Priming in visual search: Separating the effects of target repetition, distractor repetition and role-reversal. *Vision Res.* **48**:1217–1232. [10]

Krummenacher, J., A. Grubert, and H. J. Muller. 2010. Inter-trial and redundant-signals effects in visual search and discrimination tasks: Separable pre-attentive and post-selective effects. *Vision Res.* **50(14)**:1382–1395. [10]

Krupinski, E. A. 2010. Current perspectives in medical image perception. *Atten. Percept. Psychophys.* **72**:1205–1217. [10]

Kudrimoti, H. S., C. A. Barnes, and B. L. McNaughton. 1999. Reactivation of hippocampal cell assemblies: Effects of behavioral state, experience, and EEG dynamics. *J. Neurosci.* **19(10)**:4090–4101. [6]

Kunar, M., S. Flusberg, and J. Wolfe. 2008. Why don't people use memory when repeatedly searching though an over-learned visual display? *J. Vision* **8(6)**:311–311. [10]

Kusayama, T., and S. Watanabe. 2000. Reinforcing effects of methamphetamine in planarians. *NeuroReport* **11**:2511–2513. [2]

LaBar, K. S., J. C. Gatenby, J. C. Gore, J. E. LeDoux, and E. A. Phelps. 1998. Human amygdala activation during conditioned fear acquisition and extinction: A mixed-trial fMRI study. *Neuron* **20(5)**:937–945. [9]

LaBar, K. S., D. R. Gitelman, T. B. Parrish, and M. Mesulam. 1999. Neuroanatomic overlap of working memory and spatial attention networks: A functional MRI comparison within subjects. *NeuroImage* **10(6)**:695–704. [5]

Ladouceur, R., and S. Sévigny. 2005. Structural characteristics of video lotteries: Effects of a stopping device on illusion of control and gambling persistence. *J. Gambling Stud.* **21(2)**:117–131. [6]

Laming, D. 2009. Failure to recall. *Psychol. Rev.* **116**:157–186. [11]

Lamm, C., and T. Singer. 2010. The role of anterior insular cortex in social emotions. *Brain Struct. Funct.* **214(5)**:579–591. [13]

Lamme, V. A. F. 2003. Why visual attention and awareness are different. *Trends Cogn. Sci.* **7(1)**:12–18. [14]

Lamme, V. A. F., and P. R. Roelfsema. 2000. The distinct modes of vision offered by feedforward and recurrent processing. *Trends Neurosci.* **23**:571–579. [14]

Lamme, V. A. F., and H. Spekreijse. 1999. Contextual modulation in V1 and scene perception. In: The Cognitive Neurosciences, ed. M. Gazzaniga. Cambridge, MA: MIT Press. [14]

Landau, S. M., R. Lal, J. P. O'Neil, S. Baker, and W. J. Jagust. 2009. Striatal dopamine and working memory. *Cereb. Cortex* **19(2)**:445–454. [8]

Landauer, T., and S. Dumais. 1997. A solution to Plato's problem: The latent analysis theory of acquisition, induction, and representation of knowledge. *Psychol. Rev.* **104(2)**:211–240. [20]

Lang, S., A. Kroll, S. J. Lipinski, et al. 2009. Context conditioning and extinction in humans: Differential contribution of the hippocampus, amygdala and prefrontal cortex. *Eur. J. Neurosci.* **29(4)**:823–832. [9]

Langer, E. J., and J. Roth. 1975. Heads I win, tails it's chance: The illusion of control as a function of the sequence of outcomes in a purely chance task. *J. Pers. Soc. Psychol.* **32(6)**:951–955. [6]

Lansink, C. S., P. M. Goltstein, J. V. Lankelma, et al. 2008. Preferential reactivation of motivationally relevant information in the ventral striatum. *J. Neurosci.* **28(25)**:6372–6382. [6, 9]

Lansink, C. S., P. M. Goltstein, J. V. Lankelma, B. L. McNaughton, and C. M. A. Pennartz. 2009. Hippocampus leads ventral striatum in replay of place-reward information. *PLoS Biol.* **7(8)**:e1000173. [6]

Lapish, C. C., D. Durstewitz, L. J. Chandler, and J. K. Seamans. 2008. Successful choice behavior is associated with distinct and coherent network states in anterior cingulate cortex. *PNAS* **105(33)**:11,963–11,968. [9]

Lavoie, A. M., and S. J. Y. Mizumori. 1994. Spatial-, movement- and reward-sensitive discharge by medial ventral striatum neurons in rats. *Brain Res.* **638**:157–168. [6, 9]

Lazer, D., and A. Friedman. 2006. The tragedy of the network. In: International Sunbelt Social Network Conference. Vancouver: INSNA. [17]

———. 2007. The network structure of exploration and exploitation. *Adm. Sci. Q.* **52**:667–694. [17, 20]

Leavitt, H. J. 1951. Some effects of certain communication patterns on group performance. *J. Abnorm. Soc. Psychol.* **48**:38–50. [17]

———. 1962. Unhuman organizations. *Harvard Bus. Rev.* **July/Aug**:90–98. [20]

Lee, M. D. 2006. A hierarchical Bayesian model of human decision making on an optimal stopping problem. *Cogn. Sci.* **30**:555–580. [15]

Lee, M. D., S. Zhang, M. N. Munro, and M. Steyvers. 2011. Psychological models of human and optimal performance on bandit problems. *Cogn. Syst. Res.* **12**:164–174. [15]

Lehéricy, S., H. Benali, P. F. Van de Moortele, et al. 2005. Distinct basal ganglia territories are engaged in early and advanced motor sequence learning. *PNAS* **102**:12,566–12,571. [7]

Lengyal, M., and P. Dayan. 2007. Hippocampal contributions to control: The third way. *Adv. Neural Inf. Proc. Syst.* **20**:889–896. [6]

Levy, W. B. 1996. A sequence predicting CA3 is a flexible associator that learns and uses context to solve hippocampal-like tasks. *Hippocampus* **6(6)**:579–591. [6, 9]

Levy, W. B., A. Sanyal, P. Rodriguez, D. W. Sullivan, and X. B. Wu. 2005. The formation of neural codes in the hippocampus: Trace conditioning as a prototypical paradigm for studying the random recoding hypothesis. *Biol. Cybern.* **92**:409–426. [6]

Lewis, S., A. Slabosz, T. Robbins, R. Barker, and A. Owen. 2005. Dopaminergic basis for deficits in working memory but not attentional set-shifting in Parkinson's disease. *Neuropsychologia* **43(6)**:823–832. [8]

Li, J., and N. D. Daw. 2011. Signals in human striatum are appropriate for policy update rather than value prediction. *J. Neurosci.* **31(14)**:5504–5511. [12]

Li, P., C. Burgess, and K. Lund. 2000. The acquisition of word meaning through global lexical co-occurrences. In: Proc. of the 30th Child Language Research Forum, ed. E. Clark, pp. 167–178. Stanford: Center for the Study of Language and Information. [20]

Li, S.-C., U. Lindenberger, and S. Sikström. 2001. Aging cognition: From neuromodulation to representation. *Trends Cogn. Sci.* **5**:479–486. [15]

Liang, D. W., R. Moreland, and L. Argote. 1995. Group versus individual training and group performance: The mediating role of transactive memory. *Pers. Soc. Psychol. Bull.* **21(4)**:384–393. [17]

Lindsey, D. T., A. M. Brown, E. Reijnen, et al. 2010. Color channels, not color appearance or color categories guide visual search for desaturated color targets. *Psychol. Sci.* **21(9)**:1208–1214. [10]

Lisman, J. E., and A. A. Grace. 2005. The hippocampal-VTA loop: Controlling the entry of information into long-term memory. *Neuron* **46(5)**:703–713. [9]

Lisman, J. E., and N. A. Otmakhova. 2001. Storage, recall, and novelty detection of sequences by the hippocampus: Elaborating on the SOCRATIC model to account for normal and aberrant effects of dopamine. *Hippocampus* **11(5)**:551–568. [9]

Lisman, J. E., and A. D. Redish. 2009. Prediction, sequences and the hippocampus. *Phil. Trans. R. Soc. Lond. B* **364**:1193–1201. [6, 9]

Ljungberg, T., P. Apicella, and W. Schultz. 1992. Responses of monkey dopamine neurons during learning of behavioral reactions. *J. Neurophysiol.* **67**:145–163. [2]

Lloyd, G. G., and W. A. Lishman. 1975. Effect of depression on the speed of recall of pleasant and unpleasant experiences. *Psychol. Med.* **5(2)**:173–180. [9]

Loftus, E. F., and J. C. Palmer. 1974. Reconstruction of automobile destruction. *J. Verbal Learn. Behav.* **13**:585–589. [6]

Luttbeg, B. 1996. A comparative Bayes tactic for mate assessment and choice. *Behav. Ecol.* **7**:451–460. [19]

———. 2002. Assessing the robustness and optimality of alternative decision rules with varying assumptions. *Anim. Behav.* **63**:805–814. [19]

MacDonald, A. W., J. D. Cohen, V. A. Stenger, and C. S. Carter. 2000. Dissociating the role of the dorsolateral prefrontal cortex and anterior cingulate cortex in cognitive control. *Science* **288**:1835–1838. [5]

Macdonald, C., K. Lepage, U. Eden, and H. Eichenbaum. 2010. Hippocampal neurons encode the temporal organization of non-spatial event sequences. *Abstr. Soc. Neurosci.* **36**:100.15. [6, 9]

MacGregor, J. N., T. C. Ormerod, and E. Chronicle. 2000. A model of human performance on the travelling salesperson problem. *Mem. Cogn.* **7**:1183–1190. [20]

MacKay, D. J. C. 2003. Information Theory, Inference, and Learning Algorithms. Cambridge: Cambridge Univ. Press. [12]

Madole, K. L., and L. B. Cohen. 1995. The role of object parts in infants' attention to form-function correlations. *Dev. Psychol.* **31(4)**:637–648. [20]

Magno, E., J. J. Foxe, S. Molholm, I. H. Robertson, and H. Garavan. 2006. The anterior cingulate and error avoidance. *J. Neurosci.* **26(18)**:4769–4773. [5]

Maia, T. V. 2010. Two-factor theory, the actor-critic model, and conditioned avoidance. *Learn. Behav.* **38(1)**:50–67. [12]

Maljkovic, V., and Nakayama, K. 1994. Priming of popout: I. Role of features. *Mem. Cogn.* **22(6)**:657–672. [10]

Malory, S. T. 1470/1998. Le Mort d'Arthur. http://www.gutenberg.org/ebooks/1252. (accessed 17 January 2012). [10]

Mandelbrot, B. B. 1977. Fractals: Form, Chance and Direction. San Francisco: W. H. Freeman. [3]

Manes, F., B. J. Sahakian, L. Clark, et al. 2002. Decision-making processes following damage to prefrontal cortex. *Brain* **125**:624–639. [9]

Manning, C. D., and H. Schutze. 1999. Foundations of Statistical Natural Language Processing. Cambridge, MA: MIT Press. [18]

Marcel, A. J. 1983. Conscious and unconscious perception: An approach to the relations between phenomenal experience and perceptual processes. *Cogn. Psychol.* **15**:238–300. [14]

March, J. G. 1991. Exploration and exploitation in organizational learning. *Organ. Sci.* **2(1)**:71–87. [17]

Marewski, J. N., W. Gaissmaier, L. J. Schooler, D. G. Goldstein, and G. Gigerenzer. 2010. From recognition to decisions: Extending and testing recognition-based models for multi-alternative inference. *Psychon. Bull. Rev.* **17**:287–309. [15]

Markowitsch, H. J. 2000. Neuroanatomy of memory. In: The Oxford Handbook of Memory, ed. E. Tulving and F. I. M. Craik, pp. 465–484. Oxford: Oxford Univ. Press. [4]

Markus, E. J., Y. Qin, B. Leonard, et al. 1995. Interactions between location and task affect the spatial and directional firing of hippocampal neurons. *J. Neurosci.* **15**:7079–7094. [6]

Marr, D. 1971. Simple memory: A theory of archicortex. *Phil. Trans. R. Soc. Lond. B* **262(841)**:23–81. [6, 9]

Marschner, A., R. Kalisch, B. Vervliet, D. Vansteenwegen, and C. Buchel. 2008. Dissociable roles for the hippocampus and the amygdala in human cued versus context fear conditioning. *J. Neurosci.* **28(36)**:9030–9036. [9]

Marshall, J. A. R., R. Bogacz, A. Dornhaus, et al. 2009. On optimal decision-making in brains and social insect colonies. *J. R. Soc. Interface* **6**:1065–1074. [19, 20]

Marshall, J. A. R., A. Dornhaus, N. R. Franks, and T. Kovacs. 2006. Noise, cost and speed–accuracy trade-offs: Decision-making in a decentralized system. *J. R. Soc. Interface* **3**:243–254. [19]

Marshall, J. A. R., and T. G. Hinton. 2010. Beyond no free lunch: Realistic algorithms for arbitrary problem classes. In: Proc. IEEE Cong. on Computational Intelligence, pp. 1319–1324. Barcelona: IEEE. [16]

Martignon, L., and U. Hoffrage. 1999. Why does one-reason decision making work? A case study in ecological rationality. In: Simple Heuristics That Make Us Smart, ed. G. Gigerenzer, P. M. Todd, and the ABC Research Group, pp. 119–140. New York: Oxford Univ. Press. [15]

Martin, A., and L. L. Chao. 2001. Semantic memory and the brain: Structure and processes. *Curr. Opin. Neurobiol.* **11(2)**:194–201. [9]

Martin, P. D. 2001. Locomotion towards a goal alters the synchronous firing of neurons recorded simultaneously in the subiculum and nucleus accumbens of rats. *Behav. Brain Res.* **124(1)**:19–28. [6]

Mason, W. A., A. Jones, and R. L. Goldstone. 2008. Propagation of innovations in networked groups. *J. Exp. Psychol. Gen.* **137(3)**:422–433. [17]

Mata, R., and L. Nunes. 2010. When less is enough: Cognitive aging, information search, and decision quality in consumer choice. *Psychol. Aging* **25**:289–298. [15]

Mata, R., L. J. Schooler, and J. Rieskamp. 2007. The aging decision maker: Cognitive aging and the adaptive selection of decision strategies. *Psychol. Aging* **22**:796–810. [15]

Mathot, K., and L.-A. Giraldeau. 2010. Within-group relatedness can lead to higher levels of exploitation: A model and empirical test. *Behav. Ecol.* **1**:843–850. [4]

Matsumoto, M., and O. Hikosaka. 2009. Two types of dopamine neuron distinctly convey positive and negative motivational signals. *Nature* **459(7248)**:837–841. [9]

Matsumoto, M., K. Matsumoto, H. Abe, and K. Tanaka. 2007. Medial prefrontal cell activity signaling prediction errors of action values. *Nat. Neurosci.* **10(5)**:647–656. [9]

Maurer, A. P., and B. L. McNaughton. 2007. Network and intrinsic cellular mechanisms underlying theta phase precession of hippocampal neurons. *Trends Neurosci.* **30(7)**:325–333. [6, 9]

Mayer, J. S., R. A. Bittner, D. Nikolic, et al. 2007. Common neural substrates for visual working memory and attention. *NeuroImage* **36(2)**:441–453. [5]

Maynard Smith, J. 1982. Evolution and the Theory of Games. New York: Cambridge Univ. Press. [4]

Mayr, U. 2001. Age differences in the selection of mental sets: The role of inhibition, stimulus ambiguity, and response-set overlap. *Psychol. Aging* **16**:96–109. [15]

Mayr, U., E. Awh, and P. Laurey. 2003. Conflict adaptation effects in the absence of executive control. *Nat. Neurosci.* **6(5)**:450–452. [5]

Mazalov, V., N. Perrin, and Y. Dombrovsky. 1996. Adaptive search and information updating in sequential mate choice. *Am. Nat.* **148**:123–137. [19]

McDannald, M. A., F. Lucantonio, K. A. Burke, Y. Niv, and G. Schoenbaum. 2011. Ventral striatum and orbitofrontal cortex are both required for model-based, but not model-free, reinforcement learning. *J. Neurosci.* **31(7)**:2700–2705. [6, 9]

McDonald, R. J., and N. M. White. 1993. A triple dissociation of memory systems: Hippocampus, amygdala, and dorsal striatum. *Behav. Neurosci.* **107(1)**:3–22. [9]

McFadden, D. 1974. Conditional logit analysis of qualitative choice behavior. In: Frontiers of Econometrics, ed. P. Zarembka, pp. 105–142. New York: Academic Press. [18]

McGeorge, A. J., and R. L. M. Faull. 1989. The organization of the projection from the cerebral cortex to the striatum in the rat. *Neuroscience* **29**:503–537. [7]

McGlinchey-Berroth, R., M. C. Carrillo, J. D. Gabrieli, C. M. Brawn, and J. F. Disterhoft. 1997. Impaired trace eyeblink conditioning in bilateral, medial-temporal lobe amnesia. *Behav. Neurosci.* **111(5)**:873–882. [9]

McLeod, P., J. Driver, and J. Crisp. 1988. Visual search for conjunctions of movement and form is parallel. *Nature* **332**:154–155. [10]

McNair, J. 1982. Optimal giving-up times and the marginal value theorem. *Am. Nat.* **119**:511–524. [19]

McNamara, J. M. 1982. Optimal patch use in a stochastic environment. *Theor. Pop. Biol.* **21** [19]

McNamara, J. M., and E. J. Collins. 1990. The job search problem as an employer-candidate game. *J. Appl. Probab.* **27**:815–827. [19]

McNamara, J. M., L. Fromhage, Z. Barta, and A. I. Houston. 2009. The optimal coyness game. *Proc. R. Soc. B* **276**:953–960. [19]

McNamara, J. M., C. E. Gasson, and A. I. Houston. 1999. Incorporating rules for responding into evolutionary games. *Nature* **401**:368–371. [4]

McNamara, J. M., R. F. Green, and O. Olsson. 2006. Bayes' theorem and its applications in animal behavior. *Oikos* **112**:243–251. [19]

McNamara, J. M., and A. I. Houston. 1980. The application of statistical decision theory to animal behavior. *J. Theor. Biol.* **85**:673–690. [19]

———. 1985. Optimal foraging and learning. *J. Theor. Biol.* **117**:231–249. [19]

———. 1987. Foraging in patches: There's more to life than the marginal value theorem. In: Quantitative Analyses of Behavior, vol. 6, ed. M. L. Commons et al., pp. 23–39. Hillsdale, NJ: Lawrence Erlbaum. [19]

———. 1992. Risk-sensitive foraging: A review of the theory. *Bull. Math. Biol.* **54**:355–378. [15]

McNaughton, B. L., C. A. Barnes, J. L. Gerrard, et al. 1996. Deciphering the hippocampal polyglot: The hippocampus as a path integration system. *J. Exp. Biol.* **199(1)**:173–186. [6]

McNaughton, B. L., C. A. Barnes, and J. O'Keefe. 1983. The contributions of position, direction, and velocity to single unit activity in the hippocampus of freely-moving rats. *Exp. Brain Res.* **52**:41–49. [6]

McNaughton, B. L., and R. G. M. Morris. 1987. Hippocampal synaptic enhancement and information storage within a distributed memory system. *Trends Neurosci.* **10(10)**:408–415. [9]

McNaughton, B. L., and L. Nadel. 1990. Hebb-Marr networks and the neurobiological representation of action in space. In: Neuroscience and Connectionist Theory, ed. M. A. Gluck and D. E. Rumelhart, pp. 1–63. Hillsdale, NJ: Lawrence Erlbaum. [6]

McNickle, G. G., C. C. St. Clair, and J. F. Cahill, Jr. 2009. Focusing the metaphor: Plant root foraging behaviour. *Trends Ecol. Evol.* **24**:419–426. [2]

Mednick, S. 1962. The associative basis of creative problem solving process. *Psychol. Rev.* **69**:200–232. [14]

Mehta, M. R., C. A. Barnes, and B. L. McNaughton. 1997. Experience-dependent, asymmetric expansion of hippocampal place fields. *PNAS* **94**:8918–8921. [6]

Melcher, T., M. Weidema, R. M. Eenshuistra, B. Hommel, and O. Gruber. 2008. The neural substrate of the ideomotor principle: An event-related fMRI analysis. *NeuroImage* **39**:1274–1288. [14]

Menon, V., and L. Q. Uddin. 2010. Saliency, switching, attention and control: A network model of insula function. *Brain Struct. Funct.* **214**:655–667. [13]

Mensink, G. J. M., and J. G. Raaijmakers. 1988. A model for interference and forgetting. *Psychol. Rev.* **95**:434–455. [11]

Menzies, L., S. R. Chamberlain, A. R. Laird, et al. 2008. Integrating evidence from neuroimaging and neuropsychological studies of obsessive-compulsive disorder: The orbitofronto-striatal model revisited. *Neurosci. Biobehav. Rev.* **32(3)**:525–549. [9]

Merkle, T., and R. Wehner. 2010. Desert ants use foraging distance to adapt the nest search to the uncertainty of the path integrator. *Behav. Ecol.* **21**:349–355. [4]

Méry, F., A. T. Belay, A. K.-C. So, M. B. Sokolowski, and T. J. Kawecki. 2007. Natural polymorphism affecting learning and memory in *Drosophila*. *PNAS* **104**:13,051–13,055. [4]

Metcalfe, J., and W. J. Jacobs. 2010. People's study time allocation and its relation to animal foraging. *Behav. Processes* **83**:213–221. [11, 15]

Metcalfe, J., and A. P. Shimamura. 1994. Metacognition: Knowing about Knowing. Cambridge, MA: MIT Press. [15]

Miller, E. K., and J. D. Cohen. 2001. An integrative theory of prefrontal cortex function. *Ann. Rev. Neurosci.* **21**:167–202. [5, 8]

Miller, G. A., E. Galanter, and K. H. Pribram. 1960. Plans and the Structure of Behavior. New York: Holt. [15]

Miller, R. 2008. A Theory of the Basal Ganglia and Their Disorders. Boca Raton: CRC Press. [7]

Milner, A. D., and M. A. Goodale. 1995. The Visual Brain in Action. Oxford: Oxford Univ. Press. [14]

Mink, J. W. 1996. The basal ganglia: Focused selection and inhibition of competing motor programs. *Prog. Neurobiol.* **50**:381–425. [8]

Minsky, M. 1986. The Society of Mind. New York: Simon and Schuster. [4]

Mintzberg, H. 1979. The Structuring of Organizations: A Synthesis of the Research. Englewood Cliffs, NJ: Prentice-Hall. [17]

Mitchell, T. 1997. Machine Learning. New York: McGraw-Hill. [16]

Miyake, A., N. P. Friedman, M. J. Emerson, et al. 2000. The unity and diversity of executive functions and their contributions to complex "frontal lobe" tasks: A latent variable analysis. *Cogn. Psychol.* **41**:49–100. [15]

Miyazaki, K., E. Mogi, N. Araki, and G. Matsumoto. 1998. Reward-quality dependent anticipation in rat nucleus accumbens. *NeuroReport* **9**:3943–3948. [6]

Modirrousta, M., and L. K. Fellows. 2008. Dorsal medial prefrontal cortex plays a necessary role in rapid error prediction in humans. *J. Neurosci.* **28(51)**:14,000–14,005. [5, 9]

Mogenson, G. J. 1984. Limbic-motor integration with emphasis on intiation of exploratory and goal-directed locomotion. In: Modulation of Sensorimotor Activity During Alterations in Behavioral States, ed. R. Bandler, pp. 121–138. New York: Liss. [6]

Mogenson, G. J., D. L. Jones, and C. Y. Yim. 1980. From motivation to action: Functional interface between the limbic system and the motor system. *Prog. Neurobiol.* **14**:69–97. [6]

Monchi, O., M. Petrides, V. Petre, K. Worsley, and A. Dagher. 2001. Wisconsin card sorting revisited: Distinct neural circuits participating in different stages of the task identified by event-related functional magnetic resonance imaging. *J. Neurosci.* **21(19)**:7733–7741. [5]

Monsell, S. 2003. Task switching. *Trends Cogn. Sci.* **7(3)**:134–140. [5]

Moore, A. W., and C. G. Atkeson. 1993. Prioritized sweeping: Reinforcement learning with less data and less time. *Mach. Learn.* **13(1)**:103–130. [12]

Moore, D., and P. Doherty. 2009. Acquisition of a time-memory in forager honey bees. *J. Comp. Physiol. A* **195**:741–751. [4]

Morand-Ferron, J., and L.-A. Giraldeau. 2010. Learning behavioural stable solutions to producer-scrounger games. *Behav. Ecol.* **21**:343–348. [3]

Morris, R. G. M. 1981. Spatial localization does not require the presence of local cues. *Learn. Motiv.* **12**:239–260. [9]

Morris, R. G. M., P. Garrud, J. N. Rawlins, and J. O'Keefe. 1982. Place navigation impaired in rats with hippocampal lesions. *Nature* **297(5868)**:681–683. [9]

Morrison, S. E., and C. D. Salzman. 2009. The convergence of information about rewarding and aversive stimuli in single neurons. *J. Neurosci.* **29(37)**:11,471–11,483. [9]

Mueller, T., and W. F. Fagen. 2008. Search and navigation in dynamic environments: From individual behaviors to population distributions. *Oikos* **117**:654–664. [3, 4]

Muenzinger, K. F. 1938. Vicarious trial and error at a point of choice: I. A general survey of its relation to learning efficiency. *J. Genet. Psychol.* **53**:75–86. [6]

Muenzinger, K. F., and E. Gentry. 1931. Tone discrimination in white rats. *J. Comp. Psychol.* **12(2)**:195–206. [6, 9]

Muheim, R., F. R. Moore, and J. B. Phillips. 2006. Calibration of magnetic and celestial compass cues in migratory birds: A review of cue-conflict experiments. *J. Exp. Biol.* **2090**:2–17. [19]

Mulder, A. B., R. E. Nordquist, O. Orgut, and C. M. Pennartz. 2003. Learning-related changes in response patterns of prefrontal neurons during instrumental conditioning. *Behav. Brain Res.* **146**:77–88. [9]

Mulder, A. B., E. Tabuchi, and S. I. Wiener. 1999. Nucleus accumbens neuronal responses in a differentially rewarded plus maze: Comparisons of shell and core activity. *Abstr. Soc. Neurosci.* **25**:1384. [6]

———. 2004. Neurons in hippocampal afferent zones of rat striatum parse routes into multi-pace segments during maze navigation. *Eur. J. Neurosci.* **19**:1923–1932. [6]

Müller, M., and R. Wehner. 1988. Path integration in desert ants, *Cataglyphis fortis*. *PNAS* **85**:5287–5290. [4]

Muller, R. U., E. Bostock, J. S. Taube, and J. L. Kubie. 1994. On the directional firing properties of hippocampal place cells. *J. Neurosci.* **14(12)**:7235–7251. [6]

Muller-Hill, B. 1996. The *lac* Operon: A Short History of a Genetic Paradigm. New York: Walter de Gruyter. [4]

Muly, E. C., III, K. Szigeti, and P. S. Goldman-Rakic. 1998. D1 receptor in interneurons of macaque prefrontal cortex: Distribution and subcellular localization. *J. Neurosci.* **18(24)**:10,553–10,565. [5]

Murdock, B. B. 1962. The serial position effect of free recall. *J. Exp. Psychol.* **64**:482–488. [11]

Murdock, B. B., W. E. Hockley, and P. Muter. 1977. Two tests of the conveyor-belt model for item recognition. *Can. J. Psychol.* **31**:71–89. [10]

Murdock, B. B., and R. Okada. 1970. Interresponse times in single-trial free recall. *J. Exp. Psychol.* **86**:263–267. [11, 15]

Murphy, F. C., B. J. Sahakian, J. S. Rubinsztein, et al. 1999. Emotional bias and inhibitory control processes in mania and depression. *Psychol. Med.* **29(6)**:1307–1321. [9]

Murray, E. A., J. P. O'Doherty, and G. Schoenbaum. 2007. What we know and do not know about the functions of the orbitofrontal cortex after 20 years of cross-species studies. *J. Neurosci.* **27(31)**:8166–8169. [6]

Nádasdy, Z., H. Hirase, A. Czurkó, J. Csicsvari, and G. Buzsáki. 1999. Replay and time compression of recurring spike sequences in the hippocampus. *J. Neurosci.* **19(2)**:9497–9507. [6]

Nadel, L. 1991. The hippocampus and space revisited. *Hippocampus* **1(3)**:221–9. [6]

Nadel, L., and M. Moscovitch. 1997. Memory consolidation, retrograde amnesia and the hippocampal complex. *Curr. Opin. Neurobiol.* **7**:217–227. [6, 9, 11]

Nadjar, A., J. M. Brotchie, C. Guigoni, et al. 2006. Phenotype of striatofugal medium spiny neurons in parkinsonian and dyskinetic nonhuman primates: A call for a reappraisal of the functional organization of the basal ganglia. *J. Neurosci.* **26(34)**:8653–8661. [9]

Nagle, K. J., and W. J. Bell. 1987. Genetic control of the search tactic of *Drosophila melanogaster*: An ethometric analysis of rover/sitter traits in adult flies. *Behav. Genet.* **17**:385–408. [4]

Nairne, J. S. 2002. The myth of the encoding-retrieval match. *Memory* **10**:389–395. [11]

Najemnik, J., and W. S. Geisler. 2005. Optimal eye movement strategies in visual search. *Nature* **434(7031)**:387–391. [10]

———. 2008. Eye movement statistics in humans are consistent with an optimal search strategy. *J. Vision* **8(3)**:1–14. [10]

Nakayama, K., and G. H. Silverman. 1986. Serial and parallel processing of visual feature conjunctions. *Nature* **320**:264–265. [10]

Nambu, A. 2008. Seven problems on the basal ganglia. *Curr. Opin. Neurobiol.* **18(6)**:595–604. [7]

Narayanan, N. S., and M. Laubach. 2009. Delay activity in rodent frontal cortex during a simple reaction time task. *J. Neurophysiol.* **101(6)**:2859–2871. [9]

Nauta, W. J. H. 1989. Reciprocal links of the corpus striatum with the cerebral cortex and limbic system: A common substrate for movement and thought? In: Neurology and Psychiatry: A Meeting of Minds, ed. J. Mueller, pp. 43–63. Basel: Karger. [7]

Navalpakkam, V., and L. Itti. 2005. Modeling the influence of task on attention. *Vision Res.* **45(2)**:205–231. [10]

Navon, D. 1977. Forest before trees: The precedence of global features in visual perception. *Cogn. Psychol.* **9**:353–383. [14]

Nee, D. E., and J. Jonides. 2009. Common and distinct neural correlates of perceptual and memorial selection. *NeuroImage* **45(3)**:963–975. [5]

Neely, J. 1977. Semantic priming and retrieval from lexical memory: Roles of inhibitionless spreading activation and limited-capacity attention. *J. Exp. Psychol. Gen.* **106**:226–254. [2, 4]

Neisser, U. 1963. Decision time without reaction time: Experiments in visual scanning. *Am. J. Psychol.* **76**:376–385. [10]

Nelson, R. R., and S. G. Winter. 1982. An Evolutionary Theory of Economic Change. Cambridge, MA: Harvard Univ. Press. [17]

Nelson, T. O. 1996. Consciousness and metacognition. *Am. Psychol.* **51**:102–116. [15]

Nelson, T. O., R. Leonesio, R. S. Landwehr, and L. Narens. 1986. A comparison of three predictors of an individual's memory performance: The individual's feeling of knowing versus the normative feeling of knowing versus base-rate item difficulty. *J. Exp. Psychol. Learn. Mem. Cogn.* **12**:279–287. [15]

Nelson, T. O., L. Narens, and J. Dunlosky. 2004. A revised methodology for research on metamemory: Pre-judgment recall and monitoring (PRAM). *Psychol. Methods* **9**:56–69. [15]

Newell, A. 1980. Physical symbol systems. *Cogn. Sci.* **4**:135–183. [20]

Newell, A., and H. A. Simon. 1972. Human Problem Solving. Englewood Cliffs, NJ: Prentice-Hall. [15]

———. 1976. Computer science as empirical inquiry: Symbols and search. *Comm. ACM* **19(3)**:113–126. [18, 20]

———. 1987. Postscript: Reflections on the 10th Turing award lecture. In: ACM Turing Award Lectures: The First Twenty Years, ed. R. L. Ashenhurst and S. Graham, pp. 314–317. New York: ACM. [20]

Nichols, J. D. 1992. Capture-recapture models. *Bioscience* **42**:94–102. [11]

Nicola, S. M. 2010. The flexible approach hypothesis: Unification of effort and cue-responding hypotheses for the role of nucleus accumbens dopamine in the activation of reward-seeking behavior. *J. Neurosci.* **30(49)**:16,585–16,600. [6]

Nicola, S. M., I. A. Yun, K. T. Wakabayashi, and H. L. Fields. 2004a. Cue-evoked firing of nucleus accumbens neurons encodes motivational significance during a discriminative stimulus task. *J. Neurophysiol.* **91(4)**:1840–1865. [6]

———. 2004b. Firing of nucleus accumbens neurons during the consummatory phase of a discriminative stimulus task depends on previous reward predictive cues. *J. Neurophysiol.* **91(4)**:1866–1882. [6]

Nilsson, N. J. 1971. Problem Solving Methods in Artificial Intelligence. New York: McGraw-Hill. [18]

Nisbett, R. E., and Y. Miyamoto. 2005. The influence of culture: Holistic versus analytic perception. *Trends Cogn. Sci.* **9**:467–473. [15]

Niv, Y., N. D. Daw, D. Joel, and P. Dayan. 2007. Tonic dopamine: Opportunity costs and the control of response vigor. *Psychopharmacol.* **191(3)**:507–520. [8, 9]

Niv, Y., D. Joel, and P. Dayan. 2006. A normative perspective on motivation. *Trends Cogn. Sci.* **10(8)**:375–381. [6, 12]

Nobel, P. A., and R. M. Shiffrin. 2001. Retrieval processes in recognition and cued recall. *J. Exp. Psychol. Learn. Mem. Cogn.* **27**:384–413. [11]

Nobre, A. C., J. T. Coull, P. Maquet, et al. 2004. Orienting attention to locations in perceptual versus mental representations. *J. Cogn. Neurosci.* **16(3)**:363–373. [5, 9]

Nolet, B. A., and W. M. Mooij. 2002. Search paths of swans foraging on spatially autocorrelated tubers. *J. Anim. Ecol.* **71**:451–462. [4]

Nonacs, P. 2001. State dependent behavior and the marginal value theorem. *Behav. Ecol.* **2**:71–83. [4]

Nonaka, I. 1994. A dynamic theory of organizational knowledge creation. *Organ. Sci.* **5(1)**:14–37. [17]

Notebaert, W., F. Houtman, F. Van Opstal, et al. 2009. Post-error slowing: An orienting account. *Cognition* **111(2)**:275–279. [13]

Nothdurft, H.-C. 2000. Salience from feature contrast: Additivity across dimensions. *Vision Res.* **40**:1183–1201. [10]

Nyberg, L., M. Andersson, L. Forsgren, et al. 2009. Striatal dopamine D2 binding is related to frontal BOLD response during updating of long-term memory representations. *NeuroImage* **46(4)**:1194–1199. [8]

Nyberg, L., A. S. Kim, R. Habib, B. Levine, and E. Tulving. 2010. Consciousness of subjective time in the brain. *PNAS* **107(51)**:22,356–22,359. [9]

O'Doherty, J. P., P. Dayan, K. Friston, H. Critchley, and R. J. Dolan. 2003. Temporal difference models and reward-related learning in the human brain. *Neuron* **38(2)**:329–337. [7]

O'Doherty, J. P., M. L. Kringelbach, E. T. Rolls, J. Hornak, and C. Andrews. 2001a. Abstract reward and punishment representations in the human orbitofrontal cortex. *Nat. Neurosci.* **4**:95–102. [7]

O'Doherty, J. P., E. T. Rolls, S. Francis, R. Bowtell, and F. McGlone. 2001b. Representation of pleasant and aversive taste in the human brain. *J. Neurophysiol.* **85**:1315–1321. [7]

O'Doherty, J. P., E. T. Rolls, S. Francis, et al. 2000. Sensory-specific satiety-related olfactory activation of the human orbitofrontal cortex. *NeuroReport* **11**:893–897. [7]

Oei, T. P. S., and A. R. Baldwin. 2002. Expectancy theory: A two-process model of alcohol use and abuse. *J. Stud. Alcohol* **55**:525–534. [6]

O'Keefe, J. 1999. Do hippocampal pyramidal cells signal non-spatial as well as spatial information? *Hippocampus* **9(4)**:352–365. [6]

O'Keefe, J., and L. Nadel. 1978. The Hippocampus as a Cognitive Map. Oxford: Clarendon Press. [6, 9]

O'Keefe, J., and M. Recce. 1993. Phase relationship between hippocampal place units and the EEG theta rhythm. *Hippocampus* **3**:317–330. [6, 9]

O'Leary, M. B., and J. N. Cummings. 2007. The spatial, temporal, and configurational characteristics of geographic dispersion in teams. *MIS Quarterly* **31**:433–452. [17]

Olivers, C. N. L., and S. Nieuwenhuis. 2006. The beneficial effects of additional task load, positive affect, and instruction on the attentional blink. *J. Exp. Psychol. Hum. Perc. Perf.* **32**:364–379. [14]

Olton, D. S., and B. C. Papas. 1979. Spatial memory and hippocampal function. *Neuropsychologia* **17(6)**:669–682. [9]

Olypher, A. V., P. Lánský, and A. A. Fenton. 2002. Properties of the extra-positional signal in hippocampal place cell discharge derived from the overdispersion in location-specific firing. *Neuroscience* **111(3)**:553–566. [6]

O'Neill, J., T. J. Senior, K. Allen, J. R. Huxter, and J. Csicsvari. 2008. Reactivation of experience-dependent cell assembly patterns in the hippocampus. *Nat. Neurosci.* **11(2)**:209–215. [6]

O'Neill, J., T. J. Senior, and J. Csicsvari. 2006. Place-selective firing of CA1 pyramidal cells during sharp wave/ripple network patterns in exploratory behavior. *Neuron* **49**:143–155. [6]

Ongür, D., and J. L. Price. 2000. The organization of networks within the orbital and medial prefrontal cortex of rats, monkeys and humans. *Cereb. Cortex* **10**:206–219. [7]

O'Reilly, R. C., and J. L. McClelland. 1994. Hippocampal conjunctive encoding, storage, and recall: Avoiding a trade-off. *Hippocampus* **4(6)**:661–682. [9]

Osborne, K. A., A. Robichon, E. Burgess, et al. 1997. Natural behavior polymorphism due to a cGMP-dependent protein kinase of *Drosophila*. *Science* **277**:834–836. [4]

Ostlund, S. B., and B. W. Balleine. 2005. Lesions of medial prefrontal cortex disrupt the acquisition but not the expression of goal-directed learning. *J. Neurosci.* **25(34)**:7763–7770. [7]

———. 2007. Orbitofrontal cortex mediates outcome encoding in Pavlovian but not instrumental conditioning. *J. Neurosci.* **27(18)**:4819–4825. [7, 9]

Ostrom, E., T. Dietz, and P. C. Stern. 2003. The struggle to govern the commons. *Science* **302(5652)**:1907–1912. [20]

Overbeek, T. J. M., S. Nieuwenhuis, and K. R. Ridderinkhof. 2005. Dissociable components of error processing. *J. Psychophysiol.* **19(4)**:319–329. [13]

Owen, A. M., J. J. Downes, B. J. Sahakian, C. E. Polkey, and T. W. Robbins. 1990. Planning and spatial working memory following frontal lobe lesions in man. *Neuropsychologia* **28**:1021–1034. [9]

Owen, A. M., B. J. Sahakian, J. Semple, C. E. Polkey, and T. W. Robbins. 1995. Visuospatial short-term recognition memory and learning after temporal lobe excisions, frontal lobe excisions or amygdala-hippocampectomy in man. *Neuropsychologia* **33(1)**:1–24. [9]

Pachur, T., and B. Scheibehenne. 2012. Constructing preference from experience: The endowment effect reflected in external information search. *J. Exp. Psychol. Learn. Mem. Cogn.*, in press. [15]

Packard, M. G., and J. L. McGaugh. 1992. Double dissociation of fornix and caudate nucleus lesions on acquisition of two water maze tasks: Further evidence for multiple memory systems. *Behav. Neurosci.* **106(3)**:439–446. [9]

———. 1996. Inactivation of hippocampus or caudate nucleus with lidocaine differentially affects expression of place and response learning. *Neurobiol. Learn. Mem.* **65**:65–72. [6]

Padoa-Schioppa, C. 2009. Range-adapting representation of economic value in the orbitofrontal cortex. *J. Neurosci.* **29(44)**:14,004–14,014. [9]

Padoa-Schioppa, C., and J. A. Assad. 2006. Neurons in the orbitofrontal cortex encode economic value. *Nature* **441**:223–226. [6, 9, 15]

Page, S. E. 2007. The Difference: How the Power of Diversity Creates Better Groups, Firms, Schools, and Societies. Princeton: Princeton Univ. Press. [17]

Palmer, J. 1995. Attention in visual search: Distinguishing four causes of a set size effect. *Curr. Dir. Psychol. Sci.* **4(4)**:118–123. [10]

Palmer, J., P. Verghese, and M. Pavel. 2000. The psychophysics of visual search. *Vision Res.* **40(10–12)**:1227–1268. [10]

Pardon, M. C., G. G. Gould, A. Garcia, et al. 2002. Stress reactivity of the brain norad-renergic system in three rat strains differing in their neuroendocrine and behavioral responses to stress: Implications for susceptibility to stress-related neuropsychiatric disorders. *Neuroscience* **115(1)**:229–242. [9]

Parker, G. A., and J. Maynard Smith. 1990. Optimality theory in evolutionary biology. *Nature* **348**:27–33. [16, 19]

Parkhurst, D., K. Law, and E. Niebur. 2002. Modeling the role of salience in the alloca-tion of overt visual attention. *Vision Res.* **42(1)**:107–123. [10]

Parkinson, J. A., R. N. Cardinal, and B. J. Everitt. 2000. Limbic cortical-ventral striatal systems underlying appetitive conditioning. *Prog. Brain Res.* **126**:263–285. [9]

Pashler, H., and L. P. Shiu. 1999. Do images involuntarily trigger search? A test of Pillsbury's hypothesis. *Psychon. Bull. Rev.* **6(3)**:445–448. [5]

Passingham, R. 1985. Memory of monkeys (*Macaca mulatta*) with lesions in prefrontal cortex. *Behav. Neurosci.* **99(1)**:3–21. [9]

———. 1993. The Frontal Lobes and Voluntary Action. Oxford: Oxford Univ. Press. [9]

Pastalkova, E., V. Itskov, A. Amarasingham, and G. Buzsáki. 2008. Internally generated cell assembly sequences in the rat hippocampus. *Science* **321(5894)**:1322–1327. [6, 9]

Pasupathy, A., and E. K. Miller. 2005. Different time courses of learning-related activ-ity in the prefrontal cortex and striatum. *Nature* **433(7028)**:873–876. [7]

Paton, J. J., M. A. Belova, S. E. Morrison, and C. D. Salzman. 2006. The primate amyg-dala represents the positive and negative value of visual stimuli during learning. *Nature* **439**:865–870. [7]

Patricelli, G. L., J. A. C. Uy, G. Walsh, and G. Borgia. 2002. Sexual selection: Male displays adjusted to female's response. *Nature* **415**:279–280. [4]

Patterson, K. E., R. H. Meltzer, and G. Mandler. 1971. Inter-response times in catego-rized free recall. *J. Verbal Learn. Behav.* **10**:417–426. [11]

Pavlides, C., and J. Winson. 1989. Influences of hippocampal place cell firing in the awake state on the activity of these cells during subsequent sleep episodes. *J. Neurosci.* **9(8)**:2907–2918. [6]

Payne, J. W., J. R. Bettman, and E. J. Johnson. 1993. The Adaptive Decision Maker. Cambridge: Cambridge Univ. Press. [4, 15]

Payne, S. J., G. B. Duggan, and H. Neth. 2007. Discretionary task interleaving: Heuristics for time allocation in cognitive foraging. *J. Exp. Psychol. Gen.* **136**:370–388. [15]

Payzan-LeNestour, E., and P. Bossaerts. 2011. Risk, unexpected uncertainty, and es-timation uncertainty: Bayesian learning in unstable settings. *PLoS Comp. Biol.* **7(1)**:e1001048. [9]

Pennartz, C. M. A., E. Lee, J. Verheul, et al. 2004. The ventral striatum in off-line processing: Ensemble reactivation during sleep and modulation by hippocampal ripples. *J. Neurosci.* **24(29)**:6446–6456. [6]

Pereira, H. S., and M. B. Sokolowski. 1993. Mutations in the larval foraging gene af-fect adult locomotory behavior after feeding in *Drosophila melanogaster*. *PNAS* **90**:5044–5046. [4]

Peters, J., and C. Büchel. 2010. Episodic future thinking reduces reward delay dis-counting through an enhancement of prefrontal-mediotemporal interactions. *Neuron* **66(1)**:138–148. [6]

Peterson, M. S., A. F. Kramer, R. F. Wang, D. E. Irwin, and J. S. McCarley. 2001. Visual search has memory. *Psychol. Sci.* **12(4)**:287–292. [10]

Peyrache, A., M. Khamassi, K. Benchenane, S. I. Wiener, and F. P. Battaglia. 2009. Replay of rule-learning related neural patterns in the prefrontal cortex during sleep. *Nat. Neurosci.* **12(7)**:919–926. [9]

Pierce, B. D., and R. White. 1999. The evolution of social structure: Why biology matters. *Acad. Manag. Rev.* **24(4)**:843–853. [20]

Pirolli, P. 2007. Information Foraging Theory: Adaptive Interaction with Information. New York: Oxford Univ. Press. [2, 4, 11, 18]

Pirolli, P., and S. Card. 1999. Information foraging. *Psychol. Rev.* **106(4)**:643–675. [11, 18]

Pizlo, Z., E. Stefanov, J. Saalweachter, et al. 2006. Traveling salesman problem: A foveating pyramid model. *JPS* **1**:83–101. [20]

Plank, M. J., and A. James. 2008. Optimal foraging: The Lévy pattern or process. *Interface* **5**:1077–1086. [3]

Plassmann, H., J. O'Doherty, and A. Rangel. 2007. Orbitofrontal cortex encodes willingness to pay in everyday economic transactions. *J. Neurosci.* **27**:9984–9988. [7]

Plassmann, H., J. O'Doherty, B. Shiv, and A. Rangel. 2008. Marketing actions can modulate neural representations of experienced pleasantness. *PNAS* **105(3)**:1050–1054. [7]

Plato. 380 B.C.E. Meno, translated by B. Jowett. *Internet Classics Archive* http://classics.mit.edu/Plato/meno.html. (accessed 28 January 2012). [18]

Platt, M. L., and P. W. Glimcher. 1999. Neural correlates of decision variables in parietal cortex. *Nature* **400(6741)**:233–238. [9]

Plucker, J. A., and M. C. Makel. 2010. Assessment of creativity. In: The Cambridge Handbook of Creativity, ed. J. C. Kaufman and R. J. Sternberg, pp. 48–73. Cambridge: Cambridge Univ. Press. [14]

Polejack, A., and R. Tidon. 2007. Learning of courtship components in *Drosophila mercatorum* (Paterson & Wheller) (Diptera, Drosophilidae). *Rev. Brasil Entomol.* **51(1)**:82–86. [4]

Poli, R., L. Vanneschi, W. B. Langdon, and N. F. McPhee. 2010. Theoretical results in genetic programming: The next ten years? *Genet. Program. Evolvable Mach.* **11**:285–320. [16]

Pollio, H. R., R. A. Kasschau, and H. E. DeNise. 1968. Associative structure and the temporal characteristics of free recall. *J. Exp. Psychol.* **76**:190–197. [4]

Polyn, S. M., G. Erlikhman, and M. J. Kahana. 2011. Semantic cuing and the scale insensitivity of recency and contiguity. *J. Exp. Psychol. Learn. Mem. Cogn.* **37(3)**:766–775. [15]

Polyn, S. M., V. S. Natu, J. D. Cohen, and K. A. Norman. 2005. Category-specific cortical activity precedes retrieval during memory search. *Science* **310(5756)**:1963–1966. [9]

Pomiankowski, A. 1987. The costs of choice in sexual selection. *J. Theor. Biol.* **128**:195–218. [19]

Posner, M. I., and Y. Cohen. 1984. Components of visual orienting. In: Attention and Performance X: Control of Language Processes, ed. H. Bouma and D. Bouwhuis, pp. 531–556. Hillsdale, NJ: Lawrence Erlbaum. [2]

Posner, M. I., and G. DiGirolamo. 1998. Conflict, target detection and cognitive control. In: The Attentive Brain, ed. R. Parasuraman. Cambridge, MA: MIT Press. [5]

Pratt, S. C., E. B. Mallon, D. J. T. Sumpter, and N. R. Franks. 2002. Quorum sensing, recruitment, and collective decision-making during colony emigration by the ant *Leptothorax albipennis. Behav. Ecol. Sociobiol.* **52**:117–127. [19]

Preuss, T. M. 1995. Do rats have prefrontal cortex? The Rose-Woolsey-Akert program reconsidered. *J. Cogn. Neurosci.* **7**:1–24. [7]

Price, J. L. 2007. Definition of the orbital cortex in relation to specific connections with limbic and visceral structures and other cortical regions. *Ann. NY Acad. Sci.* **1121**:54–71. [9]

Pritchard, T. C., E. N. Nedderman, E. M. Edwards, et al. 2008. Satiety-responsive neurons in the medial orbitofrontal cortex of the macaque. *Behav. Neurosci.* **122(1)**:174–182. [9]

Procyk, E., and J. P. Joseph. 1996. Problem solving and logical reasoning in the macaque monkey. *Behav. Brain Res.* **82(1)**:67–78. [5, 9]

———. 2001. Characterization of serial order encoding in the monkey anterior cingulate sulcus. *Eur. J. Neurosci.* **14(6)**:1041–1046. [5]

Procyk, E., Y. L. Tanaka, and J. P. Joseph. 2000. Anterior ingulate activity during routine and non-routine sequential behaviors in macaques. *Nat. Neurosci.* **3(5)**:502–508. [5, 9]

Pycock, C. J., R. W. Kerwin, and C. J. Carter. 1980. Effect of lesion of cortical dopamine terminals on subcortical dopamine receptors in rats. *Nature* **286**:74–77. [8]

Pyke, G. H., H. R. Pulliam, and E. L. Charnov. 1977. Optimal foraging: A selective review of theory and tests. *Q. Rev. Biol.* **52(2)**:137–154. [10]

Quinlan, P. T., and G. W. Humphreys. 1987. Visual search for targets defined by combinations of color, shape, and size: An examination of the task constraints on feature and conjunction searches. *Perc. Psychophys.* **41**:455–472. [10]

Raaijmakers, J. G., and R. M. Shiffrin. 1980. SAM: A theory of probabilistic search of associative memory. In: The Psychology of Learning and Motivation, ed. G. H. Bower. New York: Academic Press. [11]

———. 1981. Search of associative memory. *Psychol. Rev.* **88(2)**:93–134. [2, 11, 15]

Raichle, M. E., A. M. MacLeod, A. Z. Snyder, et al. 2001. A default mode of brain function. *PNAS* **98(2)**:676–682. [13]

Raisch, S., and J. Birkinshaw. 2008. Organizational ambidexterity: Antecedents, outcomes, and moderators. *J. Manag.* **34(3)**:375–409. [17]

Rakow, T., B. R. Newell, K. Fayers, and M. Hersby. 2005. Evaluating three criteria for establishing cue-search hierarchies in inferential judgment *J. Exp. Psychol. Learn. Mem. Cogn.* **31(5)**:1088–1104. [15]

Ramus, S. J., J. B. Davis, R. J. Donahue, C. B. Discenza, and A. A. Waite. 2007. Interactions between the orbitofrontal cortex and hippocampal memory system during the storage of long-term memory. *Ann. NY Acad. Sci.* **1121**:216–231. [6]

Rangel, A., C. Camerer, and P. R. Montague. 2008. A framework for studying the neurobiology of value-based decision making. *Nat. Rev. Neurosci.* **9(7)**:545–556. [12]

Ratcliff, R. 1978. A theory of memory retrieval. *Psychol. Rev.* **85**:59–108. [10, 12]

Rawlins, J. N. P. 1985. Associations across time: The hippocampus as a temporary memory store. *Behav. Brain Sci.* **8**:479–496. [6, 9]

Real, L. A. 1990. Search theory and mate choice. I. Models of single-sex discrimination. *Am. Nat.* **136**:376–404. [19]

Reaume, C. J., and M. B. Sokolowski. 2009. cGMP-dependent protein kinase as a modifier of behaviour. In: cGMP: Generators, Effects and Therapeutic Implications, Handbook of Experimental Pharmacology, vol. 191, ed. H. H. W. Schmidt et al., pp. 423–443. Berlin: Springer-Verlag. [4]

Reaume, C. J., M. B. Sokolowski, and F. Méry. 2011. A natural genetic polymorphism affects retroactive interference in *Drosophila melanogaster. Proc. R. Soc. B* **278**:91–98. [4]

Redgrave, P., T. J. Prescott, and K. Gurney. 1999. The basal ganglia: A vertebrate solution to the selection problem? *Neuroscience* **89(4)**:1009–1023. [8]

Redish, A. D. 1999. Beyond the Cognitive Map: From Place Cells to Episodic Memory. Cambridge, MA: MIT Press. [6, 9]

———. 2001. The hippocampal debate: Are we asking the right questions? *Behav. Brain Res.* **127**:81–98. [6]

———. 2009. Implications of the multiple-vulnerabilities theory of addiction for craving and relapse. *Addiction* **104(11)**:1940–1941. [6]

Redish, A. D., S. Jensen, and A. Johnson. 2008. A unified framework for addiction: Vulnerabilities in the decision process. *Behav. Brain Sci.* **31**:415–487. [6, 9, 12]

Redish, A. D., S. Jensen, A. Johnson, and Z. Kurth-Nelson. 2007. Reconciling reinforcement learning models with behavioral extinction and renewal: Implications for addiction, relapse, and problem gambling. *Psychol. Rev.* **114(3)**:784–805. [5, 9]

Redish, A. D., and A. Johnson. 2007. A computational model of craving and obsession. *Ann. NY Acad. Sci.* **1104(1)**:324–339. [6]

Redish, A. D., B. L. McNaughton, and C. A. Barnes. 1998. Reconciling Barnes et al. (1997) and Tanila et al. (1997a, 1997b). *Hippocampus* **8**:438–443. [6]

Redish, A. D., E. S. Rosenzweig, J. D. Bohanick, B. L. McNaughton, and C. A. Barnes. 2000. Dynamics of hippocampal ensemble realignment: Time vs. space. *J. Neurosci.* **20(24)**:9289–9309. [6]

Redish, A. D., and D. S. Touretzky. 1997. Cognitive maps beyond the hippocampus. *Hippocampus* **7(1)**:15–35. [6]

———. 1998. The role of the hippocampus in solving the Morris water maze. *Neural Comput.* **10(1)**:73–111. [6]

Reed, J. M., and L. R. Squire. 1998. Retrograde amnesia for facts and events: Findings from four new cases. *J. Neurosci.* **18(10)**:3943–3954. [6]

Reidys, C. M., and P. F. Stadler. 2001. Neutrality in fitness landscapes. *Appl. Math. Comput.* **117**:321–350. [20]

———. 2002. Combinatorial landscapes. *SIAM Review* **44**:3–54. [20]

Reidys, C. M., P. F. Stadler, and P. Schuster. 1997. Generic properties of combinatory maps: Neutral networks of RNA secondary structures. *Bull. Math. Biol.* **59**:339–397. [20]

Rensink, R. A. 2000a. The dynamic representation of scenes. *Vis. Cogn.* **7(1)**:17–42. [15]

———. 2000b. Seeing, sensing, and scrutinizing. *Vision Res.* **40(10–12)**:1469–1487. [10]

Rensink, R. A., and J. T. Enns. 1998. Early completion of occluded objects. *Vision Res.* **38**:2489–2505. [10]

Rescorla, R. A. 1994. Transfer of instrumental control mediated by a devalued outcome. *Anim. Learn. Behav.* **22**:27–33. [7]

Rescorla, R. A., and A. R. Wagner. 1972. A theory of Pavlovian conditioning: Variations in the effectiveness of reinforcement and nonreinforcement. In: Classical Conditioning II: Current Research and Theory, ed. A. H. Black and W. F. Prokesy, pp. 64–99. New York: Appleton Century Crofts. [9, 16]

Resnick, M. 1994. Turtles, Termites, and Traffic Jams. Cambridge, MA: MIT Press. [20]

Restle, F. 1957. Discrimination of cues in mazes: A resolution of the "place-vs-response" question. *Psychol. Rev.* **64**:217–228. [6]

Reuter, M., S. Roth, K. Holve, and J. Hennig. 2006. Identification of first candidate genes for creativity: A pilot study. *Brain Res.* **1069**:190–197. [14]

Reynolds, A. M., and F. Bartumeus. 2009. Optimising the success of random destructive searches: Lévy walks can outperform ballistic motions. *J. Theor. Biol.* **260**:98–103. [3]

Reynolds, A. M., and C. J. Rhodes. 2009. The Lévy flight paradigm: Random search patterns and mechanisms. *Ecology* **90**:877–887. [3]

Rhodes, T., and M. T. Turvey. 2007. Human memory retrieval as Lévy foraging. *Physica A* **385**:255–260. [11, 19]

Rich, E. L., and M. Shapiro. 2009. Rat prefrontal cortical neurons selectively code strategy switches. *J. Neurosci.* **29(22)**:7208–7219. [9]

Ridderinkhof, K. R., B. U. Forstmann, S. A. Wylie, B. Burle, and W. P. M. van den Wildenberg. 2011. Neurocognitive mechanisms of action control: Resisting the call of the Sirens. *Wiley Interdiscip. Rev. Cogn. Sci.* **2(2)**:174–192. [13]

Rieskamp, J., and U. Hoffrage. 2008. Inferences under time pressure: How opportunity costs affect strategy selection. *Acta Psychol.* **127(2)**:258–276. [15]

Rizzolatti, G., M. Fabbri-Destro, and L. Cattaneo. 2009. Mirror neurons and their clinical relevance. *Nat. Clin. Pract. Neurol.* **5(1)**:24–34. [9]

Robbins, T. W. 1996. Dissociating executive functions of the prefrontal cortex. *Phil. Trans. R. Soc. Lond. B* **351(1346)**:1463–1470. [12]

———. 1997. Arousal systems and attentional processes. *Biol. Psych.* **45**:57–71. [9]

———. 2007. Shifting and stopping: Fronto-striatal substrates, neurochemical modulation and clinical implications. *Phil. Trans. R. Soc. Lond. B* **362(1481)**:917–932. [9]

Robbins, T. W., and B. J. Everitt. 1992. Functions of dopamine in the dorsal and ventral striatum. *Sem. Neurosci.* **4**:119–127. [9]

———. 1999. Drug addiction: Bad habits add up. *Nature* **398**:567–570. [6]

Robbins, T. W., and A. C. Roberts. 2007. Differential regulation of fronto-executive function by the monoamines and acetylcholine. *Cereb. Cortex* **17(Suppl 1)**:i151–i160. [8, 9]

Robertson, G. S., and H. A. Robertson. 1986. Synergistic effects of D1 and D2 dopamine agonists on turning behaviour in rats. *Brain Res.* **384**:387–390. [2]

Robinson, T. E., and K. C. Berridge. 2001. Mechanisms of action of addictive stimuli: Incentive-sensitization and addiction. *Addiction* **96**:103–114. [6]

———. 2003. Addiction. *Ann. Rev. Psychol.* **54**:25–53. [6]

Roche, J. P., W. Timberlake, W. E. Glanz, and D. A. Stubbs. 1998. The influence of current-visit experience within a prey patch on patch persistence. *Behav. Processes* **43**:11–25. [4]

Roesch, M. R., T. Singh, P. L. Brown, S. E. Mullins, and G. Schoenbaum. 2009. Ventral striatal neurons encode the value of the chosen action in rats deciding between differently delayed or sized rewards. *J. Neurosci.* **29(42)**:13,365–13,376. [6]

Rogers, R. D., and S. Monsell. 1995. Costs of a predictable switch between simple cognitive tasks. *J. Exp. Psychol. Gen.* **124(2)**:207–231. [5]

Rohrer, D. 1996. On the relative and absolute strength of a memory trace. *Mem. Cogn.* **24**:188–202. [11]

———. 2002. The breadth of memory search. *Memory* **10**:291–301. [11]

Rohrer, D., D. P. Salmon, J. T. Wixted, and J. S. Paulsen. 1999. The disparate effects of Alzheimer's disease and Huntington's disease on semantic memory. *Neuropsychology* **13(3)**:381–388. [11]

Rohrer, D., and J. T. Wixted. 1994. An analysis of latency and interresponse time in free recall. *Mem. Cogn.* **22**:511–524. [11]

Rohrer, D., J. T. Wixted, D. P. Salmon, and N. Butters. 1995. Retrieval from semantic memory and its implications for Alzheimer's disease. *J. Exp. Psychol. Learn. Mem. Cogn.* **21**:1127–1139. [11]

Roitman, M. F., R. A. Wheeler, and R. M. Carelli. 2005. Nucleus accumbens neurons are innately tuned for rewarding and aversive taste stimuli, encode their predictors, and are linked to motor output. *Neuron* **45(4)**:587–597. [6]

Rolls, E. T., H. D. Critchley, A. S. Browning, I. Hernadi, and L. Lenard. 1999. Responses to the sensory properties of fat of neurons in the primate orbitofrontal cortex. *J. Neurosci.* **19(4)**:1532–1540. [9]

Rolls, E. T., M. L. Kringelbach, and I. E. de Araujo. 2003. Different representations of pleasant and unpleasant odours in the human brain. *Eur. J. Neurosci.* **18**:695–703. [7]

Romanczuk, P., I. D. Couzin, and L. Schimansky-Geier. 2009. Collective motion of animal groups due to escape and pursuit behavior. *Phys. Rev. Lett.* **102(1)**:010602. [3]

Romney, A., D. Brewer, and W. H. Batchelder. 1993. Predicting clustering from semantic structure. *Psychol. Sci.* **4**:28–34. [2]

Rosen, V. M., and R. W. Engle. 1997. The role of working memory capacity in retrieval. *J. Exp. Psychol. Gen.* **126**: 211–127. [2]

Rudy, J. W. 2009. Context representations, context functions, and the parahippocampal/hippocampal system. *Learn. Mem.* **16(10)**:573–585. [6]

Runco, M. 2007. Creativity Theories and Themes: Research, Development and Practice. Burlington, MA: Elsevier Academic Press. [14]

Rundus, D. 1973. Negative effects of using list items as recall cues. *J. Verbal Learn. Behav.* **12**:43–50. [11]

Sagan, C. 1996. The Demon-Haunted World: Science as a Candle in the Dark. New York: Ballantine Books. [5]

Saimi, Y., and C. Kung. 1987. Behavioral genetics of paramecium. *Ann. Rev. Genet.* **21**:47–65. [2]

Sakai, K. 2008. Task set and prefrontal cortex. *Ann. Rev. Neurosci.* **31**:219–245. [9]

Salamone, J. D., M. S. Cousins, and B. J. Snyder. 1997. Behavioral functions of nucleus accumbens dopamine: Empirical and conceptual problems with the anhedonia hypothesis. *Neurosci. Biobehav. Rev.* **21**:341–359. [2]

Samsonovich, A. V., and G. A. Ascoli. 2005. A simple neural network model of the hippocampus suggesting its pathfinding role in episodic memory retrieval. *Learn. Mem.* **12(2)**:193–208. [6]

Samsonovich, A. V., and B. L. McNaughton. 1997. Path integration and cognitive mapping in a continuous attractor neural network model. *J. Neurosci.* **17(15)**:5900–5920. [6]

Samuelson, C. D., and D. M. Messick. 1995. When do people want to change the rules for allocating shared resources? In: Social Dilemmas: Perspectives on Individuals and Groups, ed. D. A. Schroeder, pp. 143–162. Westport, CT: Praeger. [20]

Sara, S. J. 2009. The locus coeruleus and noradrenergic modulation of cognition. *Nat. Rev. Neurosci.* **10(3)**:211–223. [8, 9]

Sayette, M. A., S. Shiffman, S. T. Tiffany, et al. 2000. The measurement of drug craving. *Addiction* **95(2)**:S189–S210. [6]

Schacter, D. L. 2001. The Seven Sins of Memory: How the Mind Forgets and Remembers. New York: Houghton Mifflin. [6]

Schacter, D. L., and D. R. Addis. 2007. Constructive memory: The ghosts of past and future. *Nature* **445**:27. [6]

Schacter, D. L., D. R. Addis, and R. L. Buckner. 2007. Remembering the past to imagine the future: The prospective brain. *Nat. Rev. Neurosci.* **8**:657–661. [6]

———. 2008. Episodic simulation of future events: Concepts, data, and applications. *Ann. NY Acad. Sci.* **1124**:39–60. [6]

Schall, J. D., V. Stuphorn, and J. W. Brown. 2002. Monitoring and control of action by the frontal lobes. *Neuron* **36(2)**:309–322. [9]

Schein, E. H. 1985. Organizational Culture and Leadership. San Francisco: Jossey-Bass. [17]

———. 1987. Process Consultation. Reading, MA: Addison-Wesley. [17]

Schilman, E. A., H. B. Uylings, Y. Galis-de Graaf, D. Joel, and H. J. Groenewegen. 2008. The orbital cortex in rats topographically projects to central parts of the caudate-putamen complex. *Neurosci. Lett.* **432(1)**:40–45. [9]

Schlosser, R. G., G. Wagner, C. Schachtzabel, et al. 2010. Fronto-cingulate effective connectivity in obsessive compulsive disorder: A study with fMRI and dynamic causal modeling. *Hum. Brain Mapp.* **31(12)**:1834–1850. [9]

Schmitzer-Torbert, N. C., and A. D. Redish. 2002. Development of path stereotypy in a single day in rats on a multiple-T maze. *Arch. Ital. Biol.* **140**:295–301. [6]

———. 2004. Neuronal activity in the rodent dorsal striatum in sequential navigation: Separation of spatial and reward responses on the multiple T task. *J. Neurophysiol.* **91(5)**:2259–2272. [6]

———. 2008. Task-dependent encoding of space and events by striatal neurons is dependent on neural subtype. *Neuroscience* **153(2)**:349–360. [6]

Schneider, J. M., and F. Vollrath. 1998. The effect of prey type on the geometry of the capture web of *Araneus diadematus*. *Naturwissenschaften* **85**:391–394. [4]

Schoenbaum, G., A. A. Chiba, and M. Gallagher. 1998. Orbitofrontal cortex and basolateral amygdala encode expected outcomes during learning. *Nat. Neurosci.* **1(2)**:155–159. [9]

Schoenbaum, G., and M. Roesch. 2005. Orbitofrontal cortex, associative learning, and expectancies. *Neuron* **47(5)**:633–636. [6]

Schöne, H. 1984. Spatial Orientation: The Spatial Control of Behavior in Animals and Man. Princeton: Princeton Univ. Press. [4]

Schulte-Mecklenbeck, M., A. Kühberger, and R. Ranyard, eds. 2011. A Handbook of Process Tracing Methods for Decision Research: A Critical Review and User's Guide. New York: Taylor & Francis. [15]

Schultz, W. 1998. Predictive reward signal of dopamine neurons. *J. Neurophysiol.* **80(1)**:1–27. [5]

———. 2006. Behavioral theories and the neurophysiology of reward. *Ann. Rev. Psychol.* **57**:87–115. [14]

———. 2007. Multiple dopamine functions at different time courses. *Ann. Rev. Neurosci.* **30**:259–288. [9]

Schultz, W., P. Apicella, E. Scarnati, and T. Ljungberg. 1992. Neuronal activity in monkey ventral striatum related to the expectation of reward. *J. Neurosci.* **12(12)**:4595–4610. [9]

Schultz, W., P. Dayan, and P. R. Montague. 1997. A neural substrate of prediction and reward. *Science* **275(5306)**:1593–1599. [9, 12]

Schuster, F. L., and M. Levandowsky. 1996. Chemosensory responses of *Acanthamoeba castellanii*: Visual analysis of random movement and responses to chemical signals. *J. Eukaryot. Microbiol.* **43**:150–158. [3]

Schyns, P. G., and L. Rodet. 1997. Categorization creates functional features *J. Exp. Psychol. Hum. Learn. Mem.* **23(3)**:681–696. [20]

Seamans, J. K., and C. R. Yang. 2004. The principal features and mechanisms of dopamine modulation in the prefrontal cortex. *Prog. Neurobiol.* **74(1)**:1–58. [9]

Sederberg, P. B., M. W. Howard, and M. J. Kahana. 2008. A context-based theory of recency and contiguity in free recall. *Psychol. Rev.* **115**:893–912. [11]

Sederberg, P. B., J. F. Miller, W. H. Howard, and M. J. Kahana. 2010. The temporal contiguity effect predicts episodic memory performance. *Mem. Cogn.* **38**:689–699. [15]

Seeley, T. D., P. K. Visscher, T. Schlegel, et al. 2012. Stop signals provide cross inhibition in collective decision-making by honeybee swarms. *Science* **335**:108–111. [20]

Seeley, W. W. 2010. Anterior insula degeneration in frontotemporal dementia. *Brain Struct. Funct.* **214(5–6)**:465–475. [13]

Seeley, W. W., R. K. Crawford, K. Rascovsky, et al. 2008. Frontal paralimbic network atrophy in very mild behavioral variant frontotemporal dementia. *Arch. Neurol.* **65(2)**:249–255. [13]

Servan-Schreiber, D., H. Printz, and J. Cohen. 1990. A network model of catecholamine effects: Gain, signal-to-noise ratio, and behavior. *Science* **249**:892–895. [8]

Shallice, T. 1982. Specific impairments of planning. *Phil. Trans. R. Soc. Lond. B* **298**:199–209. [4, 9]

Shanks, D. R., and A. Dickinson. 1991. Instrumental judgment and performance under variations in action-outcome contingency and contiguity. *Mem. Cogn.* **19**:353–360. [7]

Shannon, C. E. 1950. Programming a computer for playing chess. *Philos. Mag. Lett.* **41**:256–275. [16]

Shanteau, J. 1992. How much information does an expert use? Is it relevant? *Acta Psychol.* **81**:75–86. [15]

Shapiro, K., F. Schmitz, S. Martens, B. Hommel, and A. Schnitzler. 2006. Resource sharing in the attentional blink. *NeuroReport* **17**:163–166. [14]

Shaw, M. L., and P. Shaw. 1977. Optimal allocation of cognitive resources to spatial locations. *J. Exp. Psychol. Hum. Perc. Perf.* **3**:201–211. [2]

Shawe-Taylor, J., and N. Cristianini. 2004. Kernel Methods for Pattern Analysis. Cambridge: Cambridge Univ. Press. [20]

Shidara, M., T. Mizuhiki, and B. J. Richmond. 2005. Neuronal firing in anterior cingulate neurons changes modes across trials in single states of multitrial reward schedules. *Exp. Brain Res.* **163(2)**:242–245. [9]

Shidara, M., and B. J. Richmond. 2002. Anterior cingulate: Single neuronal signals related to degree of reward expectancy. *Science* **296(5573)**:1709–1711. [9]

Shiffrin, R. M., and M. Steyvers. 1997. A model for recognition memory: REM—Retrieving effectively from memory. *Psychon. Bull. Rev.* **4**:145–166. [11]

Shima, K., and J. Tanji. 1998. Role of cingulate motor area cells in voluntary movement selection based on reward. *Science* **282**:1335–1338. [5, 9]

Shimamura, A. P. 2008. A neurocognitive approach to metacognitive monitoring and control. In: Handbook of Memory and Metacognition, ed. J. Dunlosky and R. Bjork, pp. 373–390. Mahwah, NJ: Lawrence Erlbaum. [15]

Shin, Y. K., R. W. Proctor, and E. J. Capaldi. 2010. A review of contemporary ideomotor theory. *Psychol. Bull.* **136**:943–974. [14]

Shine, R., J. K. Webb, A. Lane, and R. T. Mason. 2005. Mate location tactics in garter snakes: Effects of rival males, interrupted trails and non-pheromonal cues. *Funct. Ecol.* **19**:1017–1024. [4]

Shore, D. I., and R. M. Klein. 2000. On the manifestations of memory in visual search. *Spat. Vis.* **14(1)**:59–75. [10]

Shuler, M. G., and M. F. Bear. 2006. Reward timing in the primary visual cortex. *Science* **311(5767)**:1606–1609. [9]

Simmons, J. M., S. Ravel, M. Shidara, and B. J. Richmond. 2007. A comparison of reward-contingent neuronal activity in monkey orbitofrontal cortex and ventral striatum: Guiding actions toward rewards. *Ann. NY Acad. Sci.* **1121**:376–394. [9]

Simon, D. A., and N. D. Daw. 2011. Neural correlates of forward planning in a spatial decision task in humans. *J. Neurosci.* **31(14)**:5526–5539. [12]

Simon, H. A. 1996. The Sciences of the Artificial, 3rd edition. Cambridge, MA: MIT Press. [16]

Simpson, S. J., A. G. Sword, P. D. Lorch, and I. D. Couzin. 2006. Cannibal crickets on a forced march for protein and salt. *PNAS* **103**:4152–4156. [3]

Sims, D. W., E. J. Southall, N. E. Humphries, et al. 2008. Scaling laws of marine predator search behaviour. *Nature* **451**:1098–1102. [3]

Singer, A. C., and L. M. Frank. 2009. Rewarded outcomes enhance reactivation of experience in the hippocampus. *Neuron* **64(6)**:910–921. [6]

Sinha, R., and S. O'Malley. 1999. Craving for alcohol: Findings from the clinic and the laboratory. *Alcohol and Alcoholism* **34(2)**:223–230. [6]

Sirotin, Y. B., D. R. Kimball, and M. J. Kahana. 2005. Going beyond a single list: Modeling the effects of prior experience on episodic free recall. *Psychon. Bull. Rev.* **12**:787–805. [11]

Skaggs, W. E., and B. L. McNaughton. 1996. Replay of neuronal firing sequences in rat hippocampus during sleep following spatial experience. *Science* **271**:1870–1873. [6]

Skaggs, W. E., B. L. McNaughton, M. A. Wilson, and C. A. Barnes. 1996. Theta phase precession in hippocampal neuronal populations and the compression of temporal sequences. *Hippocampus* **6(2)**:149–173. [6, 9]

Skals, N., P. Anderson, M. Kanneworff, C. Lofstedt, and A. Surlykke. 2005. Her odours make him deaf: Crossmodal modulation of olfaction and hearing in a male moth. *J. Exp. Biol.* **208**:595–601. [2]

Slovic, P. 1966. Risk-taking in children: Age and sex differences. *Child Dev.* **37**:169–176. [15]

Small, D. M., M. D. Gregory, Y. E. Mak, et al. 2003. Dissociation of neural representation of intensity and affective valuation in human gustation. *Neuron* **39**:701–711. [7]

Smeets, P. M., and D. Barnes-Holmes. 2003. Children's emergent preferences for soft drinks: Stimulus-equivalence and transfer. *J. Econ. Psychol.* **24(5)**:603–618. [7]

Smith, J. C., C. Lim, and J. N. Bearden. 2007. On the multi-attribute stopping problem with general value functions. *Op. Res. Lett.* **35**:324–330. [15]

Smith, S. M. 1979. Remembering in and out of context. *J. Exp. Psychol. Hum. Learn. Mem.* **5**:460–471. [11]

Sol, D. 2009. The cognitive-buffer hypothesis for the evolution of large brains. In: Cognitive Ecology II, ed. R. Dukas and J. M. Ratcliffe, pp. 111–134. Chicago: Univ. of Chicago Press. [2]

Sotthibandhu, S., and R. R. Baker. 1979. Celestial orientation by the large yellow underwing moth, *Noctua pronuba* L. *Anim. Behav.* **27**:786–800. [4]

Spelke, E. S., and K. D. Kinzler. 2007. Core knowledge. *Dev. Sci.* **10**:89–96. [20]

Squire, L. R. 1987. Memory and Brain. New York: Oxford Univ. Press. [6, 9]

Squire, L. R., and P. Alvarez. 1995. Retrograde amnesia and memory consolidation: A neurobiological perspective. *Curr. Opin. Neurobiol.* **5**:169–177. [6]

Sridharan, D., D. J. Levitin, and V. Menon. 2008. A critical role for the right fronto-insular cortex in switching between central-executive and default-mode networks. *PNAS* **105(34)**:12,569–12,574. [13]

Stamps, J., M. Buechner, K. Alexander, J. Davis, and N. Zuniga. 2005. Genotypic differences in space use and movement patterns in *Drosophila melanogaster*. *Anim. Behav.* **70**:609–618. [4]

Stasser, G., and W. Titus. 1985. Pooling of unshared information in group decision making: Biased information sampling during discussion. *J. Pers. Soc. Psychol.* **57**:67–78. [17]

———. 2003. Hidden profiles: A brief history. *Psychol. Inq.* **14(3–4)**:304–313. [17]

Steiner, A., and A. D. Redish. 2010. Orbitofrontal cortical ensembles during deliberation and learning on a spatial decision-making task. *Abstr. Soc. Neurosci.* [6, 9]

Steiner, I. 1976. Task-performing groups. In: Contemporary Topics in Social Psychology, ed. J. Thibaut et al., pp. 393–421. Englewood Cliffs, NJ: General Learning Press. [17]

Stelzel, C., U. Basten, C. Montag, M. Reuter, and C. J. Fiebach. 2010. Frontostriatal involvement in task switching depends on genetic differences in D2 receptor density. *J. Neurosci.* **30(42)**:14,205–14,212. [8]

Stephens, D. W., J. S. Brown, and R. C. Ydenberg. 2007. Foraging: Behavior and Ecology. Chicago: Univ. of Chicago Press. [2]

Stephens, D. W., and J. R. Krebs. 1986. Foraging Theory. Princeton: Princeton Univ. Press. [2, 3, 18]

Sternberg, R. J., J. C. Kaufman, and J. E. Pretz. 2002. The Creativity Conundrum: A Propulsion Model of Kinds of Creative Contributions. New York: Psychology Press. [14]

Stevens, A., and P. Coupe. 1978. Distortions in judged spatial relations. *Cogn. Psychol.* **10(4)**:422–437. [20]

Steyvers, M., and J. B. Tenenbaum. 2005. The large-scale structure of semantic networks: Statistical analyses and a model of semantic growth. *Cogn. Sci.* **29**:41–78. [2, 4]

Stuphorn, V. 2006. Neuroeconomics: Cardinal utility in the orbitofrontal cortex? *Curr. Biol.* **16(15)**:R591–593. [9]

Stuphorn, V., and J. D. Schall. 2006. Executive control of countermanding saccades by the supplementary eye field. *Nat. Neurosci.* **9(7)**:925–931. [9]

Sueur, C., O. Petit, J. L. Deneubourg, and I. D. Couzin. 2011. Group size, grooming and social cohesion in primates: A modeling approach based on group structure. *Behav. Ecol. Sociobiol.* **273**:156–166. [20]

Sugihara, G., and R. M. May. 1990. Applications of fractals in ecology. *Trends Ecol. Evol.* **5**:79–86. [3]

Sul, J. H., H. Kim, N. Huh, D. Lee, and M. W. Jung. 2010. Distinct roles of rodent orbitofrontal and medial prefrontal cortex in decision making. *Neuron* **66(3)**:449–460. [9]

Sullivan, M. S. 1994. Mate choice as an information gathering process under time constraint: Implications for behavior and signal design. *Anim. Behav.* **47**:141–151. [19]

Sunstein, C. R. 2006. Infotopia: How Many Minds Produce Knowledge. New York: Oxford Univ. Press. [17]

Suri, R. E. 2001. Anticipatory responses of dopamine neurons and cortical neurons reproduced by internal model. *Exp. Brain Res.* **140(2)**:234–240. [12]

Sutherland, G. R., and B. L. McNaughton. 2000. Memory trace reactivation in hippocampal and neocortical neuronal ensembles. *Curr. Opin. Neurobiol.* **10(2)**:180–186. [6]

Sutherland, R. J., F. Sparks, and H. Lehmann. 2011. Hippocampus and retrograde amnesia in the rat model: A modest proposal for the situation of systems consolidation. *Neuropsychologia* **48(8)**:2357–2369. [6, 9]

Sutherland, R. J., M. P. Weisend, D. Mumby, et al. 2001. Retrograde amnesia after hippocampal damage: Recent vs. remote memories in two tasks. *Hippocampus* **11**:27–42. [6]

Sutton, R. S. 1990. Integrated architectures for learning, planning, and reacting based on approximating dynamic programming. In: Proc. of the 7th Intl. Conf. on Machine Learning, pp. 216–224. Waltham, MA: Morgan Kaufmann. [12]

Sutton, R. S., and A. G. Barto. 1998. Reinforcement Learning: An Introduction. Cambridge, MA: MIT Press. [6, 9, 12]

Sutton, R. S., and B. Pinette. 1985. The learning of world models by connectionist networks. Proc. of the 7th Ann. Conf. of the Cognitive Science Society, pp. 55–64. Irvine, CA: Lawrence Erlbaum. [12]

Swanson, J., M. Kinsbourne, J. Nigg, et al. 2007. Etiologic subtypes of attention-deficit/ hyperactivity disorder: Brain imaging, molecular genetic and environmental factors and the dopamine hypothesis. *Neuropsychol. Rev.* **17(1)**:39–59. [2]

Takahashi, M., J. Lauwereyns, Y. Sakurai, and M. Tsukada. 2009a. A code for spatial alternation during fixation in rat hippocampal CA1 neurons. *J. Neurophysiol.* **102(1)**:556–567. [6, 9]

Takahashi, Y. K., M. R. Roesch, T. A. Stalnaker, et al. 2009b. The orbitofrontal cortex and ventral tegmental area are necessary for learning from unexpected outcomes. *Neuron* **62(2)**:269–280. [9]

Takahashi, Y. K., M. R. Roesch, R. Wilson, et al. 2010. Orbitofrontal cortex is required for expectancy-related changes in phasic firing of midbrain dopamine neurons. *Abstr. Soc. Neurosci.* **36**:404.2. [6]

Talmi, D., B. Seymour, P. Dayan, and R. J. Dolan. 2008. Human pavlovian-instrumental transfers. *J. Neurosci.* **28**:360–368. [7]

Tan, L., and G. Ward. 2000. A recency-based account of primacy effects in free recall. *J. Exp. Psychol. Learn. Mem. Cogn.* **26**:1589–1625. [11]

Tanaka, S. C., B. W. Balleine, and J. P. O'Doherty. 2008. Calculating consequences: Brain systems that encode the causal effects of actions. *J. Neurosci.* **28**:6750–6755. [7]

Tanaka, S. C., K. Doya, G. Okada, et al. 2004. Prediction of immediate and future rewards differentially recruits cortico-basal ganglia loops. *Nat. Neurosci.* **7**:887–893. [7]

Tarsitano, M. S., and R. Andrew. 1999. Scanning and route selection in the jumping spider *Portia labiata. Anim. Behav.* **58**:255–265. [4]

Theeuwes, J., and J. L. Kooi. 1994. Parallel search for a conjunction of shape and contrast polarity. *Vision Res.* **34(22)**:3013–3016. [10]

Thinus-Blanc, C. 1996. Animal Spatial Cognition: Behavioral and Brain Approach. Hackensack, NJ: World Scientific. [9]

Thistlethwaite, D. 1951. A critical review of latent learning and related experiments. *Psychol. Bull.* **48**:97–129. [4]

Thomas, R., M. R. Dougherty, A. Sprenger, and J. I. Harbison. 2008. Diagnostic hypothesis generation and human judgment. *Psychol. Rev.* **115**:155–185. [11, 15]

Thompson-Schill, S. L., M. D'Esposito, G. K. Aguirre, and M. J. Farah. 1997. Role of left inferior prefrontal cortex in retrieval of semantic knowledge: A re-evaluation. *PNAS* **94**:14,792–14,797. [9]

Thorn, C. A., H. Atallah, M. Howe, and A. M. Graybiel. 2010. Differential dynamics of activity changes in dorsolateral and dorsomedial striatal loops during learning. *Neuron* **66(5)**:781–795. [6]

Thorndike, E. L. 1911. Animal Intelligence: Experimental Studies. New York: Macmillan. [12]

Thornton, T. 2002. Attentional Limitation and Multiple-Target Visual Search. PhD diss., Univ. of Texas at Austin. [10]

Tiffany, S. T. 1990. A cognitive model of drug urges and drug-use behavior: Role of automatic and nonautomatic processes. *Psychol. Rev.* **97(2)**:147–168. [6]

———. 1999. Cognitive concepts of craving. *Alcohol Res. Health* **23(3)**:215–224. [6]

Tiffany, S. T., and J. Wray. 2009. The continuing conundrum of craving. *Addiction* **104(10)**:1618–1619. [6]

Tinbergen, N. 1958. Curious Naturalists. London: Country Life. [4]

Todd, P. M., and G. Gigerenzer. 2007. Environments that make us smart: Ecological rationality. *Curr. Dir. Psychol. Sci.* **16**:167–171. [19]

Todd, P. M., and G. F. Miller. 1999. From pride and prejudice to persuasion: Satisficing in mate search. In: Simple Heuristics That Make Us Smart, ed. G. Gigerenzer, P. M. Todd, and the ABC Research Group, pp. 287–308. New York: Oxford Univ. Press. [19]

Tolman, E. C. 1938. The determiners of behavior at a choice point. *Psychol. Rev.* **45(1)**:1–41. [6, 9]

———. 1939. Prediction of vicarious trial and error by means of the schematic sowbug. *Psychol. Rev.* **46**:318–336. [6]

———. 1948. Cognitive maps in rats and men. *Psychol. Rev.* **55**:189–208. [6, 12]

Torney, C., Z. Neufeld, and I. D. Couzin. 2009. Context-dependent interaction leads to emergent search behavior in social aggregates. *PNAS* **106**:22,055–22,060. [4]

Touretzky, D. S., and A. D. Redish. 1996. A theory of rodent navigation based on interacting representations of space. *Hippocampus* **6(3)**:247–270. [6]

Tourtellot, M. K., R. D. Collins, and W. J. Bell. 1990. The problem of movelength and turn definition in analysis of orientation data. *J. Theor. Biol.* **150**:287–297. [3]

Tovee, M. J. 1994. How fast is the speed of thought? *Curr. Biol.* **4**:1125–1127. [14]

Townsend, J. T. 1971. A note on the identification of parallel and serial processes. *Perc. Psychophys.* **10**:161–163. [10]

Townsend, J. T., and G. Nozawa. 1995. Spatio-temporal properties of elementary perception: An investigation of parallel, serial, and coactive theories. *J. Math. Psychol.* **39**:321–359. [11]

Townsend, J. T., and M. J. Wenger. 2004. The serial-parallel dilemma: A case study in a linkage of theory and method. *Psychon. Bull. Rev.* **10(11)**:391–418. [10, 11]

Treisman, A. M., and G. Gelade. 1980. A feature integration theory of attention. *Cogn. Psychol.* **12**:97–136. [10, 14]

Treisman, A. M., and H. Schmidt. 1982. Illusory conjunctions in the perception of objects. *Cogn. Psychol.* **14**:107–141. [10]

Treisman, M. 1975. Predation and the evolution of gregariousness. I. Models for concealment and evasion. *Anim. Behav.* **23**:779–800. [4]

Tremblay, L., and W. Schultz. 1999. Relative reward preference in primate orbitofrontal cortex. *Nature* **398(6729)**:704–708. [6, 9]

Tricomi, E., B. W. Balleine, and J. P. O'Doherty. 2009. A specific role for posterior dorsolateral striatum in human habit learning. *Eur. J. Neurosci.* **29**:2225–2232. [7]

Trimmer, P. C. 2010. The Evolution of Decision-Making: Various Modelling Approaches. PhD diss., Univ. of Bristol. [16]

Trimmer, P. C., A. I. Houston, J. A. R. Marshall, et al. 2008. Mammalian choices: Combining fast-but-inaccurate and slow-but-accurate decision-making systems. *Proc. R. Soc. B* **275**:2353–2361. [19]

Trist, E., G. Higgin, H. Murray, and A. Pollock. 1963. Organisational Choice: The Loss, Rediscovery and Transformation of a Work Tradition. London: Tavistock. [17]

Tse, D., R. F. Langston, M. Kakeyama, et al. 2007. Schemas and memory consolidation. *Science* **316(5821)**:76–82. [6, 9]

Tsodyks, M. V., W. E. Skaggs, T. J. Sejnowski, and B. L. McNaughton. 1996. Population dynamics and theta rhythm phase precession of hippocampal place cell firing: A spiking neuron model. *Hippocampus* **6(3)**:271–280. [6]

Tulving, E. 1983. Elements of Episodic Memory. New York: Oxford Univ. Press. [6]

Tulving, E., and S. A. Madigan. 1970. Memory and verbal learning. *Ann. Rev. Psychol.* **21**:437–484. [11]

Tulving, E., and Z. Pearlstone. 1966. Availability versus accessibility of information in memory for words. *J. Verbal Learn. Behav.* **5**:381–391. [11]

Tulving, E., and D. M. Thomson. 1973. Encoding specificity and retrieval processes in episodic memory. *Psychol. Rev.* **80**:352–373. [11]

Turchin, P. 1991. Translating foraging movements in heterogenous environments into the spatial distribution of foragers. *Ecology* **72**:1253–1266. [3]

Turing, A. M. 1936. On computable numbers, with an application to the Entscheidungs-problem. *Proc. Lond. Math. Soc.* **42**:240–265. [16]

———. 1950. Computing machinery and intelligence. *Mind* **59**:433–460. [16]

Turvey, M. T. 1977. Preliminaries to a theory of action with reference to vision. In: Perceiving, Acting and Knowing: Toward an Ecological Psychology, ed. R. Shaw and J. Bransford. Hillsdale, NJ: Lawrence Erlbaum. [14]

Tversky, A. 1972. Elimination by aspects: A theory of choice. *Psychol. Rev.* **79**:281–299. [15]

Ullsperger, M., H. A. Harsay, J. Wessel, and K. R. Ridderinkhof. 2010. Conscious perception of errors and its relation to the anterior insula. *Brain Struct. Funct.* **214(5)**:629–643. [13]

Unsworth, N., G. A. Brewer, and G. J. Spillers. 2010. Understanding the dynamics of correct and error responses in free recall: Evidence from externalized free recall. *Mem. Cogn.* **38**:419–430. [11]

Unsworth, N., and R. W. Engle. 2007. The nature of individual differences in working memory capacity: Active maintenance in primary memory and controlled search from secondary memory. *Psychol. Rev.* **114**:104–132. [15]

Uylings, H. B., H. J. Groenewegen, and B. Kolb. 2003. Do rats have a prefrontal cortex? *Behav. Brain Res.* **146**:3–17. [7]

Uzzi, B. 1997. Social structure and competition in interfirm networks: The paradox of embeddedness. *Adm. Sci. Q.* **42(1)** [17]

Valentin, V. V., A. Dickinson, and J. P. O'Doherty. 2007. Determining the neural substrates of goal-directed learning in the human brain. *J. Neurosci.* **27(15)**:4019–4026. [7, 12]

Valiant, L. G. 2009. Evolvability. *J. ACM* **56**:3.1–3.21. [16]

van Bergen, Y., I. Coolen, and K. Laland. 2004. Nine-spined sticklebacks exploit the most reliable source when public and private information conflict. *Proc. R. Soc. B* **271**:957–962. [4]

van der Meer, M. A., A. Johnson, N. C. Schmitzer-Torbert, and R. A. D. 2010. Triple dissociation of information processing in dorsal striatum, ventral striatum, and hippocampus on a learned spatial decision task. *Neuron* **67(1)**:25–32. [6, 12]

van der Meer, M. A., and A. D. Redish. 2009. Covert expectation-of-reward in rat ventral striatum at decision points. *Front. Integr. Neurosci.* **3(1)**:1–15. [6, 9]

———. 2010. Expectancies in decision making, reinforcement learning, and ventral striatum. *Front. Neurosci.* **4**:29–37. [6, 9]

———. 2011. Theta phase precession in rat ventral striatum links place and reward information. *J. Neurosci.* **31(8)**:2843–2854. [6, 9]

van der Meulen, J. A., R. N. Joosten, J. P. de Bruin, and M. G. Feenstra. 2007. Dopamine and noradrenaline efflux in the medial prefrontal cortex during serial reversals and extinction of instrumental goal-directed behavior. *Cereb. Cortex* **17(6)**:1444–1453. [8]

Vanderwolf, C. H. 1971. Limbic-diencephalic mechanisms of voluntary movement. Psychol. Rev. 78(2):83–113. [6]

van Duuren, E., F. A. Escamez, R. N. Joosten, et al. 2007. Neural coding of reward magnitude in the orbitofrontal cortex of the rat during a five-odor olfactory discrimination task. *Learn. Mem.* **14(6)**:446–456. [9]

van Duuren, E., G. van der Plasse, J. Lankelma, et al. 2009. Single-cell and population coding of expected reward probability in the orbitofrontal cortex of the rat. *J. Neurosci.* **29(28)**:8965–8976. [9]

Van Essen, D. C., and C. H. Anderson. 1995. Information processing strategies and pathways in the primate visual system. In: An Introduction to Neural and Electronic Networks, 2nd edition, ed. S. F. Zornetzer et al., pp. 45–76. San Diego: Academic Press. [2]

VanRullen, R. 2006. On second glance: Still no high-level pop-out effect for faces. *Vision Res.* **46(18)**:3017–3027. [10]

van Schouwenburg, M. R., E. Aarts, and R. Cools. 2010a. Dopaminergic modulation of cognitive control: Distinct roles for the prefrontal cortex and the basal ganglia *Curr. Pharm. Design* **16(18)**:2026–2032. [8]

van Schouwenburg, M. R., H. E. den Ouden, and R. Cools. 2010b. The human basal ganglia modulate frontal posterior connectivity during attention shifting. *J. Neurosci.* **30**:9910–9918. [8]

Vergassola, M., E. Villermaux, and B. I. Shraiman. 2007. "Infotaxis" as a strategy for searching without gradients. *Nature* **445**:406–409. [4]

Verghese, P. 2001. Visual search and attention: A signal detection approach. *Neuron* **31**:523–535. [10]

Vickery, W. L., L.-A. Giraldeau, J. J. Templeton, D. L. Kramer, and C. A. Chapman. 1991. Producers, scroungers and group foraging. *Am. Nat.* **137**:847–863. [3]

Vijayraghavan, S., M. Wang, S. Birnbaum, G. Williams, and A. Arnsten. 2007. Inverted-U dopamine D1 receptor actions on prefrontal neurons engaged in working memory. *Nat. Neurosci.* **10(3)**:176–184. [8]

Vinogradova, O. S. 2001. Hippocampus as comparator: Role of the two input and two output systems of the hippocampus in selection and registration of information. *Hippocampus* **11(5)**:578–598. [9]

Viswanathan, G. M., V. Afanasyev, S. V. Buldyrev, et al. 1996. Lévy flight search patterns of wandering albatrosses. *Nature* **381**:413–415. [3]

Vo, M. L. H., and J. M. Henderson. 2009. Does gravity matter? Effects of semantic and syntactic inconsistencies on the allocation of attention during scene perception. *J. Vision* **9(3)**:1–15. [10]

Vogel, E. K., A. W. McCollough, and M. G. Machizawa. 2005. Neural measures reveal individual differences in controlling access to working memory. *Nature* **438**:500–503. [15]

Von Economo, C. 1926. Eine neue art spezialzellen des lobus cinguli und lobus insulae. *Zeitschr. Ges. Neurol. Psychiatr.* **100(1)**:706–712. [13]

Voorn, P., L. J. M. J. Vanderschuren, H. J. Groenewegen, T. W. Robbins, and C. M. A. Pennartz. 2004. Putting a spin on the dorsal-ventral divide of the striatum. *Trends Neurosci.* **27(8)**:468–474. [6, 9]

Vossel, S., P. Eschenbeck, P. H. Weiss, and G. R. Fink. 2010. The neural basis of perceptual bias and response bias in the Landmark task. *Neuropsychologia* **48(13)**:3949–3954. [9]

Waage, J. K. 1978. Arrestment responses of the parasitoid, *Nemeritis canescens*, to a contact chemical produced by its host, *Plodia interpunctella*. *Physiol. Entomol.* **3**:135–146. [4]

———. 1979. Foraging for patchily distributed hosts by the parasitoid *Nemeritis canescens*. *J. Anim. Ecol.* **48**:353–371. [3, 19]

Wagenaar, W. A. 1988. Paradoxes of Gambling Behavior. London: Lawrence Erlbaum. [6]

Wajnberg, E., X. Fauvergue, and O. Pons. 2000. Patch leaving decision rules and the Marginal Value Theorem: An experimental analysis and a simulation model. *Behav. Ecol.* **11(6)**:577–586. [10]

Walcott, C. 2005. Multi-modal orientation cues in homing pigeons. *Integr. Comp. Biol.* **45**:574–581. [4]

Walker, S. C., T. W. Robbins, and A. C. Roberts. 2009. Differential contributions of dopamine and serotonin to orbitofrontal cortex function in the marmoset. *Cereb. Cortex* **19(4)**:889–898. [9]

Wallas, G. 1926. The Art of Thought. New York: Harcourt Brace. [14]

Wallis, J. D., K. C. Anderson, and E. K. Miller. 2001. Single neurons in prefrontal cortex encode abstract rules. *Nature* **411**:953–956. [9]

Wallis, J. D., and E. K. Miller. 2003. From rule to response: Neuronal processes in the premotor and prefrontal cortex. *J. Neurophysiol.* **90(3)**:1790–1806. [9]

Walton, M. E., P. L. Croxson, M. F. Rushworth, and D. M. Bannerman. 2005. The mesocortical dopamine projection to anterior cingulate cortex plays no role in guiding effort-related decisions. *Behav. Neurosci.* **119(1)**:323–328. [9]

Wang, S. H., S. B. Ostlund, K. Nader, and B. W. Balleine. 2005. Consolidation and reconsolidation of incentive learning in the amygdala. *J. Neurosci.* **25(4)**:830–835. [7]

Ward, G., L. Tan, and R. Grenfell-Essam. 2010. Examining the relationship between free recall and immediate serial recall: The effects of list length and output order. *J. Exp. Psychol. Learn. Mem. Cogn.* **36**:1207–1241. [11]

Ward, R., and J. L. McClelland. 1989. Conjunctive search for one and two identical targets. *J. Exp. Psychol. Hum. Perc. Perf.* **15(4)**:664–672. [10]

Wasserman, E. A., D. L. Chatlosh, and D. J. Neunaber. 1983. Perception of causal relations in humans: Factors affecting judgments of response-outcome contingencies under free-operant procedures. *Learn. Motiv.* **14**:406–432. [7]

Watkins, M. J., and O. G. Watkins. 1976. Cue-overload theory and the method of interpolated attributes. *Bull. Psychon. Soc.***(7)**:289–291. [11]

Wegner, D. M. 1987. Transactive memory: A contemporary analysis of the group mind. In: Theories of Group Behavior, ed. B. Mullen and G. Goethals, pp. 185–208. New York: Springer Verlag. [17]

Wehner, R. 2003. Desert ant navigation: How miniature brains solve complex tasks. *J. Comp. Physiol. A* **189**:579–588. [4]

Weissman, D. H., A. Gopalakrishnan, C. J. Hazlett, and M. G. Woldorff. 2005. Dorsal anterior cingulate cortex resolves conflict from distracting stimuli by boosting attention toward relevant events. *Cereb. Cortex* **15(2)**:229–237. [9]

Weissman, D. H., K. C. Roberts, K. M. Visscher, and M. G. Woldorff. 2006. The neural bases of momentary lapses in attention. *Nat. Neurosci.* **9(7)**:971–978. [13]

Wessel, J., C. Danielmeier, and M. Ullsperger. 2011 Error awareness revisited: Accumulation of multimodal evidence from central and autonomic nervous systems. *J. Cogn. Neurosci.* **23(10)**:3021–3036. [13]

West, M. J., and A. P. King. 1988. Female visual displays affect the development of male song in the cowbird. *Nature* **334**:244–246. [4]

Whishaw, I. Q., and B. L. Brooks. 1999. Calibrating space: Exploration is important for allothetic and idiothetic navigation. *Hippocampus* **9(6)**:659–667. [9]

White, J., T. Tobin, and W. J. Bell. 1984. Local search in the housefly *Musca domestica* after feeding on sucrose. *J. Insect Physiol.* **30**:477–487. [2]

Wiegmann, D. D., S. M. Seubert, and G. A. Wade. 2010. Mate choice and optimal search behavior: Fitness returns under the fixed sample and sequential search strategies. *J. Theor. Biol.* **262**:596–600. [19]

Wiener, J. M., M. Lafon, and A. Berthoz. 2008. Path planning under spatial uncertainty. *Mem. Cogn.* **36(3)**:495–504. [20]

Wiener, J. M., and H. A. Mallot. 2003. Fine-to-coarse route planning and navigation in regionalized environments. *Spat. Cogn. Comput.* **3(4)**:331–358. [20]

Wiener, N. 1948. Cybernetics or Control and Communication in the Animal and the Machine. Cambridge, MA: MIT Press. [15]

Wilke, A., J. M. C. Hutchinson, P. M. Todd, and U. Czienskowski. 2009. Fishing for the right words: Decision rules for human foraging behavior in internal search tasks. *Cogn. Sci.* **33**:497–529. [2, 4, 11, 15]

Williams, B. A. 1989. The effect of response contingency and reinforcement identity on response suppression by alternative reinforcement. *Learn. Motiv.* **20**:204–224. [7]

Williams-Gray, C. H., A. Hampshire, R. A. Barker, and A. M. Owen. 2008. Attentional control in Parkinson's disease is dependent on COMT val 158 met genotype. *Brain* **131(Pt 2)**:397–408. [9]

Wilson, E. O. 1974. The Insect Societies. Cambridge, MA: Belknap Press. [19]

Wilson, M. A., and B. L. McNaughton. 1993. Dynamics of the hippocampal ensemble code for space. *Science* **261**:1055–1058. [6, 9]

———. 1994. Reactivation of hippocampal ensemble memories during sleep. *Science* **265**:676–679. [6]

Wilson, R. C., Y. K. Takahashi, M. R. Roesch, et al. 2010. A computational model of the role of orbitofrontal cortex and ventral striatum in signalling reward expectancy in reinforcement learning. *Abstr. Soc. Neurosci.* **36** [6]

Winston, J. S., J. A. Gottfried, J. M. Kilner, and R. J. Dolan. 2005. Integrated neural representations of odor intensity and affective valence in human amygdala. *J. Neurosci.* **25**:8903–8907. [7]

Wise, S., E. Murray, and C. Gerfen. 1996. The frontal cortex-basal ganglia system in primates. *Crit. Rev. Neurobiol.* **10**:317–356. [9]

Witter, M. P., and D. G. Amaral. 1991. Entorhinal cortex of the monkey: V. projections to the dentate gyrus, hippocampus, and subicular complex. *J. Comp. Neurol.* **307(3)**:437–459. [9]

Wixted, J. T., and D. Rohrer. 1993. Proactive interference and the dynamics of free recall. *J. Exp. Psychol. Learn. Mem. Cogn.* **19**:1024–1039. [11]

———. 1994. Analyzing the dynamics of free recall: An integrative review of the empirical literature. *Psychon. Bull. Rev.* **1**:89–106. [11]

Wolfe, J. M. 1994. Guided search 2.0: A revised model of visual search. *Psychon. Bull. Rev.* **1**:202–238. [10, 14]

———. 1998. What do 1,000,000 trials tell us about visual search? *Psychol. Sci.* **9(1)**:33–39. [10]

———. 2001. Guided search 4.0: A guided search model that does not require memory for rejected distractors. *J. Vision* **1(3)**:349. [10]

Wolfe, J. M. 2003. Moving towards solutions to some enduring controversies in visual search. *Trends Cogn. Sci.* **7(2)**:70–76. [9, 10]

———. 2007. Guided search 4.0: Current progress with a model of visual search. In: Integrated Models of Cognitive Systems, ed. W. Gray, pp. 99–119. New York: Oxford Univ. Press. [10]

Wolfe, J. M., and S. C. Bennett. 1997. Preattentive object files: Shapeless bundles of basic features. *Vision Res.* **37(1)**:25–43. [10]

Wolfe, J. M., S. J. Butcher, C. Lee, and M. Hyle. 2003. Changing your mind: On the contributions of top-down and bottom-up guidance in visual search for feature singletons. *J. Exp. Psychol. Hum. Perc. Perf.* **29**:483–502. [10, 14]

Wolfe, J. M., K. R. Cave, and S. L. Franzel. 1989. Guided search: An alternative to the feature integration model for visual search. *J. Exp. Psychol. Hum. Perc. Perf.* **15**:419–433. [10]

Wolfe, J. M., S. R. Friedman-Hill, and A. B. Bilsky. 1994. Parallel processing of part-whole information in visual search tasks. *Perc. Psychophys.* **55(5)**:537–550. [10]

Wolfe, J. M., S. R. Friedman-Hill, M. I. Stewart, and K. M. O'Connell. 1992. The role of categorization in visual search for orientation. *J. Exp. Psychol. Hum. Perc. Perf.* **18(1)**:34–49. [10]

Wolfe, J. M., and T. S. Horowitz. 2004. What attributes guide the deployment of visual attention and how do they do it? *Nat. Rev. Neurosci.* **5(6)**:495–501. [10]

Wolfe, J. M., T. S. Horowitz, and N. M. Kenner. 2005. Rare items often missed in visual searches. *Nature* **435**:439–440. [10]

Wolfe, J. M., T. S. Horowitz , M. J. Van Wert, et al. 2007. Low target prevalence is a stubborn source of errors in visual search tasks. *J. Exp. Psychol. Gen.* **136(4)**:623–638. [10]

Wolfe, J. M., N. L. Klempen, and E. P. Shulman. 1999. Which end is up? Two representations of orientation in visual search. *Vision Res.* **39(12)**:2075–2086. [10]

Wolfe, J. M., and M. J. Van Wert. 2010. Varying target prevalence reveals two, dissociable decision criteria in visual search. *Curr. Biol.* **20(2)**:121–124. [10]

Wolfe, J. M., M. L.-H. Vo, K. K. Evans, and M. R. Greene. 2011. Visual search in scenes involves selective and non-selective pathways. *Trends Cogn. Sci.* **15**:77–84. [10]

Wolfe, J. M., K. P. Yu, M. I. Stewart, et al. 1990. Limitations on the parallel guidance of visual search: Color X color and orientation X orientation conjunctions. *J. Exp. Psychol. Hum. Perc. Perf.* **16(4)**:879–892. [10]

Wolpert, D. H. 1996. The lack of a priori distinctions between learning algorithms. *Neural Comput.* **8(7)**:1341–1390. [20]

Wolpert, D. H., and W. G. Macready. 1997. No free lunch theorems for optimization. *IEEE Trans. Evol. Comp.* **1**:67–82. [16]

Wood, E. R., P. A. Dudchenko, R. J. Robitsek, and H. Eichenbaum. 2000. Hippocampal neurons encode information about different types of memory episodes occurring in the same location. *Neuron* **27**:623–633. [6]

Wykowska, A., A. Schubö, and B. Hommel. 2009. How you move is what you see: Action planning biases selection in visual search. *J. Exp. Psychol. Hum. Perc. Perf.* **35**:1755–1769. [14]

Yeung, N., J. D. Cohen, and M. M. Botvinick. 2004. The neural basis of error detection: Conflict monitoring and the error-related negativity. *Psychol. Rev.* **111(4)**:931–959. [5]

Yeung, N., C. B. Holroyd, and J. D. Cohen. 2005. ERP correlates of feedback and reward processing in the presence and absence of response choice. *Cereb. Cortex* **15(5)**:535–544. [5]

Yeung, N., and S. Nieuwenhuis. 2009. Dissociating response conflict and error likelihood in anterior cingulate cortex. *J. Neurosci.* **29(46)**:14,506–14,510. [5]

Yin, H. H., B. J. Knowlton, and B. W. Balleine. 2004. Lesions of dorsolateral striatum preserve outcome expectancy but disrupt habit formation in instrumental learning. *Eur. J. Neurosci.* **19(1)**:181–189. [7]

Yin, H. H., S. B. Ostlund, B. J. Knowlton, and B. W. Balleine. 2005. The role of the dorsomedial striatum in instrumental conditioning. *Eur. J. Neurosci.* **22(2)**:513–523. [7, 9]

Young, C. J. 2004. Contributions of metaknowledge to retrieval of natural categories in semantic memory. *J. Exp. Psychol. Learn. Mem. Cogn.* **30**:909–916. [11]

Yu, A. J., and P. Dayan. 2005. Uncertainty, neuromodulation, and attention. *Neuron* **46(4)**:681–692. [8, 9]

Zahm, D. S., and J. S. Brog. 1992. On the significance of subterritories in the accumbens part of the rat ventral striatum. *Neuroscience* **50**:751–767. [9]

Zatorre, R. J., and A. R. Halpern. 2005. Mental concerts: Musical imagery and auditory cortex. *Neuron* **47(1)**:9–12. [9]

Zelinsky, G. 2008. A theory of eye movements during target acquisition. *Psychol. Rev.* **115(4)**:787–835. [10]

Zenger, B., and M. Fahle. 1997. Missed targets are more frequent than false alarms: A model for error rates in visual search. *J. Exp. Psychol. Hum. Perc. Perf.* **23(6)**:1783–1791. [10]

Zhang, J. X., C. M. Feng, P. T. Fox, J. H. Gao, and L. H. Tan. 2004. Is left inferior frontal gyrus a general mechanism for selection? *NeuroImage* **23(2)**:596–603. [5]

Zhang, K., I. Ginzburg, B. L. McNaughton, and T. J. Sejnowski. 1998. Interpreting neuronal population activity by reconstruction: Unified framework with application to hippocampal place cells. *J. Neurophysiol.* **79**:1017–1044. [6, 9]

Zilli, E. A., and M. E. Hasselmo. 2008. Modeling the role of working memory and episodic memory in behavioral tasks. *Hippocampus* **18(2)**:193–209. [6]

Zola, S. M., L. R. Squire, E. Teng, et al. 2000. Impaired recognition memory in monkeys after damage limited to the hippocampal region. *J. Neurosci.* **20(1)**:451–463. [9]

Zweifel, L. S., J. G. Parker, C. J. Lobb, et al. 2009. Disruption of NMDAR-dependent burst firing by dopamine neurons provides selective assessment of phasic dopamine-dependent behavior. *PNAS* **106**:7281–7288. [2]

Subject Index